Thailand
a travel survival kit

Thailand - a travel survival kit
Third edition

Published by
Lonely Planet Publications
Head Office: PO Box 88, South Yarra, Victoria, 3141, Australia
Also: PO Box 2001A, Berkeley, CA 94702, USA

Printed by
Singapore National Printers Ltd, Singapore

Photographs by
Don Campbell (DC)
Joe Cummings (JC), front cover
Bill Preston (BP)
Tony Wheeler (TW), back cover

First published
February 1982

This edition
January 1987

National Library of Australia Cataloguing in Publication Data

Cummings, Joe
Thailand, a travel survival kit

3rd ed.
ISBN 0 908086 95 4.

1. Thailand – Description and travel – 1976– – Guide-books. I. Title.

915.93'0444

Joe Cummings has been studying South-East Asia since the early '70s; he has worked as a Peace Corps volunteer in Thailand and as a translator/interpreter of Thai. He now teaches English to international students in the San Francisco area. He has also lived or travelled in Canada, China, Hawaii, Hong Kong, India, Mexico, Nepal and Western Europe.

After completing an MA degree in South and South East Asian Civilisation (Thai language/art history) at the University of California at Berkeley, Joe returned to Thailand to research the first edition of this guide in 1981 and has been returning regularly to revise and update new editions. Fluent in Thai, he has travelled well over 8000 km within the Kingdom, by bus, air, train, motorcycle, boat and foot. Joe is also the author of Lonely Planet's *Thailand Phrasebook* and a regular contributor to *The San Francisco Chronicle* and *Transitions*

Dedicated to the memory of Termpong Prateepavanich ('Trii').

Acknowledgements – this edition

Special thanks to Ken Perszyk, the Prateepavanich family, Suraphong Wajarajit, Kietiphong Kamtrakul, Prayoon Jenlapwattanakul, Phiraphong Ratanadilak Na Phuket (Max), Lynne Cummings, Jacques Paulin, Jeff Longfellow, Caravan, Sue and Toss, Boon, Porn, Gary and Shane.

The section on Thailand's national parks in the 'Facts about the Country' chapter was written by Murray D Bruce.

As usual our grateful thanks to readers who wrote to Lonely Planet with corrections, suggestions, additions and interesting snippets. Thank you:

David Stasburg (Fin), Geoff & Alison Hepplestone (UK), Derek & Jennifer Werner (USA), Jan Gustafsson (Sw), Torbjorn Andersson (Sw), Mats Svensson (Sw), Michael Brady (UK), Cindy Brown (USA), J W Saleson (USA), Les Downes (UK), David Holdcraft (Aus), Ondine Spitzel (Aus), Deanna Swaney (USA), Greg Lindeblom (USA), William Smith (T), Susan Tamaki (Isr), Dorian Benkoil (USA), Jean Heale (UK), Uwe Schlokat (D), B Wainwright (Aus), Nicki Bean (Aus), Grace Rickard (USA), Ted Jemason (USA), Allen Koshewa (J), Ellen Rothstein (T), Linda Jowsey (Aus), Beth Wetzler &. Shaun Tierney (UK), Jan Wilkman (Fin), George Bullingher (NZ), Jenni Pearson (Aus), Herty Muller (Swit), Peter Haynes (UK), Peter Roth (UK), Lamon Rutten (NL), Garry Wisnewski (NZ), Gionilla Andersson (Sw), Wilfried Fidelak (D), Berny Lottner & Tazuko Tanaka (J), Herman & Srene Eidel (D), Michael Kivikunnas, Ed Holub & Chris Moorman (USA), Ed Pores (USA), Klaas Rougoor (NL), Lothar Moltgen, Graham Wrigley & Ga Bearclerk (UK), Michael Romberg (UK), Duncan Simpson (I), Steve Growdon (USA), Bette Gallander (C), Palle Frese (Dk), Terri Henderson (Aus), Lt. Dave Pratt (HK), Dave & Angel Shiress (UK), Stewart & Ra Forsyth (NZ), Maria Santamaria (J), Claudia Simms (USA), William King (UK), Paula Deutsch (USA), Nachy Bargida (Isr), Judy Heindl (USA), Sylvia Dewit (B), G H Carlo (UK), Linda Crawford, Kathy Undin (C) & Jim Troutman (USA), Tahanga (Aus), Alan C Nobel (Aus), A Reader (USA), Joaduin Nolte (D), Grace Ross-Schnebelen (USA),

Susan Reiter (USA), Lieselotte Alfhson (Sw), Jouni Tuohi (Fin), Daphne Shye (USA), Jim Rice Jr (USA), John M Collett (Aus), Tim Carr (Aus), Sue Penco (Aus), Peter Vink (NL), Cathy Ellis (Aus), Sherman J Marcus (USA), Yung Tak Cheung (HK), Jane Vessey (J), Frankie Lim (Sing), J Bell (UK), Leigh Mabin (Aus), Emily Kopel (HK), Bente Clausen & Lars Jenson (Dk), Andreas M Faul (D), Hans Dellmo, M Hershman (USA), Anthony Healey (Aus), Susan Hansen, Lindie Lapin (USA), Leon McDonald (T).

Aus – Australia, B – Belgium, C – Canada, D – West Germany, Dk – Denmark, Fin –Finland, HK – Hong Kong, I – India, Isr – Israel, J – Japan, NL – Netherlands, NZ – New Zealand, Sw – Sweden, Swit – Switzerland, T – Thailand, UK – UK, USA – USA

Many people in the Lonely Planet office in Melbourne worked on this updated and revised edition; Fiona Boyes drew the new maps and updated the old ones; Sue Mitra edited the text; Ann Logan did the typesetting and also looked after the Thai script; Hugh Finlay proofread; Graham Imeson did the paste up and design; and Todd Pierce pasted up the corrections; the others all gave a hand.

And a Request

Travel guides are only kept up to date by travelling. If you find errors or omissions in this book we'd very much like to hear about them. As usual the best letters will score a free copy of the next edition or any other Lonely Planet guide if you prefer.

Contents

Introduction

Thailand, or Siam as it was called until the 1940s, has never been colonised by a foreign power, while all of its South-East Asian neighbours have undergone European imperialism (or more recently, ideological domination by Communism – which originated in Europe) at one time or another. True, it has suffered periodic invasions on the part of the Burmese and the Khmers and was briefly occupied by the Japanese in WW II, but the kingdom was never externally controlled long enough to dampen the Thais' serious individualism. I say serious because the Thais are so often depicted as fun-loving, happy-go-lucky folk (which they often are), but this quality is something they have worked for to achieve.

This is not to say that Thailand has not experienced any western influence. Like other Asian countries it has both suffered and benefited from contact with foreign cultures. But the everchanging spirit of Thai culture has remained dominant, even in modern city life. The end result is that Thailand has much to interest the traveller: historic culture, lively arts, exotic islands, nightlife, a tradition of friendliness and hospitality to strangers, and one of the world's most exciting cuisines.

Travel in this tropical country is fairly comfortable and down-to-earth. The rail, bus and air travel network is extensive and every place worth visiting is easily accessible. There are many places worth visiting, many sights to see, a multi-faceted culture to experience and it is all quite affordable by today's international travel standards.

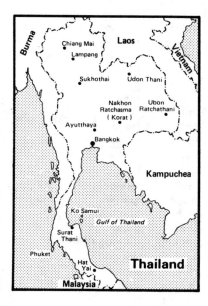

Place Names

พัทยา	Pattaya
เกาะสีชัง	Koh Si Chang
เกาะสมุย	Koh Samui
กรุงเทพ ฯ	Bangkok (Krung Thep)
ศรีอยุธยา	Ayuthaya
เชียงใหม่	Chiang Mai
เชียงราย	Chiang Rai
ชลบุรี	Chonburi
เชียงแสน	Chiang Saen
ฝาง	Fang
กำแพงเพชร	Kamphaeng Phet
กาญจนบุรี	Kanchanaburi
ขอนแก่น	Khon Kaen
กระบี่	Krabi
หัวหิน	Hua Hin
ลำพูน	Lamphun
ลพบุรี	Lopburi
มหาสารคาม	Mahasarakham
นครพนม	Nakhon Phanom
นครปฐม	Nakhon Pathom

นครราชสีมา	Nakhon Ratchasima (Khorat)
นครสวรรค์	Nakhon Sawan
นครศรีธรรมราช	Nakhon Si Thammarat
นาน	Nan
พังงา	Phangnga
พิษณุโลก	Phitsanuloke
ภูเก็ต	Phuket
ราชบุรี	Rajburi (Ratburi)
ร้อยเอ็ด	Roi Et
สระบุรี	Saraburi
สงขลา	Songkhla
สบรวก	Sop Ruak
สุโขทัย	Sukhothai
สวรรคโลก	Sawankhaloke
สุราษฎร์ธานี	Surat Thani
สุรินทร์	Surin
ศรีราชา	Si Racha
อุบลราชธานี	Ubol Ratchathani.
อุครธานี	Udorn Thani
หาดใหญ่	Hat Yai
ไชยา	Chaiya

Note that the the Thai for Rd is *Thanon*
so Phetburi Rd, for example, may be
called Thanon Phetburi on some maps.

Other terms include *Ko* or *Koh* – Island
and *Doi* – Mount or Peak.

Transliteration

As Thai uses a totally different script to
our own any Thai name has to be
transliterated into our script. Transliter-
ation is very often a matter of opinion and
this book, like anything else on Thailand,
is bound to be out of step at times.
Generally names in this book follow the
most common practice or, in the case of
hotels, for example, simply copies their
Roman script name, no matter what
devious process was used to transliterate
it! Where no Roman model was available
names were transliterated directly from
Thai.

Problems often arise when a name is
transliterated differently, even at the
same place. 'Thavee', for example, can be
Tavi, Thawee, Thavi, Thavee or various
other versions. Outside of the International Phonetic Alphabet, there is no
'proper' way to transliterate Thai – only
wrong ways. The Thais themselves are
incredibly inconsistent in this matter,
often using English letters that have no
equivalent sound in Thai: Faisal for
Phaisan, Bhumiphol for Phumiphon,
Vanich for Wanit.

Facts about the Country

HISTORY & POLITICS

The history of the geographical area now known as Thailand reaches far back into 'hoary antiquity' as they say. World renowned scholar Paul Benedict (author of *Austro-Thai Language & Culture*) found that modern linguistic theory, which ties numerous key items in ancient Chinese culture to an early Thai linguistic group, taken together . with recent archaeological finds in Thailand, enable us to establish South-East Asia 'as a focal area in the emergent cultural development of homo sapiens. It now seems likely that the first true agriculturists anywhere, perhaps also the first true metal-workers, were Austro-Thai speakers.' These proto-Thais seem to have proliferated all over South-East Asia, including the islands of Indonesia, and some may have settled in south and south-west China, later to 're-migrate' to northern Thailand to establish the first Thai kingdom in the 13th century.

With no written records or chronologies it is difficult to say with certainty what kind of cultures existed in Thailand before the Christian era. However, by the 6th century AD an important network of agricultural communities was thriving as far south as modern-day Pattani and Yala, and as far north and north-east as Lamphun and Muang Fa Daed (near Khon Kaen). Theravada Buddhism was flourishing and may have entered the region during India's Ashokan period, in the 2nd or 3rd centuries BC, when Indian missionaries were said to have been sent to a land called Suvarnabhumi – 'Land of Gold'. Suvarnabhumi most likely refers to a remarkably fertile area stretching from southern Burma, across central Thailand, to eastern Kampuchea. Two cities in the central river basin have long been called Suphanburi, 'City of Gold' and U Thong, 'Cradle of Gold'.

Dvaravati Period

This loose collection of city-states was given the Sanskritic name Dvaravati, or 'place having gates', the city of Krishna in the Indian epic *Mahabharata*. The French art historian George Coedes discovered the name on some coins excavated in the Nakhon Pathom area, which seems to have been the centre of Dvaravati culture. The Dvaravati period lasted until the 11th or 12th centuries AD and produced many fine works of art, including distinctive Buddha images (showing Indian Gupta influence), stucco reliefs on temples and in caves, some architecture (little of which remains intact), some exquisite terracotta heads, votive tablets and other miscellaneous sculpture.

Dvaravati may have been a cultural relay point for the pre-Angkor cultures of ancient Cambodia and Champa to the east. The Chinese, through the travels of the famous pilgrim Xuan Zang, knew the area as T'o-lo-po-ti, located between Sriksetra (North Burma) and Tsanapura (Sambor Prei Kuk-Kambuja). The ethnology of the Dvaravati peoples is a controversial subject, though the standard decree is that they were Mons or Mon-Khmers. The Mons themselves seem to have been descended from a group of Indian immigrants from Kalinga, an area overlapping the boundaries of the modern Indian states of Orissa and Andhra Pradesh. The Dvaravati Mons may have been an ethnic mix of these people and people indigenous to the region, ie the original Thais. In any event, the Dvaravati culture quickly declined in the 11th century under the political domin-ation of the invading Khmers who headquartered themselves in Lopburi. The area around Lamphun, then called Haripunchai, held out until the late 12th century or later as evidenced by the

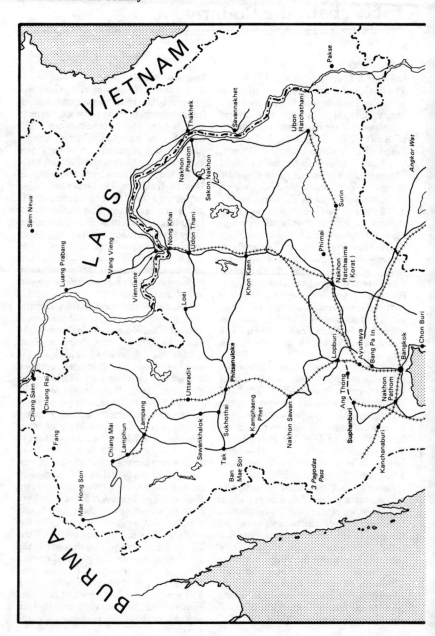

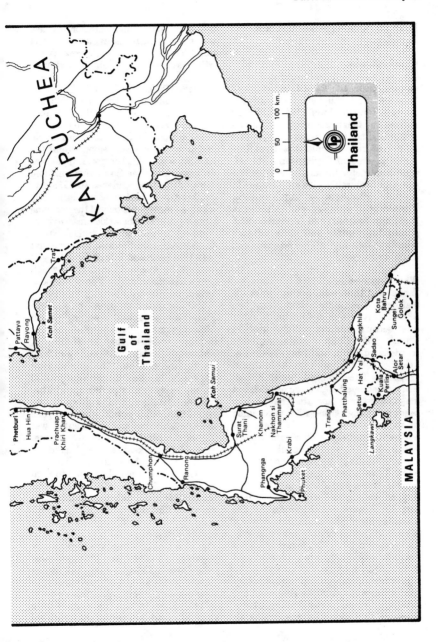

Dvaravati architecture of Wat Kukut in Lamphun.

Khmer Influence

The Khmer conquest brought Khmer cultural influence in the form of art, language and religion. Some of the Sanskrit terms in Mon-Thai vocabulary entered the language during the Khmer or Lopburi period between the 11th and 13th centuries. Monuments from this period located in Lopburi and Phimai, were constructed in the Khmer style and compare favourably with architecture in Angkor. Elements of Brahmanism, Theravada Buddhism and Mahayana Buddhism intermixed as Lopburi became a religious centre, and some of each remain to this day in Thai religious and court ceremonies.

Other Kingdoms

While all this was taking place, a distinctly Thai state called Nan Chao (650-1250 AD) was flourishing in what later became Yunnan and Szechuan in China. Nan Chao maintained close relations with imperial China and the two neighbours enjoyed much cultural exchange. The Mongols, under Kublai Khan, conquered Nan Chao in 1253, but long before they came, the Thai peoples began migrating southward, homesteading in and around what is today Laos and northern Thailand. They 'infiltrated' South-East Asia in small groups, assimilating the peoples they encountered. Some Thais became mercenaries for the Khmer armies, as depicted on the walls of Angkor Wat, in the early 12th century. The Thais were called 'Syams' by the Khmers, from Sanskrit *syam* meaning 'dark', in reference to their relatively darker skin colour. This is how the Thai kingdom eventually came to be called Syam or Siam.

Southern Thailand, the upper Malay peninsula, was under the control of the Srivijaya empire, headquartered in Sumatra, between the 8th and 13th centuries. The regional centre for Srivijaya was Chaiya, near the modern town of Surat Thani. Srivijaya art remains can still be seen in Chaiya and its environs.

Sukhothai Period

Several Thai principalities in the Mekong valley united in the 13th and 14th centuries and Thai princes took Haripunchai from the Mons to form Lan Na and the Sukhothai region from the Khmers whose Angkor government was declining fast. The Sukhothai kingdom declared its independence in 1238 and quickly expanded its sphere of influence, taking advantage not only of the declining Khmer power but the weakening Srivijaya domain in the south. Sukhothai is considered by the Siamese to be the first true Thai kingdom. It lasted until it was annexed by Ayuthaya in 1376 by which time a national identity of sorts had been forged.

The second Sukhothai king, Ram Khamheng, organised a writing system which became the basis for modern Thai, he also codified the Thai form of Theravada Buddhism, as borrowed from the Sinhalese. Many Thais today view the Sukhothai period with sentimental vision, seeing it as a golden age of Thai politics, religion and culture - an egalitarian, noble period when everyone had enough to eat and the kingdom was unconquerable. Under Ram Khamheng, Sukhothai extended as far as Nakhon Si Thammarat in the south, to Vientiane and Luang Prabang in Laos, and to Pegu in southern Burma. For a short time (1448-1486) the Sukhothai capital was moved to Phitsanuloke.

Ayuthaya Period

The Thai kings of Ayuthaya became very powerful in the 14th and 15th centuries, taking over U Thong and Lopburi, former Khmer strongholds, and moving east in their conquests until Angkor was defeated in 1431. Even though the Khmers were their adversaries in battle, the Ayuthaya kings incorporated Khmer court customs and language. One result of this was that the Thai monarch gained more absolute authority during the Ayuthaya period and assumed the title *devaraja* – 'god-king', as opposed to the then-traditional *dhammaraja* – 'dharma-king'. In the early 16th century Ayuthaya was receiving European visitors and a Portuguese embassy was established in 1511. The Portuguese were followed by the Dutch (1605), the English (1612), the Danes (1621) and the French (1662).

In the mid-16th century Ayuthaya and the independent kingdom in Chiang Mai came under the control of the Burmese, but the Thais regained rule of both by the end of the century. Ayuthaya was one of the greatest and wealthiest cities in Asia, a thriving seaport envied not only by the Burmese but by the Europeans who, by their early accounts, were in great awe of the city. It has been said that London, at the time, was a mere village in comparison.

A rather peculiar episode unfolded in Ayuthaya when a Greek, Constantine Phaulkon, became a very high official in Siam under King Narai from 1675 to 1688. He kept out the Dutch and the English but allowed the French to station 600 soldiers in the kingdom. The Thais, fearing a take-over, forcefully expelled the French and executed Phaulkon. Ironically, the word for a 'foreigner' (of European descent) in modern Thai is *farang*, an abbreviated form of *farangset*, meaning 'French'. Siam sealed itself from the west for 150 years following this experience with 'farangs'.

The Burmese again invaded Ayuthaya in 1765 and the capital fell after two years of fierce battle. This time the Burmese really did a job on the city, destroying everything sacred to the Thais, including manuscripts, temples and religious sculpture. The Burmese, despite their effectiveness in sacking Ayuthaya, could not maintain a foothold in the kingdom and Phya Taksin, a Thai general, made

himself king in 1769, ruling from the new capital of Thonburi on the banks of the Chao Phraya river opposite Bangkok. The Thais regained control of their country and further united the disparate provinces to the north with central Siam. Taksin eventually came to regard himself as the next Buddha; his ministers did not approve of this religious fanaticism and he was deposed and executed.

The Chakri Dynasty

Another general came to power, Chao Phya Chakri, and he was crowned in 1782 under the title Rama I. Rama I moved the royal capital across the river to Bangkok and ruled as the first king of the Chakri dynasty – the present king of Thailand is Rama IX and it has been prophesied that this dynasty will only have nine kings. In 1809 Rama II, son of Rama I, took the throne and reigned through to 1824. Both monarchs assumed the task of restoring the culture so severely damaged by the Burmese decades earlier. Rama III, or Phra Nang Klao (1824-1851), went beyond reviving tradition and developed trade with China while increasing domestic agricultural production.

Rama IV, commonly known as King Mongkut (to the Thais as Phra Chom Klao), was one of the more colourful and innovative of the early Chakri kings. He originally missed out on the throne in deference to his half-brother Rama III and lived as a Buddhist monk for 27 years. During his long monastic term he became adept in the Sanskrit, Pali, Latin and English languages, studied western sciences and adopted the strict discipline of local Mon monks. He kept an eye on the outside world and when he took the throne in 1851 he immediately courted diplomatic relations with European nations, while avoiding colonialisation. In addition he attempted to align Buddhist cosmology with modern science to the end of demythologising the Thai religion (a process yet to be fully accomplished), and founded the Thammayut monastic sect, based on the strict discipline he had followed as a monk. The Thammayut remains a minority sect in relation to the Mahanikai who comprise the largest number of Buddhist monks in Thailand. Thai trade restrictions were loosened by King Mongkut and many western powers signed trade agreements with the monarch. He also established Siam's first printing press and instituted educational reforms, developing a school system along European lines.

His son, King Chulalongkorn (Rama V, 1868-1910), continued Mongkut's tradition of reform, especially in the legal and administrative realm. Thailand further benefited from relations with European nations and the USA. Railways were designed and constructed, a civil service established and the legal code restructured. Though Siam still managed to avoid colonialisation, it lost some territory to French Laos and British Burma around this time. King Vajiravudh (Rama VI, 1910-25), during his rather short reign introduced compulsory education as well as other educational reforms and further 'westernised' the nation by making the Thai calendar conform to western models.

While Vajiravudh's brother King Prajadhipok (Rama VII, 1925-35) ruled, a group of Thai students living in Paris became so enamoured with democratic ideology that they mounted a successful coup d'etat against absolute monarchy in Siam. This bloodless revolution led to the development of a constitutional monarchy along British lines, with a mixed military-civilian group in power. Phibul Songkhram, a key military leader in the 1932 coup, maintained an effective position of power from 1938 until the end of WW II. Rama VIII (Ananda Mahidol), a nephew of Rama VII, ascended the throne in 1935 but was assassinated under mysterious circumstances in 1946, his brother Bhumipol Aduldej succeeded him as Rama IX. Under the influence of Phibul's government, the country's name was changed from Siam to Thailand –

officially in 1949 – rendered in Thai as *Prathet Thai*.

World War II & Post War

The Japanese outflanked the allied troops in Malaya and Burma in 1941 and the Phibul government complied with the Japanese in this action by allowing them into the Gulf of Thailand; consequently the Japanese troops occupied Thailand itself. Phibul then declared war on the US and Great Britain (1942) but Seni Pramoj, the Thai ambassador in Washington, refused to deliver the declaration. Phibul resigned in 1944 under pressure from the Thai underground resistance and after V-J day in 1945, Seni became premier.

In 1946, the year King Ananda was assassinated, Seni and his brother Kukrit were unseated in a general election and a democratic civilian group took power for a short time, only to be overthrown by Phibul in 1948. In 1951 power was wrested from Phibul by General Sarit Thanarat, who continued the tradition of military dictatorship. However, Phibul somehow retained the actual position of premier until 1957 when Sarit finally had him exiled. Elections that same year forced Sarit to resign, go abroad for 'medical treatment' and then return in 1958 to launch another coup. This time he abolished the constitution, dissolved the parliament, and banned all political parties, maintaining effective power until his death in 1963 of cirrhosis. From 1964 to 1973 the Thai nation was ruled by army officers Thanom Kittikachorn and Praphat Charusathien, during which time Thailand allowed the US to develop several army bases within her borders in support of the American campaign in Vietnam.

Reacting to political repression, 10,000 Thai students publicly demanded a real constitution in June 1973. In October of the same year the military brutally suppressed a large demonstration at Thammasat University in Bangkok, but General Krit Sivara and King Bhumiphol refused to support further bloodshed, forcing Thanom and Praphat to leave Thailand. An elected consitutional government ruled until October 1976 when students demonstrated again, this time protesting the return of Thanom to Thailand as a monk. Thammasat University again became a battlefield and a new right-wing government was installed with Thanin Kraivichien as premier. This particular incident really disillusioned many Thai students and older intellectuals not directly involved. The result being that numerous idealists 'dropped out' of Thai society and joined the insurgents in the forests. In October 1977 another coup ousted Thanin and installed Kriangsak. In 1980 the military-backed position changed hands again, leaving Prem at the stern.

If you get the idea that the coup d'etat is popular in Thailand you're on the right track: I've counted 14 successful or attempted coups since 1932 (an average of almost three per decade!), not counting election-forced resignations. There have also been 10 'permanent' constitutions enacted since the first. However, even the successful coups rarely have resulted in drastic change and the Thai commoner will tell you that things *never* change – it depends on how closely you observe politics.

Each new leader claims a renewed campaign against the communist threat within Thailand and a stronger defence against the external threat, while simultaneously promising a liberalisation of domestic repression/human rights. Freedom of speech is fairly curtailed in Thailand but appears to be improving slightly and the Bangkok curfew of the Thanin/Kriangsak years has been lifted. (Anyone who's spent the night in one of Bangkok's mosquito-infested 'detention areas' for being out past curfew will most fully appreciate this.) Every leading political figure must receive the support of the Thai military who are generally staunch reactionaries so we can't expect

any miracles in the near future. Considering Thailand's geographic position it's difficult not to understand, to some extent, the fears of this ultra-conservative group. It is a paradoxical situation that can only be worked out by the Thais themselves in cooperation with their South-East Asian neighbours. Visitors to Thailand are advised *not* to become involved in local politics in any way.

OPIUM & THE GOLDEN TRIANGLE

The opium poppy, *Papaver somnniferum*, has been cultivated and its resins extracted for use as a narcotic at least since the time of the early Greek empire. The Chinese were introduced to the drug by Arab traders during the time of Kublai Khan (1279 to 1294). It was so highly valued for its medicinal properties that hill tribe minorities in southern China began cultivating the opium poppy in order to raise money to pay taxes to their Han Chinese rulers. Easy to grow, opium became a way for the nomadic hill tribes to raise what cash they needed in transactions (willing and unwilling) with the lowland world. Many of the hill tribes that migrated to Thailand and Laos in the post WW II era in order to avoid persecution in Burma and China, took with them their one cash crop, the poppy. The poppy is well suited to hillside cultivation as it flourishes on steep slopes and in nutrient-poor soils.

The opium trade became especially lucrative in South-East Asia during the '60s and early '70s when US armed forces were embroiled in Vietnam. Alfred McCoy's *The Politics of Heroin in Southeast Asia* recounts how contact with the GI market not only expanded the immediate Asian market, but provided outlets to world markets. Before this time the source of most of the world's heroin was the Middle East. Soon everybody wanted in and various parties alternatively quarrelled over and cooperated in illegal opium commerce. Most notable were the Nationalist Chinese Army refugees living in northern Burma and northern Thailand, Burmese anti-government rebels, in particular the Burmese Communist Party, the Shan States Army and the Shan United Army. The American CIA eventually became involved in a big way, using profits from heroin runs aboard US aircraft to Vietnam and further afield to covert operations throughout Indo-China. This of course led to an increase in the availability of heroin throughout the world. Which in turn led to increased production in the remote northern areas of Thailand, Burma and Laos, where there was little government interference. This area came to be known as the 'Golden Triangle' because of local fortunes amassed by the 'opium warlords', Burmese and Chinese military-businessmen who controlled the movement of opium across three international borders. As more opium was available, more was consumed; the demand increased along with the profits – and so the cycle continues. As a result, opium cultivation became a full-time job for some hill-tribe groups within the Golden Triangle. Hill economies destabilised to the point where opium production became a necessary means of survival for thousands of people, including the less nomadic Shan people.

One of the Golden Triangle's most colourful figures is Khun Sa, aka Chang Chi-fu, aka Sao Mong Khawn, a half-Chinese, half-Shan opium warlord. He got his start in the '50s and '60s working for the Kuomintang (KMT) – Chiang Kai Shek's Nationalist Chinese troops who had fled to Burma. The KMT were continuing military operations against the Chinese Communists along the Burma-China border, financed by the smuggling of opium (with CIA protection). They employed Khun Sa as one of their prime local supporter/advisors. Khun Sa broke with the KMT in the early '60s after establishing his own opium smuggling business with heroin refineries in northern Thailand. From that time on, the history of heroin smuggling in the Golden Triangle

has been intertwined with the exploits of Khun Sa. In 1966, the Burmese government deputised Khun Sa as head of 'village defense forces' against the Burmese Communist Party (BCP), which was at maximum strength at this time and fully involved in opium trade. Khun Sa cleverly used his government backing to consolidate power and build up his own militia by developing the Shan United Army (SUA), an anti-government insurgent group heavily involved in opium throughout the Golden Triangle in competition with the BCP and KMT. When the KMT attempted to place an 'embargo' on SUA opium trade, by blocking caravan routes into Thailand and Laos, Khun Sa initiated what has come to be known as the Opium War of 1967, by attempting to thwart the embargo. However the KMT managed to chase Khun Sa, along with a contingent of SUA troops running an opium caravan routed for Thailand into Laos, where Burmese officials arrested Khun Sa and the Laotian government seized the opium. Khun Sa escaped Burmese custody by means of a carefully planned combination of extortion and bribery in 1975 and returned to take command of the SUA. About the same time, the Burmese government broke KMT control of opium trafficking and Khun Sa stepped in to become the prime opium warlord in the Triangle, working from his headquarters in Ban Hin Taek, Chiang Rai province, Thailand. Coincidentally, US forces pulled out of Indo-China at this time so there was no longer any competition from CIA conduits in Laos. Ironically since then, the primary law enforcement conflict has been between US-backed Thai forces and the SUA.

On occasions, that is whenever they receive a large financial contribution from the USA Drug Enforcement Agency (DEA), Thai Army Rangers sweep northern Thailand from Tak to Chiang Rai and Mae Hong Son, destroying poppy fields and heroin refineries but rarely making arrests. One of the most recent sweeps, a US$800,000 operation in December 1985, accomplished the destruction of 25,000 *rai* (one rai equals 1600 square metres) of poppy fields in Chiang Mai, Chiang Rai, Mae Hong Son, Tak and Nan. Hill-tribe and Shan cultivators, at the bottom of the profit scale, stood by helplessly while their primary means of livelihood was hacked to the ground. A crop substitution programme, developed by the Thai royal family in 1959 (one year after cultivation of the opium poppy for profit was made illegal), has generally been recognised as an almost complete failure. Success has only been in selected areas where crop substitution is accompanied by a concentrated effort to indoctrinate hill tribes into mainstream Thai culture.

In the late '70s and early '80s, the SUA continued to buy opium from the BCP, Shan and hill-tribe cultivators in Burma and Thailand, transporting and selling the product to ethnic Chinese syndicates in Thailand who control access to world markets. SUA strength has been estimated at between 1500 and 8000 regulars, putting it on par with the BCP and the Karen National Union, Burma's two largest insurgent groups (among the 25 different groups operating in 1983). A turning point in Khun Sa's fortunes occured in 1982 and 1983 when the Thais launched a full-scale attack on his Ban Hin Taek stronghold, forcing Khun Sa to flee to parts unknown. It's suspected that he went to the mountains of the Kok River valley across the border in Burma. Thus breaking up opium and heroin production in the Mae Salong – Ban Hin Taek area. This area is now undergoing heavy 'pacification' or Thai nationalisation efforts. At great expense to the Thai government tea, coffee, corn and Chinese herbs are now grown where opium once thrived. Whether this particular project is successful or not is another question but the government's strategy seems to be one of isolating and then pushing pockets of the opium trade out of Thailand and into Burma and Laos, where it continues uninterrupted.

The Laotian People's Revolutionary Party (LPRP), Laos' ruling group, is currently taking advantage of Thai government actions in northern Thailand to encourage an increase in opium production in Laos. They are effectively capturing some share of the market vacated by the SUA in Thailand. If the Burmese government steps up efforts to suppress poppy cultivation in Burma, as the Thai government has done in Thailand, Laos may in fact be in a position to corner the market, as it's the only government in the region with an official tolerance towards opium production. Smuggling routes for Laotian opium and heroin cross the Thai border at several points throughout the north and north-east, including the provinces of Chiang Mai, Chiang Rai, Nan, Loei, Nong Khai and Nakhon Phanom.

The cycle keeps on going with power being transferred from warlord to warlord and the hill-tribe and Shan cultivators continue to be unwilling pawns in the game. The planting of the poppy and the sale of its collected resins has never been a simple moral issue. Heroin addicts and the cultivators – who have been farming poppies for centuries – have both been exploited by governments and crime syndicates who trade in opium for the advancement of their own power. This leads to the conclusion that opium production in the Golden Triangle must be dealt with as a political, social, cultural and economic problem and not simply as a conventional law enforcement matter. So far a one-sided approach has only resulted in the unthinking destruction of minority culture and economy in the Golden Triangle area rather than an end to the opium and heroin problem. Meanwhile, opium cultivation still continues in Thailand in hidden valleys not frequented by the Thai armed forces. Any hill tribe settlement may legally plant opium poppies for its own consumption. Small plots of land are 'leased' by opium merchants who have allowed heroin production to decentralise in order for poppy resin collection to appear legal.

ECONOMY

About 76% of Thai labour is engaged in agriculture and only 7% in industry. Thailand's major exports are rice, tapioca, sugar, rubber, maize, tin, cement, pineapple and textiles. Average per capita income by the end of the '70s was US$500 per year, with a GNP growth rate (net) of 6 to 7%. Travellers should keep in mind the moderate inflation rate in Thailand; as in most countries, prices continue to rise.

The north-east of Thailand has the lowest inflation rate and cost of living. This region is generally poorer than the rest of the country and doesn't get too much tourism; therefore it offers excellent value for the traveller and is well worth a visit – a lot of good silk-weaving is done in the north-east, for example. In the south, fishing, tin mining and rubber production keep the local economy fairly stable. Central Thailand grows fruit, sugar cane and rice for export, as well as supporting some industry (textiles, food processing, wood and cement). North Thailand produces mountain or dry rice (as opposed to 'water-rice', the bulk of the crop produced in Thailand) for local use, maize, tea, certain fruits and teak.

POPULATION

The population of Thailand is 50 million and currently growing at a rate of 1.9% per annum, (as opposed to 3.3% a decade ago and 2.5% in 1977) thanks to Khun Mechai's nation-wide family planning campaign. This does not include the recent influx of Lao, Kampuchean and Vietnamese refugees. About 75% of the citizenry are ethnic Thais, 14% are Chinese, and the remaining 11% include Malays, the Yumbri, Semang, Moken ('sea gypsies'), Lawa, Kui, Karen, Meo,

Yao, Akha, Lahu, Lisu tribes (the latter six are the true hill tribes), Khmers and Mons. A small number of Europeans and other non-Asians live in Bangkok and Chiang Mai. The literacy rate of Thailand is well above 80% and increasing, and the average life expectancy is 61. In both respects Thailand is a leader in the area.

Bangkok is by far the largest city in the kingdom with a population of nearly six million – too many for the scope of its public services and what little 'city planning' exists. Chiang Mai is second but does not have nearly such a big population – just over 100,000. All other towns in Thailand have well below 100,000 with few over 20,000.

GEOGRAPHY

Thailand has an area of 517,000 square km, making it slightly smaller than the state of Texas in the USA or about the size of France. Its longest north to south distance is about 1860 km but its shape makes distances in any other direction a lot less. Its shape on the map has been compared to the head of an elephant with its trunk extending down the Malay peninsula, but it looks to me as if someone had squeezed the lower part of the 'boot' of Italy, forcing the volume into the top portion while reducing the bottom. The centre of Thailand, Bangkok, is at about 14° north latitude, putting it on a level with Madras, Manila, Guatemala and Khartoum.

The topography varies and can be divided into four main regions: the fertile centre region, dominated by the Chao Phraya river network; the north-east plateau, rising some 300 metres above the central plain and the kingdom's poorest region (thanks to 'thin' soil plus occasional droughts/floods); northern Thailand, a region of mountains and fertile valleys; the southern peninsular region, which extends to the Malaysian frontier and is predominantly rain forests. The southern region receives the most annual rainfall and the north-east the least, although the north has less general humidity. Thailand's climate is ruled by monsoons, resulting in three seasons; rainy (June to October), cool and dry (November to February), and hot (March to May). More on climate in 'Facts for the Visitor'.

RELIGION

About 95% of the Thai citizenry are Theravada Buddhists. The Thais themselves frequently call their religion *Lankavamsa* (Sinhalese lineage) Buddhism because Siam originally received Buddhism during the Sukhothai era from Sri Lanka, whereas strictly speaking (according to Thai scholars), Theravada refers to only the earliest forms of Buddhism practised during the Ashokan and immediate post-Ashokan periods in South Asia. The early Dvaravati and pre-Dvaravati forms of Buddhism are not the same as that which has existed in Siamese territories since the 13th century.

Since the Sukhothai period Thailand has maintained an unbroken canonical tradition and 'pure' ordination lineage, the only country among the Theravadin (using Theravada in its doctrinal sense) countries to do so. Ironically, when the ordination lineage in Sri Lanka broke down during the 18th century under Dutch persecution, it was Siam that restored the Sangha there. To this day the major sect in Sri Lanka is called *Siamopalivamsa* (Siam-Upali lineage, Upali being the name of the Siamese monk who led the expedition to Ceylon), or simply *Siam Nikaya*, the Siamese sect.

Basically, the Theravada school of Buddhism is an earlier and, according to its followers, less corrupted form of Buddhism than the Mahayana schools found in East Asia or in the Himalayan lands. The Theravada ('teaching of the elders') school is also called the 'southern' school since it took the southern route

from India, its place of origin, through South-East Asia (Burma, Thailand, Laos and Cambodia in this case), while the 'northern' school proceeded north into Nepal, Tibet, China, Korea, Mongolia, Vietnam and Japan. Because the southern school tried to preserve or limit the Buddhist doctrines to only those canons codified in the early Buddhist era, the northern school gave Theravada Buddhism the name Hinayana, or the 'lesser vehicle'. They considered themselves Mahayana, the 'great vehicle', because they built upon the earlier teachings, 'expanding' the doctrine in such a way so as to respond more to the needs of lay people, or so it is claimed.

Theravada or Hinayana doctrine stresses the three principal aspects of existence; *dukkha* (suffering, unsatisfactoriness, dis-ease), *anicca* (impermanency, transiency of all things) and *anatta* (non-substantiality or non-essentiality of reality: no permanent 'soul'). These concepts, when 'discovered' by Siddhartha Gautama in the sixth century BC, were in direct contrast to the Hindu belief in an eternal, blissful, Self or *Paramatman*, hence Buddhism was originally a 'heresy' against India's Brahmanic religion.

Gautama, an Indian prince-turned-ascetic, subjected himself to many years of severe austerities to arrive at this vision of the world and was given the title Buddha, 'the enlightened' or 'the awakened'. Gautama Buddha spoke of four noble truths which had the power to liberate any human being who could realise them. These four noble truths are:

1 The truth of suffering – 'Existence is suffering'.

2 The truth of the cause of suffering – 'Suffering is caused by desire'.

3 The truth of the cessation of suffering – 'Eliminate the cause of suffering (desire) and suffering will cease to arise'.

4 The truth of the path – 'The eight-

fold path is the way to eliminate desire/extinguish suffering'.

The 'eight-fold path' (*atthangika-magga*) consists of: (1) right understanding, (2) right mindedness (or 'right thought'), (3) right speech, (4) right bodily conduct, (5) right livelihood, (6) right effort, (7) right attentiveness and (8) right concentration. These eight limbs belong to three different 'pillars' of practice: morality or *sila* (3 to 5); concentration or *samadhi* (7 and 8); and wisdom or *panna* (1 and 2). Some Buddhists believe the path, called the Middle Way since ideally it avoids both extreme austerity as well as extreme sensuality is to be taken in successive stages, while others say the pillars and/or limbs are interdependent.

The *summum bonum* of Theravada Buddhism is *nibbana* (Sanskrit: nirvana) which literally means the 'blowing-out' or 'extinction' of all causes of *dukkha*. Effectively it means an end to all corporeal existence – an end to that which is forever subject to suffering and which is conditioned from moment to moment as *karma*, action. In reality, most Thai Buddhists aim for rebirth in a 'better' existence rather than the supramundane goal of nibbana, which is highly misunderstood by Asians as well as westerners. Many Thais express the feeling that they are somehow unworthy of nibbana. By feeding monks, giving donations to temples and performing regular worship at the local *wat* (temple) they hope to improve their lot, acquiring enough merit (Pali: *punna*, Thai: *bun*) to prevent, or at least lessen the number of rebirths. The making of merit (*tham bun*) is an important social as well as religious activity in Thailand. The concept of reincarnation is almost universally accepted in Thailand, even by non-Buddhists, and the Buddhist theory of karma is well expressed in the Thai proverb '*tham dii, dai dii; tham chua, dai chua*' – 'do good and receive good; do evil and receive evil'.

The *triratna*, or Triple Gems, highly respected by Thai Buddhists, include the Buddha, the Dhamma (the teachings) and the Sangha (the Buddhist brotherhood). Each is quite visible in Thailand. The Buddha in his myriad and omnipresent sculptural form is found on a high shelf in the lowliest roadside restaurants and in the lounges of the expensive Bangkok hotels. The Dhamma is chanted morning and evening in every wat and taught to every Thai citizen in primary school. The Sangha is seen everywhere in the presence of orange-robed monks, especially in the early morning hours when they perform their alms-rounds, in what has almost become a travel-guide cliche in motion. Socially, every Thai male is expected to become a monk for a short period in his life, optimally between the time he finishes school and starts a career or marries. Men or boys under 20 years of age may enter the Sangha as novices and this is not unusual since a family earns great merit when one of its sons takes robe and bowl. Traditionally the length of time spent in the wat is three months, during the Buddhist lent (Thai *phansaa*) beginning in July. However, nowadays men may spend as little time as a week or 15 days to accrue merit as monks. There are about 20,000 monasteries in Thailand and 150,000 monks; many of these monks ordain for a lifetime. Of these a large percentage become scholars and teachers, while some specialise in healing and/or folk magic.

The Sangha is divided into two sects, the Mahanikai and the Thammayut. The latter is a minority sect (one Thammayut to 35 Mahanikai) begun by King Mongkut and patterned after an early Mon form of monastic discipline which he had practised as a *bhikkhu*. Generally discipline for Thammayut monks is stricter, for example, they eat only once a day, before noon and must eat only what is in their alms-bowls, whereas Mahanikais eat twice before noon and may accept side dishes. Thammayut monks are expected to attain proficiency in meditation as well as Buddhist scholarship or scripture-study; the Mahanikai monks typically 'specialise' in one or the other.

An increasing number of foreigners come to Thailand to ordain as Buddhist monks, especially to study with the famed meditation masters of the forest wats in north-east Thailand.

Recommended books about Buddhism in Thailand:
Buddhism in Transition by Donald K Swearer
Buddhism in the Modern World ed by Heinrich Dumoulin
Buddhism, Imperialism, and War by Trevor Ling
World Conqueror and World Renouncer by Stanley Tambiah
Living Buddhist Masters by Jack Kornfield
Buddhism Explained by Phra Khantipalo

General books about Buddhism:
What the Buddha Taught by Walpola Rahula
The Central Conception of Buddhism by Th Stcherbatsky
Buddhist Dictionary by Mahathera Nyanatiloka

There is a Buddhist bookstore selling English-language books across the street from the main entrance of Wat Bovornives in Bangkok. If you wish to find out more about Buddhism you can contact the World Fellowship of Buddhists, 33 Sukhumvit Rd (between Soi 1 and Soi 3. There's an English meditation class here on Wednesday evenings, all are welcome.

Minority Religions

Most of the Malays in the south as well as a small percentage of Thais are followers of Islam, amounting to about 4% of the total population. The remaining 1% are Confucianists, Taoists, Mahayana Buddhists, Christians and Hindus. Muslim mosques (in the south) and Chinese temples are both common enough that you will probably come across some in your travels in Thailand. Before entering *any* temple, sanctuary or mosque you must remove your shoes, and in a mosque your head must be covered.

FESTIVALS & HOLIDAYS

31 January to 1 February
> *Phra Buddhabaht Fair* Annual pilgrimage to the Temple of the Holy Footprint at Saraburi, 236 km north-north-east of Bangkok. Quite an affair, with music, outdoor drama, many other festivities. The shrine is worth visiting even in the 'off-season', if you're in the area.

February
> *Flower Carnival in Chiang Mai* Colourful floats and parades exhibiting Chiang Mai's cultivated flora.

February
> *Magha Puja* Held on the full moon of the third lunar month to commemorate the preaching of the Buddha to 1250 enlightened monks who came to hear him 'without prior summons'. A public holiday throughout the country culminating in a candlelit circum-ambulation of the main chapel at every *wat*.

6 April
> *Chakri Day* Public holiday commemorating the founder of the Chakri dynasty, Rama I.

13 to 15 April
> *Songkran Festival* The New Year's celebration of the lunar year in Thailand. Buddha images are 'bathed', monks and elders receive the respect of younger Thais by the sprinkling of water over their hands and a lot of water is tossed about for fun. Songkran generally gives everyone a chance to release their frustrations and literally cool off during the peak of the hot

season. Hide out in your room or expect to be soaked; the latter is a lot more fun.

5 May

Coronation Day Public holiday. The King and Queen preside at a ceremony at Wat Phra Kaew in Bangkok, commemorating their 1946 coronation.

May (Full Moon)

Visakha Puja Falls on the 15th day of the waxing moon in the 6th lunar month, which is considered the date of the Buddha's birth, enlightenment and *parinibbana*, or passing away. Activities are centred around the *wat*, with candlelit processions, much chanting and sermonising, etc. Public holiday.

Mid-July

Asalha Puja Full moon is a must for this holiday, too, commemorating the first sermon preached by the Buddha. Public holiday.

Mid-to-late July

Khao Phansaa (beginning of Buddhist 'lent') The traditional time of year for young men to enter the monkhood for the rainy season and for all monks to station themselves in a single monastery for the three months. A good time to observe a Buddhist ordination. Public holiday.

12 August

Queen's birthday Public holiday.

Mid-October to mid-November

Thawt Kathin A one month period at the end of 'lent' during which new monastic robes and requisites are offered to the Sangha.

23 October

Chulalongkorn Day Public holiday in commemoration of King Chulalongkorn (Rama V).

October– November

Loi Krathong On the proper full moon night, small lotus-shaped baskets or boats made of banana leaves containing flowers, incense, candles and a coin are floated on Thai rivers, lakes and canals. This is a peculiarly Thai festival.

Third weekend in November

Annual elephant round-up in Surin. Pretty touristy these days, but no more so than the 'running of the bulls' in Pamplona, Spain.

5 December

King's birthday Public holiday, celebrated with some fervour in Bangkok.

31 December– 1 January

New Year's Day A rather recent public holiday in deference to the western calendar.

Note: The official year in Thailand is reckoned from 543 BC, the beginning of the Buddhist Era, so that 1982 AD = 2525 BE.

ARTS/MUSIC

The following scheme is the standard one used to categorise styles of Thai art, principally sculpture and architecture (since very little painting prior to the 19th century has survived).

Dvaravati style	6th to 11th century
Srivijaya style	8th to 13th century
Lopburi style	11th to 14th century
U Thong style	12th to 15th century
Sukhothai style	13th to 15th century
Chiang Saen style	12th to 20th century
Ayuthaya style	15th to late 18th century
Bangkok style	late 18th century to present

A good way to acquaint yourself with these styles, if you are interested, is to visit the National Museum in Bangkok, where works from each of these periods are on display. Then as you travel upcountry and view old monuments and sculpture you'll know what you're seeing, as well as what to look for.

Sites of historical interest for art and architecture are: Thonburi, Lamphun, Nakhorn Pathom, Nan, Rajburi, Sukhothai, Ayuthaya, Si Satchanalai, Lopburi, Kampaeng Phet, Chaiya, Sawankhaloke, Chiang Mai, Phitsanuloke, Chiang Saen and Phimai.

Some recommended books are *Arts of Thailand* by A B Griswold and *A Concise History of Buddhist Art in Siam* by Reginald LeMay. Several good English-language books on Thai art are for sale at the National Museum, also.

Music

From a western perspective, traditional Thai music is some of the most bizarre on the planet and is an acquired taste for most of us. Fortunately I've acquired it and suggest that it is well worth the effort! The classical stuff is spicy, like Thai food, and features an incredible array of textures and subtleties, hair-raising tempos and pastoral melodies. The classical orchestra is called the *piphat* and can include as few as five players or more than 20.

Among the more common instruments is the *pi*, a woodwind instrument which uses a reed mouthpiece and is heard prominently at Thai boxing matches. The *pi* is a relative of a similar Indian instrument, as is the *pin*, a banjo-like string instrument descended from the Indian *vina*. A bowed instrument similar to ones played in China and Japan is aptly called the *saw*. The *ranaad ek* is the wooden percussion instrument resembling the western xylophone. An instrument of tuned gongs arranged in a semi-circle is the *gong wong yai*. There are also several different kinds of drums, some played with the hands, some with sticks.

The *piphat* was originally developed to accompany classical dance-drama *(khon)* and shadow theatre *(nang)* but can be heard in straightforward performance these days, in temple fairs as well as concerts. One reason classical Thai music may sound strange to the western ear is that it does not use a tempered scale as we have been accustomed to hearing since Bach's time. In fact, they do have an eight-note octave but it is arranged in seven full intervals, with no 'semi-tones'.

In the north and north-east several types of reed instruments with multiple bamboo pipes, functioning basically like a mouth-organ, are popular. Chief among these is the *khaen*, which originated in Laos and when played by an adept musician sounds like a rhythmic, churning calliope.

Popular Thai music has borrowed much from popular American music but still retains a distinct flavour of its own, even though modern Thai musicians may play electric guitars, saxophones, drum kits and electronic keyboards. Some of the musicians in Bangkok, however, have succeeded in losing all vestiges of Thai tradition in their music and can play fair copies of everything from Hank Williams to Olivia Newton-John. As far as I have been able to tell, the only good jazz played in Bangkok is played by Filipinos. To me this is ironic since I would put some of the wilder *pi*-players up against John Coltrane anytime!

If you're interested in learning how to play traditional Thai instruments, contact the Bangkok YMCA, (tel 286 1542 or 286 2580) to inquire about their weekly classes taught by M R Pranai Navarat.

Some recommended books are *The Traditional Music of Thailand* by David Morton and *Thai Music* by Phra Chen Duriyanga.

Spirit Houses

Every Thai house or building has to have a spirit house to go with it – a place for the spirits of the site to live in. Without this vital structure you're likely to have the spirits living in the house with you and that can cause all sorts of trouble. Spirit houses look rather like a birdhouse-sized Thai temple mounted on a pedestal. At least your average spirit house does – a big hotel may have a spirit house as big as an average house.

How do you ensure that the spirits take up residence in your spirit house rather than in the main house with you? Mainly by making the spirit house a better place to live than the main house. Most important it should have the best location and should not be shaded by the main house. Thus the spirit house's position has to be planned from the very beginning. The spirit house has to be installed with due ceremony and if your own house is improved or enlarged then the spirit house should be as well.

LANGUAGE

During your travels in Thailand, meeting and getting to know Thai people can be a very rewarding experience. I would particularly urge shoestring travellers, young and old, to make the effort to meet Thai college and university students. Thai students are, by and large, eager to meet their peers from other countries. They will often know some English, so communication is not as difficult as it may be with merchants, civil servants, etc, plus they are generally willing to show you useful Thai words and phrases. Learning some Thai is indispensable for travelling in the kingdom; naturally, the more language one picks up, the closer one comes to Thailand's culture and people. Foreigners who speak Thai are so rare in Thailand that it doesn't take much to impress most Thais with a few words in their own language. Don't let laughter at your linguistic attempts discourage you; this amusement is an expression of their appreciation.

Thai is one of the oldest languages in East and South-East Asia; according to

linguist/anthropologist Paul Benedict it may even pre-date Chinese, at least in its prototypical form. Many of the so-called 'loan words' thought to be borrowed from Chinese by the Thais, actually have an Austro-Thai origin. At any rate, Chinese and Thai have many similarities, since both are monosyllabic tonal languages. In Thai the meaning of a single syllable may be altered by means of five different tones (in standard, central Thai): level or mid tone; high tone; low tone; falling tone and rising tone. Consequently, the syllable *mai*, for example, can mean, depending on the tone, 'new', 'burn', 'wood', 'not?' or 'not'. This makes it rather tricky to learn at first, for those of us who come from more or less non-tonal language traditions. Even when we 'know' what the correct tone in Thai should be, our tendency to denote emotion, verbal stress, the interrogative, etc, through tone modulation, often interferes with speaking the correct tone. So the first rule in learning to speak Thai is to divorce emotions from your speech, at least until you have learned the Thai way to express them without changing essential tone value.

The Thai script, a fairly recent development in comparison with the spoken language (King Rham Khamheng introduced the script in 1283), consists of 44 consonants (but only 21 separate *sounds*) and 48 vowel and diphthong possibilities (32 separate *signs*) and is of Sanskrit origin. Written Thai proceeds from left to right, though vowel-signs may be written before, above, below, 'around' (before, above *and* after), *or* after consonants, depending on the sign. Though learning the alphabet is not difficult, the writing system itself is fairly complex, so unless you are planning a lengthy stay in Thailand it should perhaps be foregone in favour of learning to actually speak the language. Included in this book is a list of prominent place-names in Thai script as well as in Roman script, so that you can at least 'read' the names of destinations at a pinch, or point to them if necessary.

For the following phrase section I have used some common English punctuation marks to indicate the corresponding Thai tones. The level or mid tone is pronounced 'flat', at the relative middle of the speaker's vocal range.

The falling tone is pronounced as if we were emphasising a word, or calling someone's name from afar. Generally in English an exclamation mark (!) is used to indicate this kind of stress, so it serves well as a symbol for the falling tone. Example *mai!* means 'no' or 'not'.

The rising tone sounds like the inflection English-speakers generally give to a question – 'You like soup?' – so the question mark (?) will serve for the rising tone. Example *saam?* is 'three'.

The low tone is 'flat' like the mid tone, but pronounced at the relative *bottom* of one's vocal range. It is low, level and with no inflection. Linguists sometimes call it the 'period' tone, so I have used the period mark (.) for its designation. Example: *baat.* means 'Baht' (the Thai currency).

The high tone is usually the most difficult for westerners. It is pronounced near the relative top of the vocal range, as level as possible. I have used the apostrophe mark (') for the high tone. Example: nii' is 'this'.

On a visual curve the tones might look like this:

—	⌢	⌣	—	—
Mid	Falling	Rising	Low	High

Words in Thai that appear to have more than one syllable are usually compounds made up of two or more word units, each with its own tone. They may be words taken directly from Sanskrit or Pali, in which case each syllable must still have its own tone. Sometimes the tone of the first syllable is not as important as that of the last, so for these I am omitting the tone mark.

Here is a guide to the phonetic system which has been used in this book.

Consonants

th	t as in English 'tea'
ph	p as in English 'pup'
kh	k as in English 'kite'
k	g as in English 'good' or k in 'cuckoo'
t	like English 't' but unaspirated or 'unexploded'; close to 'd' but unvoiced
p	similar to 'p' in 'put', unvoiced, unaspirated
ng	as in English 'sing'; used as an initial consonant in Thai

All the remaining consonants correspond closely to their English counterparts.

Vowels

i	as in English 'it'
ii	as in English 'feet' or 'tea'
ai	as in English 'pipe' or 'I'
aa	long 'a' as in 'father'
a	half as long as 'aa' above
ae	as in English 'bat' or 'tab'
e	as in English 'hen'
er	as in English 'her'
u	as in English 'flute'
uu	as in English 'food'
eu	as in French 'deux'
eua	diphthong of 'eu' and 'a'
ao	as in English 'now' or 'cow'
aw	as in English 'jaw'
o	as in English 'phone'
oh	as in English 'toe'

Words & Phrases

When being polite the speaker ends his/her sentence with *khrap'* (for men) or *kha!* (for women). It is the gender of the *speaker* that is being expressed here; it is also the common way to answer 'yes' to a question or show agreement.

greetings	*sawat.dii (khrap'/kha!)*
how are you?	*pen yangai*
I'm fine	*sabaay.dii*
you	*khun* (for peers) *thaan!* (for elders, people in authority)

I	*phom?* (for men)
	diichan? (for women)
thank you	*khawp. khun*
do you have?	*... mii mai?*
	(subject goes first, eg *kuaythiaw? mii mai?* means 'Do you have noodles?')
I, you, he/she/it does not have	*mai! mii*
No	*mai! chai!*
No?	*mai? or chai! mai?*
where is ... ?	*... yuu. thii! nai?* (subject first)
when?	*meuarai* (or *meu!arai*)
how much?	*thao! rai*
It doesn't matter	*mai! pen rai*
how much is this?	*nii' thao! rai* (or *kii. baat.*)
What is this?	*nii' arai*
go	*pai*
will go	*ja. pai*
come	*maa*
will come	*ja. maa*
What is your name?	*khun cheu! arai*
My name is ...	*phom? cheu! ...* (men), *diichan? cheu! ...* (women)
(I) like	*chawp! ...*
(I) do not like ...	*mai! chawp! ...*
(I) would like (+ verb)	*yaak. ja.*
(I) would not like	*mai! yaak. ja.*
(I) would like to eat	*yaak. ja. thaan*
(I) would like (+ noun)	*yaak. dai! ...*
I would like a ticket	*yaak. dai! tua?*
I would like to go ...	*yaak. ja. pai ...*
today	*wan nii'*
tomorrow	*prung! nii'*
yesterday	*meua! waan*
too expensive	*phaeng pai*
cheap, inexpensive	*thuuk.*
a little	*nit' nawy.*
I understand	*khao! jai*
Do you understand?	*khao! jai mai?*

I don't understand	*mai! khao! jai*
food (rice)	*khao!*
bathroom	*hawng! nam'*
toilet	*hawng! suam!*
room	*hawng!*
motorcycle	*rot' mohtohsai*
train	*rot' fai*
bus	*rot' me*
car	*rot' yon*
hotel	*rohng raem*
station	*sathaa?nii*
post office	*praisanii*
restaurant	*raan' aahaan?*
hospital	*rohng phayaabaan*
hot	*rawn'*
cold	*nao?*
bath/shower	*aap. nam'*
airport	*sanaam? bin*
market	*talaat.*
beach	*haat.*

Numbers

one	*neung.*
two	*sawng?*
three	*saam?*
four	*sii.*
five	*haa!*
six	*hok.*
seven	*jet.*
eight	*paet.*
nine	*kao!*
10	*sip.*
11	*sip.et.*
12	*sip.sawng?*
13	*sip.saam?*
14	*sip.sii.*
20	*yii!sip.*
21	*yii!sip.et.*
22	*yii!sip.sawng?*
23	*yii!sip.saam?*
30,40,50	*saam?sip.,sii,sip., haa!sip*
100	*neung.rawy'*
200	*sawng?rawy'*
300	*saam?rawy'*
1000	*neung. phan*

Your first attempts to speak the language will probably meet with mixed success, but keep trying. When learning new words, phrases or sentences, listen carefully to the way the Thais themselves use the various tones – you should catch on quickly.

For expanding your travel vocabulary, I recommend *Robertson's Practical English-Thai Dictionary* since it has a phonetic guide to pronunciation, with tones and is compact in size. Published by Charles E Tuttle Co, Suido 1-chome, 2-6, Bunkyo-ku, Tokyo, it may be difficult to find.

For more serious language-learners there is Mary Haas' *Thai-English Student's Dictionary* and George McFarland's *Thai-English Dictionary* (the cream of the crop), both published by Stanford University Press, Stanford, California.

For a more complete selection of phrases and basic vocabulary and grammar for travel in Thailand, see Lonely Planet's *Thailand Phrasebook*.

NATIONAL PARKS

Despite Thailand's rich diversity of flora and fauna, it has only been in recent years that most of the 48 national parks have been established. Few animal species enjoy full protection, even the endangered tiger can be hunted.

A number of national parks are easily accessible for visitors. There is usually somewhere to stay, sometimes meals are provided but it's a good idea to take your own sleeping bag or mat; and basic camping gear is useful if there is not much accommodation. You should also take a torch (flashlight), rain gear, insect repellent, a water container and a small medical kit.

Most parks charge a small fee to visit. Advance bookings are advisable at the more popular parks especially at holidays and weekends. In Bangkok the reservations office is at the National Parks Division of the Royal Forest Department, Phaholyothin Rd, Bang Khen (north from Siam Square); (tel 579 4842, 579 0529). Bookings are paid in advance.

Khao Yai National Park

This is the oldest national park in Thailand and one of the world's best. It has some of Asia's largest remaining areas of rain forest and is rich in wildlife, with elephant, tiger, deer, gibbons and other large mammals. There are over 500 km of hiking trails and visitor facilities are very good.

Accommodation can be arranged with the Tourism Authority of Thailand, but may be expensive; you may be able to sleep on the floor at the Forestry HQ. Coolest months are December-January.

The park is 205 km north-east of Bangkok. Take a bus to Pak Chong from the Northern Bus Terminal (or a train from Krung Thep station). From Pak Chong a large truck with seats in the back leaves at noon on weekdays, 10.30 am on weekends (15B).

Erawan National Park
Sai Yok National Park
Srinagarind National Park

These three parks form one main complex, north-west of Kanchanaburi. Large mammals and many birds can be found in this region. Best time to visit is November-February.

Erawan is best known for its waterfall and the spectacular Phrathat Cave. Buses run daily from Kanchanaburi to the market near the park; from there it's two km – hire a minibus, hitch or walk. Try to avoid weekends.

Srinagarind is also noted for its waterfall. To reach the park continue on the dirt road north from the Erawan HQ; or hire a boat at Tha Kradan 24 km past the junction to Srinagarind Dam, for a 1½-hour ride.

Sai Yok is between Erawan and the Burmese border. It has the world's smallest mammal – a bat weighing just two grams, discovered in 1973.

From Kanchanaburi daily buses going north on Highway 323 pass the park entrance and from there it is about one km.

Khao Chamao-Khao Wong National Park

This park of only 83 square km has an abundance of wildlife for whom it is a refuge from the habitat destruction caused by forestry in surrounding areas.

From Rayong take a minibus to Ban Khao Din, where minibuses to the park are available. Best time is November-February.

Khao Sam Roi Yot National Park

This offers the largest variety of easily accessible attractions. It is on the east coast, north of Prachuap Khiri Khan and consists of a series of striking limestone hills rising from the sea. Wildlife includes the serow, a goat-antelope that lives on the limestone crags; also monkeys, porcupines and leopards.

From Bangkok take a bus to Pran Buri, from there you can hitch a ride; trucks go the 35 km to the park HQ several times daily. Best time: November-February.

Doi Suthep-Pui National Park

This became a national park only in 1981. In spite of the heavy human use which has displaced the larger animals, some trails off the side of the road to the summit offer pleasant walking after a visit to the famous Wat Phrathat. It is described in more detail in the North Thailand chapter.

Doi Inthanon National Park

Doi Inthanon is Thailand's highest mountain (2565 metres). Off the new 47-km road to the summit there are many trails to explore and several impressive waterfalls.

From Chiang Mai take a minibus to Chom Tong, then a *songthaew*. Ask for Doi Inthanon and say you want to get off at km 31. From the park HQ there is plenty of traffic for hitching.

Doi Khuntan National Park

In this seldom visited park, the trail to the summit of Khuntan (1273 metres) offers great views and a good chance of seeing large mammals, including black bear, serow, tiger and sambar.

The only access is by train from Chiang Mai to Khuntan station (one to two hours); the train makes only a quick stop, so be careful not to miss it (watch for the tunnel near the station). Weekdays are best; try to arrive by noon to reach the bungalows (2 ½ km above the HQ) before dark. Best time is November-February.

Ramkhamhaeng National Park

The mountains here are famous as the birthplace of the Thai nation over 700 years ago. One notable animal seen here is the scaly pangolin, a strange anteater the size of a small dog. Plan to spend at least two days and camp on the summit of Khao Luang.

From Sukhothai take a bus to Kamphaeng Phet and get off after 22 km at a police post opposite a hospital sign. From there it's 16 km by unsealed road to the park; hitching is usually the best way to reach the HQ. Best time is November-February.

Lansang National Park

This small park is a popular local recreation spot, with a large hill-tribe centre on the west side. Several trails meander to waterfalls. It's a pleasant stopover along the Bangkok-Chiang Mai Highway.

From Chiang Mai get out at Tak and take a bus for Mae Sot; the park HQ is reached after 18 km. Best time is November-January.

Nam Nao National Park

One of Thailand's most beautiful and valuable parks. Rumours of rhinoceros persist (last seen 1971) and the bizarre fur-coated Sumatran Rhinoceros may survive here.

From Sukhothai take a bus to Chum Phae; the park HQ is 55 km after passing through Lom Sak. Daily buses run through the park from Lom Sak or Khon Kaen. Best time is November-February.

Thaleban National Park

Thailand's southernmost park, bordering on Malaysia. The beautiful, unspoilt forests support a great variety of wildlife and there are good trails too.

The park HQ is only two km from the border. It is about 90 km south of Hat Yai; coming from Malaysia it's about 75 km from Alor Star. Best time is December-March.

Tarutao National Park

The 51 islands off the south-west coast offer beaches, coral reefs and rain forest. Turtles nest on Adang Island around September-December. The park HQ on Tarutao Island includes an outdoor museum, an aquarium and turtle-rearing ponds. There is a store selling basics and snorkelling gear can be hired.

Share taxis run from Hat Yai to the Visitor Centre at Pak Bara. No boats can be hired on Tarutao so arrange the return trip in advance; best if you can organise with a group as boat rates start at about 3000B. Best time is November-April.

Hat Nai Yang National Park

A marine park protecting the north-west portion of Phuket Island. Turtles nest here around November-February. There are facilities for day visitors; bring your own snorkelling gear if you can.

Park HQ is 1½ km from Phuket Airport. From Phuket Town minibuses can be hired at the central market for the 32-km ride to Hat Nai Yang. Best time is September-December.

Phangnga Bay National Park

The forested limestone pillars of Phangnga Bay, made famous by the James Bond film 'Man with the Golden Gun' are the major attraction. The park is 96 km from Phuket Town and nine km from Phangnga Town where a minibus can be hired at the market. Alternatively, organise a day tour from Phuket.

Khao Laem Ya – Mu Ko Samet National Park

Officially declared a National Park in 1981, the Samet Island group and Laem (Cape) Ya have only recently had a park headquarters installed (1985). The main islands of the Samet group are Samet, Chan, Makham, Kruai, Plai Tin, Kut and Thalu. Laem Ya is opposite Samet on the mainland, south-west of Ban Phe. There are many places to stay along the mainland sections of the park, as well as on Samet Island, while the other islands may be visited on day trips from Samet. Admission to the National Park is 5B.

This section on national parks was contributed by Murray D Bruce

Facts for the Visitor

VISAS

Transit visas cost US$5, tourist visas cost US$10 and three passport photos must accompany applications. A transit visa is valid for 30 days, a tourist visa for 60 days. People arriving in Thailand without a visa may be granted a 15-day stay, no extension allowed, with proof of onward ticket and sufficient funds. Non-immigrant visas are good for 90 days, must be applied for in your home country, cost US$15 and are not difficult to get if you can offer a good reason for your visit.

Tourist visas may be extended at the discretion of Thai Immigration, Soi Suan Phlu, Sathorn Tai Road, Bangkok. No extension of the 15-day transit visa is allowed unless you hold a passport from a country that has no Thai embassy. The 30-day transit visa cannot be extended for any reason.

If you need a re-entry visa for an out-and-back trip to Burma or the like, apply at the Immigration Office on Soi Suan Phlu. Cost is 300B.

Thailand does not issue 'multiple-entry' visas. If you want a visa that enables you to leave the country and then return, the best you can do is to obtain a visa permitting two entries and this will cost double the single-entry visa. For example: a two-entry three-month non-immigrant visa will cost US$30 and will allow you six months in the country as long as you cross the Malaysian border (or any other border with immigration facilities) by the end of your first three months. The second half of your visa is validated as soon as you re-cross the Thai border, no need to go to a Thai embassy/consulate abroad.

Bangkok is a good place to collect visas for westward journeys. See Embassies in the Bangkok section.

A couple of travellers' comments:

If you fail to get your passport stamped on arrival, as has happened to people arriving by long-tail boat at Satul in the south of Thailand, you can take your sorry story to the immigration office in Bangkok and after filling out countless forms and showing a ticket out of the country you might get away with not being fined. If you overstay your 15 day limit the practice at Don Muang Airport, it is said, seems to be to fine you 10B per day of your overstay.

If you want to stay longer a non-immigrant visa is the one to get. Extending it is very much up to how the officials feel about you, if they like you then they will. Money doesn't come in to it. An Australian teaching English in Thailand recounted how he had to collect various signatures and go through various interviews which resulted in a 'provisional' extension. Back in his province he then had to report to the local office every 10 days for the next three months until his actual extension came through. 'Extensions needn't be expensive', he reported, 'you just have to say nice things and smile to a lot of people'. Becoming a monk doesn't necessarily mean you'll get a longer visa either, again it depends on whom you see and how they feel about you.

If you are travelling from Nepal and purchase your Thailand tourist visa there, it will cost Rs 135.

MONEY

US$1	= 26 Baht	10 Baht	= US$0.36
A$1	= 17 Baht	10 Baht	= A$0.58
£1	= 40 Baht	10 Baht	= £0.25

There are 100 satang in 1 baht; coins include 25 and 50 satang pieces, baht in 1B and 5B coins. There are several denominations of paper currency; notes come in 10B, 20B, 50B, 100B and 500B denominations. 500B bills can be hard to change in small towns, but banks will always change them.

No more than 500 baht in Thai currency may be legally brought into Thailand by an individual. There is no black market money exchange for baht, so there is no reason to bring in any Thai currency. Banks or legal money-changers offer the best exchange rate within the country. The baht is firmly attached to the American dollar and as stable.

Twenty-five satang equals one 'saleng' in colloquial Thai, so if you're quoted a price of six saleng in the market, say, for a small bunch of bananas or bag of peanuts, this means 1½B.

Exchange rates are given in the *Bangkok Post* everday. Note that you can't exchange Indonesian Rupiah or Nepalese Rupees into Thai currency. Visa credit card holders can get a cash advance of up to US$200 through some branches of the Thai Farmers Bank and some Thai Commercial Banks. If you try to use a Visa card at hotels upcountry (very common in the south, even at the smaller hotels), the staff may try to tell you that only Visa cards issued by Thai Farmers Bank are acceptable. With a little patience, you should be able to make them understand that Thai Farmers Bank will pay the hotel and that your bank will pay Thai Farmers – that any Visa card issued anywhere in the world is indeed acceptable. A few hotels will charge an extra 3% for using credit cards. American Express card holders can also get an advance but only in travellers' cheques. The Amex agent is SEA Tours, Room 414, Siam Centre, 965 Rama I Rd.

COSTS

Food and accommodation outside of Bangkok is cheap and even in Bangkok it's quite low, especially considering the value *vis a vis* other countries in South and South-East Asia.

Legally any traveller arriving in Thailand must have at least the following amounts of money in cash, travellers' cheques, bank draft, or letter of credit, according to visa category:

– Non-immigrant visa: US$500 per person or US$1000 per family
– Tourist visa: US$250 per person or US$500 per family
– Transit visa or no visa: US$125 per person or US$250 per family

This may be checked if you arrive on a one-way ticket or if you look as if you're at 'the end of the road'.

Outside of Bangkok, budget travellers should be able to get by on 100B or less per day if you really watch your baht, varying, of course, from place to place. With travel experience it can be done for even less, if you live like a Thai of modest means. Add another 40 to 45B per day for every beer you drink. In Bangkok there's almost no limit to the amount you *could* spend, but if you live frugally, avoid the tourist ghettos and ride the public bus system you could get by on the same or just a little bit more. Typically though, the traveller spends over 100B per day in Bangkok for accommodation – this is generally the absolute minimum for air-conditioning. However, accommodation can be found in Bangkok for as little as 40B per person. The noise, heat and pollution in Bangkok drives many visitors to seek more comfort than they might otherwise need upcountry.

Food is somewhat more expensive in Bangkok; however, in Thonburi, where I lived for some time, many dishes are often *cheaper* than they are upcountry, due to the availability of fresh ingredients. Bangkok is the typical 'primate city' cited by sociologists, meaning that most goods produced by the country as a whole end up in Bangkok. The glaring exception is western food, which Bangkok has more of than anywhere else in the kingdom but charges the most for it. Eat only Thai and Chinese food if you're trying to spend as little as possible. After all, why go to Thailand to eat steak and potatoes?

Good bargaining, which takes practice, is another way to cut costs. Anything bought in a market should be bargained for, as well as accommodation. Some more specific suggestions concerning costs can be found under 'Accommodation' and 'Things to Buy'.

Transportation between cities and within them is very reasonable; again, bargaining can save you a lot of baht. See 'Getting Around'.

TIPPING

Tipping is not a normal practice in Thailand although they're getting used to it in expensive hotels and restaurants. Elsewhere don't bother. In taxis where you have to bargain the fare, it certainly isn't necessary.

CLIMATE

Thailand basically has three more or less distinct seasons: hot (March to June); rainy (July to October) and cool/dry (November to February). Some people say the rainy season begins in June, some say in July. The truth is it depends on the monsoons in any given year; 'officially' the rains begin in July. It rains more and longer in the south, so that the wet season effectively lasts through January. The temperature is more even all year-round in the south, when it is 35°C in Bangkok it may be only 32°C in Phuket. The hot season is the hottest in the north-east plain, easily reaching 37°C in the daytime and only a few degrees less at night. Most of Thailand is very humid, the mountains in the north being the exception. The temperature can drop to 13°C at night during the cool season in Chiang Mai – if you're visiting the north during the cooler months, long-sleeved shirts and pullovers would be in order.

In central Thailand it rains the most during August and September, though there may be floods in October since the ground has reached full saturation by then. If you are in Bangkok in early October don't be surprised if you find yourself in hip-deep water in certain parts of the city. In 1983, when the floods were reputed to be the worst in 30 years, it

was in every part of the city! It rains a little less in the north, August being the peak month. The north-east gets a bit less rain and periodically suffers droughts. In Phuket it rains most in May (average 21 out of 30 days) and in October (22 out of 30), undergoing two monsoons. Generally travelling in the rainy season is not unpleasant at all, but unpaved roads may close down occasionally.

Best overall time to visit Thailand would be between November and February – during these months it rains least and is not so hot. See the south during the coolest months, December and January, the north in February when it begins warming up, elsewhere (Bangkok included) in November. Of course, if you can't choose your time so carefully, come anytime, but be prepared to roast in April and to do some wading in September/ October. There is a slight increase in the total number of tourists in Thailand during the optimum months.

HEALTH

There are no health requirements for Thailand in terms of required vaccinations unless you are coming from an infected area. Travellers should have a cholera immunisation prior to arriving and a tetanus booster would be a good idea as well in case you injure yourself while travelling. You should also check if vaccinations are required by any countries you are going to after visiting Thailand.

As with any Asian country, care should be taken in consuming food or drink. Besides malaria, really serious diseases are not too common in Thailand. Bacteriological dysentery, or traveller's diarrhoea, strikes most visitors who stay for any length of time outside of Bangkok. Thai soft drinks are safe to drink, as is the weak Chinese tea served in most restaurants. Ice is probably not safe, but is very difficult to resist in the hot season. It is best to buy fruit that you can peel and slice yourself (cheaper, too), but most fare at foodstalls is reasonably safe.

Top: Wat Jong Klang, Mae Hong Son (JC)
Left: Opium poppies and bulbs (JC)
Right: Fasting Buddha at Wat U Mong, Chiang Mai (JC)

Top: Chicken stew vendor, Chiang Mai (JC)
Left: A well-stocked Thai restaurant (JC)
Right: Several varieties of shrimp paste, Chiang Mai (JC)

Malaria

Malaria suppressants should be taken before, during and after one's visit to Thailand. Malaria, a mosquito-carried disease is on the increase all over the country and unfortunately most of the strains are chloroquine-resistant, including the deadly *Plasmodium falciparum*. Taking a malaria prophylactic and a few other simple precautions can greatly reduce your chances of contracting any kind of malaria.

There is much controversy surrounding the use of certain malarial prophylaxis, in particular Fansidar. It must be stressed that it is very important to use anti-malarials when travelling in malaria-infected regions. Before leaving it is wise to get in contact with an Infectious Diseases Hospital or Government health body to find out the latest information regarding malarial prophylaxis and then to consult with a general practitioner for a prescription. Factors such as your length of stay and the areas you plan to visit are relevant in helping to prescribe anti-malarials. Also, persons allergic to sulphonamides should not take Fansidar.

In fact, the use of Fansidar as a prophylactic has been associated with severe and in some cases, fatal reactions amongst travellers who have used the drug in multiple doses (ie two to five doses of Fansidar). For this reason there's now a move by many medical authorities away from the prescription of Fansidar as a malarial prophylactic. Although the incidence of severe reaction is not high, lack of information about the drug, suggests that other malarial prophylactics should be used before considering Fansidar. Further information can be found from the article by the *Centres for Disease Control* (CDC), April 12 1985, Volume 34/No 14, titled, *Revised Recommendations For Preventing Malaria in Travellers to Areas with Chloroquine-Resistant Plasmodium falciparum*.

A good mosquito repellent called Skeetolene is sold in Thailand (manufactured by the British Dispensary in Bangkok), to be applied to skin and clothes and mosquito coils do an excellent job of repelling mosquitoes in your room. Day mosquitoes do not carry malaria, so it is only in the night that you have to worry – the day variety do carry some six strains of dengue fever, but dengue is not so dangerous an affliction, usually subsiding after a few days.

The Malaria Centre Region II in Chiang Mai gives the following advice on malaria:

1. If your travels are limited to urban areas you do not have to worry about malaria. 2. If you go to an area where you will be at risk, in the hills and forests for example, you should take a malarial prophylactic. Since malaria-carrying mosquitoes only bite from early evening to early morning you should sleep under a mosquito net even if you see only a few mosquitoes. If you are outside during the biting hours use an insect repellent. 3. If you do develop a fever have a blood check for malaria.

Hospitals

There are several good hospitals in Bangkok and Chiang Mai:

Bangkok:
   Bangkok Christian Hospital, 124 Silom Rd (tel 2336981-9).
   Seventh Day Adventist Hospital, 430 Phitsanuloke Rd.
   Ramathibodi Hospital, Rama VI Rd, (tel 2813566, 2811364, 2819110, 2819110, 2811616).
   Sumitivej Hospital, Soi 49, Sukhumvit Rd.

Chiang Mai:
   McCormick Hospital, Nawarat Rd.
   Ariawongse Clinic, Changmoi Rd.
   Chiang Mai Hospital, Suan Dawk Rd.

Insurance

As with travelling anywhere in the world a good travel insurance policy is a very wise idea. A motorcycle accident can make an expensive and nasty end to your travels. 'After paying the hospital bills, damage to the bike I hit and goodwill contribution to the local police,' wrote one, fortunately not irreparably damaged traveller, 'I wished I had been insured'.

GENERAL INFORMATION
Business Hours

Most government offices are open 8.30 am to 4.30 pm, Monday to Friday but closed 12 noon to 1 pm for lunch. Banks are open 8.30 am to 3.30 pm Monday through Friday but in Bangkok in particular several banks are now opening special foreign exchange offices which are open longer hours and every day of the week.

Businesses usually work 8.30 am to 5 pm, Monday to Friday, and sometimes Saturday morning as well. Larger shops usually open 10 am to 6.30 or 7 pm but smaller shops will open earlier and close later.

Time

Thai time is seven hours ahead of GMT (London). Thus 12 noon in Bangkok is 3 pm in Sydney, 1 pm in Perth, 5 am in London, 1 am in New York and 10 pm the previous day in Los Angeles.

Electricity

Electric current is 220 volts, 50 cycles.

Postal Services

Thailand has a very efficient postal service and within the country it's also very cheap. Bangkok's Central GPO on New Road is open from 8 am to 8 pm Monday through Friday and from 9 am to 1 pm weekends and holidays. There is a telegram service 24 hours a day. Outside of Bangkok, most post offices close at 4.30 pm on weekdays and only the larger ones are open a half day on Saturday.

The poste restante service is also very reliable. Note, however, that as with many Asian countries confusion at poste restantes is most likely to arise over given names and surnames. Ask people who are writing to you to print your surname clearly and to underline it. If you're certain a letter should be waiting for you and it cannot be found it's always wise to check it hasn't been filed under your given name.

Telephone

The telephone system in Thailand is quite efficient and from Bangkok you can usually direct dial most major centres with little difficulty. The opposite may not always apply and in smaller centres it's often best to go to the local telephone exchange and make calls from there.

ACCOMMODATION

Places to stay are abundant, varied, and reasonably priced in Thailand.

Hostels, Guest Houses, YMCA/YWCA's

These are generally the cheapest accommodation but they are not found everywhere in Thailand. There are more and more hostels and guest houses opening in Bangkok, including the two Y's, at this writing, one Y in Chiang Mai (but *many* guest houses and youth hostels), and one official Thai Youth Hostel in each of the following towns: Ayuthaya, Chiang Mai, Chonburi, Kanchanaburi, Lopburi, Nakhon Nayok, Nakhon Pathom, Nakhon Sawan, Phitsanuloke and Saraburi.

The rates for this type of accommodation range from 30B to 50B per night per person in dormitories or, occasionally, in single or double rooms. Most serve meals or can arrange for them. Guest houses vary quite a bit in facilities and are particularly popular in Bangkok and Chiang Mai. Guest house type accommodation is also spreading to other provinces, particularly in the north. Some are especially good value, while others are mere flophouses.

Chinese-Thai Hotels

The standard Thai hotels, often run by Chinese-Thai families, are the easiest accommodation to come by and generally are very reasonable in rates. They may be located on the main street of town and/or near bus and train stations. The most economical ones to stay in are those without air-conditioning; typical rooms are clean and include a double bed and a ceiling fan, some have attached Thai-style bathrooms (this will cost you a little more). Rates may or may not be posted; if not, they may be increased for the *farang*, so it is worthwhile to try bargaining. It is best to have a look around before agreeing to check in, to make sure the room *is* clean, that the fan and lights work, etc. If there is any problem request another room or a good discount.

Some of these hotels may double as brothels; the perpetual traffic in and out can be a bit noisy but is generally bearable. The best (cheapest) hotels have Thai or Chinese names posted in the scripts of both languages (newer hotels may have the name in Romanised script as well), but you will learn how to find and identify them with experience. Many of these hotels have restaurants downstairs; if they don't, there are usually restaurants and noodle-shops nearby.

Government-owned Guest Houses/ Bungalows

At Phu Kradung National Park near Loei and at Khao Yai National Park near Nakhon Nayok there are government-owned guest houses/bungalows, very nice, with moderate to high rates (200B to 1000B). Other government accommodation is available near the Sukhothai old city ruins.

Universities/Schools

College and university campuses may be able to provide inexpensive accommodation during the summer vacation (March to June). Outside of Bangkok there are teacher's colleges in almost every sizeable town in Thailand, called *withayalai khru* in Thai. There are universities in Chiang Mai, Nakhon Pathom, Khon Kaen, Mahasarakham and Songkhla.

Tourist Class Hotels

These are found only in the main tourist destinations: Chiang Mai, Bangkok, Pattaya, Songkhla, Phuket, Hat Yai, plus a few in towns near former US military bases: Tak, Udorn and Sattaheep. They start at around 300B outside of Bangkok and Chiang Mai and proceed to 1000B or more – genuine tourist class hotels in Bangkok start at 500B or so and go to 2000B if you can pay it. These will all have air-con and western-style toilets.

Temples

If you are a Buddhist or can make a good show of it, you may be able to stay overnight in some temples for a small donation. Facilities may be very basic though and early rising is expected. They are usually for men only, unless the *wat* has a place for lay women to stay. In addition the World Fellowship of Buddhists (33 Sukhumvit Rd) has a list of several meditation wats around the country that will accommodate lay students for periods of several weeks if you are interested.

FOOD

Some people take to the food in Thailand immediately while others don't; Thai dishes can be pungent and spicy – a lot of garlic and chillies are used, especially *phrik kii noo*, or 'mouse-shit peppers'. These are the small torpedo-shaped devils which can be pushed aside if you are timid about 10-alarm curries. Almost all Thai food is cooked with fresh ingredients, including vegetables, poultry, pork and some beef. Plenty of rice, lime juice, lemon grass and fresh coriander leaf are added to give the food its characteristic tang and fish sauce (generally made from anchovies), or shrimp paste to make it salty.

Other common seasonings include 'laos' root (Thai: *khaa*), black pepper, ground peanuts (more often a condiment), tamarind juice *(nam makhaam)*, ginger *(khing)* and coconut milk *(kati)*. The Thais eat a lot of what could be called Chinese food which is generally, but not always, less spicy. In the north and northeast 'sticky' or glutinous rice is common and is traditionally eaten with the hands.

Where to Eat

Restaurants or foodstalls outside of Bangkok usually do not have menus, so it is worthwhile memorising a standard 'repertoire' of dishes. Most provinces have their own local specialities in addition to the standards and you might try asking for 'whatever is good', allowing the proprietors to choose for you. Of course, you might get stuck with a large bill this way, but with a little practice in Thai social relations you may get some very pleasant results.

The most economical places to eat and the most dependable, are noodle-shops and night markets. Most towns and villages have at least one night market and several noodle-shops. The night market(s) in Chiang Mai have a slight reputation for over-charging (especially for large parties), but on the other hand I have never been over-charged for food anywhere in Thailand. It helps if you speak Thai as much as possible.

What to Eat

Thai food is served with a variety of condiments, including ground red pepper, ground peanuts, vinegar with sliced peppers, fish sauce with peppers *(nam plaa phrik)*, a spicy red sauce called *nam phrik si raachaa* (from Si Racha, of course), and any number of other special sauces for particular dishes. Soy sauce *(nam sii-yu)* can be requested.

Except for the 'rice plates' and noodle dishes, Thai meals are usually ordered family style, which is to say that two or more people order together, sharing different dishes. Traditionally, the party orders one of each kind of dish, eg one chicken, one fish, one soup, etc. One dish is generally large enough for two people. One or two extras may be ordered for a large party. If you come to eat at a Thai restaurant alone and order one of these 'entrees', you had better be hungry or know enough Thai to order a small portion. This latter alternative is not really too acceptable socially; Thais generally consider eating alone in a restaurant unusual. But then as a *farang* you're an exception anyway.

Thais eat with a fork and spoon, except for noodles which are eaten with spoon and chopsticks *(ta-kiap)* and sticky rice, which is rolled into balls and eaten with hands, along with the food accompanying it.

A list follows of standard dishes in Thai script with a transliterated pronunciation guide using the system outlined in the Language section and English translation/description.

Beverages

plain water	*nam. plao.*	น้ำเปล่า
boiled water	*nam' tom!*	น้ำต้ม
ice	*nam' khaeng?*	น้ำแข็ง
weak Chinese tea	*nam' chaa*	น้ำชา
hot water	*nam' rawn'*	น้ำร้อน
cold water	*nam' yen*	น้ำเย็น
Chinese tea	*chaa jiin*	ชาจีน

iced tea with milk & sugar	*chaa yen*	ชาเย็น
iced black tea with sugar (thai tea)	*chaa dam yen*	ชาดำเย็น
no sugar (command)	*mai! sai. nam'-taan*	ไม่ใส่น้ำตาล
hot Thai tea with sugar	*chaa dam rawn'*	ชาดำร้อน
hot Thai tea with milk & sugar	*chaa rawn'*	ชาร้อน
hot coffee with milk & sugar	*kaafae rawn'*	กาแฟร้อน
iced coffee with sugar, no milk	*oh-lieng'*	โอเลี้ยง
Ovaltine	*ohwantin*	โอวัลติน
orange soda	*nam' som!*	น้ำส้ม
plain milk	*nom jeud.*	นมจืด
yoghurt	*nom priaw!*	นมเปรี้ยว
beer	*bia*	เบียร์
iced lime juice with sugar (usually with salt too)	*nam'manao*	น้ำมะนาว
no salt (command)	*mai! sai. kleua*	ไม่ใส่เกลือ
rice whiskey	*mae khong?* (brand name)	แม่โขง

Curries

rich, spicy curry with chicken or beef	*kaeng mat'-sa-man*	แกงมัสหมั่น
mild,'Indian-style' curry with chicken	*kaeng kari. kai.*	แกงกะหรี่ไก่
hot Thai chicken curry	*kaeng phet. kai.*	แกงเผ็ดไก่
fish & vegetable curry	*kaeng som!*	แกงส้ม
'green' curry, made with fish, chicken or beef	*kaeng khiaw?wann?*	แกงเขียวหวาน
savoury curry with chicken or beef	*kaeng phanaeng*	แกงพะแนง
beef curry	*kaeng neua'*	แกงเนื้อ
catfish curry	*kaeng plaa duk*	แกงปลาดุก

Soups

mild soup with vegetables & pork	*kaeng jeud.*	แกงจืด
same as above, with bean curd	*kaeng jeud. tao!hu!*	แกงจืดเต้าหู้
delicious soup with chicken, 'Laos', & coconut	*tom! khaa. kai.*	ต้มข่าไก่
shrimp & lemon grass soup with mushrooms	*tom! yam kung!*	ต้มยำกุ้ง
fishball soup	*kaeng jeud, luuk! chin'*	แกงจืดลูกชิ้น
rice soup with fish/chicken/shrimp	*khao! tom! plaa/ kai./kung!*	ข้าวต้มปลา/ไก่/กุ้ง

Eggs

hard-boiled egg	*khai. tom!*	ไข่ต้ม
fried egg	*khai. dao*	ไข่ดาว
scrambled egg or plain omelette	*khai. jiaw*	ไข่เจียว
omelette stuffed with vegetables & pork	*khai. yat' sai!*	ไข่ยัดไส้

Rice Dishes

fried rice with pork/chicken/shrimp	*khao! phat.muu?/kai./kung!*	ข้าวผัดหมู/ไก่/กุ้ง

boned, sliced chicken with marinated rice	*khao! man kai.*	ข้าวมันไก่
chicken with sauce over rice	*khao! naa! kai.*	ข้าวหน้าไก่
roast duck over rice	*khao! naa! pet.*	ข้าวหน้าเป็ด
'red' pork with rice	*khao! muu? daeng*	ข้าวหมูแดง

Noodles

wide rice noodle soup with vegetables & meat	*kuaytiaw? nam'*	ก๋วยเตี๋ยวน้ำ
same as above without broth	*kuaytiaw? haeng!*	ก๋วยเตี๋ยวแห้ง
same noodles served on plate with gravy	*raat! naa!*	ก๋วยเตี๋ยวแห้ง ราคหน้า
thin rice noodles fried with vegetables, egg, peanuts	*phat. thai*	ก๋วยเตี๋ยวแห้ง ผัดไทย
fried thin noodles with soy sauce	*phat. siyu'*	ก๋วยเตี๋ยวแห้ง ผัดซีอิ๊ว
wheat noodles in broth, with vegetables & meat	*bamii. nam'*	บะหมี่น้ำ
same as above without broth	*bamii. haeng!*	บะหมี่แห้ง

Seafood

sweet & sour fish	*plaa priaw! waan?*	ปลาเปรี้ยวหวาน
steamed crab	*puu neung!*	ปูนึ่ง
steamed crab claws	*kaam! neung!*	ก้ามนึ่ง
shark fin soup	*huu? chalaam?*	หูฉลาม
crisp-fried fish	*plaa tawt!*	ปลาทอด
fried prawns	*kung! tawt!*	กุ้งทอด
batter-fried prawns	*kung! chup'baeng! tawt!*	กุ้งชุบแป้งทอด
steamed fish	*plaa neung!*	ปลานึ่ง
grilled fish	*plaa phao?*	ปลาเผา
cellophane noodles baked with rice	*wun'sen! op. puu*	วุ้นเส้นอบปู

Miscellaneous

stir-fried vegetables	*phat.phak. lai? yang.*	ผัดผักหลายอย่าง
morning-glory vine fried in garlic & bean sauce	*phak. bung! phat.*	ผักบุ้งผัด
spring rolls	*paw-pia'*	ปอเปี๊ยะ
beef in oyster sauce	*neua' phat. nam'man hawy?*	เนื้อผัดน้ำมันหอย
duck soup	*pet. tun?*	เป็ดตุ๋น
roast duck	*pet. yang!*	เป็ดย่าง
chicken fried in holy basil	*kai. phat. bai ka-phrao*	ไก่ผัดใบกะเพรา
roast chicken	*kai. yang!*	ไก่ย่าง
chicken fried with chillies	*kai. phat. phrik'*	ไก่ผัดพริก
fried chicken	*kai. tawt!*	ไก่ทอด
'satay' or skewers of barbequed meat, sold on street	*sate'*	สะเต๊ะ
spicy green papaya salad	*som! tam*	ส้มตำ

noodles with fish curry	*nam' yaa*	น้ำยา
chicken with vegetable & peanut sauce	*phra'raam lonngsong? kai*	พระรามลงสรงไก่
chicken fried with cashews	*kai.phat. met'mamuang!*	ไก่ผัดเม็ดมะม่วง
prawns fried with chillies	*kung! phat. phrik' phao?*	กุ้งผัดพริกเผา
chicken fried with ginger	*kai. phat khing?*	ไก่ผัดขิง
fried wonton	*kiaw' krawp.*	เกี๊ยวกรอบ
cellophane noodle salad	*yam wun'sen!*	ยำวุ้นเส้น
spicy beef salad	*laap! neua'*	ลาบเนื้อ
hot & sour grilled beef salad	*yam neua'*	ยำเนื้อ
chicken with bean sprouts	*kai. sap.tua. ngawk!*	ไก่สับถั่วงอก
fried fish cakes with cucumber sauce	*tawt! man plaa*	ทอดมันปลา

Sweets ขนม

Thai custard	*sang?kha-yaa?*	สังขยา
coconut custard	*sang?kha-yaa?maphrao'*	สังขยามะพร้าว
sweet shredded egg yolk	*fawy? thawng*	ฝอยทอง
egg custard	*maw! kaeng*	หม้อแกง
banana in coconut milk	*kluay! buat. chii*	กล้วยบวดชี
'Indian -style' banana, fried	*kluay!khaek.*	กล้วยแขก
sweet palm kernels	*luuk!taan cheuam!*	ลูกตาลเชื่อม
Thai 'jello' with coconut cream	*takoh!*	ตะโก้
sticky rice with coconut cream	*khao! niaw? daeng*	ข้าวเหนียวแดง
sticky rice in coconut cream & ripe mango	*khao! niaw? mamuang!*	ข้าวเหนียวมะม่วง

Fruit

watermelon	*taeng moh*	แตงโม
mangosteen	*mang-khut'*	มังคุด
rambutan	*ngaw'*	เงาะ
rose-apple	*chom phuu!*	ชมพู่
banana; there are over 20 varieties - *kluay!-hawm?* is the best	*kluay!*	กล้วย
pineapple	*sap. pa.rot'*	สับปะรด
'sapota'; eating too much of this plum-like fruit can irritate the stomach	*lamut'*	ละมุด
'rambeh', sweet, apricot-like	*mafai*	มะไฟ
mango, several varieties & seasons	*ma-muang!*	มะม่วง
durian, held in high esteem by the Thais, but most Westerners dislike this fruit. There are several varieties, so keep trying.	*turian*	ทุเรียน
pomelo	*som! oh*	ส้มโอ
longan	*lam yai*	ลำไย
papaya	*ma'la'kaw*	มะละกอ
custard-apple	*nawy'naa!*	น้อยหน่า

ALCOHOL

Drinking in Thailand can be expensive but it is relative to the cost of other consumer goods in the country. The Thai government has placed increasingly heavy taxes on liquor and beer, so that now about 30B out of the 40B to 45B that you pay for a beer is tax. Whether this is an effort to raise more tax revenue (the result has been a sharp decrease in the consumption of alcoholic beverages for perhaps a net decrease in revenue) or to discourage consumption (if that's the case it works), drinking can wreak havoc with your budget. One large bottle (630 ml) of Singha beer costs more than half the minimum daily wage of a Bangkok worker (54B) as of 1986.

Beer

Four brands of beer are brewed in Thailand: Singha, Khun Phaen, Amarit and Kloster. Singha is by far the most common beer in Thailand, with Kloster a close second. Khun Phaen and Amarit are hard to find, though Khun Phaen is worth asking for since it costs about 5B to 10B less per bottle than Singha and tastes almost exactly the same (I can't tell the difference). Amarit is also fairly similar, with no price difference. Kloster is quite a bit lighter in taste than Singha and generally costs 5B more, but it is a good-tasting brew. Boon Rawd Breweries, makers of Singha, have introduced a new lighter beer called Singha Gold in an effort to compete with Kloster, which is becoming increasingly popular in Thailand. At this writing the Gold only comes in small bottles; most people seem to prefer either Kloster or regular Singha over the Singha Gold, which is a little on the bland side.

Spirits

Rice whiskeys are a big favourite in Thailand and somewhat more affordable than beer for the average Thai. They have a sharp, sweet taste not unlike rum, with an alcoholic content of 35%. The two major liquor manufacturers are Suramaharas Co. and the Surathip Group. The first produces the famous Mekhong and Kwangthong brands, the second the 'Hong' ('swan') labels such as Hong Thong, Hong Ngoen, Hong Yok, Hong Tho, etc. Mekhong and Kwangthong cost around 60B for a large bottle (called *klom* in Thai) or 35B for the flask-sized bottle (called *baen*). The Hong brands are considerably less expensive. In March of 1986, the two liquor giants met and formed a common board of directors to try to end the fierce competition brought about when a government tax increase in 1985 led to a 40% drop in Thai whiskey sales. This may result in an increase in whiskey prices but probably also in better distribution – Mekhong and Kwangthong have generally not been available in regions where the Hong labels are marketed and vice versa.

A third company produces a true rum, that is, a distilled liquor made from sugar cane, called Sang Som. Alcohol content is 40% and the stock is supposedly aged, drawn from the leftovers of a rum called Tara that was popular in the '70s. Sang Som costs a few baht more than the rice whiskeys, but for those who find Mekhong and the like unpalatable, it is an alternative worth trying.

A cheaper alternative is *lao khao*, or 'white liquor', of which there are two broad categories: legal and contraband. The legal kind is generally made from sticky rice and is produced for regional consumption. Like Mekhong and Kin, it is 35% alcohol, but sells for 30B to 35B per *klom*, or roughly half the price. The taste is sweet and raw and much more aromatic than the amber stuff – no amount of mixer will disguise the distinctive taste.

The illegal kinds are made from various agricultural products including sugar palm, coconut milk, sugar cane, taro and rice. Alcohol content may vary from as little as 10 to 12% to as much as 95%. Although it is generally weaker in the south and stronger in the north and north-east. This is the choice of the many Thais who can't afford to pay the heavy government liquor taxes; prices vary but 10B worth of the stronger concoctions will intoxicate three or four people. These types of home-brew or moonshine are generally taken staight with pure water as a chaser. In smaller towns, almost every garage-type restaurant (except, of course, for Muslim restaurants) keeps some under the counter for sale.

PHOTOGRAPHY

Film is expensive in Thailand so bring enough to last throughout your visit. Also it is best to wait until you return home to have film processed, as the Thais are not known for their excellence in non-commercial film-processing. However, a Dutch traveller wrote to say that film prices are much lower than in the Netherlands and he thought the developing and printing quality was excellent and very cheap so obviously opinions differ.

Pack some silica gel with your camera to prevent mould growing on the inside of your lenses. Hill tribespeople in some of the more visited areas expect money if you photograph them, while certain Red Karens will not allow you to point a camera at them.

A polarising filter could be useful to cut down on tropical glare at certain times of day, particularly around water or highly-polished glazed tilework. Keep an eye on your camera – they are very expensive in Thailand and are thus tempting to thieves.

BATHING IN THAILAND

Upcountry the typical Thai bathroom consists of a tall earthen water jar fed by a spigot and a plastic or metal bowl. You bathe by scooping water out of the water jar and sluicing it over the body. It's very refreshing during the hot and rainy seasons, but takes a little stamina during the cool season if you're not used to it. If the 'bathroom' has no walls, or if you are bathing at a public well or spring in an area where there are no bathrooms, you should bathe while wearing the *phaakamaa* or *phaasin*; bathing nude would offend the Thais.

Which brings me to:

Nudity on Beaches

Regardless of what the Thais may (or may not) have been accustomed to centuries ago, they are quite offended by public nudity today. Bathing nude at beaches in Thailand is illegal. If you are at a truly deserted beach and are sure no Thais may come along, there's nothing stopping you – however, at most beaches (Phuket, etc) travellers should be suitably attired. Recently, when staying in Phuket for an extended period (Kata-Karon-Naiharn area), I talked with a few Thai bungalow/restaurant proprietors who said that nudity on the beaches was what bothered them most about foreign travellers. These Thais took nudity as a sign of disrespect on the part of the travellers for the locals, rather than as a libertarian symbol or modern custom. I was even asked to make signs that they could post forbidding or discouraging nudity – I declined, forgoing a free bungalow for my stay. Thais are extremely modest in this respect (despite racy billboards in Bangkok) and it should not be the traveller's purpose to 'reform' them.

CONDUCT

The TAT put out a useful handout on do's and don'ts in Thailand starting with the warning that the monarchy is held in considerable respect in Thailand (they are) and visitors should be respectful too.

There are several guidelines to correct behaviour in temples most important of which is to dress neatly and take your shoes off when you enter the inner compound or buildings. At the temple on Doi Suthep near Chiang Mai you can see a whole snapshot photo gallery of 'inappropriately dressed' visitors. Buddha images are sacred objects, don't pose in front of them for pictures and definitely do not clamber upon them.

Thais greet each other not with a hand shake but with a prayer-like palms together gesture known as a *wai*. The feet are the lowest part of the body (spiritually as well as physically) so don't point your feet at people or point at things with your feet. In the same context, the head is regarded as the highest part of the body, so don't touch Thais on the head either. Thais are often addressed by their first name with the honorific *Khun* or a title preceding it. As in most parts of Asia anger and emotions are rarely displayed and generally gets you nowhere. In any argument or dispute, remember the paramount rule is to keep your cool.

INFORMATION & EMBASSIES

The Tourist Authority of Thailand has several offices within the country and others overseas.

Bangkok
    4 Ratchadamnoen Nok Avenue, Bangkok 1, (tel 282 1143-7)
Chiang Mai
    135 Praisani Rd, Chiang Mai (tel 235334)
Hat Yai
    1/1 Soi 2, Niphat Uthit 3 Rd, Hat Yai (tel 243747, 245986)
Kanchanaburi
    Saengchoto Rd, Kanchanaburi (tel 511200)
Khorat
    53/1-4 Mukkhamontri Rd, Nakhon Ratchasima Khorat (tel 243427)
Pattaya
    Chai Hat Rd, Pattaya Beach, Chonburi (tel 418750)
Songkhla
    9 Prachatipat Rd, Songkhla (tel 243747)

Australia
    12th Floor, Exchange Bldg, Pitt & Bridge St, Sydney NSW 2000 (tel 277540, 277549)
France
    c/o Royal Thai Embassy, 8 Rue Greuze 75116, Paris (tel 7043221)
Japan
    Hibiya Mitsui Bldg, 1-2 Yrakucho 1-chome, Choyoda-ku, Tokyo 100 (tel (03) 5806776)
Singapore
    c/o Royal Thai Embassy, 370 Orchard Rd (tel 372158)
UK
    9 Stafford Ct, London W1X 3FE (tel 01 499 7670, 499 7679)
USA (east)
    5 World Trade Ctr, Suite 2449, New York, NY 10048 (tel 434 20433)
USA (west)
    3400 Wilshire Blvd, Suite 1101, Los Angeles, California, 90010
West Germany
    4th floor Bethmann Strasse, 58/Ecke Kaiserstrasse 15, 6000 Frankfurt/M 1 (tel 0611-295704-295804)

BOOKS & BOOKSHOPS
Guides

Two travel guides with some good stuff on history, culture, art, etc are *Nagel's Encyclopedia-Guide to Thailand*, an expensive little book published in Switzerland and *Guide to Thailand* by Achille Clarac, edited and translated by Michael Smithies.

The *Insight Guide to Thailand* (Apa Productions, Singapore) is beautifully appointed and well-written although it's a little hefty to carry around as a travel guide.

If you can get hold of a copy of *Hudson's Guide to Chiang Mai & the North* you will learn a lot about this area that is unknown to the average traveller. Some of the information is out of date (since the book is long out of print) but it makes interesting reading and has the best Thai phrase section of any guide published – 218 phrases *with* tone marks. (Phrase sections without tone marks are next to worthless.)

Recently a number of locally produced Thai guidebooks have emerged. *The Shell Guide to Thailand* is basically a directory of hotels, restaurants and service stations but provides many useful addresses and phone numbers and has some good maps.

Hill Tribes

If you are interested in detailed info on hill tribes, get *The Hill Tribes of Northern Thailand* by Gordon Young (Monograph No 1, The Siam Society). Young was born among Lahu tribespeople of third-generation Christian missionaries, speaks several tribal dialects and is even an honorary Lahu chieftain with the highest Lahu title, the 'Supreme Hunter'. The monograph covers 16 tribes, including descriptions, photographs, tables and maps. *From the Hands of the Hills* by Margaret Campbell also has lots of beautiful pictures.

General Books

Additional serious reading: *The Indianized States of South-East Asia* by George Coedes – classic work on South-East Asian history; *The Thai Peoples* by Erik Seidenfaden; *Siam in Crisis* by Sulak Sivaraksa, currently one of Thailand's leading intellectuals (available at DK Books in Bangkok) and *Political Conflict in Thailand: Reform, Reaction, Revolution* by David Morrell and Chai-anan Samudavanija, probably the single best book available on modern Thai politics.

Culture Shock! Thailand & How to Survive It by Robert and Nanthapa Cooper is an interesting outline on getting along with the Thai way of life. *Letters from Thailand* by Botan (translated by Susan Fullop) has also been recommended. *Cooking Thai Food in American Kitchens* by Malulee Pinsuvana is 'great because it has pictures and diagrams so you can identify your meals'!

Maps

Latest Tour's Guide to Bangkok & Thailand has a bus map of Bangkok on one side and a fair map of Thailand on the other, usually priced around 30B. The bus side is quite necessary if you spend much time at all in Bangkok and want to use the very economical bus system. It is available at most bookstores in Bangkok

which carry English-language materials. A better map of the country is published by APA Productions which costs around US$7, also available at many Bangkok bookstores, as well as overseas.

Even better is the four-map set issued by Thailand's Dept of Highways. For 65B you get a very detailed road map of the central, northern, north-eastern and southern regions. The maps include information on 'roads not under control by the Highway Department'; for example, many of the roads you may travel on in the Golden Triangle. Bookstores sometimes sell this set for 200B, including a mailing tube, but the Highway Department on Si Ayuthaya Rd and the Bangkok Tourist Authority of Thailand office on Ratchadamnoen Nok offer the set at the lower price. The mailing tube is not worth 135B.

The Highway Department maps are more than adequate for most people. At DK Books in Chiang Mai, however, you can also purchase Thai military maps, which focus on areas no larger than the *amphoe*, or local district, complete with elevations and contour lines. These may be of use to the on-your-own trekker, but cost 60B upwards per map. DK also publishes special maps for hill-tribe trekkers. See the section on Hill Tribe Treks under North Thailand.

There is also Nancy Chandler's very useful city maps of Bangkok and Chiang Mai, which are actually more than just maps. Her colourful maps serve as up-to-date and informative guides as well, spotlighting local sights, noting local markets and their wares, outlining local transport and even recommending restaurants.

NEWSPAPERS

There are four English-language newspapers available in Bangkok and Chiang Mai: *Bangkok Post, Nation* (morning) and *Bangkok World, International Herald Tribune* (afternoon).

RADIO & TV

Bangkok's national public radio station *(Sathani Withayu Haeng Prathet Thai)* broadcasts English language programmes over the FM frequency 97 MHz from 6 am to 7.30 pm. Most of the programmes comprise local, national and international news, sports, business and special news-related features. There is some music on the channel between 9 am and 11.15 am, interspersed with hourly English news broadcasts. For up-to-date news reports this is the station to listen to.

FM 107 is another public radio station, it is affiliated with Radio Thailand and Channel 9 on Thai public television. They broadcast Radio Thailand English-language news at 7 am, 6 pm and 7 pm. At 6 am and 8 pm there are also English translation voice-overs of the local, national and world news on television channels 3 and 9. From 5 am to 2 am daily, there are surprisingly good music programmes with British, Thai and American disc jockeys.

Chulalongkorn University broadcasts classical music at FM 101.5 MHz from 9.30 to 11 pm nightly. A schedule of the evening's programmes can be found in the *Nation* and *Bangkok Post* newspapers. The Voice of America, BBC World Service and Radio Australia all have English and Thai-language broadcasts over short wave radio. The radio frequencies and schedules which change hourly, also appear in the *Post* and the *Nation*.

There are four television networks in Bangkok. Channel 9 is the national public television station and broadcasts from 6 am until midnight. Channel 3 is privately owned and is on the air from 4 pm until midnight. Channel 5 is a military network (the only one to operate during *coups*), it broadcasts from 4 pm to midnight as well. Channel 7 is military-owned but broadcast time is leased to private companies, hours of operation are noon to midnight. Upcountry cities will generally receive only two networks, channel 9 and a local private network with restricted hours.

THINGS TO BUY

There are a lot of good bargains awaiting you in Thailand if you have the space to carry them back.

Fabrics

Possibly the best all-round buy in Thailand in my opinion. Thai silk is considered the best in the world and can be purchased cheaply in the north-east where it is made or, more easily, in Bangkok. Excellent and reasonably-priced tailor shops can make your choice of fabric into almost any pattern. Cottons are also a good deal – common items like the *phaakamaa*, which is reputed to have over a hundred uses in Thailand and the *phaasin*, the slightly larger female equivalent, make great tablecloths and curtains. Good ready-made cotton shirts are available, for example, the *maw hawm* (Thai work shirt) and the *kuay haeng* ('Chinese' style shirt), see the section on Pasang in the north and Koh Yaw in the south. Nice batik is available too. Always bargain for these items.

Shoulder Bags

Thai shoulder bags or *yaams*, are generally quite well made. The *yaam* comes in many varieties, some woven by hill tribes, others by Thai cottage industry. Chiang Mai has a good selection, but Bangkok has the best prices – try the Indian district (Pahurat) for these as well as anything else made of cloth.

The best *yaams* are made by the Lahu hill-tribes, whom the Thais call 'Musoe'. The weaving is more skillful and the bags tend to last longer than those made by other tribes.

Antiques

Real antiques cannot be taken out of Thailand without a permit from the Department of Fine Arts. No Buddha image, new or old, may be exported without permission – refer to Fine Arts again, or, in some cases, the Department of Religious Affairs, under the Ministry of Education. Too many private collectors smuggling and hording Siamese art (Buddhas in particular) around the world have caused this situation to arise.

Chinese and Thai antiques are sold in Chinatown in an area called Wang Burapha – the streets with Chinese 'gates' over the entrance. Some antiques (and many fakes) are sold at the Weekend Market, Chatuchak Park. Objects for sale in the tourist antique shops are well over-priced, as can be expected.

Jewellery
Thailand is one of the world's largest exporters of gems and ornaments, rivalled only by India and Sri Lanka. The biggest importers of Thai jewellery are the US, Japan and Switzerland. One of the results of the remarkable growth of the gem industry – in Thailand the gem trade has increased nearly 10% every year for the last decade – is that the prices are rising rapidly. If you know what you are doing you can make some really good buys in both unset gems and finished jewellery. Gold ornaments are sold at a good rate as labour costs are low. The best bargains in gems are jade, rubies and sapphires. Buy from reputable dealers only, unless you're a gemologist. I've heard of *farangs* that scored really big but be careful. Shop around.

Hill-tribe Crafts
Interesting embroidery, clothing, bags and jewellery from the north, can be bought in Bangkok at Narayan Phand, (a store on Larn Luang Rd, at the Queen's Hillcrafts Foundation in the Sapatum Palace compound behind the Siam Centre) and at various tourist shops around town. The International School of Bangkok, on Soi Ruam Chai (Soi 15) off Sukhumvit Rd, has regular hill-tribe craft sales, often featuring good selections and the prices

are good. These are usually held once a month but check with the school to find out the latest schedule. In Chiang Mai there are shops selling handicrafts all along Thapae Rd and there is a shop sponsored by missionaries near Prince Royal College. There is a branch of the Queen's Hillcrafts Foundation in Chiang Rai. It is worthwhile to shop around for the best prices and bargain. The all-round best buys on northern hill-tribe crafts are at the Chiang Mai night bazaar.

Lacquerware
Thailand produces some good Burmese-style lacquerware and sells some of the Burmese stuff itself, along the northern Burmese border. Try towns like Mae Sot and Mae Hong Son for the best values.

Fake or Pirated Goods
In Bangkok, Chiang Mai, Pattaya, Phuket and Hat Yai, there is a black market street trade in fake designer goods; particularly LaCoste ('crocodile') polo shirts and Rolex, Dunhill and Cartier watches. No one pretends they're the real thing, at least not the vendors themselves. The European manufacturers are applying heavy pressure to the Asian governments involved to get this stuff off the street.

Prerecorded cassette tapes are another slightly illegal bargain in Thailand. The tapes are 'pirated', that is, no royalties are paid to the copyright owners.

THINGS TO BRING
As little as possible – one medium-size shoulder bag or backpack should do it. Pack light, wash-and-wear, natural-fabric clothes, unless you're going to be in the north in the cool season, in which case you should have a sweater/pullover. Pick up a *phaakamaa* (short Thai-style sarong for men) or *phaasin* (same made for women but longer) to wear in your room, on the beach, or when bathing outdoors. These can be bought at any local market

(different patterns/colours in different parts of the country) and the sellers will show you how to tie them. The *phaakamaa/ phaasin* is a very handy item, it can be used to sleep on or as a light bedspread, as a make-shift 'shopping bag', as a turban-scarf to keep off the sun and absorb perspiration, as a towel, as a small hammock and as a device with which to climb coconut palms – to name just a few of its many functions. (It is not considered proper street attire, however.)

Sunglasses are a must for most people, they can be bought cheaply in Bangkok. Slip-on shoes or sandals are highly recommended – besides being cooler than tie shoes, they are easily removed before entering a Thai home or temple. A small torch (flashlight) is a good idea, makes it easier to find your way back to your bungalow at night if you are staying at the beach or at a government guest house. A couple of other handy things are a compass and a fits-all sink plug. Sunscreen and mosquito repellent can be purchased in Thailand, as can toothpaste, soap and most other toiletries.

SAFETY

Several insurgent groups have been operating in Thailand since the 1920s and 1930s – the Communist Party of Thailand (CPT) with its tactical force, the People's Liberation Army of Thailand (PLAT) in rural areas all over Thailand, as well as the Malay separatists and Muslim revolutionaries in the extreme south. These groups have been mainly involved in propaganda activity, village infiltration and occasional clashes with Thai government troops. Very rarely have they had any encounters with foreign travellers. Aside from sporadic terrorist bombings – mostly in railway stations in the south and sometimes at up-country festivals – 'innocent' people have not been involved in the insurgent activity.

In 1976, the official government estimate of the number of active guerrillas in Thailand was 10,000. By the end of the 1970s however, many CPT followers had surrendered under the government amnesty programme. In the 1980s new military strategies, as well as political measures, reduced the number to around two to three thousand. In the south, traditionally a hot spot, communist forces have been all but limited to Camp 508 in a relatively inaccessible area along the Surat Thani-Nakhon Si Thammarat provincial border.

In the north and north-east, the government claims that armed resistance has been virtually eliminated and this appears to be verified by independent sources. Part of the reason for the CPT's dwindling influence stems from the 1979 split between the CPT and the Chinese Communist Party over policy differences regarding Indochinese revolution – CPT cadres used to get training in Kunming, China. New highways in previously remote provinces such as Nan and Loei have contributed to improved communications, stability and central (Bangkok) control. This means that routes in these provinces closed to foreigners in the 1970s, are now open for travel, eg

Phitsanuloke to Loei via Nakhon Thai. Within the next two years or so, travellers should be able to travel from Nan to Loei by bus and from Chiang Rai to Nan via Chiang Muan. A new road between Phattalung and Hat Yai has cut travel time between those two cities considerably.

Whether this signals a long-lasting trend or not is difficult to say. The battle is between government and anti-government forces. As long as you are not directly associated with either side there is little danger in travelling through guerrilla territory, wherever it may or may not exist in the future.

Border Areas

Probably the most sensitive areas in Thailand now are the border areas. Most dangerous is the Thai-Kampuchean border area, especially since the Vietnamese-backed Heng Samrin regime has instituted its 'K-5' plan to seal the border with heavy armament, land mines and booby traps. Most but not all of the latter are planted inside Kampuchean territory, so it is imperative that you stay away from this border. The armed guards, booby traps and mines make it impossible to safely visit the Phra Viharn ruins just inside Kampuchea near Ubon. Anyway, you would probably be stopped by Thai troops at Kantharalak on approach.

The Thai-Lao border is not nearly as dangerous but you should avoid walking along the Mekhong River at night, as this is when Thai and Lao troops occasionally trade fire. As with Kampuchea, it is not a good idea to try and cross into Laos illegally – you might very well be accused of espionage and end up in prison or worse.

The Burmese border is fairly safe in most places, but there is occasional shelling between Mae Sot and Mae Sarieng coming from Burmese troops in pursuit of Karen rebels. The rebels are trying to maintain an independent nation

called Kawthoolei along the border with Thailand. If you cross and are captured by the Burmese, you will automatically be suspected of supporting the Karen. If you are captured by the Karen, you will probably be released though they may demand money

Moving to the Thai-Malaysian border; it is fairly safe except for the area in the Yala province around Betong, where the Communist Party of Malaysia have established themselves in some numbers. Thai and Malaysian government troops occasionally carry out joint operations in this area in pursuit of the insurgents. They are particularly in search of so-called Target 1, a company-sized camp and possible headquarters of the CPM believed to be somewhere in the mountains near Betong.

Precautions

Although Thailand is in no way a dangerous country to visit, it's wise to be a little cautious in Thailand, particularly if you're a solo woman traveller. In that case take special care on arrival at Bangkok airport particularly at night. Don't take one of Bangkok's often very unofficial taxis by yourself – better the Thai International bus, or even the public bus. Women in particular, but men also, should ensure their rooms are securely locked and bolted at night. Inspect cheap rooms with thin walls for strategic peepholes. Take care with the police, reported several women travellers. And watch out for the monks said one!

Take caution when leaving valuables in hotel safes. One traveller reported his experience of leaving valuables in a Chiang Mai hotel safe while trekking. On return home to the USA, a bill arrived for about US$1000. This was for jewellery charged to his Visa card in Bangkok while his card had supposedly been secure in the hotel safe! Many travellers have reported similar experiences, especially in Chiang Mai. Make sure you obtain an itemised receipt for property left in hotel safes – note the exact quantity of travellers cheques and all other valuables.

On trains, particularly the Hat Yai-Bangkok service, beware of friendly strangers offering cigarettes, coffee or sweets (candy). Several travellers have reported waking up with a headache sometime later to find their valuables have disappeared. One recent letter reported how a would be druggist consider-ably overdid it with what looked like a machine wrapped, made-in-England Cadbury's chocolate. His girlfriend spat it out immediately, he woke up nine hours later in hospital having required emergency resuscitation after his breathing nearly stopped. This happened on the Surat Thani-Phuket bus. Conclusion – don't accept gifts from strangers.

Getting There

BY AIR

The expense of getting to Bangkok per air km, varies quite a bit depending on your point of departure. However, you can take heart in the fact that Bangkok is one of the cheapest cities in the world to fly out of, due to the Thai government's loose restrictions on air fares and the close competition between airlines and travel agencies. The result is that with a little shopping around, you can come up with some real bargains. If you can find a cheap one-way ticket to Bangkok, take it, because you are virtually guaranteed to find one of equal or lesser cost for the return trip once you get there.

From most places around the world your best bet will be budget, excursion or Apex (advance purchase) fares – when enquiring from airlines ask for the various fares in that order. Each carries its own set of restrictions and it's up to you to decide which set works best in your case. Fares are going up and down with regularity these days, but in general they are cheaper from September through to April than during the rest of the year.

Fares listed below should serve as a guideline – don't count on them staying this way for long (they may go down!).

From Australia

Regular one-way economy fare from Australia to Bangkok is A$1143 from Sydney or Melbourne, A$953 from Perth. There are one-way and return advance purchase fares which must be booked and paid for 21 days in advance. Two seasons apply to advance purchase tickets, the peak is 10 December to 10 January, all the rest of the year is off-peak.

One-way advance purchase fares are A$601 from Sydney or Melbourne (A$727 peak), A$439 from Perth (A$532 peak). The return fares are A$924 from Sydney or Melbourne (A$1118 peak), A$680 from Perth (A$820 peak). Through travel agents specialising in discount tickets you should be able to knock a bit off these fares although you will still need to book in advance.

From Europe

London 'bucket shops' will have tickets to Bangkok available for around £180 one-way or £360 return. It's also easy to stop-over in Bangkok between London and Australia with fares for around £380 to the Australian east coast. Good travel agents to try for these sort of fares are Trailfinders on Earls Court Rd or STA on Old Brompton Rd. Or you can simply check the travel ads in *Time Out* or the *News & Travel Magazine*.

From North America

If you can fly from the West Coast, you can get some great deals. First and foremost among the bargains is *OC Tours*, their new address is 1366 San Mateo Ave, South San Francisco, CA 94080. Toll-free from outside California is now (tel (800) 227 5988), inside CA, (tel (800) 632 4739). OC Tours is a Chinese-operated corporation which mainly serves the heavy Chinese traffic between San Francisco and Hong Kong. This company even puts out an interesting monthly newspaper which is the 'largest trilingual monthly in America' (English, Chinese, Japanese) and which contains a full listing of routes (extensive) and fares (quite low). OC Tours suspended its charter service early in 1983 but is now doing charters again. Charters start at US$739 return.

Other airways to check, all cheapest from the West Coast are: Thai International, China Airlines, Korean Airlines, Pan Am and CP Air. Each of these airlines has a budget and/or 'super Apex' fare that runs US$900 to US$1100 round-trip from Los Angeles, San Francisco or Seattle. Thai International offers the best all-round service, both in terms of flight departures and in-flight facilities, food and entertainment. Several of these airlines also fly out of New York and Chicago – add another US$100 to US$200 to their lowest fares.

From Asia

There are regular flights to Bangkok from every major city in Asia and it's not so tricky dealing with inter-Asia flights as most airlines offer about the same fares. Here is a sample of current estimated fares:

Singapore-Bangkok	US$200
Hong Kong-Bangkok	US$140
Kuala Lumpur-Bangkok	US$100
Taipei-Bangkok	US$243
Calcutta-Bangkok	US$125 to US$150
Kathmandu-Bangkok	US$160
Colombo-Bangkok	US$250
New Delhi-Bangkok	US$280
Manila-Bangkok	US$300+

Hong Kong-Bangkok tickets can be booked at substantially lower fares than US$140 through Air India or Air Lanka.

Tickets in Bangkok

Although other Asian centres are now competitive with Bangkok for buying discounted airline tickets this is still a good place for shopping around. Note however, that some Bangkok travel agents have a shocking reputation. Taking money and then delaying or not coming through with the tickets, providing tickets with very limited time life or severe use restrictions are all part of the racket. There are a lot of perfectly straight up and down agents but beware of the rogues.

Some typical fares being quoted out of Bangkok include:

Around Asia

Calcutta	3220B
Colombo	4130B

Delhi	4490B
Kathmandu	4320B
Rangoon	1925B
Kuala Lumpur	2300B
Penang	2395B
Singapore	2420B
Hong Kong	3415B
Jakarta	4560B
Jakarta*	2500B

Australia & New Zealand

Sydney or Melbourne	9000B
Darwin*	6150B
Perth*	7950B
Auckland*	9120B

Europe

Athens, Amsterdam, Rome, Paris	8390B
London, Frankfurt	9220B
London**	7935B

USA – Los Angeles

direct	US$515
via Australia	US$760

*	from Singapore
**	from New Delhi

Departure Tax

Airport departure tax is now 120B, see the Airport section in the Bangkok chapter for more details.

BY LAND

Trains, buses and taxis enter Thailand from Malaysia, either from the western point of entry, Padang Besar, or the eastern, Sungai Kolok. See the section on South Thailand for train fares between Bangkok and Singapore, Bangkok and Butterworth, etc. The crossing at Sungai Kolok is scheduled to be replaced or superceded by a new crossing at Tak Bai in Narathiwat province, which will shorten the road link between Thailand and Malaysia by at least 60 km. The new town, which has been under construction since 1982 and is to be open by September 1987, will have a boat jetty and ferry dock for boat service across the Kolok River, as well as Customs and Immigration Offices.

There is currently no land passage allowed betwen Burma and Thailand (legally) and likewise Kampuchea and Laos, although we can look for Laos to open in the near future at the Vientiane crossing.

BY SEA

Frequent boats go between Perlis (Kuala Perlis) in Malaysia (departure point for Langkawi Island) and Satun, Thailand. The trip takes about one to 1½ hours and costs M$4 or 40B. Be sure to go to the Immigration Office in Satun to have your passport stamped – there is no office at the pier itself.

Getting Around

BUSES
Government Buses
Several different types of buses ply the roads of Thailand. The cheapest and slowest are the ordinary government-run buses. For some destinations – smaller towns – these are your only choice. The faster, more comfortable, government-run 'tour buses' (*rot tua* or *rot air*), usually with air-con, only run between certain major cities. If these are available to your destination, they are your very best choice since they don't cost that much more than the ordinary stop-in-every-town buses. The government bus company is called *Baw Kaw Saw* as an abbreviation for *Borisat Khon Song* – literally the Transportation Company. Every city and town in Thailand linked by bus transportation has a *Baw Kaw Saw*-designated terminal, even if it's just a patch of dirt by the side of the road.

Private Buses
Charter buses are available between Bangkok and major tourist destinations: Chiang Mai, Surat, Hat Yai, Pattaya and a few others. These are called 'tour' buses although there is no tour involved. To Chiang Mai, for example, there are several companies running buses out of Bangkok every day. These can be booked through most hotels or any travel agency. Fares may vary a little bit from company to company but usually not more than a few baht. However, fare differences between the government and private bus companies can be substantial. Using Chaing Mai as an example again; the state-run buses from the Northern Bus Terminal are 133B for ordinary bus, 150B air-con, while the private companies charge about 200B. On the other hand, AC buses to Phuket are all the same price, 299B (ordinary bus is 165B)

As a result of passenger complaints concerning certain bus lines with regard to delayed or non-existent departures, poor baggage service, theft etc, all buses in Thailand are required to be licensed by *Baw Kaw Saw*, which now oversees all bus operations.

There are also chartered buses running between major destinations within the various regions, eg Nakhon Si Thammarat to Hat Yai in the south, and Chiang Mai to Sukhothai in the north. New companies are cropping up all the time. The numbers did seem to peak in the early '80s but are now somewhat stabilised. Where once there were at least 10 different companies running buses to Phuket, at this writing there are only four, ie, fewer companies are running more buses.

The tour buses are somewhat more comfortable than the state buses, if you don't mind narrow seats and a hair-raising ride. The trick the tour companies use to make their buses seem more comfortable is to make you think you're not on a bus, by turning up the air-con until your knees knock, handing out pillows and blankets and serving free soft drinks. On long overnight journeys the buses usually stop somewhere en route and passengers are awakened to dismount the bus for a free meal of fried rice or rice soup. One company running buses from Songkhla to Bangkok (booked through the Choke Dee Hotel) treats you to a fabulous seafood meal at Samila Beach *before* you take off for Bangkok, which is really nice. In general, food service seems to be getting better on the long overnight trips.

Bus Safety The main trouble with the tour buses is that statistically, they seem to meet with a lot of accidents. Head-ons with trucks and turnovers as they round a bad curve are probably due to the inexperience of their drivers on a particular route. This in turn is probably a result of the companies opening and folding so frequently and because they try hard to make good time – fares are sold on a reputation for speed.

As fares are higher than the government-run buses they attract a better-heeled clientele among the Thais, as well as foreign tourists. One result is that a tour bus loaded with money or the promise of money has become a temptation for upcountry bandits. Hence tour buses occasionally get robbed by bands of thieves, but these incidents have become increasingly rare due to increased security in the provinces under the Prem administration. The most dangerous route now seems to be the road between Surat and Phuket, though this is more so because of the old drugged food/drink/cigarette trick than because of armed robbery. (See Precautions under 'Facts for the Visitor' for details.) In an effort to prevent this menace, which began to increase rapidly during the early '80s, Thai police now board tour buses plying the southern roads at unannounced intervals, taking photos and videotapes of the passengers and asking for IDs. Reported druggings are now on the decrease. Another dangerous area is in Yala province between Yala and Betong on the Malaysian border, where the Communist Party of Malaysia insurgents and Thai Muslim separatists occasionally hijak public vehicles.

Large-scale robberies never occur on the ordinary buses, very rarely on the state-run air-con buses and rarely on the trains, the Southern route being the most dangerous for trains. Accidents are not unknown to happen on the state-run buses, so the train still comes out the safest means of transport in Thailand.

Now that you've decided not to go to Thailand after all let me point out that robberies and accidents are relatively infrequent considering the number of buses taken daily (though they are more frequent than they should be) and I've

never been on a bus that's suffered either mishap – the odds are on your side. Travellers to Thailand should know the risk of tour bus travel against the apparent convenience, especially when there are alternatives. Some travellers really like the tour buses though, so the private companies will continue to do good business.

Keep an eye on your bags when riding buses – thievery by stealth is still the most popular form of robbery in Thailand (eminently preferable to the forceful variety in my opinion), though again the risks are not that great – just be aware. The place you are most likely to be 'touched' is on the crowded buses in Bangkok. Razor artists abound, particularly on the buses in the vicinity of the Hualamphong railway station. These dexterous thieves specialise in slashing your knapsack, shoulder bag or even your pant's pockets with a sharp razor and slipping your valuables out unnoticed. Hold your bag in front of you, under your attention and carry money in a front shirt pocket, preferably (as the Thais do) maintaining a tactile and visual sensitivity to these areas if the bus is packed shoulder to shoulder. Seasoned travellers don't need this advice as the same precautions are useful all over the world – the trick is to be relaxed but aware, not tense.

TRAINS

The railway network in Thailand, run by the Thai government, is surprisingly good. After travelling several thousand km by train and bus, I have to say that the train wins hands down as the best form of public transport in the kingdom. It is not possible to take the train everywhere in Thailand but if it were that's how I'd go. If you travel third class, it is often the cheapest way to cover a long distance; by second class it's about the same as a 'tour bus' but much safer and more comfortable. The trains take a bit longer than a chartered bus but, on overnight trips especially, it is worth the extra time it takes.

The trains offer many advantages; there is more space, more room to breathe and stretch out – even in third class, than there is on the best buses. The windows are big and usually open, so that there is no glass between you and the scenery – good for taking photos – and more to see. The scenery itself is always better along the rail routes compared to the scenery along Thai highways – the train regularly passes small villages, farmland, old temples, etc. Decent, reasonably priced food is available and served at your seat. The pitch-and-roll of the railway cars is much easier on the bones, muscles and nervous system than the quick stops and starts, the harrowing turns and the pot-hole jolts endured on buses. The train is safer in terms of both accidents en route and robberies. Last, but certainly not least, you meet a lot more interesting people on the trains, or so it seems to me.

Lines

There are four main rail lines; the Northern, Southern, North-eastern and Eastern routes. There are several side routes, notably between Nakhon Pathom and Nam Tok (stopping in Kanchanaburi) in the west central region, another between Tung Song and Kan Tang (stopping in Trang) in the south, and between Hat Yai and Songkhla in the south. The Southern line splits at Hat Yai, one route going to Sungai Kolok in Malaysia, through Yala, one route going to Padang Besar in the west, also on the Malaysian border. Within the next few years, there will be a line running from Kiriratnikom to Phuket in the south, establishing a rail link between Surat Thani and Phuket.

Booking Trains

The disadvantage of travelling by train, in addition to the time factor mentioned above, is that they can be difficult to

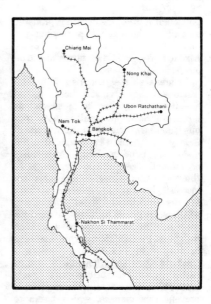

book. This is especially true around holiday time, eg the middle of April approaching Songkran festival, since a lot of Thais prefer the train, too. Trains out of Bangkok should be booked as far in advance as possible – a week minimum for such popular routes as the Northern (to Chiang Mai) and Southern (to Hat Yai) lines, especially if you want a sleeper. For the North-eastern and Eastern lines a few days will suffice.

To book tickets in advance go to the Hualamphong station in Bangkok, walk through the front of the station house and go straight to the back right-hand corner where a sign says 'Advance Booking'. The other ticket windows, on the left-hand side of the station, are for same-day purchases, mostly third class. In the Advance Booking office you will receive a numbered reservation form, white for the Southern line, green for North, North-eastern and Eastern. Then proceed into the ticketing room, taking the blank reservation form to the appropriate counter. At this point you do *not* wait for your number to be called but must fight for a place at the counter so one of the railway clerks can fill in the forms for you, according to available space on the train you want. This done, you take the filled-out form to the desk indicated by the clerk, separate your numbered stub from the form and spindle the form on the nail standing upright on that desk. Then you must wait until your number is called (most likely in Thai, so keep an eye on the numbers around you), at which point the agent at the desk will give you your ticket and collect the money. It's not as bad as it sounds, but takes some time.

Note that buying a return ticket does not guarantee you a seat on the way back, it only means you do not have to buy a ticket for the return. If you want a guaranteed seat reservation it's best to buy a one-way ticket for the return immediately upon arrival at your destination, not to buy a return ticket at your starting point. Kind of an odd system.

Booking trains back to Bangkok is generally not as difficult as booking trains out of Bangkok; however some stations can be quite difficult, eg, buying a ticket from Surat Thani to Bangkok.

Tickets between any stations in Thailand can be purchased at Hualamphong. Ticket offices for the State Railway of Thailand are open from 8.30 am to 6 pm on weekdays, 8.30 am to 12 noon on weekends and public holidays. Train tickets can also be purchased at certain travel agencies in Bangkok, such as Airland on Phloenchit Rd or at the Viengthai Hotel in Banglamphu. It is much simpler to book trains through these agencies than to book them at the station.

Classes & Charges

There is a 30B surcharge for Express trains *(rot duan)* and 20B for Rapid trains *(Rot raew)*. These trains are somewhat faster than the ordinary trains, as they make fewer stops. On the Northern line during the daytime there may be a 40B surcharge for air-con in second class.

The charge for second class sleeping berths is 150B for an upper berth and 180B for a lower berth. The difference is that there is a window next to the lower berth and a little more headroom. The upper berth is still quite comfortable. No sleepers are available in third class.

On the north and north-eastern lines, all first-class rooms are air-conditioned and a two-bed room costs 210B per person while a single-bed room is 320B. On the southern line, AC first class is the same but there are also a few non-AC first class rooms available, all with two beds, for 130B per person. Obviously, if you're travelling south as a couple, it's cheaper to get a non-AC first class room for two than it is to get two second class berths.

Third class is not too bad, seats are harder than in second and it can be more crowded, but it costs about half as much as second class. Recommended for shorter journeys.

Train fares in Thailand continue to increase regularly so train travel is not quite the bargain it once was, especially considering that the charge for second class berths is higher than the cost of most hotel rooms outside Bangkok. You can figure on 500 km costing around 180B in second class (not counting surcharges for rapid/express service), twice that in first class, less than half in third. For any journey over 200 km you are allowed a stopover of two days anywhere along the route (for a return ticket, in either or both directions, as long as the one-way distance is over 200 km) but the ticket must be endorsed by the stationmaster (fee of 1B) when you get off the train. Don't forget to keep the fee receipt, you'll need it to get back on the train.

The main railway stations in Bangkok (Hualamphong), Phitsanuloke, Chiang Mai and Hat Yai have baggage storage services. The rates and hours of operation vary from station to station.

Information Accurate up-to-date information on train travel is available at the Rail Travel Aids counter in Hualamphong station. There you can pick up timetables or ask questions about fares and scheduling – one person behind the counter usually speaks a little English. There are two types of timetable available: a 'condensed timetable' in English with fares, schedules and routes of rapid and express trains on the four trunk lines; and complete, separate timetables for each trunk line, with side lines as well, in Thai. These latter timetables give fares and schedules for all trains, ordinary, rapid and express.

AIR

Domestic air services in Thailand are operated by Thai Airways, a quite efficient small airline. They cover major centres throughout Thailand and also make international connections to adjoining countries – in particular to Penang and Kuala Lumpur in Malaysia, to Vientiane in Laos and to Hanoi in Vietnam.

Thai Airways operate Boeing 737s on all their main routes but they also have Avro 748s on some smaller routes and to the more remote locations, particularly in the north and north-east, there are small Shorts 330s and 360s. Some of the fares to these remote locations are subsidised.

The accompanying chart shows some of the fares on more popular routes. These prices though can only be guaranteed by Thai Airways until May 1986. Where routes are operated by 737s and by Avro 748s or Shorts 330s and 360s the 737 fares will be higher. Note that through fares are generally less than the combination fares – Chiang Rai-Bangkok, for example, is less than the addition of Chiang Rai-Chiang Mai and Chiang Mai-Bangkok fares. This does not always apply to international fares however. It's much cheaper to fly from Bangkok to Penang via Phuket or Hat Yai than direct, for example.

Thai Airways no longer has a run between Udon Thani and Ubon Ratchathani. Thai Air now has special night fares on certain routes which are 20% below day fares (eg Bangkok-Chiang Mai 880B as against 1100B).

Offices of Thai Airways are:

Bangkok
6 Larn Luang Rd (tel 2827151-60, 2827640-43, 2827756-60 (Head office); 2811633, 2815600-5 (Reservations); 5238271-3 (Don Muang Airport).

Chiang Mai
240 Prapokklao Rd (tel 211541, 211420, 211044-7).

Chiang Rai
870 Phaholyothin Rd (tel 311179).

Hat Yai
166/4 Niphat Utit 2 Rd (tel 245851, 246165, 233433).

Khon Kaen
183/6 Maliwan Rd (tel 236523, 239011, 238803).

Lampang
314 Sanambin Rd (tel 217078).

Mae Hong Son
71 Sinhanatbamrung Rd (tel 611297).

Nan
34 Mahaprom Rd (tel 710377).

Nong Khai
453 Prachak Rd (tel 411530).

Pattani
9 Preeda Rd (tel 349149).

Phitsanulok
209/27-28 Bromtrailonknart Rd (tel 258020).

Phrae
42-44 Rasdamner Rd (tel 511123).

Phuket
78 Ranong Rd (tel 211195).

Songkhla
2 Soi 4 Saiburi Rd (tel 311012).

Surat Thani
3/27-28 Karoonrat Rd (tel 273710, 273355).

Trang
31/1 Viseskul Rd (tel 218066).

Ubol
292/9 Chayanggoon Rd (tel 254431).

Udorn
60 Makkang Rd (tel 221004).

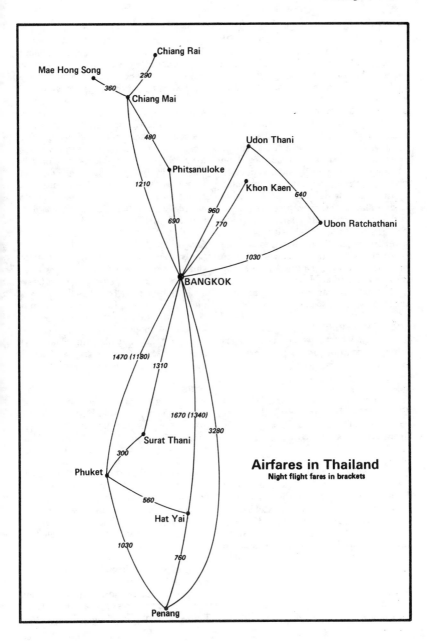

Chiang Rai

Mae Hong Song

290

360 Chiang Mai

Udon Thani

480

Phitsanuloke

Khon Kaen *640*

1210

960

770 Ubon Ratchathani

690

1030

BANGKOK

1470 (1180)

1310

1670 (1340)

3290

Surat Thani

300

Phuket

Airfares in Thailand
Night flight fares in brackets

560

Hat Yai

1030

760

Penang

In early 1986, a new domestic airlines began operations in competition with Thai Air. The newcomer is Bangkok Airways and at this writing they have four daily flights along the Bangkok-Khorat and Bangkok-Surin routes. They also plan flights between Bangkok and Krabi as soon as the Krabi airport is renovated and also between Bangkok and Samui Island when the 200-*rai* Samui airport is completed. The Samui airport will be privately owned by a group of Thai investors who are mostly medical doctors, financiers and retired military, who plan to allow landing rights for charter flights from Malaysia and Singapore in addition to domestic traffic. Bangkok Air fares are competitive with Thai Air's but the company is small and it remains to be seen whether or not it will survive to become a seious contender. At the moment it's like . Mekhong and Hong Thong whiskey, each concentrating on a different share of the market.

LOCAL TRANSPORT

The Bangkok Getting Around section has more information on various forms of local transport.

Buses

In many larger cities, Bangkok and Chiang Mai in particular, there are extensive local bus services, generally operating at very low costs.

Taxi

Many regional centres, apart from Bangkok, have taxi services but, as in Bangkok itself, although there may well be meters they're never used. Establishing the fare before departure is essential. Try and get an idea from a third party what the fare should be and be prepared to bargain. In general fares are reasonably low.

Samlors

Samlor means three (*sam*) wheels (*lor*) and that's just what they are – three-wheeled vehicles. There are two types of samlors, motorised and non-motorised. You'll find motorised samlors throughout the country, they're small utility vehicles, powered by a horrendously noisy two-stroke engine – if the noise and vibration doesn't get you the pollution will. These samlors are often known as *tuk tuks* from the noise they make. The non-motorised version, on the other hand, are bicycle rickshaws, just like you find, in various forms, all over Asia. There are no bicycle samlors in Bangkok but you will find them elsewhere all over the country. In either form of samlor the fare must be established, by bargaining if necessary, before departure.

Songthaews

Songthaew means two rows – they're small pickup trucks with two rows of bench seats down the sides. A songthaew could be a samlor or a small Japanese pickup, just like an Indonesian *bemo* and akin to a Filipino *jeepney*. Songthaews sometimes operate fixed routes, just like a bus, but they may also run a share taxi type of service or even be booked individually just like a regular taxi.

Boats

As any flight over Thailand will reveal there is plenty of water down there and you'll probably get opportunities to get out on it from time to time. The true Thai river transport is the 'long-tail boat', so called because the propellor is driven by a long extension off the end of the engine. The engine, which can run all the way from a small marine engine to a large car engine, is mounted on gimbals and the whole engine is swivelled to steer the boat. They can travel at a phenomenal speed.

Car & Motorcycle Rental

Cars and motorcycles can be rented in Bangkok, Chiang Mai, Phuket and Hat Yai. Check with travel agencies or large hotels for rental locations. Rental rates vary considerably from one agency to another and from city to city. Since there is a glut of motorcycles for rent in Chiang Mai these days, they can be rented there for as little as 80B per day. Motorcycles in Phuket cost up to 200B per day. A substantial deposit is usually required to rent a bike or car. Bicycles can also be hired in some locations, particularly Chiang Mai where they are the ideal form of transport. One traveller wrote in with this warning though, carefully note the condition of the bike before hiring, if it breaks down you are responsible and parts can be very expensive.

Bangkok บางกอก or กรุงเทพมหานคร

Population: 6,000,000

There is a lot to see and do in Bangkok if you can tolerate the traffic, noise, heat (in the hot season), floods (in the rainy season) and somewhat polluted air. The city is incredibly urbanised, but beneath its modern veneer lies an unmistakable Thai-ness. To say that Bangkok is not Thailand, as has been superciliously claimed by some, is like saying that New York is not America, Paris is not France, or London not England.

The capital of Thailand was established at Bangkok in 1782 by the first king of the Chakri dynasty, Rama I. The name Bangkok means 'place of olives' (not the European variety) and refers to the original site which is only a very small part of what is today, called Bangkok by foreigners. The official Thai name is *Krungthepmahanakhornbowornrattan-akosinmahintarayuthayamahadilok-popnopparatratchathaniburiromudom-ratchhaniwetmahasathan*, quite a tongue-twister. Fortunately it is shortened to Krung Thep, 'city of angels', in everyday usage. Metropolitan Krung Thep includes Thonburi, the older part of the city (and predecessor to Bangkok as the capital), which is across the Chao Phraya River to the west.

Bangkok caters to diverse interests: there are temples, museums and other historic sites for those interested in traditional Thai culture, an endless variety of good restaurants, clubs, international culture and social events, movies in several different languages and a modern art institute for those seeking contemporary Krung Thep.

Information

Tourist Information & Maps The TAT (Tourist Authority of Thailand) has a desk in the arrivals area at Bangkok airport. Their main office (tel 282 1143) is at Ratchadamnoen Nok Avenue. The TAT produces the usual selection of colourful brochures but they're also one of the best tourist offices in Asia for putting out useful hard facts – on plain but quite invaluable duplicated sheets. The TAT also maintains a Tourist Assistance Centre for matters relating to theft or other such mishaps. The para-military arm of the TAT, the Tourist Police, can be quite effective in dealing with such matters, particularly 'unethical' business practices (which sometimes turn out to be cultural misunderstandings). The centre can be contacted by phone (tel 281 5051 and 281 0372).

A map is essential for finding your way around Bangkok and the vital one is *Latest Tour's Guide to Bangkok & Thailand* because it clearly shows all the bus routes. The map costs 35B (some places ask 40B) and although it's regularly updated some bus routes will inevitably be wrong, so take care.

A second map to consider is *Nancy Chandler's Map of Bangkok* which costs 60B. This map has a whole host of out of the way and unusual information including lots of stuff on where to buy unusual things around the city. There's a similar companion map to Chiang Mai. Still more – well, the Fine Arts Commission of the Association of Siamese Architects produce a pack of four unusual and interesting maps showing temples and important places of cultural interest. The maps are *Bangkok*, *Grand Palace*, *Canals of Thonburi* and *Ayuthaya*.

Bookshops Bangkok has many good bookshops. Some of the best include Chalermnit in the Erawan Arcade on Ploenchit Rd by the Erawan Hotel. Chalermnit has many interesting second-hand books on Asia as well as new books and there is a second branch nearby. Continue along Ploenchit, which changes names and you'll come to the excellent Asia Books on Sukhumvit Rd, Soi 15. Between the two is the small Yajimaya in the shopping centre by the corner of Sukhumvit and Wit Thayu Rd. Other bookshops include DK (Duang Kamol) Bookstore, Siam Square and the new Bookseller, 81 Patpong Rd.

Bangkok also has some good libraries – like the National Library or the main library at Chulalongkorn University. They're perfectly quiet with air-conditioning and have many books and periodicals in English.

Money The Thai Farmers Bank has four currency exchange offices which are open 8.30 am to 8 pm every day of the year. They're located in Nana Nua, Bangkapi, Patpong and Surawongse Rd. If you're after currency for other countries in Asia, particularly for places like Burma where it is illegal to import currency and it can, therefore, be bought at a considerable discount, then check the money changers along New Rd near the GPO.

Post Office The GPO is on Charoen Krung (New) Rd. The poste restante counter opens 8 am to 8 pm, Monday to Friday and 8 am to 1 pm, Saturday and Sunday. They charge 25 satang per letter you collect and they're very efficient. There's also a packaging service at the post office where they'll wrap parcels for you for about 20B. You can also send letters or parcels from the adjacent Central Telegraph Office after the GPO is the shut.

Travel Agents Bangkok is packed with travel agents of every manner and description but if you're looking for cheap airline tickets it's wise to be cautious. Some of Bangkok's agents are quite notorious and should be avoided at all costs. Ask other travellers' advice about agents. The really bad ones change their

names frequently so saying this week that J Travel, for example, is not to be recommended is useless when they're called something else next week. Wherever possible try to see the tickets before you hand over the money. The STA (Student Travel Australia) agent in Bangkok is Tour Centre (tel 281 0731) at the Thai Hotel, 78 Prachatipatai Rd.

Embassies

Bangkok is an important place for gathering visas for onward travel. If you're heading on to Burma or India you'll definitely need a visa, if you're going to Nepal it's much better to have a visa although they are granted on entry. Both the Burmese and Nepalese embassies keep your passport overnight. Addresses of some of the Bangkok embassies include:

Argentina
    20/85 Soi 49 Sukhumvit Rd, (tel 259 0401-2)
Australia
    37 Sathon Tai Rd, (tel 286 0411)
Austria
    14 off Nandha Soi Attakarnprasit, Sathon Tai Rd (tel 286 3011, 286 3019)
Bangladesh
    8 Soi 63 Sukhumvit Rd, (tel 391 8069-70)
Belgium
    44 Soi Pipat, Silom Rd, (tel 233 0840-1)
Bulgaria
    11 Soi Lumpetch, Huamark, (tel 314 3056)
Brunei
    26/50 Orakarn Bldg. Soi Chitlom Phloenchit Rd, (tel 250 1483-4)
Brazil
    8/1 Sukhumvit 15, (tel 252 6043, 252 6023)
Britain
    1031 Wireless Rd, (tel 253 0191-9)
Burma
    132 Sathon Nua Rd, (tel 233 2237, 234 4698)
Canada
    138 Silom Rd, (tel 234 1561-8)
Chile
    15 Soi 61 Sukhumvit Rd, (tel 391 8443)
China
    Ratchadaphisek Rd, (tel 245 7030-49)

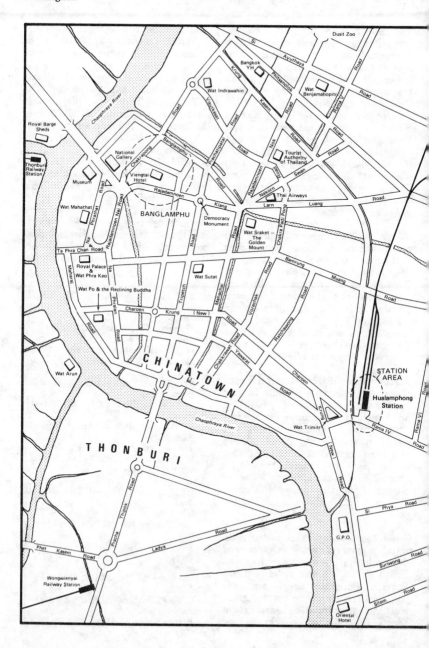

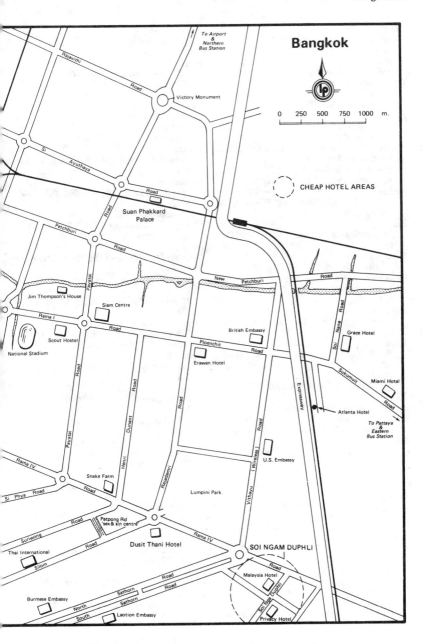

Bangkok

0   250   500   750   1000   m.

CHEAP HOTEL AREAS

To Airport & Northern Bus Station

Rajavithi

Road

Victory Monument

Si

Ayuthaya

Road

Petchburi

Road

Suan Phakkard Palace

Payatai

New   Petchburi

Road

Jim Thompson's House

Siam Centre

Rama I

Road

British Embassy

Nana   Road

Grace Hotel

Scout Hostel

Ploenchit   Road

Soi

Sukumvit

Road

National Stadium

Erawan Hotel

Road

Miami Hotel

Dunant

Road

Payatai

Henri

Expressway

Atlanta Hotel

To Pattaya & Eastern Bus Station

Rama IV

Rajadamri

U.S. Embassy

Si Phya Road

Snake Farm

Road

Vithayu (Wireless) Road

Lumpini Park

Road

Patpong Rd 'sex & sin centre'

SOI NGAM DUPHLI

Suriwong

Road

Rama IV

Thai International

Dusit Thani Hotel

Road

Silom

Road

Road

Malaysia Hotel

Burmese Embassy

North   Sathorn

Road

Soi Ngam Duphli

South   Sathorn

Laotion Embassy

Privacy Hotel

Czechoslovakia
197/1 Silom Rd, (tel 234 1922, 233 4535
Denmark
10 Soi Attakarnprasit, Sathon Tai Rd,(tel 286 3930, 286 3942-4)
Dominican Consulate
92/6 Changwattana Rd, Laksee, Bangkhen (tel 579 1130, 521 0737)
Egypt
49 Soi Ruam Ruddee, Phloenchit Rd, (tel 252 6139, 252 7767)
European Communities Commission Delegation for South-East Asia
9th and 10th floor, Thai Military Bank Bldg. Phyathai Rd, (tel 282 1452)
Finland
3rd floor Vithayu Place, 89/17 Wireless Rd, (tel 252 3636-7)
France
35 Customs House Lane, New Rd, (tel 234 0950-6)
Germany (West)
9 Sathon Tai Rd, (tel 286 4223-7)
Greece Consulate
1977-87 New Petchburi Rd, (tel 314 7333, 314 7778)
Hungary
28 off Sukchai Soi, 42 Sukhumvit Rd, (tel 391 2002-3)
India
46 Soi Prasarnmit, Sukhumvit Rd, (tel 258 0300-6)
Indonesia
600-602 Phethburi Rd, (tel 252 3135-40)
Iran
140 Wireless Rd, (tel 251 4925)
Iraq
47 Pradipat Rd, (tel 278 5335-8)
Israel
31 Soi Langsuan, Phloenchit Rd, (tel 252 3131-4)
Italy
399 Nang Linchee Rd, (tel 286 4844-6)
Japan
1674 New Phetburi Rd, (tel 252 6151-9)
Jordanian Consulate
47 Soi 63 Sukhumvit Rd, (tel 391 7142)
Korea
28/1 Surasak Rd, (tel 234 0723, 235 8339)
Laos
193 Sathon Tai Rd, (tel 286 0010)
Malaysia
35 Sathon Tai Rd, (tel 286 1390-2)
Monaco Consulate
3rd Floor Nailert Bldg, 888 Phetchburi Rd, (tel 252 8106 ext 46)

Nepal
189 Soi Phuengsuk Soi 71 Sukhumvit Rd, (tel 391 7240)
Netherlands
106 Wireless Rd, (tel 252 6103-5)
New Zealand
93 Wireless Rd, (tel 251 8165)
Norway
690 Sukhumvit Rd, (tel 258 0531-33)
Oman Consulate
134/1-2 Silom Rd, (tel 235 8868-9)
Pakistan
31 off Soi 3, Sukhumvit Rd, (tel 253 0288-90)
Philippines
760 Sukhumvit Rd, (tel 390 0993, 258 5382)
Peru Consulate
Louis T Leonowens Bldg, 723 Siphya Rd, (tel 233 5910-7 ext 25)
Poland
61 Soi 23 Sukhumvit Rd, (tel 258 4112-3)
Portugal
26 Bush Lane, New Rd, (tel 234 0372)
Romania
39 Soi 10 Sukhumvit Rd, (tel 252 8515, 251 2242-3)
Saudi Arabia
138 Boon Mitr Bldg, Silom Rd, (tel 233 7941-2, 235 2171-2)
Singapore
129 Sathon Tai Rd, (tel 286 2111, 286 1434)
Spain
104 Wireless Rd, (tel 252 6112)
Sri Lanka
1/7-8 Soi 10 Sukhumvit Rd (tel 251 8062, 251 0803)
Sweden
138 Boonmitr Bldg, Silom Rd, (tel 234 3891, 233 0295)
Switzerland
35 Wireless Rd, (tel 252 8992-4, 253 0156-60)
Taiwan visa office
Chiengnuan Bldg, 140 Wireless Rd, (tel 251 9274-6)
Turkey
153/2 Soi Mahadlekluang, Rajdamri Rd, (tel 251 2987-8)
USA
95 Wireless Rd, (tel 252 5040-9)
USSR
108 Sathon Nua Rd, (tel 234 9824, 234 2012, 235 5599)

Top: Brahma shrine at the Erawan Hotel, Bangkok (JC)
Left: Wat Arun, Temple of the Dawn, Thonburi (TW)
Right: Rama I Rd, Bangkok (JC)

Top: Wat Phra Keo, Bangkok (JC)
Left: Wat Saket, The Golden Mount, Bangkok (JC)
Right: Wat Indrawihan, Bangkok (TW)

Vietnam
    83/1 Wireless Rd, (tel 251 7201-3, 251
    5838)
Yugoslavia
    28 Soi 61 Sukhumvit Rd, (tel 391 9090-1)

Orientation

The east side of the river, Bangkok
proper, can be divided into two by the
main north-south rail line. The portion
between the river and the railway is old
Bangkok, where most of the older temples
and the original palace is located, as well
as the Chinese and Indian districts. That
part of the city east of the railway, which
covers more than twice as much area as
the old districts, is 'new' Bangkok. This
latter part can be divided again into the
business and tourist district wedged
between New Rd (Charoen Krung Rd)
and Rama IV Rd and the sprawling
residential and tourist district stretching
along Sukhumvit and Phetburi Extension
(New Phetburi) Rds.

This leaves the hard-to-classify areas
below Sathorn Tai Rd (which includes
Klong Toey, Bangkok's main port) and
the area above Rama IV Rd between the
railway and Withayu Rd, which comprises
an infinite variety of businesses, several
movie theatres, civil service offices, the
shopping area of Siam Square, Chulalongkorn University and the National
Stadium.

TEMPLES

There are close to 400 *wats* or temple-
monasteries in Bangkok. Below are listed
some of the most interesting, though you
may easily discover others on your own.
Shoes should be removed before entering
the main chapel *(bot)* in any temple
compound. Since the wat is a sacred place
to Thai Buddhists, visitors should dress
and behave decently for their visit.

Wat Phra Keo & Grand Palace

Also called the Temple of the Emerald
Buddha, this wat adjoins the Grand
Palace on common ground which was
consecrated in 1782, the first year of
Bangkok rule. Together they have been
added to by the different Thai monarchs
and consequently feature several different
types of architecture, most of it in the
Bangkok or Ratanakosin style. A very
colourful place, the wat has a mural
depicting scenes from the Ramakien, the
Thai version of the Indian epic *Ramayana*,
along the inside walls of the compound.
Originally painted during Rama III's
reign (1824 to 1850), the mural has
undergone more than one restoration,
including a major one finished in time for
the 1982 Bangkok/Chakri dynasty
bicentennial.

The so-called Emerald Buddha, 60 cm
to 75 cm high (depending on how it is
measured), is actually made of a type of
jasper or perhaps nephrite, a type of jade,
depending on whom you believe. An aura
of definite mystery surrounds the image,
enhanced by the fact that it cannot be
examined closely – it sits in a glass case,
on a pedestal high above the heads of
worshippers – and photography within
the chapel is forbidden. Its mystery
further adds to the occult significance of
the image, which is considered the
'talisman' of the Thai kingdom, the
legitimator of Thai sovereignty.

It is not known for certain where the
image originated or who sculpted it but it
first appeared on record in 15th century
Chiang Rai; stylistically it seems to be
from the Chiang Saen period. It is said
that the image was covered with plaster
and gold leaf at that time and located in
Chiang Rai's own Wat Phra Keo (literally
'temple of the jewel holy image'). While
being transported elsewhere after a storm
had damaged the *chedi* (in which the
image had been kept), the image
supposedly lost its plaster covering in a
fall. It next appeared in Lampang where
it enjoyed a 32-year stay (again at a Wat
Phra Keo) until it was brought to Wat
Chedi Luang in Chiang Mai.

Laotian invaders took the image from
Chiang Mai in the mid-16th century and

brought it to Luang Prabang in Laos. Later it was moved to Vientiane and when the Thai king Taksin waged war against Laos 200 years later the image was taken back to the Thai capital of Thonburi by General Chakri, who later succeeded Taksin as Rama I, the founder of the Chakri dynasty. Rama I had the Emerald Buddha moved to the new Thai capital in Bangkok and had two royal robes made for it, one to be worn in the hot season and one for the rainy season. Rama III added another to the wardrobe – to be worn in the cool season. The three robes are still changed at the beginning of each season by the king himself.

The palace itself is only used by the king on certain ceremonial occasions (eg Coronation Day), as his residence is now Chitlada Palace in the northern part of the city. The Grand Palace was the headquarters for the attempted coup by General San Chitpatima in April 1981.

Admission to Wat Phra Keo is free on Saturdays and Sundays but on those days only the exterior area is open. On other days admission is 60B. Hours are 8.30 am to 11.30 am and 1 pm to 3.30 pm.

Wat Mahathat

A very old monastery, Wat Mahathat is worth a visit as it is right across the street from Wat Phra Keo, on the west side of Sanam Luang. This wat is a national centre for the Mahanikai monastic sect and houses one of Bangkok's two Buddhist universities. Check out the pigeons in the courtyard behind the main temple.

The temple is officially open to visitors from 9 am to 5 pm everyday and on *wan phra* – Buddhist holy days (the full and new moons every fortnight). There is an admission charge. There is an open-air market which features traditional Thai herbal medicine.

Those interested in learning about Buddhist meditation or *vipassana* should contact the monks in Section 5 within the temple compound, English-language instruction is usually available.

Wat Pho (Wat Phra Jetuphon)

A long list of superlatives for this one: the oldest and largest wat in Bangkok, it features the largest reclining Buddha and the largest collection of Buddha images in Thailand and was the earliest centre for public education. As a temple site Wat Pho dates back supposedly to the 16th century but its current history really begins in 1781 with the renovation of the original monastery.

Narrow Jetuphon Rd divides the grounds in two; each portion is surrounded by huge whitewashed walls but the most interesting portion is the northern compound, which includes a very large *bot* enclosed by a gallery of Buddha images and four *wiharns*, four large *chedis*, commemorating the first four Chakri kings, 91 smaller chedis, an old *tripitaka* library, a sermon-hall, the large *wiharn* which houses the reclining Buddha and a school building for classes in *abhidhamma* (Buddhist philosophy), plus several less important structures. A massage school of sorts convenes in the afternoons at the west end of the compound.

The tremendous reclining Buddha, 46 metres long and 15 metres high, illustrates the passing of the Buddha into final nirvana. The figure is modelled of plaster around a brick core and finished in gold leaf. Mother-of-pearl inlay ornaments the eyes and feet of the colossal image, the feet displaying 108 different auspicious *laksanas* or characteristics of a Buddha. The images on display in the four wiharns surrounding the main bot in the eastern part of the compound are interesting. Particularly the Phra Jinaraj and Phra Jinachi Buddhas, located in the west and south chapels, both from Sukhothai. The galleries extending between the four chapels feature no less than 394 gilded Buddha images.

The temple rubbings for sale at Wat Pho and elsewhere in Thailand come from the reliefs sculpted in the base of the large bot, which are carved in marble and were obtained from the ruins of Ayuthaya. The rubbings are no longer taken directly from the panels but are rubbed from cement casts of the panels made years ago.

The golden image can be seen every day from 9 am to 5 pm, admission is free.

Wat Traimit

The 'Temple of the Golden Buddha' is situated where Yaowarat Rd and Charoen Krung Rd intersect, near the Hualamphong Railway Station. The attraction at this old wat is, of course, the impressive three-metre tall, 5½ tonne solid gold Buddha image, which gleams like no other gold artefact I've ever seen.

Sculpted in the graceful Sukhothai style, the image was 'rediscovered' some 30 years ago beneath a stucco or plaster exterior when it fell from a crane while being moved to a new building within the temple compound. It has been theorised that the covering was added to protect it from 'marauding hordes' either during the late Sukhothai period or later in Ayuthaya when the city was under siege by the Burmese. The temple itself is said to date to the early 13th century.

The golden image can be seen every day from 9 am to 5 pm, admission to Wat Traimit is free.

Wat Arun

The 'Temple of Dawn' is named after the Indian god of dawn, Aruna. It appears in all the tourist brochures and is located on the Thonburi side of the Chao Phraya River. The tall, 82-metre *prang* was constructed during the first half of the 19th century by Rama II and Rama III. It is composed of a brick core with a plaster covering embedded with a mosaic of broken Chinese porcelain. The present wat is built on the site of Wat Chang, which was the palace and royal temple of King Taksin when Thonburi was the Thai capital; hence, it was the last home of the Emerald Buddha before Rama I brought it across the river to Bangkok.

The temple looks more impressive from the river than it does up close, though the peaceful wat grounds make a very nice retreat from the hustle and bustle of Bangkok. The main tower can be climbed by means of steep stairs to over half its height and provides a fine view of Thonburi and the river.

Wat Arun is open daily; the admission fee is 5B.

Getting There To reach Wat Arun from the Bangkok side catch a river taxi going downriver from the pier at Na Phra Lan Rd (near Wat Phra Keo) or the one at Thai Wang Rd (near Wat Pho) and it will stop at the Wat Arun landing.

Wat Benchamabophit

On Si Ayuthaya and Rama V Rds, this wat of white Carrara marble was built at the turn of the century under Chulalong-korn (Rama V). The large *bot* at Wat Ben is a prime example of modern Thai architecture. The courtyard behind the bot exhibits 53 Buddha images, most of which are copies of famous images and styles from all over Thailand and other Buddhist countries – an education in itself if you're interested in Buddhist iconography.

Admission is free and the wat is open daily.

Wat Saket

Saket is an undistinguished temple except for the Golden Mount (Phu Khao Thong) on the west side of the grounds which provides a good view of Bangkok rooftops. The artificial hill was created when a large *chedi* under construction by Rama III collapsed because the soft soil beneath would not support it. The resulting mud-and-brick hill was left to sprout weeds until Rama IV built a small chedi on its crest.

Later his son, Rama V, added to the structure and housed a Buddha relic from India (given to him by the British government) in the chedi. The concrete walls were added during WW II to prevent the hill from eroding. Every November there is a big festival on the grounds of Wat Saket, which includes a candle-lit procession up the Golden Mount.

Admission to Wat Saket is free except for the final approach to the summit of the Golden Mount, which costs 1B.

Wat Rajanadda

Across Mahachai Rd from Wat Saket and behind the Chalerm Thai movie theatre, this temple dates to the mid-19th century. It was built under Rama III and is an unusual specimen, possibly influenced by Burmese models. There is a well-known amulet market here selling all sizes, shapes and styles of Buddhist amulets or magic charms, (called *phra phim* in Thai) which feature not only images of the Buddha but famous Thai monks and Indian deities.

This is a very expensive place to purchase a charm, but it is a good place to look; these images are purported to protect the wearer from physical harm though some can act as 'love charms'. Those amulets that are considered to be particularly powerful tend to cost thousands of baht and are worn by soldiers, taxi drivers and other Thai believers working in high-risk professions.

Wat Bowonniwet (Bowornives)

On Phra Sumen Rd, Wat Bowon is the national headquarters for the Thammayut monastic sect, the minority sect in relation to Mahanikai. King Mongkut, founder of the Thammayuts, began a royal tradition by residing here as a monk – in fact he was the abbot of Wat Bowon for several years. Bangkok's second Buddhist university, Mahamakut University, is housed here and there are meditation and dhamma classes in English on a regular basis. There is an English-language Buddhist bookstore across the street from the main entrance to the wat.

Other Temples

On Wisut Kasat Rd, near its junction with Samsen Rd just north of Banglamphu is **Wat Indrawihan**, marked by its enormous standing Buddha figure. At **Sao Ching-Cha**, the 'giant swing', a spectacular Brahmin festival in honour of the Hindu god Shiva used to take place each year but it was stopped during the reign of Rama VII. The giant swing is a block south of the Democracy Monument. Nearby is **Wat Suthat** with interesting Buddha images and panels illustrating incidents in the Buddha's life.

At the corner by the Erawan Hotel is a small Brahmin shrine **San Phra Prom** which attracts a steady stream of worshippers. Many of them make an offering by commissioning the musicians and dancers who are always on hand to make an impromptu performance. There's a similar Brahmin shrine at **Wat Khaek** by the Narai Hotel.

There are also numerous temples on the Thonburi side of the river, which are comparatively untouristed. See the *Canals of Thonburi* map for more information. They include **Wat Kanlayanimit** with its towering Buddha statue and, outside, the biggest bronze bell in Thailand. **Wat Phailom** on the banks of the Chao Phraya in Prathumthani Province is noted for the tens of thousands of open billed storks that nest in the temple area from December to June.

Temples aren't all Bangkok has to offer, there are plenty of other attractions in the city:

National Museum

On Na Phrathat Rd, west side of Sanam Luang, the National Museum is said to be the largest museum in South-East Asia, and it is an excellent place to learn something about Thai art before heading upcountry. All periods and styles are represented from Dvaravati to Ratanakosin and English-language literature is available.

Free English tours of the museum are

given on Tuesdays (Thai culture), Wednesdays (Buddhism) and Thursdays (Thai art), beginning at 9.30 am. These guided tours are excellent value and numerous people have written to recommend them. The tours in German have also been recommended. The museum is open 9 am to noon and 1 pm to 4 pm every day except Monday and Friday; admission is 20B.

Lak Muang Shrine

The 'City Pillar' is across the street from the east wall of Wat Phra Keo, at the south end of Sanam Luang. This shrine encloses a wooden pillar erected by Rama I to represent the founding of the new Bangkok capital. The spirit of the pillar is considered the city's guardian deity and receives the daily supplications of countless Thai worshippers, some of whom commission classical Thai dancers to perform at the shrine. Some of the offerings include severed pigs' heads with sticks of incense sprouting from the forehead area.

Royal Barges

The royal barges are fantastically ornamented boats used in ceremonial processions on the river. They are kept in the royal barge sheds on the Thonburi side of the river. They're on Khlong Bangkok Noi, near the Phra Pin Klao Bridge. *Suphanahong*, the king's personal barge, is the most important of the boats. The barge shed is open daily from 8.30 am to 4.30 pm and admission is 10B.

Jim Thompson's House

On Soi Kasem San 2, Rama I Rd this is a great place to visit, even though it sounds hokey when described, for its authentic Thai residential architecture. Located at the end of an undistinguished Bangkok *soi* next to Khlong San Saep, the premises once belonged to the American silk entrepreneur Jim Thompson, who deserves most of the credit for the current world-wide popularity of Thai silk. Thompson

disappeared in the Cameron Highlands of west Malaysia under quite mysterious circumstances in 1967 and has never been heard from since. On display in the main house is his splendid little Asian art collection as well as his personal belongings.

An excellent book on Thompson, his career, residence and intriguing disappearance is available: *The Legendary American – The Remarkable Career & Strange Disappearance of Jim Thompson* by William Warren (Houghton Mifflin Co, Boston, 1970).

The house is open Monday to Friday from 9 am to 4 pm, admission is 80B (proceeds go to Bangkok's School for the Blind) but you may wander around the grounds for free. Ask about student discounts. The rather sleazy *khlong* at the end of the soi is one of Bangkok's most lively.

Wang Suan Phakkard

The 'Lettuce Farm Palace' is a collection of five traditional wooden Thai houses containing a varied collection of art, antiques and furnishings in a beautiful garden with a pavilion. Special exhibitions include seashells and Ban Chiang pottery. The gardens are a peaceful oasis from the noise and confusion of Bangkok, complete with ducks and swans and a semi-enclosed garden reminiscent of Japan.

The palace is open daily except Sunday from 9 am to 4 pm and admission is 50B. It's on Si Ayuthaya Rd, quite close to the Victory Monument.

Chinatown (Sampeng)

Off Yaowarat and Ratchawong Rds, Bangkok's Chinatown comprises a confusing and crowded array of jewellery, hardware, wholesale food, automotive and fabric shops, as well as dozens of other small businesses. It's a good place to shop since goods here are cheaper than almost anywhere else in Bangkok and the Chinese proprietors like to bargain. Chinese and Thai antiques in various grades of age and authenticity are available in the so-called Thieves' Market or Nakhorn Kasem, better for browsing than buying these days.

At the edge of Chinatown around the intersection of Pahuraht and Chakraphet Rds is a small but thriving Indian district, generally called **Pahuraht**. Here dozens of Indian-owned shops sell all kinds of fabric and clothes. This is the best place in the city to bargain for such items, especially silk. The selection is unbelievable, and Thai shoulder bags *(yahms)* sold here are the cheapest in Bangkok, perhaps in Thailand. Behind the more obvious store fronts along these streets, in the 'bowels' of the blocks, is a seemingly endless Indian bazaar selling not only fabric, but household items, food and other necessities. There are some good, reasonably priced Indian restaurants in this area, too, and a Sikh temple off Chakraphet Rd.

National Theatre

This is on Na Phrathat and Chao Fa Rds. Check here if you are interested in Thai classical drama, *lakhorn*. Performances are usually excellent and admission fees very reasonable, around 30B depending on the seating. Attendance at a *khon* performance (masked dance-drama based on stories from the Ramakien) is highly recommended. On the last Friday of every month, there are special public exhibitions of Thai classical dance-drama at 5 pm. Contact the National Theatre at 221 5861 for details and for other current programming. Opposite the theatre is the National Arts Gallery which displays traditional and contemporary art. It's closed Mondays and Fridays, open 9 am to 12 noon and 1 pm to 4 pm on other days. Admission is free.

Ancient City (Muang Boran)

The Ancient City (Muang Boran) covers over 80 hectares and presents outstanding scaled-down facsimiles of many of the Kingdom's most famous monuments. For students of Thai architecture, it's worth a

day's visit (it takes an entire day to cover the area). The owner is Bangkok's largest Mercedes Benz dealer, who has an avid interest in Thai art. The Ancient City Co. (tel 222 8143, 221 4495) also puts out a lavish bilingual periodical devoted to Thai art and architecture called *Muang Boran*. It's edited by some of Thailand's leading art historians. Ancient City is located 33 km from Bangkok in Samut Prakarn, along the Sukhumvit highway. Admission to the site is 50B. Fare by public bus from the Eastern Bus Terminal (Soi Ekamai, Sukhumvit) should be about 15B, or transportation can be arranged through the Bangkok office, which is near the Mercedes Benz dealer on Ratchadamnoen Avenue (close to the Democracy Monument).

In the same area there is a **Crocodile Farm**, where you can even see – oh my my – crocodile wrestling! The crocodile farm is open 8 am to 6 pm daily, the reptiles get their dinner between 5 pm and 6 pm, admission is 80B.

Thai Boxing

Muay Thai, or Thai boxing, can be seen at two boxing stadiums, Lumpini (on Rama IV Rd near South Sathorn Rd) and Ratchadamnoen (on Ratchadamnoen Nok Rd, next to the TAT office). Admission fees vary according to seating – cheapest in Bangkok is now around 180B and ringside seats cost 800B or more. Monday, Wednesday, Thursday and Sunday, the boxing is at Ratchadamnoen and Tuesday, Wednesday, Friday and Saturday it is at Lumpini. The Ratchadamnoen matches begin at 6 pm, except for the Sunday shows which start at 5 pm, while the Lumpini matches all begin at 6.20 pm. Afficionados say the best-matched bouts are reserved for Tuesday nights at Lumpini and Thursday nights at Ratchadamnoen.

Almost anything goes in this martial sport, both in the ring and in the stands. If you don't mind the violence (in the ring) a Thai boxing match is worth attending for the pure spectacle – the wild musical accompaniment, the ceremonial beginning of each match and the frenzied betting around the stadium. The restaurants on the north side of the entrance to Ratchadamnoen Stadium are well-known for their delicious *kai yang* and other north-eastern dishes.

Thai Classical Dancing

If you are not able to catch a free performance at the Lak Muang or Erawan Hotel shrines or one at the National Theatre, there are several restaurants and hotels that specialise in performances for tourists. Admission charges range from 140B to 180B and include a sumptuous Thai meal as well as martial art and sword-fighting demonstrations. One of the better places is the *Baan Thai* on Soi 32 (Soi Baan Thai) Sukhumvit Rd – the food is very good and is served in a traditional manner with diners seated at low tables. If you're looking for a splurge this might be it.

The historic Oriental Hotel on Charoen Krung Rd offers dance/martial art performances (the Kodak Siam Show) in the riverside garden every Sunday and Thursday at 11 am for 80B.

Floating Markets & Canal Tours

Travellers who have been to the Thonburi floating market on Khlong Dao Kanong in recent years are divided in their opinons as to whether the trip is worth the early rising to get there by 7 to 7.30 am. There are still plenty of boats out there, selling fresh produce and ready-to-eat foods, but there may be as many boat-loads of tourists, not to mention lots of tourist shops.

If you're set on going it might be best to take one of the floating market tours that leave from the Oriental pier (Soi Oriental) or Tha Phra Chan beside Thammasat University – your only alternative is to hire a boat of your own (at the Oriental pier) to go up Khlong Dao Kanong and that can be quite expensive these days.

Khlong Dao Kanong is located in south Thonburi, across the river from the terminus of Charoen Krung Rd, below Krung Thep Bridge. Floating market tours cost from 50B up but the cheapest tours probably only give you 20 minutes or so at the market.

There is a more lively and less touristed floating market on Khlong Damnoen Saduak in Rajburi province, 104 km south-west of Bangkok, between Nakhorn Pathom and Samut Songkhram. See Nakhon Pathom in the Around Bangkok section for more details.

The terminus of the Chao Phraya River Taxi is no longer at Thanon Tok, as the Latest Tours Guide bus map indicates, but at Soi Khlongsung, closer to town. Several different buses run to Soi Khlongsung and from here you can take the riverboat all the way to the end of its run at Nonburi, although, of course, you can also board it anywhere along the way.

Another good boat trip is the Bangkok Noi canal taxi route which leaves from Tha Phra Chan next to Thammasat University. The fare is only a few baht and the further up Khlong Bangkok Noi you go, the better the scenery gets – teak houses on stilts, old wats, plenty of greenery – as if you were upcountry and, in a sense, you are. It is possible to go as far from Bangkok as Suphanburi and Ratburi (Ratchaburi) by boat, though this may involve many boat connections. Beware of 'agents' who will try to put you on the boat and rake off an extra commission. Before travelling by boat, establish the price – you can't bargain when you're in the middle of the river.

Finally, if you're really a canal freak, I suggest you lay out 150B for *50 Trips Through Siam's Canals* by Geo-Ch Veran (translated from French into English by Sarah Bennett, 1979, Editions Duang Kamol). The book contains 25 detailed maps and clear instructions on how to take the various trips – some of which are very time consuming.

Weekend Market

In 1982 the Weekend Market moved from Sanam Luang, near Wat Phra Keo, to keep the grounds clear for Bangkok's bicentennial celebration. The market is now located at Chatuchak Park, off Phahonyothin Rd, just above the Saphan Khwai district in north Bangkok, across from the Northern Bus Terminal. Air-con bus Nos 3, 9, 10 and 13 all pass the market – just get off before the Northern Bus Terminal. A dozen other ordinary city buses also pass the market.

Like the old weekend market at Sanam Luang, the new one is the Disneyland of markets. Everything is sold here, from live chickens and snakes to opium pipes and herbal remedies. Thai clothing such as the *phaakamaa* (wraparound for men) and the *phaasin* (same for women), *kang kaeng jin* (Chinese pants) and *maw hawm* (blue cotton farmer's shirt) are good buys. Best bargains of all are on household goods like pots and pans, dishes, drinking glasses, etc. If you're moving to Thailand for an extended period, this is the place to pick up stuff for your kitchen. There is plenty of interesting and tasty food for sale if you're feeling hungry. Don't forget to try out your bargaining skills.

The market is in operation all day Saturday and Sunday.

Other Markets

Atok Market Just across Kamphaeng Phet Rd from the new Weekend Market. Open every day of the week with a selection similar to the Weekend Market, including flowers and potted plants. **Klong Toey Market** At the intersection of Rama IV and At Narong Rds in the Kong Toey district, under the super highway. Possibly the cheapest all-purpose market in Bangkok, best on Wednesdays. **Pratunam Market** Intersection of Phetburi and Ratchaprarop Rds. This market runs every day and is very crowded, but has great deals in new, cheap clothing. Good eating, too. **Samyan Market** north-west

corner of the intersection of Rama IV and Phayathai Rds, near Chulalongkorn University. All the usual stuff, but worth a special trip for the tasty and cheap seafood restaurants along the first soi on the right off Phayathai Rd above Rama IV.

Snake Farm

At the Pasteur Institute, Rama IV Rd, venomous snakes are milked every day at 11 am to make snake bite antidotes which are then distributed throughout the country. Boring to some, exciting to others.

The 'farm' is open 8.30 am to 4 pm daily, admission is 10B. An additional 20B is charged for camera use.

Siam Society

At 131 Soi Asoke, Sukhumvit 21, are the publishers of the renowned *Journal of the Siam Society* and valiant preservers of traditional Thai culture. The Society headquarters is a good place to visit for those with a serious interest in Thailand – a reference library is open to visitors and Siam Society monographs are for sale. Almost anything you'd want to know about Thailand (outside the political sphere, since the Society is sponsored by the royal family) can be researched here. An ethnological museum of sorts, exhibiting Thai folk art is located on the Siam Society grounds in the Kamthieng House. Ban Kamthieng is open Tuesday to Saturday from 9 am to 12 noon and 1 pm to 5 pm. Admission is 25B.

Other Attractions

The **Dusit Zoo** (Khao Din Wana) may be of interest to zoo enthusiasts. It's a big, quite pleasant zoo. The collection of animals is not very interesting, but it's a nice place to get away from the noise of the city and to observe how the Thais amuse themselves – by eating mainly. Food is very good and cheap at the zoo! **Vimanek Royal Palace** is built of teak and set in peaceful gardens. It only opened in late 1985 and it's behind the National Assembly building and admission is 50B for a 1½ hour tour.

Bangkok has a host of artificial tourist attractions including **Timland** (Thailand in Miniature), an example of the 'see the whole country in half an hour' park which every South-East Asian country seems to have. The **Rose Garden Country Resort** is south of Bangkok on the Thachin River and includes a Thai cultural village. Admission to the garden area is 10B, another 140B for the 3 pm performances in the cultural village. The garden is open from 8 am to 6 pm daily.

Bangkok also has a **Science Museum** and a **Planetarium**, both on Sukhumvit Rd. At Meen Buri **Siam Park** is a huge recreational park with pools, water slides, a wave pool and the like. Admission is 60B.

Places to Stay – bottom end

There is really quite a variety of places to stay in Bangkok, only some are harder to find than others. Your choice actually depends on what part of the city you want to be located in – the tourist ghetto of Sukhumvit Rd, the 'world traveller' ghetto of Soi Ngam Duphli around the Malaysia Hotel off Rama IV, the Siam Square area, Chinatown, or up-and-coming 'world traveller' centre Banglamphu (north of Ratchadamnoen Klang).

Chinatown/Hualamphong and Banglamphu are the best all-round areas for seeing the real Bangkok and are the cheapest districts for eating and sleeping. The Siam Square area is also well located, in that it's more or less in the centre of Bangkok – this, coupled with the good selection of city buses that pass through the Rama I-Phayathai Rd intersection, makes even more of the city accessible. In addition, Siam Square has a good bookstore, several banks, cheap foodstalls and excellent middle-priced restaurants, travel agencies and three movie theatres. Don't confuse Siam Square with the Siam Centre across the street, a huge air-conditioned shopping complex for foreigners and rich Thais.

Soi Ngam Duphli This area, off Rama IV Rd, where the Malaysia, Boston Inn, and Privacy Hotels are located, is where most budget travellers come on their first trip to Bangkok. These places are not cheap and are sometimes full but the area is easy to deal with for first-timers since just about everyone speaks English. The entrance to this *soi* is on Rama IV Rd, near the intersection with Sathon Tai Rd, within walking distance of the imposing Dusit Thani Hotel and Lumphini Park. As a travellers' centre Soi Ngam Duphli is falling from favour as it has simply become too expensive for many backpackers. Banglamphu is probably now the main travellers' centre.

If, however, you have a lot of visa collection and airline ticket business to do then it's definitely worth considering Soi Ngam Duphli. It's close to many of the embassies and the main airline office area (Silom Rd). Banglamphu is a good 45 minute bus ride from the area.

The Malaysia Hotel (tel 286 3582, 286 7263) at 54 Soi Ngam Duphli was once Bangkok's most famous travellers' hotel. It's 120 air-con rooms now go for 298B single, 336B twin, 374B triple and all rooms have hot water. The Malaysia has a swimming pool which may be used by visitors for 50B per day. The notice-board which used to be full of the most amazing information and mis-information from all over Asia is now strictly second rate. In fact the Malaysia seems to be making a conscious effort to distance itself from the travellers' market. It's been jazzed up a bit – the lobby area has noisy video game machines – and a backpack is starting to look rather out of place. A big sign out front advertises 'Day-Off International Club – Paradise for Everyone – You'll Never be Alone Again', which gives you an idea what kind of clientele the Malaysia is trying to lure these days.

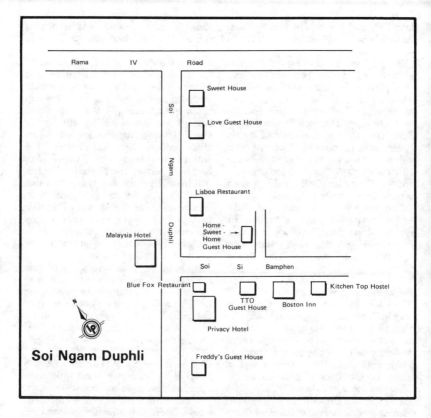

Soi Ngam Duphli

The *Privacy* (tel 286 2339, 286 8811) is also fully AC and costs 195B for a double. Many 'short-time' residents here give the place a sleazy kind of feel, but its actually quieter than the Malaysia, less of a 'scene'. It's right across the road.

The *Boston Inn* is on Soi Si Bamphen, off Soi Ngam Duphli. Singles here are 120B with ceiling fan, 140B for a double. Air-con rooms for 130B single, 190B double. A triple with fan and attached bath costs 160B, or 210B with air-con. There are also dorm beds for 60B. The staff are friendly, rooms are clean and it's the best value in the Ngam Duphli area. It's noticeboard is now far superior to the Malaysia's.

Also along Soi Ngam Duphli are the *Flower* and *White House* guest houses, both charging 60B single, 80B double. Then there's *Windy Guest House* and *Sweet House*, both 60B/90B single (with or without bath) or 90B/120B double. All of the above offer cramped but adequate quarters. A bit better but on the short-time circuit is the *LA Hotel* (English sign just says 'Hotel') for 120B for large rooms with bath and fan. The *TTO Guest House* is 60B/80B single/double or 100B for an AC room.

The rates at *Freddy's*, on Soi Bamphen are now 80B/100B. The D Guest House is now called the *K Guest House*. It's on Soi Si Bamphen just past Yen Akat Rd on the right. Still great rooms at 90B for a room with fan, 150B AC. The *Kitchen Top Hostel* is 50B/80B single/double. New guest houses on Soi Si Bamphen include the *Welcome* and the *Lee*, both with rates at 50B/90B. A very friendly new place is *Madame Guest House* on Si Bamphen, it's run by an older Thai woman who goes out of her way to be helpful to travellers. She charges 60B and 100B for single/doubles.

Banglamphu If you're really on a tight budget, head for Khao San Rd, near the Democracy monument, parallel to Ratchadamnoen Klang Rd – a No 17 or 56 bus will get you there. This is becoming much more the main travellers' centre these days and new guest houses are springing up all the time. A landmark here, although it's in a much higher price bracket, is the big *Viengtai Hotel*. The prices here are far lower than Soi Ngam Duphli and although some of the basic places are just that, basic, many others are excellent value.

The *VS Guest House* has two locations, at 136 Tanao Rd (an alley off Khao San Rd) and 1/3 Prachatipotai Rd, near the Thai Hotel. Both are 30B per person or doubles for 60B, dark and not particularly clean, but adequate. Close to the first VS is the *ET Guest House* (they're very big on initials here), another small guest house.

The *Bonny Guest House* is on Khao San Rd, an English sign points the way. It costs 40B per person, several beds per room, fairly clean, friendly proprietors but not much English spoken. More rooms have been added recently; 80B doubles and 50B singles now available and a small breakfast menu is served. The *Top Guest House* (tel 281 9954) is next door to the Bonny GH and owned by the same family. It also costs 40B per person, similar arrangement. Bigger rooms in front are available for 70B a single or 80B a double.

The *New Sri Phranakhorn Hotel*, 139 Khao San Rd, is owned by Chinese. It's clean and costs 120B for a room with fan and bath, 150B for air-con, complete with 'short term' horizontal mirrors in some rooms! Next door to New Sri Phranakhorn Hotel on Khao San Rd is the *Nit Jaroen Suke* or Nith Charoen Suke (tel 281 9872). A very clean double costs 120B, with fan and bathroom. It's back off the road a little so it's reasonably quiet. Recommended, 'best value on our entire trip' was one traveller's comment.

The *VIP Guest House* is on Khao San Rd, near Bonny and Tum GH; look for a restaurant in front. This costs 40B per person in small dorms, 80B for a double with fan and 60B for a single with fan. The people here are nice, it's clean and good value, but usually full. The *160 Guest House* at 160 Khao San has also been recommended.

PB Guest House, 74 Khao San Rd, at the back of the pool hall. Mr Lu, the proprietor, speaks pretty good English and is very helpful to travellers. It costs 60B for a room with two beds or 30B in a 20-bed dorm. You can get both Thai and western food here with most Thai dishes at 10B.

The *Ponderosa Guest House*, 66 Khao San Rd, is much the same as the rest, with nothing to distinguish it from the crowd except if others are full. It has three or four-bed dorms for 40B per person, two singles for 70B and a double for 100B. All rooms have a bath and fan.

Suneeporn Guest House is on a short soi between Khao San and Rambutri Rds. Nothing special for 50B per person, but they have a long-term luggage storage service. They also have a 'guest house office' travel agency at 178 Khao San Rd. There are entrances to the soi at both ends. Next door to Suneeporn and identical in price and facilities is the very clean *Lek Guest House*. There is a good Thai restaurant in the courtyard behind these two.

The *Central Guest House* (tel 282 0667) is just off Tanao Rd, look for the

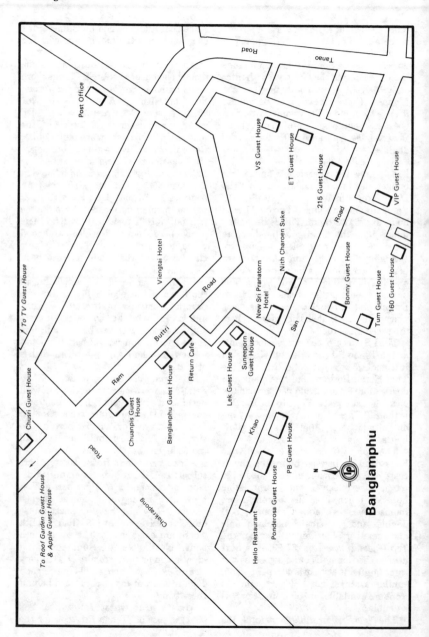

Banglamphu

rather inconspicuous signs. This is a very pleasant guest house, clean, quiet and well kept with rooms at 40B per person. There are some bigger, more spacious doubles here. *Chuanpis Guest House* (tel 282 9948) at 86 Chakrapong Rd, behind the police station at the end of Khao San Rd has also been recommended. The usual 50B per person price. The *Chusri Guest House* at 61/1 Soi Rambutri off Chakrapong Rd also received a recent recommendation, it is 40B per person for two-bed rooms or 30B per person in a dorm and is located on a fairly quite soi.

The *Siam Guest House* in Ram Buttri Rd has adequate rooms for 60B single, 80B double; one traveller wrote in to say that the people here are very friendly and the place is kept clean. Nearby is the *New Hawaii Guest House* which is quite similar. The *Sweety Guest House* is on a soi next to the bank where everyone changes money on Ratchadamnoen Avenue, near Democracy Monument. Guest houses are multiplying all over this area and you can walk down just about any street or soi in the Chakrapong-Khao San-Tanao area in Banglamphu and stumble on new guest houses. During the height of the tourist season (January to February) it can be difficult to find a bed, but keep trying because there seems to be no end to the ingenuity and enterprise of the folks in Banglamphu.

Around Banglamphu More guest houses have started to pop up elsewhere in the Banglamphu area. Guest houses have started sprouting up along Trok Rong Mai (*trok* means alley) off Phra Athit Rd opposite UNICEF. This area is convenient to the Bangkok Noi train station across the river, the National Museum and the National Theatre. Nearby restaurants are tasty and cheap. Most have only two-bed rooms. Proceeding down Trok Rong Mai:

The *Apple Guest House*, 10/1 Trok Rong Mai may not look the best but it's very popular at 40B per person. Some-

times they put people up in the corridor for 20B if it's really full. The family who run it are very helpful, there's a good noticeboard, good food and a garden to sit in. There's also an *Apple Guest House II* closeby, which one traveller recommended as being better. The *Ngam Pit*, 28/2 Trok Rong Mai is also pretty good, it serves food, and costs the same as the Apple.

The *Roof Garden Guest House*, 28/6 Trok Rong Mai is the pick of the pack – very clean doubles for 80B or 40B per person, with fan and shared bath. The rooms are a bit box-like and bare though. On the roof you can get an aerial view of Bangkok and the Chao Phraya River plus dry your laundry.

Two other popular guest houses can be found by heading north up Samsen Rd (the extension of Chakrapong Rd) from Khao San Rd. The new *TV Guest House* (tel 282 7451) is at 7 Soi Phra Sawat, just off Samsen Rd to the right (east). Very good value at 40B for a dorm bed or 80B for a double in this clean and modern guest house.

Continue another km or so to the place where Phitsanulok Rd dead ends on Samsen and where Si Ayuthaya Rd crosses Samsen. Just beyond this junction is the National Library. At 71 Si Ayuthaya on the river side of Samsen Rd is the very popular *Sawatdee*, an extremely friendly family-run guest house. It's very basic but clean and well kept, the rooms have fans and there's a nice atmosphere here. Plus it's fairly quiet. Dorm beds are 40B, singles are 50B, doubles 80B. There's a good market right across the road.

The *Bangkok International Youth Hostel*, is at 25/2 Phitsanuloke Rd. Dorm beds are 30B, rooms are 50B without bath and 100B with. Add a 10B surcharge if you don't have a Youth Hostel card.

Chinatown-Hualamphong This area is central and colourful although rather noisy. There are numerous cheap hotels but it's not a travellers' centre like Soi Ngam Duphli or Banglamphu. Watch your pockets and bag around the Hualamphong area, both on the street and on the bus. The cream of the razor artists operates here as the railway passengers make good pickings.

The *Empire Hotel* (tel 234 6990-6) is at 572 Yaowarat Rd, near the intersection of Yaowarat and New Rd (Charoen Krung Rd), a short walk from Wat Traimit. Doubles are 120B – a bit noisy but a great location if you like Chinatown. Other rooms go up to 300B. The Empire is a favourite among Thais from the southern region.

Other Chinatown hotels, most without English signs out front, can be found along Yaowarat, Chakraphat and Ratchawong Rds. The *Burapha*, at the intersection of Chakraphat and Charoen Krung on the edge of Chinatown, is not too bad, rates are about the same as the Empire.

The *Sri Hualamphong Hotel* is at 445 Rong Muang Rd, the road is alongside the Hualamphong Railway Station and has several Thai hotels. This is one of the better ones – 100B single, 140B double with fan. The *Sahakit Hotel* is a few doors down from the Sri Hualamphong towards Rama IV Rd. Rooms from 90B up.

The *Jeep Sieng*, at 462-64 Rong Muang Rd (tel 214 2808) is not too clean but it's adequate. Rooms are 80B and up. The *No Name Hotel* has no name out front, in *any* language. This one's down at the far end of Rong Muang and is pretty basic but only 70B for a room. The Thai Song Greet, one of the longest running hotels in this area and a rock bottom travellers' favourite for many years, has now disappeared.

Many travellers have written to strongly recommend a new guest house which has opened near Hualamphong. Turn left out of the station along Rama IV Rd and you'll soon see signs to the *TT Guest House* (tel 235 8006). It's about 10 minutes walk, at 138 Soi Watmahaphrutt-haram, Sipraya Manakorn Rd. It's a bit difficult to find as it's in a little alley but if you follow the signs it's worth the effort as it's very clean and friendly, singles 60B, doubles 100B. They also run a 'left luggage service' which is cheaper than the one at the airport and they also have a laundry service.

There are also several guest houses in the 'India-town' area of Pahurat, on or off Chakraphet Rd. On Chakraphet is the *Amarin Guest House*, with a sign in English, Thai, Hindi and Arabic. Rooms are 70B up and fairly clean. Further down towards the well-known Royal India restaurant there is a soi (off to the left if you're walking from the pedestrian bridge) on which are located the *Moon*, *Kamal*, *Bobby's* and *Tony's Fashion*, all offering similar accomodation for 80B to 100B per room. They cater to mostly South Asian guests, but are happy to take anyone. It's an economical alternative if you need to be in this part of town.

Another Indian guest house a bit further away from Chinatown is the *Silom Lodge*, on Vaithi Lane off Silom Rd, not far from the Saiva temple. It's quite a walk down Vaithi Lane and rooms are 100B upstairs, somewhat lower downstairs, but it does have the advantage of being far removed from big street traffic. The proprietor is a very friendly Indian man from Madras, a retired gem dealer and his kitchen serves delicious south Indian food.

Siam Square Area There are several good places in this central area. The *Scout Hostel* is on Rama I Rd, next to the National Stadium. Dorm beds are 30B per night here.

The *Star Hotel* is at 36/1 Soi Kasem San 1, off Rama I Rd. At the end of the soi, the Star is a real Thai hotel. Fairly clean, comfortable AC rooms with bath cost 250B to 300B for a double. The *Reno Hotel* between the Muangphol Building and the Star on Soi Kasem 1, costs 250B/300B for a single/double room, similar facilities to the Muangphol.

The *Muangphol Building* on the corner of Soi Kasem San 1 and Rama I Rd (931/8 Rama I Rd) has doubles for 280B. It's good value for the discriminating traveller who can afford it – air-con, restaurant downstairs, friendly staff and good service. Bathrooms have hot water and western-style toilets, both of which function well. Muangphol has the same comfort as, say, the Miami, Viengtai or Liberty, but is better located and lower priced. Travellers have also recommended the *Krit Thai Mansion*, 931/1 Rama I Rd (across from the National Stadium). For 380B the facilities include hot water, private bath, AC and even free newspapers in the lobby.

Sukhumvit Area Nothing much can be said for this area – staying here puts you in the newest part of Bangkok and the furthest from the old Bangkok near the river. Buses take longer to get here and taxis to or from Sukhumvit Rd cost more since it is known as a residential area for *farangs*. The majority of the hotels in this area are in the middle price range, well above the more basic bottom end places.

The *Atlanta* at Soi 2 (Soi Phasak), Sukhumvit Rd has undergone several improvements during the past two years in the areas of cleanliness and service. Rooms are now fairly clean and maid service regular. Rooms with shared bath and fan cost 150B single, 200B double. A few rooms have private baths for 50B extra. Small singles with fan and shared bath are available for 120B. Air-con rooms are 250B single, 300B double and 350B triple.

The *Miami* (tel 252 5140-2, 252 4759, 252 5036), Soi 13, Sukhumvit has become a favourite among Arab tourists (rivalling the *Rajah, Nana* and *Grace Hotels* on Soi 3) who are driving the prices up. Rooms with fan and bath are 160B to 200B single, 200B to 250B double and 350B triple. For air-con add 100B to each category. The new wing has deluxe air-con singles for 380B and doubles for 450B. It's comfortable, clean and has a swimming pool.

The *Crown*, Soi 29, Sukhumvit costs 196B for a 'budget' room, 219B for a 'deluxe', 296B for a 'super deluxe'. All rooms have air-con and private bath and the hotel has a swimming pool. Good deal. The *Golden Palace Hotel*, 15 Soi 1, Sukhumvit has a swimming pool, is well situated and costs 308B for a double with air-con and bath. The clientele here are mostly middle-class tourists 'on a budget'.

At Soi 4 (Soi Nana Tai) in Nana Plaza there are two places offering AC carpeted rooms with hot water, *Nana Guest House* (200B) and the *Royal Siam Guest House* (300B). The atmosphere is rather wild, as these two are located amidst a three-storey array of recently established Patpong-type bars. This obviously appeals to some, as rooms are often full. A recent letter recommended *Mermaids Rest* on Soi 8, rooms from 125B and a swimming pool. Another place that has been recommended is the *Ruamchitt Mansion Co*, 1-15 Soi 15, Sukhumvit. Rooms range from 120B to 350B and there is hot water, fridge, AC or fans, communal kitchen and a supermarket just below. Between Soi 25 and Soi 27 is the cheapest hotel on Sukhumvit this side of Phrakanong – no name, just a chalkboard out front that reads, in Thai, 'Temporary Use – 50B; All Night – 110B'. Use your own discretion.

The Ys Bangkok has a YMCA and YWCA. The *YMCA* (tel 286 5134-5, 286 5971-3) is at 27 Sathorn Tai Rd and has air-con singles at 300B, doubles at 425B. The *YWCA* (tel 286 1936) is at 13 Sathorn Tai Rd and has slightly cheaper air-con rooms, 165B single, 390B double and 150B for a dorm bed. There is also a new Youth Hostel at 25/2 Phitsanulok Rd (tel 282 0950, 281 0361).

Places to Stay – top end
Bangkok has all sorts of expensive hotels from the straightforward package places to some of Asia's classic hotels. The riverside *Oriental* is one of the most

famous hotels in Asia, right up there with the Raffles in Singapore. What's more it's also rated as one of the very best hotels in the world, as well as being just about the most expensive in Bangkok. It's worth wandering in if only to see the string quartet playing in the lobby! The *Bangkok Peninsula* is a close rival to the Oriental in price.

Other well known hotels include the big *Dusit Thani*, the gracious old *Erawan* and (convenient for the airport) the new *Airport Hotel*. The new *Hyatt Central Plaza* is also out towards the airport. There's no single area for top end hotels although you'll find quite a few of them around the Siam Square area or along the parallel Surawongse/Silom Rds while many of the cheaper 'international standard' places are scattered along Sukhumvit Rd.

Airport Hotel (tel 523 9177), opposite Don Muang Airport, 300 rooms, singles/doubles 1450B/1550B

Amarin Hotel (tel 252 9810-9), 526 Ploenchit Rd, 217 rooms, singles/doubles 800B/1000B

Ambassador Hotel (tel 251 0404, Soi 11, Sukhumvit Rd, 1000 rooms, singles/doubles 900B to 2000B/1100B to 2200B

Asia Hotel (tel 281 1433, 281 5905, 282 0121), 296 Phya Thai Rd, 300 rooms, singles/doubles 1000B to 1400B/1200B to 1600B

Bangkok Centre Hotel (tel 235 1780, 235 1799), Rama IV Rd, 232 rooms, singles/doubles 800B to 1200B/900B to 1300B

Bangkok Palace Hotel (tel 252 5700), New Petchburi Rd, 650 rooms, singles/doubles 1200B to 1300B/1400B to 1500B

Baron Hotel (tel 245 5020, 245 5544), 544 Soi Huaykwang Ratchadapisek Rd.

Century Hotel (tel 245 3271-3), 9 Rajaprarob Rd, 96 rooms, singles/doubles 540B/660B

Continental Hotel (tel 278 1596-8), 971/16 Phaholyothin Rd, 122 rooms, singles/doubles 550B to 605B /695B to 750B

Dusit Thani Hotel (tel 233 1130), Rama IV Rd, 560 rooms, singles/doubles 1870B to 2420B/2090B to 2860B

Erawan Hotel (tel 252 9100), 494 Rajadamri Rd, 250 rooms, singles/doubles 1320B to 1430B/1430B to 1650B

Federal Hotel (tel 252 5143), 27 Sukhumvit Rd, 95 rooms, singles/doubles 340B to 500B/380B to 600B

First Hotel (tel 252 5010-9), Petchburi Rd, 222 rooms, singles/doubles 1000B/1100B

Florida Hotel (tel 245 3221-4, 245 1816-9), 43 Phya Thai Square, Phya Thai Rd, 107 rooms, singles/doubles 500B/600B

Fortuna Hotel (tel 251 5121), 19 Sukhumvit Rd, 110 rooms, singles/doubles 450B/515B

Golden Dragon (tel 588 4414-5), 20/21 Ngarm Wongvarn Rd, 114 rooms, singles/doubles 540B/640B

Golden Horse Hotel (tel 281 7388), 5/1 Dumrongrak Rd, 130 rooms, singles/doubles 700B/800B

Grace Hotel (tel 252 9170/3), 12 Nana North (Soi 3), Sukhumvit Rd, 350 rooms, singles/doubles 500B to 770B/560B to 825B

Hilton International Bangkok (tel 251 0856, 252 8166), Nai Lert Park, Wireless Rd, 398 rooms, singles/doubles 1800B to 2400B/2250B to 3000B

Hyatt Centra Plaza Bangkok (tel 230 1820), Phaholyothin Rd, 600 rooms, singles/doubles 1700B/1900B

Impala Hotel (tel 390 1210-4), Soi 24, Sukhumvit Rd, 220 rooms, singles/doubles 680B/780B

Imperial Hotel (tel 252 0450, 252 8070), Wireless Rd, 400 rooms, singles/doubles 1940B/2130B

Indra Regent (tel 251 1111, 252 1111), Rajaprarob Rd, 500 rooms, singles/doubles 1300B to 1500/1500B to 1700B

Liberty Hotel (tel 279 8913-7), 215 Sapan Kwai Pratipat Rd, 209 rooms, singles/doubles 370B to 540B/460B to 670B

Mandarin Hotel (tel 233 4980-9), 662 Rama IV Rd, 419 rooms, singles/doubles 1250B to 1400B/1400B to 1500B

Hotel Manhattan (tel 252 7141-9), Soi 15, Sukhumvit Rd, 206 rooms, singles/doubles 950B to 1050B/1050B to 1250B

Manohra Hotel (tel 234 5070), 412 Surawongse Rd, 250 rooms, singles/doubles 900B to 1000B/1100B to 1300B

Marakot Hotel (tel 314 0761-3), 2802 New Petchburi Rd, 121 rooms, singles 350B to 460B/400B to 525B

Menam Riverside Resort Hotel (tel 289 3814-8), 2074 New Rd, Yannawa, 800 rooms, singles/doubles 1500B to 1900B/1700B to 2100B

Miramar Hotel (tel 222 4191-5), 777 Minson Corner, Samyod Rd, 150 rooms, singles/doubles 450B to 600B

Montien Hotel (tel 234 8060), 54 Surawongse Rd, 600 rooms, singles/doubles 1800B to 2170B/1900B to 2350B

Nana Hotel (tel 250 1210-9, 250 1380-9), 4 Nana Tai, Sukhumvit Rd, 224 rooms, singles/doubles 550B/590B

Narai Hotel (tel 233 3350), 222 Silom Rd, 500 rooms, singles/doubles 1400B/1600B

New Amarin Hotel (tel 245 2661-7), 477 Si Ayuthaya Rd, 201 rooms, singles/doubles 700B/840B to 1000B

New Trocadero Hotel (tel 234 8920-9), Surawongse Rd, 140 rooms, singles/doubles 580B to 700B/700B to 800B

The Oriental Bangkok (tel 234 8620-9), 48 Oriental Ave, 406 rooms, singles/doubles 2700B to 3500B/3000B to 3800B

Park Hotel (tel 252 5110-3), 6 Soi 7, Sukhumvit Rd, 128 rooms, singles/doubles 500B/600B

President Hotel – The Regent of Bangkok (tel 252 9880-9), 135/26 Gaysorn Rd, 400 rooms, singles/doubles 1480B to 1900B/1700B to 2100B

Prince Hotel (tel 251 6171-6), 1537/1 New Petchburi Rd, 140 rooms, singles/doubles 300B to 400B/400B to 500B

Rajah Hotel (tel 252 5102-9), 18 Soi 4, Sukhumvit Rd, 450 rooms, singles/doubles 950B/1050B

Rama Garden Hotel (tel 579 5400), 9/9 Viphavadee-Rangsit highway, Bangkaen, 369 rooms, singles/doubles 1300B to 1500B/1400B to 1600B

The Rama Tower (tel 234 1010), 981 Silom Rd, 518 rooms, singles/doubles 1300B to 1700B/1400B to 1800B

The Regent Bangkok (tel 256 1627), 155 Rajadamri Avenue, 424 rooms, singles/doubles 2600B/3000B

Rex Hotel (tel 391 0100), 762/1 Sukhumvit Rd, 131 rooms, singles/doubles 500B/750B

R S Hotel (tel 281 3644, 281 3004), 269 Larn Luang Rd, 142 rooms, singles/doubles 620B to 700B/760B to 840B

Rose Hotel (tel 233 7695-7), 118 Surawongse Rd, 105 rooms, singles/doubles 420B/540B

Royal Hotel (tel 222 9111-7), 2 Rajdamnoen Ave, 138 rooms, singles/doubles 506B/570B

The Royal Orchid (tel 234 5599), 2 Capt Bush Lane, Siphya Rd, 776 rooms, singles/doubles 1900B to 2200B/2100B to 2400B

Sheraton-Bangkok Hotel (tel 233 5160), 60 Surawongse Rd, 265 rooms, singles/doubles 1500B to 1760B/1600B to 1860B

Siam Hotel (tel 252 5081), 1777 Petchburi Rd, 120 rooms, singles/doubles 650B/750B

Hotel Siam Inter-Continental (tel 252 9040, 252 9060), Rama I Rd, 411 rooms, singles/doubles 1800B to 2200B/2100B to 2400B

Thai Hotel (tel 282 2833), 78 Prajatiphatai Rd, 100 rooms, singles/doubles 520B/620B

Victory Hotel (tel 233 9060-2), 322 Silom Rd, 125 rooms, singles/doubles 540B/620B to 800B

Viengtai Hotel (tel 281 5788), 42 Tanee Rd, 240 rooms, singles/doubles 785B to 910B

Windsor Hotel (tel 391 5300), 3 Soi 20, Sukhumvit Rd, 212 rooms, singles/doubles 1050B/1165B

Places to Eat

Banglamphu & Democracy Monument

There are lots of cheap eating establishments in Banglamphu – most of the noodle shops along Khao San Rd close at night, but around the corner on Ban Tanao Rd are several good places to eat at night. The *Hello Restaurant* has gone downhill since it began serving farangs but still serves sandwiches and spaghetti for the homesick. Better food can be found in the stalls along the soi on which the VIP and 160 ('Marco Polo') guest houses are found, off Khao San Rd. Also on the next street north of Khao San there are several open air restaurants serving excellent Thai food at low prices

There is a decent floating restaurant serving seafood at the Samphraya pier in Banglamphu called *Yok Yok*. They have an English menu.

There are many good, inexpensive restaurants and food stalls along Phra Athit Rd near Trok Rong Mai – *Taew* across from the alley entrance is very good. Good curry and rice for 7B is available at the outdoor dining hall at Thammasat University nearby, open lunch only. Good north-eastern food is served at restaurants next door to the boxing stadium on Ratchadamnoen Nok Rd, near the TAT office.

Across Ratchadamnoen Klang Ave, at the south-east side of the Democracy Monument, is one of Bangkok's best Thai restaurants – the *Sarn Daeng*. Fish is prepared well here, and the restaurant is famous for its *tawt man plaa*, fried fish cakes. Prices are reasonable and I believe there is an English menu available. One traveller wrote to complain, however, that the servings were so small 'you had to imagine where your food was'.

Soi Ngam Duphli This area has several world traveller hangouts, eg the *Lisboa* and *Blue Fox*, both air-con and slightly high-priced since they cater for such western tastes as toast and scrambled eggs. Better are the open-air restaurants on Soi Si Bamphen (near the Boston Inn) which are low to moderate in price, have English menus and decent food – mostly Thai and Chinese. In this area, the curry shops out on Rama IV are best for cheap nutrition – 7B to 8B for curry and rice – check the ones near the pedestrian bridge. Also cheap eats can be had across Rama IV in the daily market, look for a cluster of umbrellas. *Robinson's Department Store* has been recommended by a traveller as being the best fast food place in Bangkok. It's at the northern end of Silom Rd, at the junction with Rama IV, next to the Dairy Queen.

Station & Siam Square There is no shortage of cheap places to eat on Rong Muang Rd in Hualamphong, especially if you like north-eastern Thai food – steamed innards and the like.

Excellent foodstalls can be found in the alleys between Siam Square sois – *khao man kai* or other rice-plates, plus tea, for 8B to 10B. The big noodle restaurant on the last soi, facing Henri Dunant Rd, called *Co-Co*, is really good for Chinese food. There is a very good, cheap, small restaurant on the south-east corner of the Rama I-Phayathai intersection called *Nam Chai* (no English sign) where most rice dishes cost 10B. It's next door to the watch shop. Of course there's the usual assortment of mobile noodle shops in the area.

The Mawbukhrong Food Centre, on the 6th floor of the shopping centre directly across from Siam Square on Phayathai Rd (top floor of Tokyo Department Store), has dishes from all over Thailand at prices averaging 20B per plate. The food is good and the place is air-conditioned. They also serve farang food.

The open-air *Kloster Beer Garden* operates in the parking area next to the Siam Centre during the cool season, roughly mid-November to mid-February. The food is good and reasonably priced and Kloster draft beer sells for 100B per large pitcher or 20B per glass.

At the end of Soi Lang Suan, near Lumphini Park, there is a large Thai-Chinese seafood restaurant called *Nguan Lee* that is very good and not expensive.

Last and certainly not least, this area has seen an epidemic of American-style fast food eateries in recent years. Siam Square has *Mister Donut, Dunkin Donuts, Pizza Hut, A&W Root Beer* and *Kentucky Fried Chicken*. The Sogo Dept Store on Ploenchit Rd has a *McDonalds*. Prices are close to what you would pay in the country of origin.

Vegetarian Restaurants On Lang Suan Rd, off Rama I Rd more or less equi-distant from the Siam Centre, Sukhumvit and Silom Rd, is the *Whole Earth Restaurant*. It's a good Thai and Indian vegetarian restaurant but a bit pricey if you're on a tight budget. Another Thai veggie restaurant is *Prakai* in the new Fuji Hotel on Suriwong Rd. The Bangkok Adventist Hospital cafeteria (430 Phitsanulok Rd) also serves inexpensive veggie fare. All the Indian restaurants in town have vegetarian selections on their menus.

Sukhumvit On Sukhumvit try the *Yong Lee Restaurant* at Soi 15, near Asia Books. Excellent Thai and Chinese food and good service at reasonable prices has made Yong Lee a favourite among Thai and farang residents alike.

One of the very best restaurants in Bangkok, not too well known yet among farangs, is *Laikhram* (tel 392 5867) at Soi

49/4, 11/1 Sukhumvit, near Samitiwet Hospital. To get there take a bus out Sukhumvit to Soi 49, walk down the soi until it appears to end, bear left and then take the next right, heading towards the hospital (you are still on Soi 49 actually). Across from the hospital go right down Soi 49/4 – the restaurant will be on the left. This is a fairly long walk, so you may want to take a *tuk-tuk* from the mouth of Soi 49 for 10B to 15B. The food here is authentic gourmet Thai, but not outrageously priced – better than any of the more famous restaurants in Bangkok like *Jit Pochana* or any of the first class hotel restaurants. One of the house specialities is *haw mok hawy*, a thick fish curry steamed with mussels inside the shell – exquisite. *Somtam*, spicy green papaya salad, is also excellent here, as is *khao man*, rice cooked with coconut milk and *bai toei* or pandanus leaf. Hours are 10 am to 9 pm Monday to Saturday, 10 am to 3 pm Sunday.

There are many restaurants around the major hotels on Sukhumvit with Thai-Chinese-European-American menus, most of average quality and average prices, like the *Number One Restaurant*, good if you're not used to Thai food. *Dusita Restaurant*, 135/7-8 Gaysorn Rd, near the President Hotel, has been recommended for having good Thai food, cheap prices and 'a traditional atmosphere'.

Several rather expensive west European restaurants (Swiss, French, German, etc) are also found along tourist Sukhumvit. *Crown Pizza*, round the corner from the Crown Hotel, between Soi 29 and 31 has been recommended – it's open fairly late and is air-con. *Chit Pochana Restaurant* at Soi 20 has also been recommended for a splurge and the expensive *Sea Food Market & Restaurant* at 388 Sukhumvit. A few Indian-Pakistani-Middle Eastern restaurants are cropping up on Soi 3 – medium to high prices.

There are three food centres on Sukhumvit Road, the latest eating fashion among young Thais. All are good places to initiate oneself into Thai cuisine, or to pick up inexpensive, good-tasting Thai food in fairly hygienic surroundings. The first is the *Gaysorn Food Mall* next to the President Hotel, located on Ploenchit Rd (which turns into Sukhumvit a few blocks east) between Ratchadamri Rd and Soi Chit Lom. The second is the *Ma-Chim Food Centre* underneath the Din Daeng superhighway entrance/exit near Soi 1 Sukhumvit. Third is the *Ambassador City Food Centre* at Soi 11, in the Ambassador Hotel complex. All are about the same in price and quality, though the Ambassador seems to have a better selection than the others. Dishes average around 15B to 20B and there are photographs of the foods which are labelled in English and Thai, making it easier to know what you are ordering. One buys coupons upon entry rather than paying the cooks. Any unused coupons may be returned for a refund.

Victory Monument There are a couple of large but good Thai-Chinese restaurants near the Victory Monument at the intersection of Rajwithi and Phayathai Rds. Especially recommended is *Nquan Lee* on the north-west corner. A good place for beer and Maekhong whiskey with *kap klaem* – finger food for drinkers.

Indian Restaurants The best Indian restaurant in town, frequented almost exclusively by Indian residents, is the *Royal India* at 392/1 Chakraphet Rd in Pahurat, the Indian fabric district. It is very crowded at lunchtime, so it might be better to go there after the standard lunch hour or at night. The place has very good *dahl*, curries, Indian breads, *raita* and *lassi*, etc for both vegetarian and non-vegetarian eaters at quite reasonable prices. Definitely better value than the *Muslim Restaurant* on New Rd, which costs more and has watery curries but has been a traveller's standby.

There are at least two more Indian restaurants down alleys off Chakraphat Rd, no names and difficult to find, that are downright cheap. Vegetable *samosas* can be bought in the street in Pahuraht. The *Moti Mahal Restaurant* at the old Chartered Bank near the Swan Hotel has good Muslim/Indian food, great yoghurt and reasonable prices.

For south Indian food (*dosa, idli, vada*, etc), try the *Silom Lodge* at 92/1 Vaithy (or Vaithi) Lane, off Silom Rd near the Narai Hotel. Worth the long walk down Vaithi Lane for the delicious coconut *chatni*. Another place serving South Indian (in addition to North Indian) food is *Simla Cafe* at 382 Soi Tat Mai (opposite Borneo & Co) off Silom, not far from New Rd.

Patpong & Silom Rd On Patpong Rd the *Thai Room*, a Thai-Chinese-Mexican-Farang place, is favoured by Thai-farang couples, Peace Corps volunteers and off-duty barmaids. Prices are reasonable. If you crave German or Japanese food, there are plenty of places serving these cuisines on and around Patphong Rd. *Bobby's Arms*, an Aussie-Brit pub, has good fish-and-chips.

Out on Silom Rd there are a couple of good restaurants. The medium-priced *Talaad Nam Restaurant* has great Thai food – especially soups and *laap kai* – and is air-conditoned upstairs, open downstairs. The place is nicely decorated in bamboo, with Thai *bongs* (*ganja* waterpipes), hill-tribe crossbows, etc hanging on the walls. Across the street from the Taalad Nam look for the *Charuvan*, 70-72 Silom Rd, a glassed-in Thai restaurant advertising Singha beer for 38B; inside find two rooms, one aircon, one *au naturel* (sweaty in the hot season) – very good low-priced Thai food with discount beer.

Down Sala Daeng Rd, off Silom, are several different places to eat – noodle shops, street vendors, an ice cream parlour, and the tiny air-con *Irrawaddy Restaurant*, with 'American fried rice' (Thai fried rice with ketchup), 'American breakfasts', but also Thai noodle dishes, and good chicken fried in holy basil.

At the other end of Silom, across from the Narai Hotel is a south Indian (Tamil) temple near which street vendors sell various Indian snacks. Around the corner of Silom on New Rd is the *Moslem Restaurant* mentioned above. Better but more expensive North Indian food is available at the *Himali Cha-Cha* (1229/11 New Rd) nearby. Also off Silom are two restaurants serving south Indian style food – see Indian Restaurants above.

Pratunam Pratunam, the market district at the intersection of Phetburi and Ratchaprarop, down from the Indra Regent, is a good hunting ground for Thai food. Check out the night markets behind Ratchaprarop Rd storefronts near the Phetburi Rd overpass and in the little sois near this intersection. These are all great places to eat real Thai food and see 'pure' (non-western) urban Thai culture. The Pratunam markets are open with corrugated tin roofs high above the tables and rustic kitchens, all bathed in fluorescent light. The market on the east side of Ratchaprarop is more like a series of connected tents – one speciality here is a tangy fish stomach soup, *kaphaw plaa*. Four people can eat a large meal, drinking beer or rice whiskey and nibbling away for hours and only spend around 150B to 200B, cheaper if it's rice whiskey rather than beer. Night markets in Bangkok, as elsewhere in Thailand, have no menus so you had better have your Thai in shape before venturing out for an evening – or better, get a Thai friend to accompany you.

Expensive Places The *Siam Intercontinental Hotel* has an all-you-can-eat buffet of well-prepared Thai food, including your choice of seafood steamed on the spot. The buffet costs 100B and is open 12 noon to 2.30 pm, Monday to

Friday only, in the *Talay Thong* restaurant. The *Oriental Hotel* does a 'marvellous buffet lunch for 200B, a real touch of class for the weary traveller'. The Terrace Restaurant here is also very good, and has one of the best sunset views in Bangkok.

The pinnacle of Thai cuisine in Bangkok, according to Thai gourmets who can afford it (though it is not expensive at all by European standards), is served at *Bussaracum Restaurant* (pronounced 'boot-sa-ra-kam') at 35 Soi Pipat off Convent Rd. Every dish is prepared only when ordered, from all-fresh ingredients and freshly ground spices. The menu is in Thai and English and anything you order will be near-perfect, like the service. Live solo classical Thai music, played at a subdued volume is provided as well. A fancy place, recommended for a splurge. Two can eat for 400B to 500B.

Ice Cream There are several Sala Foremost Ice Cream shops in Bangkok – one at Siam Square, one on Ploenchit Rd, a couple on Charoen Krung, one on Ratchaprarop Rd in Pratunam, they're springing up everywhere. Good ice cream and other delicacies at *Pan Pan*, there's one on Sukhumvit at Soi 33 and another near the Siam Society.

Nightlife

Bangkok is loaded with coffeeshops, nightclubs and massage parlours, many of them left over from the days when the City of Angels was an R&R stop for GIs serving in Viet Nam. By and large they are seedy, expensive and cater to men only. All the major hotels have flashy nightclubs too, less seedy but more expensive. Many feature live music – rock, C&W, Thai pop music and jazz, the latter usually played by good Filipino bands.

Bars The girlie bars are concentrated along Sukhumvit Rd from Soi 21 on out; off Sukhumvit on Soi Nana (including the infamous Grace Hotel); and on Patpong Rds I and II, between Silom and Suriwong Rds. Most are pretty tame nowadays, at least in terms of the excitement you get for your money, though Soi Cowboy (off Sukhumvit between Soi 22 and 23) still gets pretty wild some nights. Check the price of drinks first, beers are usually 30B to 40B.

There is a new bar area called Nana Plaza on Soi 4 (Soi Nana Tai) Sukhumwit Rd. One bar here, *Woodstock*, plays some of the best recorded music in town over a good sound system and they don't seem to mind if you come and just listen either, ie, the girls keep a low profile.

Massage Parlours Massage parlours have been a Bangkok attraction for many years now, though the Tourist Authority of Thailand tries to discourage the city's reputation in this respect. Massage as a healing art is a tradition that is centuries old in Thailand (check out Wat Po) and it is still possible to get a really legitimate massage in Bangkok – despite the commercialisation of recent years. That many of the massage parlours also deal in prostitution is well-known; less well-known is the fact that many (but by no means all) of the girls working in the parlours are bonded labour – they are not there by choice. It takes a pretty sexist male not to be saddened by the sight of 50 girls/women behind a glass wall with numbers pinned to their dresses. Should male travellers avail themselves of more than a massage and come down with something they hadn't bargained for, there are plenty of VD clinics located along Ploenchit Rd.

Theatre & Cinema For more high-brow entertainment, there is the Alliance Francaise, next to the YMCA on Sathorn Tai Rd, which shows several French films each week. Show times are usually 8 pm (titles and show times are posted outside the main building) and admission is 20B for members, 30B for non-members. There are also a dozen or more Thai movie theatres around town showing Thai, Chinese, Indian and occasional Western (European and American) movies. These theatres are air-conditioned and quite comfortable, with reasonable rates. All movies in Thai theatres are preceded by the Thai national anthem along with pictures of King Bhumiphol and other members of the royal family projected on the screen. Everyone in the theatre stands quietly for the duration of the anthem (written by the king, incidentally) in respect for the monarch.

Films are listed in the daily *Bangkok Post* newspaper – look for other cultural events in the paper, too, there are occasional classical music performances, rock concerts, Asian music/theatre ensembles on tour, art shows, international buffets, etc. Boredom should not be a problem in Bangkok, at least not for a short-term visit; however, save some money for your upcountry trip!

Getting There
Bus See the introductory Getting Around section for more details on bus travel in Thailand. Bangkok is the centre for bus services that fan out all over the kingdom. There are basically three types of buses. First there are the regular public buses, then the air-con buses. These both go from the main bus stations, leave regularly and provide a good service to all the centres. Third choice is the many private air-con services which leave from various

offices and hotels all over the city and provide a de-luxe service for those people for whom simple air-con isn't enough!

There are three main public bus stations. The North Bus Station (tel 279 6621-5) is on Phahonyothin Rd on the way up to the airport, lots of buses heading north go by it. Buses depart from here to Chiang Mai and other northern centres as well as to Ayuthaya, Lopburi and other places close to Bangkok but north of the city. Buses to Aranyaprathet also go from here, not from the East Bus Station as you might expect.

The East Bus Station (tel 392 2391),

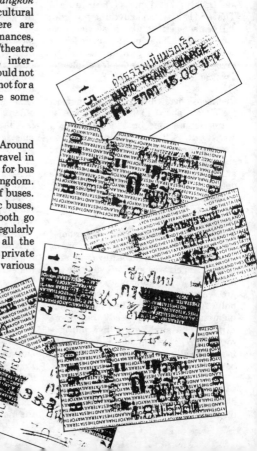

สู่จุดหมาย ด้วยบริการใหม่ของ
SHORTS 330
OFFERS NEW SERVICES TO YOUR
DESTINATION.

โปรดคอยที่ห้องพักผู้ –
โดยสารขาออกจนกว่าจะ
เชิญท่านขึ้นเครื่องบิน
PLEASE WAIT IN THE
DEPARTURE LOUNGE FOR
BOARDING.

เงินตากาศไทย
Thai Airways

บัตรขึ้นเครื่องบิน
BOARDING PASS
เที่ยวบิน FLT. NO.
H 108
ที่นั่งด้านหน้า
FORWARD SECTION
ที่นั่งด้านหลัง
A SECTION
15 B

from where buses go to Pattaya amongst other places, is a long way out Sukhumvit Rd, at Soi 40 opposite Soi 63. The South Bus Station (tel 411 4978-9) for buses to Phuket, Surat Thani and closer in centres like Nakhon Pathom and Kanchanaburi, is across the river in Thonburi. It's on Charan Sanitwong Rd, near the Bangkok Noi or Thonburi railway station. The North and East Bus Stations (South too?) both have good left luggage facilities.

When travelling on night buses take care with your belongings. One traveller wrote in to say that on the night bus from Chiang Mai to Bangkok all of their travellers cheques were stolen (US$650). The tourist police and Amex were very helpful and they received US$500 back from Amex on the same day.

Train See the introductory Getting Around section for more details about rail travel throughout Thailand. Bangkok is the terminus for rail services to the south, north and north-east. There are two main railway stations. The big Hualamphong Station on Rama IV Rd handles services to the north, north-east and some of the services to the south. The Thonburi or Bangkok Noi Station handles some services to the south. If you're heading south make certain which station your train departs from.

Air Bangkok is a major centre for international flights throughout Asia and Bangkok's airport is a busy one. Bangkok is also a major centre for buying discounted airline tickets – see the introductory Getting There section for details but also note the re-iterated warning about crooked travel agency operators. Domestic flights operated by Thai airways also fan out from Bangkok all over the country. Addresses of airline offices are:

Aeroflot
7 Silom Rd, (tel 233 6965-7)
Air France
3 Patpong Rd, (tel 233 7100-19, resv 234 7901-5)
Air India
287 Silom Rd, (tel 233 8950-4, resv 234 7558)
Air Lanka
1 Patpong Rd, (tel 235 6800, 235 0133-4)
Alia the Royal Jordanian Airline
56 Silom Rd, (tel 235 4800)
Alitalia
138 Silom Rd, (tel 233 4000-4, resv 234 5253-7)
Bangladesh Biman
Chongkolnee Bldg, 56 Suriwongse Rd, (tel 233 6178, 235 7643-4),
British Airways
133/19 Rajaprasong Rd, (tel 252 9871-9)
Burma Airways
208 Surawongse Rd, (tel 234 9692, 233 3052)
Cathay Pacific Airways
109 Suriwongse Rd, (tel 235 6022, resv 233 6105-9)
China Airlines
Siam Centre, Rama I Rd, (tel 251 9656-9, resv 252 1748-9)
Egyptair
120 Silom Rd (tel 235 8964, resv 233 7601-3)
Garuda
944/19 Rama IV Rd (tel 233 3873, resv 233 0981-2)
General Administration of Civil Aviation of China
134/1-2 Silom Rd (tel 235 6510-1, 235 1880-2)
Gulf Air
9 Decho Rd, (tel 233 5039, 235 5605)
Indian Airlines
2/1 Decho Rd, (tel 233 3890-2)
Iraqi Airlines
29/3 Soi Saladaeng 1, Silom Rd (tel 233 3271-4, 233 0569)
Japan Airlines
1 Patpong Rd, (tel 234 9105-18, resv 234 9113-18

KLM Royal Dutch Airlines
2 Patpong Rd, (tel 235 5150-9)
Korean Airlines
Dusit Thani Bldg, Silom Rd, (tel 234 9283-9)
Kuwait Airways
159 Rajadamri Rd, (tel 251 5855)
Lao Aviation
56 Chongkolnee Bldg, Surawongse Rd, (tel 233 7950, resv 234 0300)
Lot Polish Airlines
585/11-12 Silom Rd, (tel 235 2223-7, 235 7092-4)
Lufthansa
331/1-3 Silom Rd, (tel 234 1350-9)
Malaysian Airlines System
98-102 Suriwongse Rd, (tel 234 9795-9, resv 234 9790-4)
Pakistan International Airlines
52 Suriwongse Rd, (tel 234 2961)
Philippine Airlines
Chongkolnee Bldg, Suriwongse Rd, (tel 233 2350-2),
Qantas
Charns Issara Tower, 942/51 Rama IV Rd, (tel 236 9193-6)
Royal Brunei Airlines
c/o Thai International, 485 Silom Rd, (tel 234 3110-9)
Royal Nepal Airlines
1/4 Convent Rd, (tel 233 3921-4)
SAS Scandinavian Airlines System
412 Rama I Rd, (tel 252 4181)
Sabena Airlines
109 Suriwongse Rd, (tel 233 5940-1)
Saudi Arabian Airlines
Ground Fl, CCT Bldg, 109 Surawongse Rd, (tel 235 7930-9)
Singapore Airlines
12 Fl, Silom Centre Building, 2 Silom Rd, (tel 236 0303, resv 236 0440)
Swiss Air Transport
1 Silom Rd, (tel 233 2930-4, resv 233 2935-8)
Tarom Romanian Air Transport
Zuellig Bldg, 1-7 Silom Rd, (tel 235 2668-9)
Thai Airways Co Ltd
Thai Airways Bldg, 6 Larn Luang Rd, (tel 282 7600, 282 7151, resv 281 1633),
Thai Airways International
89 Vipavadi Rangsit Rd, 485 Silom Rd, (tel 234 3100, resv 511 0821)
Vietnam Airlines
83/1 Wireless Rd, (tel 251 7202)

Getting Around

Getting around in Bangkok may be difficult at first for the uninitiated but once you've got the bus system down the whole city is accessible. Bangkok was once called the Venice of the East, but the canal system is fast disappearing to give way to more road construction – with 10% of Thailand's population living in the capital, water transportation, with few exceptions, is a thing of the past. Those canals that do remain are hopelessly polluted and will probably be filled in by the end of the century.

Bus You can save a lot of money in Bangkok by sticking to the public buses, which are 2B for any journey under 10 km on the ordinary, non-AC buses or 5B on the air-con lines. The fare on ordinary buses is 3B for longer trips, eg from Chulalongkorn University to King Mongkut's Institute of Technology in Thonburi on bus no 21 and for AC buses the fare can go as high as 15B, eg from Silom Road to Don Muang airport on AC bus No 4. The AC buses are not only cooler but are usually less crowded (all bets off during rush hours).

To do any serious bus riding you'll need a Bangkok bus map – easiest to read is the one put out by Suwannachai (*Latest Tour's Guide to Bangkok & Thailand*) which also has a decent map of the whole country on the flip side. The bus numbers are clearly marked in red, air-con buses in larger types. Don't expect the routes to be 100% correct, a few have changed since the map came out last, but it'll get you where you're going most of the time. This map usually retails for 30B or sometimes 40B.

Taxis Taxis in Bangkok have meters but the drivers do not use them. The fare must be decided before you get in the cab unless you really want to get taken for a ride. Fares to most places within central Bangkok should not exceed 50B – add 5B to 10B if it's rush hour or after midnight.

Short distances should be under 40B – Siam Square to Silom Rd, for example, should be 30B to 35B in relatively light traffic.

To get these fares you must bargain well. There is an over-supply of taxis in Bangkok so just wave a driver on if he won't meet a reasonable fare and flag down another cab. It gets easier with practice and better results are obtained if you speak some Thai. Petrol prices are high in Thailand and they are increasing. About 90% of Bangkok taxis have switched over from gasoline fuel to LP gas in recent years. Most cabs are now air-conditioned, too, so fares continue to rise. Better to take a bus if you are really counting baht, save the taxi for when you're in a genuine hurry.

Tuk-tuks These three-wheeled taxis, which sound like power saws gone berserk, are good only for very short distances. For longer distances they may charge more than the four-wheel variety and there have been some instances of *tuk-tuk* drivers robbing their fares at night. Bangkok residents often talk of the tuk-tuks as a nuisance, even a menace, to their already suffering environment. Some have even been trying to get a ban on tuk-tuks enacted. A few years ago the city supposedly forbade the further production of any new three-wheel taxis, but on a recent trip there I saw more than a few brand new ones. It's a bit of a moral dilemma actually, since the tuk-tuk drivers are usually poor north-easterners who can't afford to rent the quieter, less polluting Toyota auto-taxis.

River Transport Although Bangkok's canals (*klongs*) are disappearing there is still plenty of transport along and across the Chao Phya River and up adjoining canals. River transport is one of the nicest ways of getting around Bangkok as well as, quite often, being much faster than any road-based alternatives. For a start you get a quite different view of the city,

Main stops of the Chao Phya Express

1 Oriental Hotel
2 Wat Muang Kai — for GPO
3 Siphya
4 Ratchawong — for Chinatown
5 Memorial Bridge
6 Rachini
7 Thai Tien — for Wat Pho
8 Tha Chang — for Wat Phra Keo
9 Maharaj — for Thammasart
    University
10 Prannock
11 Rot Fai — Bangkok Noi Railway
    Station
12 Wat Daowadung
13 Samphya — for Banglamphu
14 Wisut Kasat
15 Thewait — for National Library &
    Sawatdee Guest House

The boat does not stop at every landing if there are no passengers

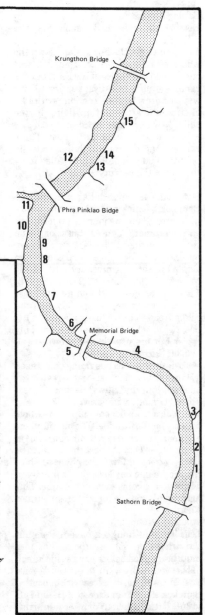

secondly, it's far less hassling than tangling with the polluted, noisy, traffic-crowded streets. And just try getting from Banglamphu to the GPO as fast by road.

First step to successfully using river transport is to know your boats. The main ones you'll want to use are the rapid Chao Phya Express or *rua duan*, a sort of river bus service. They cost 3B, 5B or 7B depending on the distance you travel and follow a regular route up and down the river – note that they do not necessarily stop at every stop if there are no people there or wanting to get off. You buy your tickets on the boat. The Chao Phya Express is a big, long boat with a number on the roof:

Chao Phya express river taxi

From the main Chao Phya stops and also from almost every other jetty there are slower cross-river ferries (*rua kham fak*) which simply shuttle back and forth across the river. The standard fare is 50 satang and you usually pay this at the entrance to the jetty. Be careful, there will probably be a pay window at the jetty and also a straight through aisle for people taking other boats:

Ferry to cross Chao Phya River

Finally there are the long-tail taxis (*rua hang yao*) which operate a share-taxi system off the main river and up the smaller *klongs*. Fares usually start from around 3B – you've really got to know where you're going on these. There are also river taxis where you really do take the whole boat – find them at certain jetties, like the Oriental Hotel and charter them for trips to the floating market or other attractions. Bargain hard.

Long - tailed taxis

Cars & Motorcycles Cars and motorcycles can easily be rented in Bangkok if you can afford it and have steel nerves. Rates are around 300B per day, less for a motorcycle, not including insurance. An International Driver's Permit and passport are required.

For cross-country trips of some duration, you might consider buying a new or used motorcycle and reselling it when you leave – this can end up being cheaper than renting, especially if you buy a good used bike.

Here are the names and addresses of a few car rental companies:

Bangkok Car Rent
   83/2 Witthayu Rd, (tel 252 9729)
Choke Dee Car Rent
   2/6 Soi 30, Sukhumvit Rd, (tel 392 2082)
Grand Car Rent
   144/3-4 Silom Rd, (tel 234 9956, 234 6867)
Hertz Car Rent
   1620 New Phetburi Rd, (tel 252 4903-6)
Highway Car Rent
   6/2 Rama IV Rd, (tel 234 0832, 235 5132, 235 7746-7)
Inter Car Rent
   45 Sukhumvit Rd, near Soi 3, (tel 251 4910, 252 9223)
Klong Toey Car Rent
   2149 Rama IV Rd, (tel 250 1141, 250 1361, 250 1930)
Krung Thai Car Rent
   233-5 Asoke-Din Daeng Rd, (tel 245 0909, 245 1894)
New First Car Rent
   Soi 1, 1 Sukhumvit Rd, (tel 392 4422)
Petchburi Car Rent
   2317 Petchburi Rd, (tel 317 6782, 314 7360)
Rama Transport (Avis)
   981 Silom Rd, (tel 234 0350, 235 7742, 234 4300)
Royal Car Rent
   2/7 Soi 20, Sukhumvit, (tel 391 6240, 391 3502)
Siam Car Rent
   45-49 Sukhumvit Rd, (tel 251 1850)
Sintat
   16/23 North Sathorn Rd, (tel 233 0397, 235 7028)
Super Car Rent
   Soi 7-9, 131/2 Sukhumvit Rd, (tel 252 4214, 252 4215)

There are several more car rental agencies along Witthayu Rd – many of these rent motorcyles, too.

Don Muang International Airport
Don Muang Airport is 25 km north of Bangkok and there are several ways of getting from there to the city.

Taxis Taxis will ask an outrageous amount to transport you to your destination but will usually go for a 100B or so (up to 150B if your bargaining is weak or there aren't many taxis around), not too bad if you're looking for the fastest way in, or have a few other travellers with whom to share the fare. Taxis flagged down on the highway that passes in front of the airport are cheaper – 80B to 100B. Thai International offer their airport limousine service for 280B – just a glorified air-con taxi service really.

The taxis which wait near the arrival area of the airport are illegal taxis run by Mafioso-type syndicates and are not recommended simply because you have no legal recourse if you are somehow cheated. These taxis have white and black plates. The syndicates won't let their licensed brothers into this area so you have to go upstairs to the departure area to get a real taxi. Don't follow the touts waiting near the customs exit if you want a taxi; go straight upstairs.

Taxis going to the airport from Bangkok generally ask for a higher fare than taxis coming back – count on 25B to 50B more.

Private Bus Thai International has a minibus that goes to most major hotels (and some minor ones if the driver feels like it) for 80B per person.

There are direct AC buses to Pattaya from the airport twice daily at 11 am and 9 pm; the fare is 190B one way.

Public Bus Cheapest of all are the public buses which stop on the highway to Bangkok, out front. The ordinary No 29 bus is only 3B but often crowded – it comes straight down Phahonyothin Rd after entering the city limits. This road soon turns into Phayathai Rd, meanwhile passing Phetburi Rd (where you'll want to get off to change buses if you're going to the Democracy Monument area), Rama I Rd (for buses out Sukhumvit, or to walk to the Star Hotel, Reno Hotel, or

Muangphol Lodging), and finally turning right on Rama IV Rd to go to the Hualamphong district (where Bangkok's main railway station is located). You'll want to go the opposite way on Rama IV for the Malaysia, Boston Inn, etc. Bus No 59 goes straight to the Democracy Monument area from the airport.

The air-conditioned public bus No 4 can also be boarded at the airport for 15B to most destinations in Bangkok; it costs less if you're getting off in north Bangkok (say, for the Liberty Hotel in Saphan Khwai district) though this must be established before you pay the fare. Unless you're really strapped for baht, it's worth the extra 12B for the air-con and almost guaranteed seating on the No 4, especially in the hot season, since the trip downtown by bus can take an hour or more.

The No 4 bus does a route parallel to the No 29 – down Mitthaphap Rd to Ratchprarop/Ratachadamri Rd, crossing Phetburi, Rama I, Ploenchit, and Rama IV Rds, then down Silom, left on Charoen Krung, and across the river to Thonburi. You ought to have some kind of map of Bangkok before attempting the buses so you'll know approximately where to get off. The air-con No 13 also goes to Bangkok from the airport, coming down Phahonyothin (like No 29), turning left at the Victory Monument to Ratchaprarop, then south to Ploenchit, where it goes east out Sukhumvit Rd all the way to Bang Na.

Train You can also get into Bangkok from the airport by train. Just leave the airport building, cross the road by the pedestrian bridge, turn left and walk about a hundred metres towards Bangkok. Right opposite the big Airport Hotel is a small railway station from where trains depart regularly to Bangkok. Third class fare is 5B.

Departure Tax Airport departure tax is now 150B. Don't complain; the Thais have to pay a 2000B departure tax when they leave the country. You're exempted from paying the tax if you're only in transit and have not left the airport building. You have to fill in a declaration form if this is the case – ask for it.

Airport Facilities Bangkok airport is not the most modern and convenient in Asia but it's also far from the worst. It's major problem is that few of the aircraft bays are reached by skybridges, you have to take buses out for most flights. A new international terminal is under construction. The new domestic terminal is south of the international terminal.

In the international terminal there's a good value restaurant/snack bar upstairs which provides (by airport standards) excellent food at fairly reasonable prices. There's no real price advantage in using the self service section. By contrast there is very little food available on the other side of the wall in the departure/transit lounge area – just over-priced soft drinks and terrible pre-wrapped sandwiches.

The airport has the usual bank, post office, left luggage facilities and a tourist information counter in the arrival area. The hotel counter here makes reservations for THA (Thai Hotel Association) members. That doesn't go below the Miami-Malaysia standard of hotel. The Thai Military Bank at the airport gives a good rate of exchange.

If you leave the airport building area and cross the freeway on the pedestrian bridge you'll find yourself in the Don Muang town area where there are all sorts of shops, a market, lots of small restaurants and food stalls, even a wat, all within a hundred metres or so of the airport. What there isn't is a cheap hotel although the expensive *Airport Hotel* is only a hundred metres or so away.

Thai Boxing

Most of what is known about the early history of Thai boxing comes from the Burmese accounts of warfare between Burma and Thailand during the 15th and 16th centuries. The earliest reference (1411 AD) mentions a ferocious style of unarmed combat that decided the fate of Thai kings. A later description tells how Nai Khanom Tom, Thailand's first famous boxer and a prisoner of war in Burma, gained his freedom by roundly defeating a dozen Burmese warriors before the Burmese court. To this day, many martial art afficionados consider the Siamese style the ultimate in hand-to-hand fighting.

King Naresuan the Great (1555 to 1605) was supposed to have been a top-notch boxer himself. He made *muay thai* ('Thai boxing') a required part of military training for all Thai soldiers. Later another Thai king, Phra Chao Seua ('the Tiger King') further promoted Thai boxing as a national sport by encouraging prize fights and the development of training camps in the early 18th century. There are accounts of massive wagers and bouts to the finish during this time. Phra Chao Seua is said to have been an incognito participant in many of the matches during the early part of his reign. Combatants' fists were wrapped in thick horsehide for maximum impact with minimum knuckle damage. They also used cotton soaked in glue and ground glass and later hemp. Tree bark and seashells were used to protect the groin from lethal kicks.

The high incidence of death and physical injury led the Thai government to institute a ban on *muay thai* in the 1920s, but in the '30s, the sport was revived under a modern set of regulations based on the international Queensbury Rules. Bouts were limited to five rounds of three minutes duration each with a two-minute break inbetween. Contestants had to wear international-style gloves and trunks (always in red or blue) and their feet were taped but no shoes worn. There are 12 weight divisions in Thai boxing, from flyweight to heavyweight, with the best fighters said to be in the welterweight division (67 kg max). As in international-style boxing, matches take place on a 7.3 metre square canvas-covered floor with rope retainers supported by four padded posts, rather than the traditional dirt circle. In spite of these concessions to safety, today, all surfaces of the body are still considered fair targets and any part of the body may be used to strike an opponent, except the head. Common blows include high kicks to the neck, elbow thrusts to the face and head, knee hooks to the ribs and low crescent kicks to the calf. A contestant may even grasp an opponent's head between his hands and pull it down to meet an upward knee thrust. Punching is considered the weakest of all blows and kicking merely a way to 'soften up' one's opponent; it is the knee and elbow strikes that are decisive in most matches.

The training of a Thai boxer and particularly the relationship between boxer and trainer is highly ritualised. When a boxer is considered ready for the ring, he is given a new name by his trainer, with the name of the training camp as his surname. For the public, the relationship is perhaps best expressed in the *ram muay* or 'boxing dance' that takes place before every match. The *ram muay* ceremony usually lasts about five minutes and expresses obeisance to the fighter's guru (*khru*), as well as to the guardian spirit of Thai boxing. This is done through a series of gestures and body movements performed in rhythm to the ringside musical accompaniment of Thai oboe (*pii*) and percussion. Each boxer works out his own dance, in conjunction with his trainer and in accordance with the style of his particular camp. The woven headbands and armbands worn into the ring by fighters are sacred ornaments which bestow blessings and divine protection; the headband is removed after the *ram muay* ceremony, but the armband, which actually contains a small Buddha image, is worn throughout the match. After the bout begins, the fighters continue to bob and weave in rhythm until the action begins to heat up. The musicians continue to play throughout the match and the volume and tempo of the music rise and fall along with the events in the ring.

It is said that Thai-style boxing is becoming commercialised and that there is an increasing number of bouts staged for tourists. Nonetheless, there are hundreds of authentic matches taking place every day of the year at the major Bangkok stadiums and in the provinces.

The places that follow could all be visited in day trips from Bangkok but in most cases they make better stepping stones to places further afield. You can, for example, pause in Ayuthaya on the way north to Chiang Mai or Nakhon Pathom if you're heading south.

AYUTHAYA (population 52,000)
จังหวัดศรีอยุธยา or พระนครศรีอยุธยา

Approximately 86 km north of Bangkok, this city was the Thai capital from 1350 to 1767. Prior to 1350, when the capital was moved there from U Thong, it was a Khmer outpost.

Thirty-three kings of various Siamese dynasties reigned in Ayuthaya until it was conquered by the Burmese. During its heyday, Thai culture and international commerce flourished in the kingdom – the Ayuthaya period has so far been the apex of Thai history – and Ayuthaya was courted by Dutch, Portuguese, French, English, Chinese and Japanese merchants. All visitors claimed it to be the most illustrious city they had ever seen.

The present-day city is located at the confluence of three rivers, the Chao Phraya, the Pa Sak and the smaller Lopburi. A wide canal joins them and makes a complete circle around the town. Long-tail boats can be rented from the boat landing across from Chandra Kasem (Chan Kasem) Palace for a tour around the river/canal; several of the old *wat* ruins (Wat Phanam Choeng, Wat Phuttaisawan, Wat Kasatrathira and Wat Chai Wattanaram) may be glimpsed at in this way, as well as a picturesque view of river life. Outside of the historic ruins and museums, Ayuthaya is not particularly interesting but it is one of three cities in Thailand known for their 'gangster' activity. Foreigners now have to pay a 20B admission price to each historical site they visit.

National Museum

There are two, the main one being the Chao Sam Phraya Museum, which is near the intersection of Rojana Rd (Ayuthaya's main street, connecting with the highway to Bangkok) and Si Sanphet Rd, opposite the city hall near the centre of town. It is open 9 am to 12 noon and 1 pm to 4 pm, Wednesday to Sunday.

The second, Chan Kasem Palace *(Phra Ratchawong Chan Kasem)*, is a museum piece itself, built by the 17th king of Ayuthaya – Maha Thammaraj – for his son Prince Naresuan. It is in the Chan Kasem Palace in the north-east corner of the town, near the river. Hours are the same there as at the other museum. Pick up a good map/guide of Ayuthaya at the museum for 15B.

Wat Phra Si Sanphet

This was the largest temple in Ayuthaya in its time, it was used as the Royal Temple-Palace for several Ayuthaya kings. Built in the 14th century, the compound once contained a 16-metre standing Buddha covered with 250 kg of gold, which was melted down by the Burmese conquerors. It is mainly known for the *chedis* erected in the quintessential Ayuthaya style, which has come to be identified with Thai art more than any other single style.

Wiharn Phra Mongkol Bopit

Near Si Sanphet, this monastery contains one of Thailand's largest Buddha images. The present *wiharn* was built in 1956.

Wat Phra Maha That

This wat, located at the corner of Chee Kun and Naresuan Rds, dates back to the 14th century. Despite extensive ruin – not much was left standing after the Burmese hordes – the *prang* is still impressive.

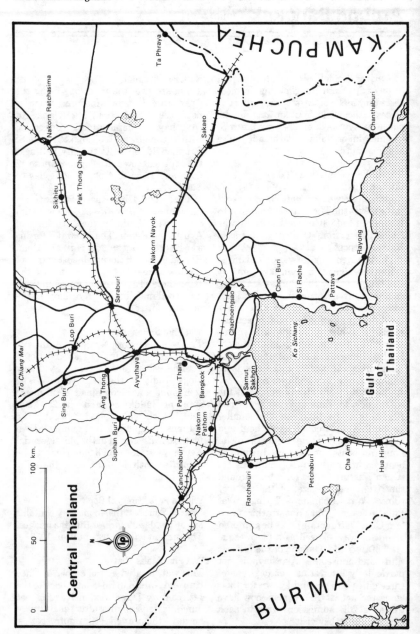

Wat Rajburana

Counterpart ruins to Maha That across the road, however the *chedis* are not quite as dilapidated.

Wat Phra Chao Phanam Choeng

This one was built before Ayuthaya became a Siamese capital and it is right on the Chao Phraya River outside the town proper to the south-east. The main *wiharn* contains a highly revered 19-metre sitting Buddha image.

Wat Na Phra Mane (Phra Meru)

Across from the old Royal Palace *(wang luang)* grounds is a bridge which can be crossed to arrive at Wat Phra Mane. This temple is notable because it escaped destruction in 1767, though it has required restoration over the years anyway. Recommended.

Wat Thammik Raj

To the west of the old palace grounds, inside the river loop, Thammik Raj features overgrown *chedi* ruins and lion sculptures.

Wat Yai Chai Mongkol

Wat Yai, as the locals call it, lies outside the city to the south-east but can be reached by minibus for 3B to 4B. It's a quiet old place that was once a famous meditation wat, built in 1357 by King U Thong. The compound contains a very large *chedi* from which the wat takes its popular name (*yai* = big), and there is a community of *mae chee* or Buddhist nuns (actually laywomen since the Sangha does not officially admit women into the order) residing here.

Places to Stay & Eat

Most visitors stay at the *U Thong* (tel 251136) on U Thong Rd near the boat landing and Chan Kasem Palace. Rooms cost from 80B to 200B per night, some are air-con. The *Thai Thai* (tel 251505), at 13/1 Naresuan Rd, between Wat Rajburana and the road to Wat Phra

Men, has rooms from 80B to 180B with air-con. The *Cathay* (tel 251562), near the U Thong towards Hua Raw market is 80B to 120B for a room with fan. 'Clean and friendly,' wrote one traveller, 'they lent us money and refused offers of passports as guarantee'. *Si Samai Bungalow*, 12/19 Naresuan Rd (tel 251104) is near the Thai Thai and costs 90B for a room with fan and bath, 150B air-con.

Best places to eat are the Hua Raw market, on the river near Chan Kasem Palace and the Chao Phrom market on Chao Phrom Rd east of Wat Rajburana. There are quite a few restaurants on the main road into Ayuthaya, Rojana Rd, and there are two floating restaurants on the Pa Sak River, one on either side of the Pridi Damrong Bridge. Food is fairly expensive and not all that good.

Getting There

Ayuthaya can be reached by bus, train or boat.

Bus Daily buses leave from the Northern Bus Terminal in Bangkok every 10 minutes, 5 am to 7 pm, the fare is 17B and the trip takes 1½ hours.

Train Trains to Ayuthaya leave Bangkok's Hualamphong station about every half hour between 4.30 am and 8 pm, with additional trains at 10 pm and 11.05 pm. Third class fare is 15B for the one hour, 15 minute trip; it's hardly worth taking a more expensive seat for this short trip. Train schedules are available at the information booth at Hualamphong station.

Boat Boats to Ayuthaya leave Bangkok from Tha Thien pier near Thammasat daily at about 10 am but the trip is rather long going upriver. Better to take the boat back from Ayuthaya – about three hours or so. Check at the landing near Chan Kasem Palace in Ayuthaya for the current fare and departure time. A typical round-trip charter fare for a long-

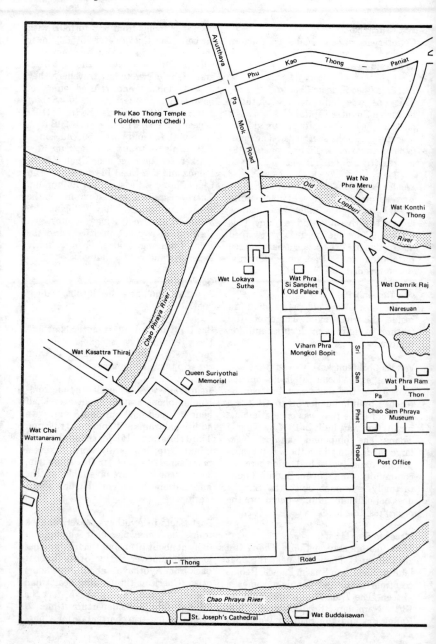

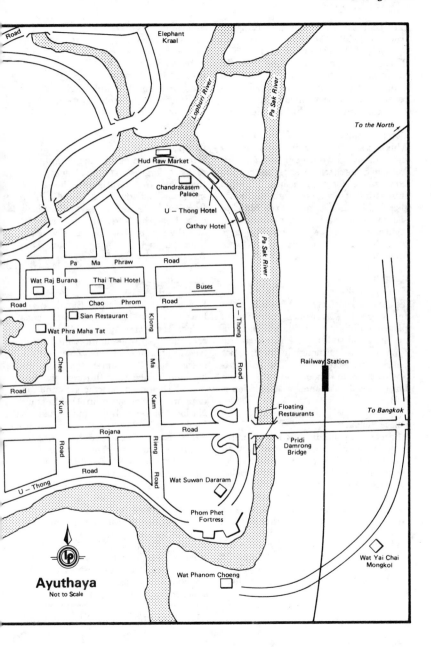

Elephant Kraal

Lopburi River

Pa Sak River

To the North

Hud Raw Market

Chandrakasem Palace

U – Thong Hotel

Cathay Hotel

Pa Sak River

Pa   Ma   Phraw   Road

Wat Raj Burana   Thai Thai Hotel

Buses

Road

Chao   Phrom   Road

Sian Restaurant

Klong

Wat Phra Maha Tat

U – Thong

Chee

Ma

Kam

Railway Station

Road

Road

Floating Restaurants

To Bangkok

Kun

Rieng Road

Rojana   Road

Pridi Damrong Bridge

Road

Road

Wat Suwan Dararam

U – Thong

Phom Phet Fortress

Wat Yai Chai Mongkol

Ayuthaya
Not to Scale

Wat Phanom Choeng

tail boat Bangkok-Ayuthaya-Bangkok would be 1200B. You can get a water taxi Ayuthaya to Bang Pa In for around 150B. There's a tour boat operating from the Oriental Hotel to Ayuthaya for around 570B. You can go by bus or boat and return by the opposite mode of transport. Lunch is included on this de-luxe tour.

Getting Around
Minibuses from the train station to any point in Ayuthaya should be 3B to 5B. You can hire a *samlor* or *songthaew* by the hour to explore the ruins. It's also interesting to hire a boat from the palace pier to do a circular tour of the island to see some of the less accessible ruins. Ayuthaya covers a surprisingly large area, it's not a place where you walk around.

BANG PA IN
อำเภอบางปะอิน
Twenty km south of Ayuthaya is Bang Pa In, which has a curious collection of palace buildings in a wide variety of architectural styles. It's a nice boat trip from Ayuthaya although in itself it's not particularly noteworthy. The palace is open 8.30 am to 12 noon and 1 pm to 4 pm but is closed on Mondays. Admission is 10B.

Palace Buildings
The postcard building here is a pretty little Thai pavilion in the centre of a small lake by the palace entrance. Inside the palace grounds the Chinese-style **Wehat Chamrun Palace** is the only building open to visitors. The **Withun Thatsana** building looks like a lighthouse with balconies. It was built to give a fine view over gardens and lakes. There are various other buildings, towers and memorials in the grounds plus an interesting example of topiary where the bushes have been trimmed into the shape of a small herd of elephants.

Wat Nivesthamapravat
Across the river and south from the palace grounds this unusual wat looks much more like a gothic Christian church than anything from Thailand. It was built by Rama V (Chulalongkorn). You get to the wat by crossing the river in a small trolley-like cable car. The crossing is free.

Getting There
Bang Pa In can be reached by minibus, really a large *songthaew* truck rather than a bus, from Ayuthaya's Chao Phom market, Chao Phom Rd, for 6B. From Bangkok there are buses every half hour or so from the Northern Bus Terminal and the fare is 14B. You can also reach Bang Pa In by train or by boat from Bangkok, or by boat from Ayuthaya.

LOPBURI (population 37,000)
จังหวัดลพบุรี
Exactly 154 km north of Bangkok, the town of Lopburi has been inhabited since at least the Dvaravati period (6th to 11th centuries AD) when it was called Lavo. Nearly all traces of Lavo culture have been erased by Khmer and Thai inhabitants since the 10th century, but many Dvaravati artefacts found in Lopburi can be seen in the Lopburi National Museum. Ruins and statuary in Lopburi span 12 centuries.

The Khmers extended their Angkor empire in the 10th century to include Lavo. It was during this century that they built the Prang Khaek (Hindu Shrine), San Phra Kan (Kala Shrine) and Prang Sam Yot (Three-Spired Shrine) – the current symbol of Lopburi province which appears on the back of the 500B note, as well as the impressive *prang* at Wat Phra Sri Ratana Mahathat.

Power over Lopburi was wrested from the Khmers in the 13th century as the Sukhothai kingdom to the north grew stronger, but the Khmer cultural influence remained to some extent throughout the Ayuthaya period. King Narai fortified

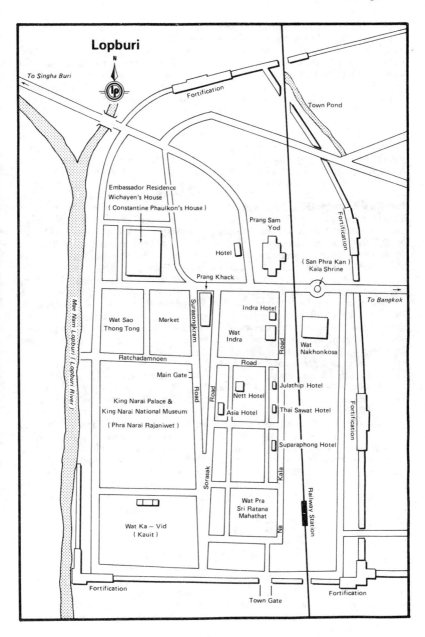

Lopburi

N

To Singha Buri

Fortification

Town Pond

Fortification

Embassador Residence
Wichayen's House
(Constantine Phaulkon's House)

Prang Sam
Yod

Hotel

(San Phra Kan)
Kala Shrine

Prang Khack

Mae Nam Lopburi (Lopburi River)

Surasongkram

To Bangkok

Indra Hotel

Wat Sao
Thong Tong

Market

Wat
Indra

Wat
Nakhonkosa

Ratchadamnoen

Road

Road

Main Gate

Road

Julathip Hotel

Nett Hotel

Thai Sawat Hotel

King Narai Palace &
King Narai National Museum
(Phra Narai Rajaniwet)

Road

Asia Hotel

Fortification

Suparaphong Hotel

Sorasak

Kala

Wat Ka – Vid
(Kauit)

Wat Pra
Sri Ratana
Mahathat

Na

Railway Station

Fortification

Fortification

Town Gate

Lopburi in the mid-17th century to serve as a second capital when the kingdom of Ayuthaya was threatened by a Dutch naval blockade. Narai's palace in Lopburi was constructed in 1665 and he died there in 1688.

The new town of Lopburi was begun in 1940. It's some distance east of the old fortified town and is centred around two large traffic circles. There is really nothing of interest in the new section; so you should try to stay at a hotel in the old town. All the historical sites in Lopburi can be visited on foot in a day or two.

Phra Narai Rajaniwet (King Narai's Palace) This is probably the best place to begin a tour of Lopburi. After King Narai's death in 1688, the palace was used only by King Phetracha (Narai's successor) for his coronation ceremony and it was then abandoned until King Mongkut ordered restoration in the mid-19th century.

The palace took 12 years to build (1665-1677). French architects contributed to the design and Khmer influence was still strong in central Thailand at that time. It's hardly surprising then that the palace exhibits an unusual blend of Khmer and European style – but it works.

The main gate into the palace, Pratu Phayakkha, is off Sorasak Rd, opposite the Asia Lopburi Hotel. The grounds are well kept, planted with trees and shrubbery and serve as a kind of city park for local children and young lovers. Immediately on the left as you enter are the remains of the king's elephant stables, with the palace water reservoir in the foreground. In the adjacent quadrangle to the left is the royal reception hall and the Phra Chao Hao, which probably served as a *wiharn* for a valued Buddha image. Passing through more stables, one comes to the south-west quadrangle with the Suttha Sawan pavilion in the centre. The north-west quadrangle contains many ruined buildings which were once an audience hall, various *salas* and residence quarters for the king's harem.

The Lopburi National Museum is located here in two separate buildings. The museum houses an excellent collection of Lopburi period sculpture, as well as an assortment of Khmer, Dvaravati, U Thong and Ayuthaya art. *A Guide to Ancient Monuments in Lopburi* by M C Subhadradis Diskul, Thailand's leading art historian, is available free from the counter on the second floor of the museum. Admission into the museum is 5B; open Wednesday to Sunday, 9 am to 12 pm and 1 pm to 4 pm.

Wat Phra Sri Ratana Mahathat
Directly across from the railway station, this very large 12th century Khmer wat is currently undergoing restoration by the Fine Arts Department. A very tall laterite *prang* still stands and features a few intact lintels, as well as some ornate stucco. A large *wiharn* added by King Narai also displays a ruined elegance. Several *chedis* and smaller prangs dot the grounds, some almost completely restored, some a little worse for wear, and there are a few ruined parts of Buddha images laying about.

Wat Nakhon Kosa
Just north of the railway station, near San Phra Kan, this was built by the Khmers in the 12th century and may originally have been a Hindu shrine. U Thong and Lopburi images found at the temple (now in the Lopburi museum) are thought to have been added later. There's not much left of this one, though the foliage growing on the brick ruins makes an interesting image. However, half-hearted attempts to restore it with modern materials and motifs detract from the overall effect.

Wat Indra & Wat Racha
Wat Indra, across the street from Wat Nakhon Kosa. Little is known of its history and it's now a pile of rubble. Wat Racha, off Phra Ya Jamkat Rd, is another pile of bricks with little known history.

Wat Sao Thong Thong

Located north-west of the palace centre, behind the central market, the buildings here are in pretty poor shape. The *wiharn* and large seated Buddha are from the Ayuthaya period; King Narai restored the wiharn, changing the windows to an incongruous but intriguing Gothic style so that it could be used as a Christian chapel. Niches along the inside walls contain Lopburi style *naga* Buddhas.

Chao Phraya Wichayen (Constantine Phaulkon Residence)

Across the street north-east of Wat Sao Thong Thong, King Narai built this eclectic Thai-European palace as a residence for foreign ambassadors, of whom the Greek Constantine Phaulkon was the most famous. Phaulkon became one of King Narai's principal advisors and was eventually a royal minister. In 1688, as Narai lay dying, Phaulkon was assassinated by Luang Sorasak, who wanted all the power of Narai's throne for himself.

San Phra Kan (Kala Shrine)

Across the railway tracks to the north of Wat Nakhon Kosa, this unimpressive shrine contains a crude gold-leaf laden image of Kala, the Hindu god of time and death. A virtual sea of monkeys surrounds this shrine, falling out of the tamarind trees and scurrying along the steps leading to the sanctuary. They are getting fat on hand-outs.

Prang Sam Yod

Opposite the Kala shrine, near the Muang Thong Hotel, this shrine represents classic Khmer-Lopburi style and is another Hindu-turned-Buddhist temple. Originally the three *prangs* symbolised the Hindu *trimurti* of Shiva, Vishnu and Brahma. Now two of them contain ruined Lopburi-style Buddha images. Some Khmer lintels can still be made out and some appear unfinished.

A rather uninteresting U Thong/ Ayuthaya imitation Buddha image sits in the brick sanctuary in front of the linked *prangs*. At the back, facing the Muang Thong Hotel, are a couple of crudely restored images, probably once Lopburi style. The grounds allotted to Prang Sam Yod by the city are rather small and make the structure difficult to photograph. The grounds are virtually surrounded by modern buildings as well. The best view of the monument would probably be from one of the upper floors of the Muang Thong.

Music & Dance

For those interested in Thai classical music and dance, there is a fine arts college *(Withayalai Kalasilpa Lopburi)* on Pha Ya Jamkat Rd, not far from the palace. Here you can watch young dancers practicing the rudiments of classical dance with live accompaniment.

Places to Stay

Lopburi is best visited as a day trip from Ayuthaya, but if you want to stay overnight try:

Asia Lopburi, corner of Sorasak and Phra Yam Jamkat Rds, overlooking King Narai's palace. This place is clean, comfortable, has good service and two Chinese restaurants downstairs. Rooms are 100B with fan and bath.

Muang Thong, across from Prang Sam Yot, has noisy but adequate rooms for 70B with fan and bath. Rooms without bath are also available for 50B.

The *Indra* on Na Kala Rd is across from Wat Nakhon Kosa and costs 70B for passable rooms with fan and bath. Also on Na Kala Rd, the *Julathip* is near the Indra but closer to the railway station, and has no English sign. This one is 60B with fan and bath – ask to see a room first. Also on Na Kala Rd, the *Suparaphong* is not far from Wat Phra Sri Ratana Mahathat and the train station. This costs 70B and is much the same as the Julathip and Indra hotels.

A few shops down from Julathip on the

same street is the *Thai Sawat* which, at 40B per room, is Lopburi's cheapest.

The *Nett Hotel* at 17/1-2 Ratchadamnoen Rd is actually on a *soi* between Ratchadamnoen and Phra Yam Jamkat, parallel to Sorasak Rd. It's 90B for clean, quiet rooms with fan and bath.

You can also pay a visit to the *Travellers Drop in Centre* at 34 Wichayen Rd, Soi 3 Maung. It is run by a New Zealander, his Thai wife and their three children. Here travellers can meet Thais at the informal English classes held here three times daily. After the class, the students go with travellers and share a meal in a restaurant. They also run a small Guest House for travellers – there are two double rooms; cost is 50B for one person or 60B to 70B for two. They also hire out bicycles.

Behind the bus station in the new part of the city is the *Srisawat*. The rooms here are grubby and cost 80B, but the Chinese owners are friendly. However, it's not recommended unless you have to be in the new city or arrive late at night by bus.

There are so many hotels along Na Kala Rd that bargaining should be possible. Ask if they have a 'cheaper room'. The Thai for this is *Mii hawng! tuuk. kwaa. mai?*

Places to Eat

Several Chinese restaurants operate along Na Kala Rd, parallel to the railway, especially near the Julathip and Thai Sawat hotels. The food is good but they tend to overcharge a bit. Restaurants on the side streets of Ratchadamnoen and Phra Yam Jamkat can be better value. The Chinese-Thai restaurant next to the Asia Lopburi Hotel on Sorasak Rd, across from the main gate to Narai's palace, makes excellent *tom yam kung* (shrimp-lemon grass soup), *kai phat bai kaphrao* (chicken fried in holy basil) and *kuaytiaw raat naa* (fried rice noodles with vegetables and sauce). There are also plenty of cheap curry vendors down the alleys and along the smaller streets in old Lopburi.

The day and night market off Ratchadamnoen and Surasongkhram Rds (just north of the palace) is a great place to pick up food to eat in your hotel room – *kai thawt* or *kai yang* (fried or roast chicken) with sticky rice, *haw mok* (fish and coconut curry steamed in banana leaves), *kluay khaek* ('Indian-style' fried bananas), a wide selection of fruits, *satay, khao kriap* (crispy rice cakes), *thawt man plaa* (fried fish cakes) and other delights.

Getting There

Bus Buses leave for Lopburi every 10 minutes from Ayuthaya, or, if you're coming from Bangkok, about every 20 minutes (5.21 am to 8.29 pm) from the Northern Terminal. It's a three-hour ride which costs 32B or 60B air-con.

Lopburi can also be reached from the west via Kanchanaburi or Suphanburi. If you're coming from Kanchanaburi, you'll have to take a bus first to Suphanburi from the Kan bus station. The trip lasts two hours, costs 21B, and has great scenery all the way. In Suphanburi, get off the bus along the city's main drag, Malimaen Rd (has English signs), at the intersection which has an English sign pointing to Sri Prachan. This is also where you catch the bus to Singhburi, across the river from Lopburi and a necessary stop.

The Suphanburi-Singhburi leg lasts about 2½ hours for 20B and the scenery gets even better – you'll pass many old traditional Thai wooden houses – late Ayuthaya style, countless cool rice paddies and small wats of all descriptions. Finally, at the Singhburi bus terminal, catch one of the frequent buses to Lopburi for 7B – takes about 30 minutes.

Train An Express train leaves for Lopburi from Bangkok every day at 6 pm, arriving in Lopburi at 8.25 pm. Fares are 111B first

class, 57B second class and 28B third.
There is a 30B express surcharge. Ordinary
trains (no surcharge) depart every half
hour or so between 4.30 am and 8 pm and
take only 13 minutes longer than the
express! No first class either.

There are also regular trains from
Ayuthaya to Lopburi which take about
one hour and cost 13B third class. One
could leave Ayuthaya in the morning,
have a look around Lopburi during the
day (leaving your bags in the Lopburi
Railway Station) and then carry on to
Chiang Mai on one of the night trains
(departure times are at 6.12 pm and at
8.26 pm).

Getting Around

Samlors will go anywhere in Lopburi for
5B.

SARABURI (population 46,000)
จังหวัดสระบุรี

There's nothing of interest in Saraburi
itself but between Lopburi and here you
can turn off to the **Phra Buddhabat**. It's
also known as Phra Phutthabat. This
small and delicately beautiful shrine
houses a revered Buddha footprint. Like
all genuine Buddha footprints it is
massive and identified by its 108 auspicious
distinguishing marks.

Places to Stay

Try the *Tanin* at Amphoe Phra Buddha
Baht. In Saraburi there's the *Keaw Un*
(tel 211222) on Phahonyothin Rd where
rooms with fan cost from 100B, with air-
con from 200B. Other hotels include the
slightly cheaper *Saraburi* (tel 211646,
211500) opposite the bus stand or the
Saen Suk (tel 211104) on Phahonyothin
Rd.

ANG THONG (population 10,000)
จังหวัดอ่างทอง

Between Lopburi and Suphanburi there
are some places of interest outside this
small town including **Wat Pa Mok** with its
22 metre long reclining Buddha.

Places to Stay

Rooms cost from 80B in the *Bua Luang*
(tel 611116) on Ayuthaya Rd. The *Ang
Thong Bungalow* (tel 611767-8) at 19 Ang
Thong Rd is more expensive.

Getting There

A bus from the Northern Bus Terminal in
Bangkok costs 25B.

SUPHANBURI (population 23,000)
จังหวัดสุพรรณบุรี

Almost 70 km north-east of Kanchanaburi,
Suphan is a very old Thai city that may
have had some connection with the semi-
mythical *Suvarnabhumi* mentioned in
early Buddhist writings. Today the town
is a prosperous, typical central Thai town
with a high proportion of Chinese among
the population. There are some noteworthy Ayuthaya period *chedis* and one
Khmer *prang*. If you're passing through
Suphan on a trip from Kanchanaburi to
Lopburi, you might want to stop off for a
couple of hours, see the sights, eat and
rest.

Entering Suphan from the direction of
Kan, you'll see **Wat Palelai** on the right at
the city limits. Several of the buildings
are old, originally built during the U
Thong period, and the *bot* is very
distinctive for its extremely high whitewashed walls. Looking inside, you'll
realise the building was designed that
way in order to house the gigantic late U
Thong or early Ayuthaya style seated
Buddha image inside. Exotic-looking
goats roam the grounds of this semi-
abandoned wat.

Further in towards the city centre on
the left side of Malimaen Rd is **Wat Phra Si
Ratana Mahathat** (this must be the most
popular name for wats in Thailand), set
back off the road a bit. This quiet wat
features a fine Lopburi-style Khmer
prang on which much of the stucco is still
intact. There is a staircase inside the
prang leading to a small chamber in the
top.

Two other wats this side of the new

town, **Wat Phra Rup** and **Wat Chum**, have venerable old Ayuthaya *chedis*.

Places to Stay

The *King Pho Sai* (tel 511412) at 678 Nane Kaew Rd has rooms from 80B or from 125B with air-con. Other similarly priced hotels are the *K A T* (tel 511619, 511639) at 433 Phra Phan-va-sar and the *Suk San* (tel 511668) at 1145 Nang Pim Rd.

Getting There

See Getting There – Lopburi. A bus from the Northern Bus Terminal in Bangkok costs 47B.

KHAO YAI NATIONAL PARK

อุทยานแห่งชาติเขาใหญ่

This is a beautiful park with good walks. You can get a rather inaccurate trail map from the park headquarters. It is easy to get lost on the longer trails so it's advisable to hire a guide. The charge will be 100B per day no matter how many people go. He's liable to ask for a tip. If you do plan to go walking, it is a good idea to take walking boots as leeches are a problem – apparently though, mosquito repellent does help to keep leeches away.

Places to Stay

There's a clean and modern hotel with rooms from 380B with an attached bath. It's near the bus station in Pak Chong. Dormitory accommodation is available, it costs 10B without a mosquito net and 20B with a mosquito net. Groups can also hire cottages from the HQ, it will cost 600B or more for six to 15 people.

Getting There

Take a bus from the Northern Bus Station to Pak Chong, from where you can hitch or take a *songthaew* to the park gates. A park car will take you from there. You can also take a direct bus from Bangkok.

Don Chedi

อำเภอดอนเจดีย์

Seven km west past Suphanburi off Route 324 on the way to Kanchanaburi is the road to Don Chedi, a very famous battle site and early war memorial. It was here that King Naresuan, then a prince, defeated the Prince of Burma on elephant back in the late 16th century. In doing so he freed Ayuthaya from domination by the Pegu Kingdom. The *chedi* or pagoda itself was built during Naresuan's lifetime but was neglected in the centuries afterwards. By the reign of King Rama V (Chulalongkorn) at the beginning of this century, its location had been forgotten. Rama V began a search for the site but it wasn't until three years after his death in 1913 that Prince Damrong, an accomplished archaeologist, rediscovered the chedi in Suphan province.

The chedi was restored in 1955 and the area developed as a national historic site. Every year during the week of January 25 (Thai Armed Forces Day), there is a week-long Don Chedi Monument Fair which features a full costume re-enactment of the elephant battle that took place four centuries ago

During the Fair there are regular buses to Don Chedi from Suphanburi, the nearest place to stay. Transportation from Bangkok can also be arranged through the bigger travel agencies in Bangkok.

NAKHON PATHOM (population 45,000)

จังหวัดนครปฐม

Only 56 km west of Bangkok, Nakhon Pathom is regarded as the oldest city in Thailand. It was the centre of the Dvaravati kingdom, a loose collection of city states that flourished between the 6th and 11th centuries AD in the Chao Phraya River valley. The area has probably been inhabited at least since India's Ashokan period (3rd century BC), as it is theorised that Buddhist missionaries from India visited Nakhon Pathom at that time.

Phra Pathom Chedi

The central attraction here is the famous Phra Pathom Chedi, the single tallest Buddhist monument in the world, rising to 127 metres. The original monument, buried within the massive orange-glazed dome, was erected in the early 6th century by the Theravada Buddhists of Dvaravati, but in the early 11th century the Khmer King Suryavarman I of Angkor conquered the city and built a Brahman *prang* over the sanctuary. The Pagan Burmese, under King Anuruddha, sacked the city in 1057 and it was in ruins until King Mongkut had it restored in 1860, building a larger *chedi* over the remains according to Buddhist tradition, adding four *wiharns*, a *bot*, a replica of the original chedi and assorted *salas*, *prangs* and other embellishments. There is even a Chinese temple attached to the outer walls of the Phra Pathom Chedi, next to which outdoor *lakhon* (classical Thai dance-drama) is sometimes performed.

On the east side of the monument, in the bot, is a Dvaravati style Buddha seated in 'European pose', that is, in a chair, similar to the one in Wat Phra Men in Ayuthaya. It may, in fact, have come from Phra Men.

Opposite the bot is a museum, open Wednesday to Sunday from 9 am to noon and 1 pm to 4 pm, it contains some interesting Dvaravati sculpture.

Other

Beside the chedi, the other foci of the city are **Silpakorn University**, west of the chedi off Phetkasem Highway and **Sanam Chan**, adjacent to the University. Sanam Chan is a pleasant park with a canal passing through it, formerly the grounds for Rama VI's palace. The somewhat rundown palace still stands in the park but entrance is not permitted.

Floating Market

ตลาดน้ำดำเนินสะดวก

If the commercialisation of Bangkok's floating market puts you off there is a much more lively and less touristed floating market on **Khlong Damnoen Saduak** in Rajburi province, 104 km south-west of Bangkok, between Nakhon Pathom and Samut Songkhram.

There are direct buses from Bangkok's Southern Bus Terminal (No 78) to Damnoen Saduak every 20 minutes beginning at 6 am but you'll have to get one of the first few buses so as to arrive in Damnoen Saduak by 8 or 9 am when the market's at its best. Fare is 40B air-con or 25B for an ordinary bus. From the pier nearest the bus station, take a 10B water taxi to the *talaat nam*, floating market, or simply walk east from the station along the canal until you come to the market area. On either side of the Damnoen Saduak canal are the two most popular markets, **Talaat Ton Khem** and **Talaat Hia Kui**. There is another less crowded market on a smaller canal a bit south of Damnoen Saduak, called **Talaat Khun Phitak**. To get there, take a water taxi going south from the pier on the south side of Thong Lang canal, which intersects Damnoen Saduak near the larger floating market and ask for Talaat Khun Phitak.

Another way is to spend the night in Nakhon Pathom and catch an early morning bus out of Nakhon Pathom headed for Samut Songkhram, asking to be let out at Damnoen Saduak. Or, from the opposite direction, spend the night in Samut Sakhon.

To get to Damnoen Saduak from Samut Sakhon, take a local bus to Kratum Baen and then take a local bus a few km north to Kratum Baen and walk west to the pier on the right bank of the Tha Chin River. From the pier (called Tha Angton), catch a ferry boat across the river to the Damnoen Saduak canal, which runs west off the Tha Chin. From the Bang Yang lock, where ferry passengers disembark and you have a 30 km trip by *hang yao* (long-tailed boat) to the floating market. The fare is 16B and includes a boat change half-way at Ban

Phaew – worth it for what is one of Thailand's most beautiful stretches of waterway.

Places to Stay

Near the west side of the Phra Pathom Chedi, next to a furniture store, is the *Mitsamphan*. It's 80B for a clean room with fan and bath.

The *Mittaowan* is on the right as you walk towards the chedi from the train station. This costs 90B for a room with fan and bath, or 150B with air-con.

The *Mitphaisan* (tel 242422) – English sign reads, incorrectly, Mitfaaisal – is further down the alley to the right from Mittaowan. Rooms here are 100B for fan and bath and 170B with air-con. All three of the 'Mit' hotels are owned by the same family. Price differences reflect differences in cleanliness and service. I'd recommend Mittaowan.

West of the chedi, several blocks beyond Mitsamphan, is the *Siam Hotel*, but the staff here are unfriendly and it costs 100B for a room with fan and bath, or 200B for air-con.

Places to Eat

Nakhon Pathom has an excellent fruit market along the road between the train station and the Phra Pathom Chedi. The *khao lam* (sticky rice and coconut steamed in a bamboo joint) sold here is reputed to be the best in Thailand. There are many good restaurants in this area – cheap, too. The province has its own bottled drinking water. Ask for 'UPC' *(yew pee see)*.

A very good Chinese restaurant, *Ha Seng*, is located along the south side of the road which intersects the road from the train station to the chedi. Turn right if walking from the chedi and walk about 20 metres.

Getting There

Bus Buses for Nakhon Pathom leave the Southern Bus Terminal in Bangkok every 10 minutes from 6.30 am to 8.20 pm, fare is 13B for the one-hour trip.

Buses to Kanchanaburi leave throughout the day from the left side (coming from the Nakhon Pathom train station) of the Phra Pathom Chedi – get bus No 81.

Train Trains leave the Bangkok Noi railway station daily at 8 am, arriving in Nakhon Pathom at 9.08 am. Third class fare, recommended for such a short distance, is 14B.

There are also ordinary trains to Nakhon Pathom from the Hualamphong Station at 9 am and 1.40 pm, same third class fare as from Bangkok Noi. Don't bother taking rapid or express trains; travel time for this distance is the same but you'd have to pay the rapid or express surcharges which cost more than the ordinary third class fares alone.

KANCHANABURI (population 30,000)
จังหวัดกาญจนบุรี

Kanchanaburi is 130 km west of Bangkok in the slightly elevated valley of the Mae Klang River amidst hills and sugar cane plantations. It was originally established by Rama I as a first line of defence against the Burmese who might use the old invasion route through the Three Pagodas Pass on the Thai-Burmese border. It's still a popular smuggling route into Burma today.

During WW II the Japanese occupation in Thailand used Allied prisoners of war to build the infamous Death Railway along this same invasion route, in reverse, along the Khwae Noi River to the pass. Thousands and thousands of prisoners died as a result of brutal treatment by their captors, a story chronicled by Boulle's book *The Bridge Over the River Kwai* and popularised by a movie based on the same. The bridge is still there to be seen (still in use, in fact) and so are the graves of the Allied soldiers. The river is actually spelled and pronounced Khwae, like 'quack' without the '-ck'.

The town itself has a charming atmosphere and is a great place to hang out for a while. The weather here is

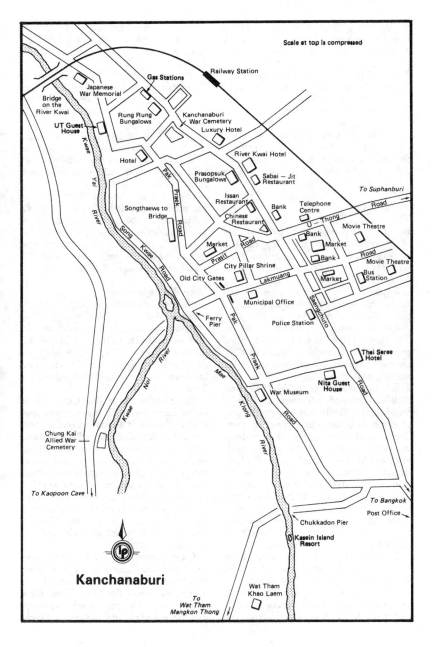

Scale at top is compressed

Japanese War Memorial

Gas Stations

Railway Station

Bridge on the River Kwai

Rung Rung Bungalows

Kanchanaburi War Cemetery

UT Guest House

Luxury Hotel

Kwae Yai River

Hotel

Pak Praek Road

River Kwai Hotel

Prasopsuk Bungalows

Sabai – Jit Restaurant

To Suphanburi

Issan Restaurant

Bank

Telephone Centre

Road

Songthaews to Bridge

Song Kwae Road

Chinese Restaurant

Road

U – Thong

Bank

Movie Theatre

Market

Prasit Road

Market

Bank

Road

City Pillar Shrine

Bank

Movie Theatre

Old City Gates

Lakmuang

Market

Bus Station

Ferry Pier

Municipal Office

Police Station

Pak Praek Road

Saengchuto

Kwae Noi River

Mae Klong River

Thai Seree Hotel

War Museum

Nita Guest House

Road

Chung Kai Allied War Cemetery

To Kaopoon Cave

To Bangkok

Post Office

Chukkadon Pier

Kasein Island Resort

Kanchanaburi

To Wat Tham Mangkon Thong

Wat Tham Khao Laem

slightly cooler than in Bangkok and the evenings are especially pleasant. Although Kan (as the locals call it; also Kan'buri) gets enough tourists to warrant its own tourist office, not many western visitors make it here – most tourists are Hong Kong/Singapore Chinese or Japanese who blaze through on air-con buses, hitting the River Khwae Bridge, the cemetery on Saengchuto Rd, the Rama River Kwai Hotel, and then they're off to the nearby sapphire mines or one of the big waterfalls before heading north to Chiang Mai or back to Bangkok.

The Bridge

The so-called Bridge over the River Kwai may be of interest to war historians but really looks quite ordinary. It spans the Khwae Yai River, a tributary of the Mae Klong River, a couple of km north of town – *Khwae Yai* literally translates as 'large tributary'. It is the story behind the bridge that is dramatic. The materials for the bridge were brought from Java by the Japanese during their occupation of Thailand. In 1945 the bridge was bombed several times and was only rebuilt after the war – the curved portions of the bridge are original.

It is estimated that 16,000 POWs and 49,000 impressed labourers died while building the 'Death Railway' to Burma, of which the bridge was only a small part. Train nuts may enjoy the 'railway museum' in front of the bridge, with engines which were used during WW II on display. Although the statistics of the number of POWs who died during the Japanese occupation is horrifying, the figures for the labourers, many from Malaysia and Indonesia, are even worse. It is thought that in total 100,000 to 150,000 coolies died in the area.

The best way to get to the bridge from town is to catch a *songthaew* along Pak Raek Rd (parallel to Saengchuto Rd towards the river) heading north. If you're standing at the River Kwai Hotel, just cross Saengchuto Rd, walk to the right, turn left at the first street and walk until you come to Pak Praek Rd. The regular songthaews are 3B and stop at the Bridge.

Every year during the first week of December there is a nightly light and sound show at the Bridge, commemorating the Allied attack on the Death Railway in 1945. It's a pretty big scene, with the sounds of bombers and explosions, fantastic bursts of light etc. The town gets a lot of Thai tourists during this week, so book early if you want to witness this spectacle.

There are a couple of large outdoor restaurants near the bridge, on the river, but these are for tour groups that arrive *en masse* throughout the day. If you're hungry, better to eat with the tour bus and songthaew drivers in the little noodle places at the head of Pak Praek Rd.

Allied War Cemeteries

There are two cemeteries containing the remains of Allied POWs who died in captivity during WW II; one is north of town off Saengchuto Rd, just before the railway station, and the other is across the Mae Klong River west of town, a few km down the Khwae Noi ('little tributary') River.

The Kanchanaburi War Cemetery is better cared for, with green lawns and healthy flowers. It's usually a cool spot on a hot Kanchanaburi day. To get there, catch a songthaew anywhere along Saengchuto Rd going north – fare is 3B. Jump off at the English sign in front of the cemetery on the left, or ask to be let off at the *susaan* (Thai for cemetery). Just before the cemetery on the same side of the road is a very colorful Chinese cemetery with burial mounds and inscribed tombstones.

To get to the other cemetery, the Chung Kai Allied War Cemetery, take a 2B ferry boat from the pier at the west end of Lak Muang Rd across the Mae Klong, then follow the curving road through picturesque corn and sugarcane fields until you reach the cemetery on your left. This is a fairly long walk, but the scenery along the way is pleasant. Thai border police frequent this half-paved, half-gravel road and may offer rides to or from the pier.

Like the more visited cemetery north of town, the Chung Kai Cemetery burial plaques carry the names, military insignia and short epitaphs for Dutch, British, French and Australian soldiers.

Very near the Chung Kai Cemetery is a dirt path that leads to **Wat Tham Khao Pun**, one of Kanchanaburi's many cave temples. The path is approximately one km long and passes through thick forest with a few wooden houses along the way.

JEATH War Museum

This odd museum at Wat Chaichunphon is worth visiting just to sit on the cool banks of the Mae Klong. Phra Maha Tomson Tongproh, a Thai monk who devotes much energy to promoting the museum, speaks some English and can not only answer questions about the exhibits but can supply information about what to see around Kan and how best to get there. If you show him this book, he'll give you a 5B discount off the usual 20B admission.

The museum itself consists of a replica example of the bamboo-atap huts used to house Allied POWs in the Kanchanaburi area during the Japanese occupation. The long huts contain various photographs taken during the war, drawings and paintings by POWs, maps, weapons and other war memorabilia. According to Phra Tomson, the acronym JEATH represents the fated meeting of Japan, England, Australia/America, Thailand and Holland at Kanchanaburi during WW II.

The War Museum is at the end of Wisuttharangsi (Visutrangsi) Rd, near the TAT office, next to the main compound of Wat Chaichumphon. If you're coming from Saengchuto Rd, you'll pass the Nita Guest House on the left.

Lak Muang Shrine

Like many other older Thai cities, Kanchanaburi has a *lak muang*, or city pillar/phallus, enclosed in a shrine at what was originally the town centre. Kan's lak muang is appropriately located on Lak Muang Rd, which intersects Saengchuto Rd two blocks north of the TAT office.

The bulbous-tipped pillar is covered with gold leaf and is much worshipped. Unlike Bangkok's lak muang you can get as close to this pillar as you like – no curtain.

Within sight of the pillar, towards the river, stands Kanchanaburi's original city gate.

Wat Tham Mongkorn Thong
วัดถ้ำมงคลทอง

The 'Cave Temple of the Golden Dragon' is well known because of the 'Floating Nun' – a 70+ year old *mae chee* who meditates while floating on her back in a pool of water. If you are lucky you might see her as she seems to be doing this less frequently nowadays. Thais come from all over Thailand to see her float and to receive her blessings which she bestows by whistling onto the top of a devotee's head. A sizable contingent of young Thai nuns stay here under the old nun's tutelage.

A long and steep series of steps with dragon-sculpted handrails lead up the craggy mountainside behind the main *bot* to a complex of limestone caves. Follow the string of light bulbs through the front cave and you'll come out above the wat with a view of the valley and mountains below. One section of the cave requires crawling or duck-walking, so wear appropriate clothing. Bats squeak away above your head and the smell of guano permeates the air.

In front of the caves sits a Chinese hermit with a long white beard who prepares and sells ancient Chinese herbal remedies. He won't allow his picture to be taken.

Another cave wat is off this same road about one or two km from Wat Tham Mongkorn Thong towards the pier. It can be seen on a limestone outcropping back from the road some 500 metres or so. The name is **Wat Tham Khao Laem**. The cave is less impressive than that at Wat Tham Mongkorn Thong but there are some interesting old temple buildings on the grounds.

Getting There Heading towards Bangkok down Saengchuto Rd from the TAT office, turn right on Chukkadon Rd (marked in English – about half-way between TAT and the central post office), or take a *samlor* (5B) from the town centre to Tha Chukkadon pier at the end of Chukkadon Rd. Cross the Mae Klong by ferry (2B per pedestrian) and follow the road on the other side three or four km until you see the wat on the left.

If you can, cross the river with someone who has a car, jeep, truck or motorcycle who can drop you off at Wat Tham Mongkorn Thong; if you pay the driver's ferry crossing (20B per vehicle), he or she will be glad to take you right to the wat, as there is only one road leading from the river to the villages west of Kan. There is no charge for people riding in or on a motor vehicle. The road to Wat Tham is long and dusty so hitching a ride is advisable. Rather infrequent buses (actually large *songthaews*) also cross the river here and stop at the wat – 4B per person.

The road to the wat passes sugarcane fields, karst formations, wooden houses, cattle and rock quarries.

Waterfalls

There are seven major waterfalls in Kanchanaburi province, all north of the capital. They are Erawan, Pha Lan, Traitrung, Khao Pang, Sai Yok, Pha That and Huay Khamin. Of these, the three most worth visiting – if you're looking for grandeur and swimming potential – are Erawan, Sai Yok and Huay Khamin. The

Erawan Falls are the easiest to get to from Kanchanaburi city, while Sai Yok and Huay Khamin are best visited only if you are able to spend the night in the vicinity of the falls. They are too far for a comfortable day trip from Kan.

Any of the waterfalls described below could be visited by motorcycle. The Suzuki dealer in the main business district/market on the east side of Saengchuto Rd will rent bikes – offer 150B per day.

Erawan Falls น้ำตกเอราวัณ The first bus to Erawan leaves Kan bus station at 8.40 am, takes 1½ hours and costs 17B per person. Ask for *rot thammada pai nam tok erawan* (ordinary bus to Erawan Falls). Take this first bus, as Erawan takes a full day to appreciate. The last bus back to Kan leaves Erawan at 4 pm.

The bus station/market at Erawan is a good 1½ km from the **Erawan National Park** which contains the falls. Once in the park, you'll have to walk two km from the trail entrance to the end of seven levels of waterfalls. The trails weave in and out of the numerous pools and falls, sometimes running alongside the water, sometimes leading across footbridges, splitting in different directions. Wear good walking shoes or sneakers. Also bring a bathing suit as several of the pools beneath the falls are great for swimming.

There are foodstalls near the park entrance and at the bus station/market, outside the park. The peak crowds at Erawan come in mid-April around Songkran time. The falls here, as elsewhere in Kanchanaburi, are best visited during the rainy season or in the first two months of the cool season, when the pools are full and the falls most impressive.

Huay Khamin Falls น้ำตกห้วยขมิ้น
These falls are about 25 km north of Erawan. To get there, take a bus to Si Sawat, either from Kan city or from Erawan. Fare from Erawan should be about 10B, from Kan 27B.

Top: Bridge over the River Kwai (TW)
Bottom: Pattaya Beach (JC)

Top: Wat Phra Maha That, Ayuthaya (TW)
Left: Wat Phra Si Sanphet, Ayuthaya (TW)
Right: Phra Pathom Chedi, Nakhon Pathom (TW)

Huay Khamin ('Turmeric Stream') has what are probably Kanchanaburi province's most powerful falls and the pools under the falls are large and deep. An excellent place for swimming.

Sai Yok Falls น้ำตกไทรโยค About 100 km north-west of Kan city, Sai Yok is well-known for the overnight raft trips that leave from here along the Khwae Noi River – the falls empty directly into the river. The trips are not cheap, but those who have gone say they're worth the money. There is fishing and swimming as well as jungle scenery and wildlife. It was near here that the famous Russian roulette scenes in the movie *The Deer Hunter* were filmed.

Near Sai Yok are the **Daowadung Caves** (20 minutes north by boat) and **Hin Dat Hot Springs** (40 minutes further north by boat). The hot springs (Thai: *baw nam rawn*) are looked after by a Buddhist monastery so only men are permitted to bathe there.

Sai Yok can be reached by boarding a bus in Kan bound for Thong Pha Phum. Tell the driver you're going to Sai Yok and he'll let you off at the road to the falls, on the left side of Route 323. The trip takes about two hours and costs 25B. You can also contact Khun Manop at 280/1 Pak Praek Rd in Kanchanaburi, who does bookings for the raft houses at Sai Yok – he can arrange transportation to Sai Yok if enough people are interested.

Three Pagodas Pass
พระเจดีย์สามองค์
Three Pagodas Pass (*Chedi Sam Ong* in Thai), was the planned terminus of the Death Railway in WW II and is a major smuggling point for the Thai-Burmese black market trade today. It's an untame place that the TAT and the Thai government would rather you'd forget about (much like Mae Salong in the north some years ago). But you can go there, either by public transport or on a rented motorcycle. It's an all-day journey and will require

that you spend at least one night in **Sangkhlaburi** อำเภอสังขละบุรี , a somewhat interesting off-the-track destination. The distance between Kan and Sangkhlaburi alone is about 200 km, so if you take a motorcycle it is imperative that you fill up before you leave Kan and stop for petrol again in Tong Pha Phum, the last town before Sangkhlaburi. The paved road ends in Thong Pha Phum. From Thong Pha Phum to Sangkhla, as well as on to Three Pagodas, it is mostly laterite and dust (or mud, if you're foolish enough to go there during the rainy season). Best time to go is during the mid-to-late part of the cool season, January to February. During the rainy season nearly the whole of Sangkhlaburi is under water and travel is difficult. Note that if you're travelling on your own and using the Kanchanaburi Tourist Office's 'Outskirts Map', there is only one road to Sangkhlaburi from Thong Pha Phum, the one that heads north out of town. The road that begins west of Thong Pha Phum on the map no longer reaches its original destination.

There is a cheap hotel in Sangkhlaburi where you can stay the night before heading on to the pass. To the west and south-west of Sangkhla is a huge lake created by the Khao Laem Dam at its southern tip. Sangkhla can in fact be reached by water transport from Kan or from Sai Yok (see raft trips). You can also catch a public bus to Sangkhla from the Kan bus station.

In the morning you can either hop a *songthaew* or ride your motorcycle on to Three Pagodas Pass, which is about 50 slow km from Sangkhla. You'll find very little English spoken out this way and in fact you may hear as much Burmese, Karen and Mon as Thai. The pagodas themselves are rather small but it is the 'wild west atmosphere' of this black market outpost that draws a few intrepid travellers. The Burmese side of the border is controlled by the Karen National Union and Three Pagodas is one of several 'toll gates' along the Thai-Burmese border where the KNU collects a 5% tax on all merchandise which passes. They use the funds to finance armed resistance against the Burmese government which has recently increased efforts to regain control of the border area. The Karen also conduct a huge multi-million dollar business in illegal mining and logging, the products of which are smuggled into Thailand by the truckload under the cover of night. Not without the palms-up cooperation of the Thai police, of course.

Raft Trips

The number of small-time enterprises offering raft trips up and down the Mae Klong River and its various tributaries in Kanchanaburi province continues to multiply. The typical raft is a large affair with a two-storey shelter that will carry 15 to 20 people. Average cost for a two-day trip from one of the piers in Kan town is 2000B to 2500B for the whole raft, or roughly 100B to 160B per person. Such a trip would include stops at Tha Aw beach, Wat Tham Mongkorn Thong, Khao Boon Cave and the Chung Kai Allied War Cemetery, plus all meals and one night's accommodation on the raft. Drinks are usually extra. Add more nights and/or go further afield and the cost can escalate quite a bit. It is possible to arrange trips all the way to Three Pagodas Pass, for example. Inquire at Nita Guest House, the Sunya Rux Restaurant, the TAT or at the main pier at the end of Lak Muang Rd on the river. Perhaps the best trips are arranged by groups of travellers who get together and plan their own raft excursions with one of the raft operators. I expect that in the future Kanchanaburi raft trips will join Chiang Mai hill-tribe treks as one of Thailand's big hustles.

Places to Stay

There are numerous places to stay in Kan in every price range. On Visutrangsi Rd,

on the way to JEATH War Museum, is *Nita Guest House*, a friendly place that is current favourite among travellers. Rates are 35B dorm, 50B single and 60B double. Sleeping accommodations are spacious and there is plenty of room to lounge about elsewhere in the compound. They also serve food and can help arrange raft trips, waterfall outings etc.

Another nice guest house is the *U.T.*, which is near the River Khwae Bridge on Pak Praek Rd. A *samlor* from the railway station should be about 10B; from the bus station 20B. UT charges a flat 50B per person for accommodation, whether in a two-bed room or in the 10-bed dormitory.

You can also stay on the river in a raft house for 30B to 50B per person depending on the raft. If you travel with a lot of valuables, note that this is not one of Kan's safest places to stay, although the proprietors can keep valuables for you during your stay. One person who has raft houses for rent is Sanyarak; contact him at his family's little tourist restaurant; (no tourist prices! reads one of the signs out front), *Sunya Rux*, next to the Rama River Kwai Hotel.

There are two River Kwai Hotels in Kan, one next to the other on Saengchuto Rd. The *Rama River Kwai,* 284/4-6 Saengchuto Rd, (tel 511269) has air-con rooms starting at 530B, while the *River Kwai 2*, 284/3 Saengchuto, (tel 511565) has clean and spacious fan-cooled rooms with bath starting at 90B. The latter hotel keeps a monkey and an *iihen* ('palm civet' – a cat-racoon-monkey type of creature) in the lobby for your entertainment.

Prasopsuk Bungalows (tel 511777) at 677 Saengchuto Rd is across from the River Kwai hotels. These are good 90B bungalows, situated off the road a bit, plus a friendly staff, restaurant and night club – a Thai scene at night. *Wang Thong Bungalows*, 60/3 Saengchuto Rd (tel 511046) and *Boon Yang Bungalows* offer similar rooms for 90B up. In case you haven't figured this out on your own, 'bungalows' (not the beach kind) are the upcountry equivalent of Bangkok's 'short-time' hotels. They're located off the road for the same reason that their Bangkok equivalents have heavy curtains over the carports: so that it will be difficult to spot license plate numbers. Still, they function well as tourist hotels too.

Other hotels in town include the *Sri Muang Kan*, at the north end of Saengchuto, 131/113 Saengchuto Rd, (tel 511609), rooms with fan and bath for 90B and the *Thai Seree* at the south end of the same road, near the Visutrangsi Rd intersection and the TAT office, somewhat dilapidated but adequate rooms for 70B.

The *Luxury Hotel* (tel 511168) at 284/1-5 Saengchuto is a couple of blocks north of the River Kwai Hotels, not as centrally located, but good value. Clean rooms with fan and bath start at 70B

Perhaps the last word in comfort is *Kasem Island Resort*, which is located on an island in the middle of the Mae Klong River just a couple of hundred metres from Tha Chukkadon pier. The tastefully designed thatched cottages and house-rafts are cool, clean, quiet and go for 450B. Four people can rent a house-raft for 700B a night and eight people, 1350B. There are facilities for swimming, fishing and rafting as well as an outdoor bar and restaurant. The Resort has an office near Tha Chukkadon pier where you can arrange for a free shuttle boat out to the island.

Out of Town Thirty-eight km south-west of Kan city at Ban Khao is the *River Kwai Farm*, a resort that attempts to duplicate for tourists the natural simplicity of jungle life. The bamboo bungalows are without electricity and the daily rate, including three meals a day, is 450B per person. This is where Bangkok yuppies come to clear out their lungs. Reservations can be made through River Kwai Farm, 68/2 Sathorn Neua Rd, Bangkok (tel 234

0358, 233 9651) or through the private tour agency on Saengchuto Rd just north of the TAT office.

The *River Kwai Village* is a 60-room air-con resort 70 km from Kan near Tam Tok, on the Kwae Noi River. They also have a few raft-houses. Accommodation (count on 600B) can be booked through their office in Bangkok, 1054/4 Petchburi Rd (tel 251 7522, 251 7828) or through any Kan travel agency.

Other high-end raft-house type accommodation is in the Sai Yok Falls National Park area: *River Kwai Rafts* (Bangkok tel 251 5290) at 500B per person including all meals and *River Kwai Jungle Rafts* (Bangkok tel 252 5492) 300B per person. On the Khwae Yai River towards Si Sawat and the Si Nakarin Dam are *Kwai Yai River Hut* (Bangkok tel 392 3286) at 500B per person including meals and *Kwai Yai Island Resort* (Bangkok tel 521 2389; Kan tel 511261) at 450B to 700B per person. These can also probably be booked in Kanchanaburi through one of the travel agencies near the bus station. There are several other raft houses and bungalow operations along the Khwae Yai and near Sai Yok Falls on the Khwae Noi.

Places to Eat

The greatest proliferation of inexpensive restaurants in Kan is along the north end of Saengchuto Rd near the River Kwai hotels. From here south to where U Thong Rd crosses Saengchuto are many good Chinese, Thai and *issan-style* restaurants. As elsewhere in Thailand, the best are generally the most crowded.

One of the most popular is *Esan* (English spelling), which has good *kai yang-khao niaw-somtam* etc, as well as other Thai and local specialities. The *kai yang* is grilled right out front and served with two sauces – the usual sweet and sour *nam jim kai* and the salt-garlic-fish sauce-roast red pepper sauce, *nam phrik phao*. The menu here is extensive and includes *aahaan baa* ('forest food') which is popular all over Kan province, characterised by very, very spicy curries without coconut milk and seafood specialities such as *haw mok* ('serpent-fish curry steamed in banana leaves) and *po taek* (literally, 'broken fish-trap'), a gourmet clay-pot soup of crab claws, clams, shrimp, squid and other seafood. Esan also serves good appetisers or 'drinking food' (called *kap klaem* in Thai), like fried cashews/peanuts, fried potatoes, *yam*, etc. To go along with the great food, the jukebox in this place features funky, north-eastern pop music with its almost Caribbean or African Hi-Life style rhythms. The beer is ice-cold and an English menu is available, although it's not as complete as the Thai-language menu, which sits under a roll of toilet paper on each table. A whole roast chicken for 50B, a half kg of sticky rice for 15B (10B worth is probably more than enough rice), *somtam* for 10B, and you have a feast for three to four people. On the downside, the service at Esan can be a little indifferent these days. Apparently, the restaurant became so successful in recent years that the original cook/owner split for Bangkok to pursue his dream career as an actor. Another restaurant worth trying is *Sunya Rux*.

The Chinese restaurant on the north-west corner of U Thong and Saengchuto (look for the old marble-topped tables) has good noodles. In the early mornings some of the smaller, older food stalls on the east side of Saengchuto serve *pathong-ko* (Chinese 'doughnuts') with hot sweet Thai tea *(cha rawn)* and clear *(nam cha)* as a chaser – 8B will get you through the morning. As usual, the *pathong-ko* disappears by 9 am.

Good, inexpensive eating can also be found in the markets along Prasit Rd and between U Thong and Lak Muang Rd east of Saengchuto.

The *Sabai-jit* restaurant, next to the River Kwai Hotel, has an English menu. Beer and Maekhong whiskey are sold here at quite competitive prices and the food is

consistently good. Other Thai and Chinese dishes are served beyond those listed on the English menu. If you see someone eating something not listed, point.

Down on the river there are several large floating restaurants where the quality of the food varies. Most of them are pretty good according to locals, but if you go don't expect western food or large portions – if you know what to order, you could have a very nice meal here. There are several smaller food stalls which open shop along the road next to the river in the evenings where you can eat cheaply. This is a festive and prosperous town and people seem to eat out a lot.

Getting There

Bus Buses leave Bangkok every 20 minutes daily for Kanchanaburi from the Southern Bus Terminal on Charan Sanitwong Rd in Thonburi beginning at 5 am, last bus at 7.30 pm. The trip takes about two hours and costs 28B. Buses back to Bangkok leave Kan beginning 5.10 am with the last bus at 7.50 pm.

Air-con buses leave Bangkok's Southern Bus Terminal hourly from 6 am to 9.30 pm for 53B. These same buses depart Kan for Bangkok from opposite the police station on Saengchuto Rd, not from the bus station.

There are frequent buses throughout the day from nearby Nakhon Pathom. Bus No 81 leaves from the east side of the Phra Pathom Chedi, costs 22B, and takes about 1½ hours.

Train Ordinary trains leave the Bangkok Noi train station at 8 am and 2 pm, arriving at 10.32 am and 4.42 pm. Only third class fare is available and the fare is 28B. Trains return to Bangkok from Kan at 8.05 am, 1.38 pm and 2.26; arriving at the Bangkok Noi station at 10.50 am, 5.35 pm and 5 pm respectively. The second train is slower because it is a mixed freight and passenger train.

You can also ride the train from the Kan station out to the River Kwai Bridge,

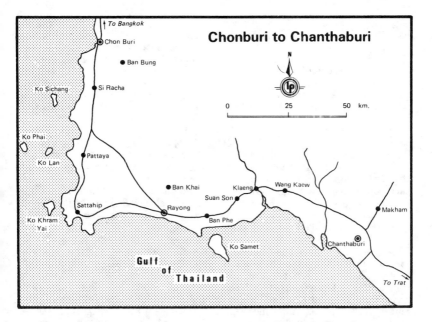

Chonburi to Chanthaburi

a three-minute ride for 1B, there is one train only at 10.34 am (No 171).

The same train, No 171, goes to the end of the railway line to Nam Tok, which is very near Sai Yok Falls. You can catch the train at the Bridge (10.35 am); the fare is the same, 17B. Nam Tok is eight km from Khao Pang Falls and 12 km from the River Kwai Village. Two other trains also make the trip to Nam Tok daily, but do not stop at the bridge, leaving Kan at 11.25 am and 4.42 pm. The trip to Nam Tok takes about two hours. Coming back from Nam Tok, there are trains at 6.10 am, 10.35 am, 12.35 pm and 3.20 pm.

Excursion Train There is a special tourist train from Hualamphong station on weekends and holidays which departs Bangkok at 6.15 am and returns at 7.30 pm. The fare is 60B for adults, 33B for children round-trip. It includes a 40-minute stop in Nakhon Pathom to see the Phra Pathom Chedi, 30 minutes at the Bridge over the River Kwai, a three-hour stop at Nam Tok for lunch, a 2B minibus to Khao Pang waterfall and 45 minutes at the Kanchanaburi War Cemetery, before returning to Bangkok. This ticket should be booked in advance although it's worth trying on the day even if you're told it's full. Ordinary train tickets to Kan can be booked the day of departure.

Getting Around
Prices are very reasonable in Kan, especially for food and accommodation, if you are your own tour guide – don't even consider letting a *samlor* driver show you around, they want big money. The city is not very big so getting around is easy. A samlor to anywhere in Kan should be 5B for one person. *Songthaews* run up and down Saengchuto Rd for 3B per passenger.

Motorcycles can be rented at the Suzuki dealer near the bus station. Expect to pay about 150B per day, though they may ask for more. Motorcycles can be taken across the river by ferry for a few baht.

SI RACHA - KOH SI CHANG
อำเภอศรีราชา - เกาะสีชัง
(population 22,000)

About 105 km from Bangkok on the east coast of the Gulf of Thailand is the small town of Si Racha, home of spicy Si Racha sauce (*nam phrik si rachaa*). Some of Thailand's best seafood, accompanied by this sauce, can be bought here, especially the local oysters. The motor *samlors* in this fishing town are unlike those seen anywhere else - more like motorcycles with a side-car in the rear.

On **Koh Loi**, a small rocky island which is connected to the mainland by a long jetty, there is a Thai-Chinese Buddhist temple. Further off shore is a large island called **Koh Si Chang** flanked by two smaller islands, **Kham Yai** to the north and **Khang Kao** to the south. As this provides a natural shelter from the wind and sea, it is used by large incoming freighters as a harbour. Smaller boats transport goods to the Chao Phraya delta some 50 km away.

Si Chang island itself makes a nifty getaway. There is only one town on the island, facing the mainland; the rest of the island is practically deserted and fun to explore. The small population is made up of fishermen, retired and working mariners and government workers who are stationed with the Customs Office or with one of the aquaculture projects on the island.

There is a monastic hermitage along the island's centre ridge, ensconced in limestone caves and palm huts. The hermit caves make an interesting visit but should be approached with respect - monks from all over Thailand come here to take advantage of the peaceful environment for meditation. Be careful that you don't fall down a limestone shaft; some are nearly covered with vines.

On the opposite side of the island, facing out to sea, are some decent beaches with good snorkelling - take care with the tide and the sea urchins, though. There is also a more public beach at the western end of the island near the old palace grounds. The beach is called **Hat Tha Wang** and Thai residents and visitors from the mainland come here for picnics.

The palace was once inhabited by King Chulalongkorn (Rama V) during the summer months but was abandoned when the French briefly occupied the island in 1893. Little remains of the various palace buildings but there are a few remnants to see. The main palace building was moved to Bangkok many years ago, but the stairs leading up to it are still there; if you follow these stairs to the crest of the hill overlooking Tha Wang, you'll come to a stone outcropping wrapped in holy cloth. The locals call it 'Bell Rock' because if struck with a rock or heavy stick it rings like a bell. Flanking the rock are what appear to be two ruined *chedis*. The large chedi on the left actually contains **Atsadangnimit Temple**, a small consecrated chamber where King Rama V used to meditate. The unique Buddha image inside was fashioned 50 years ago by a local monk who now lives in the cave hermitage.

Not far from Wat Atsadangnimit is a large limestone cave called **Tham Saowapha** which appears to plunge deep into the island. If you have a flashlight with you, the cave might be worthwhile exploring.

To the east of town, high on the hill overlooking the sea, is a large and much-frequented Chinese temple. During Chinese New Year in February, the island is overrun with Chinese visitors from the mainland. This is one of Thailand's most interesting Chinese temples, with shrine-caves, several different temple levels and a good view of Si Chang and the ocean. It's a long and steep climb from the road below.

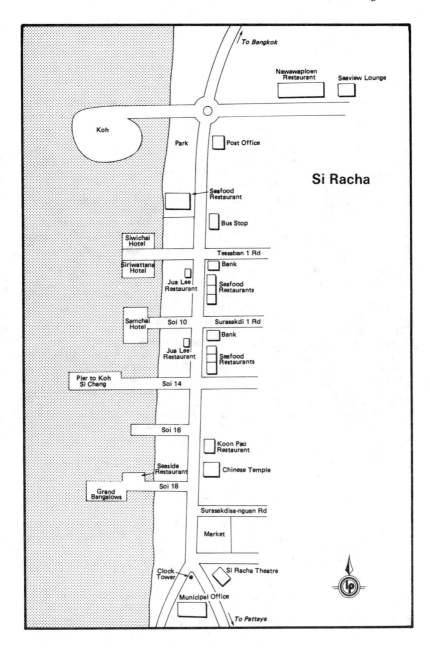

To Bangkok

Nawawaploen Restaurant

Seeview Lounge

Koh

Park

Post Office

Si Racha

Seafood Restaurant

Bus Stop

Siwichai Hotel

Tessaban 1 Rd

Siriwattana Hotel

Bank

Jua Lee Restaurant

Seafood Restaurants

Samchai Hotel

Soi 10

Surasakdi 1 Rd

Bank

Jua Lee Restaurant

Seafood Restaurants

Pier to Koh Si Chang

Soi 14

Soi 16

Koon Pao Restaurant

Chinese Temple

Seaside Restaurant

Soi 18

Grand Bangalows

Surasakdisa-nguan Rd

Market

Clock Tower

Si Racha Theatre

Municipal Office

To Pattaya

Places to Stay & Eat

Si Racha Best places to stay in Si Racha are the hotels built on piers over the waterfront. Three of them are similar in price and quality: *Siriwattana* and *Siwichai*, across from Tessaban 1 Rd and the Bangkok Bank and *Samchai*, on Soi 10, across from Surasakdi 1 Rd. All have rooms from 100B up and the Samchai has some AC rooms as well. The Siriwattana seems to be the cleanest and the service is very good. All three are open and breezy with outdoor tables where you can bring food in the evening from nearby markets.

On Soi 18, the *Grand Bungalows* rent bungalows of various sizes, built off the pier for 600B to 1000B. Each one sleeps several people and they are very popular among Thais and Chinese on holidays

There is plenty of good seafood in Si Racha, but you have to watch the prices (though eating here is not as dangerous as Pattaya). Most well known is the Chinese-owned *Chua Lee* on Jermjompol Rd next to Soi 10, across from the Krung Thai Bank. Their seafood is great but probably the most expensive in town. Next door and across the street are several seafood places with similar fare at much more reasonable prices. The *Koon Pao* restaurant is pretty good. It's located near the Chinese temple on Jermjompol across from Soi 16 and 18. On the pier at Soi 18 is the *Rim Thale* or Seaside Restaurant which is a good place to have a beer.

Most economical place to eat is in the markets near the clock tower at the southern end of town. The food here is quite good and they have everything from noodles to fresh seafood, from morning until night.

Outside of town, off Sukhumvit Highway on the way to Pattaya, there are a couple of cheap but good fresh seafood places. Locals favour a place near Laem Chabang called *Sut Thang Rak* or 'End of love Road', about 10 km south of Si Racha. Nearer to town is Ao Udom, a small fishing bay where there are several open-air seafood places.

Koh Si Chang There are three hotels now on Koh Si Chang, none of which have English signs out front. All are located toward the southern end of town (turn left after disembarking on the pier), on the way to Hat Tha Wang. The first two, on the left side of the road are 100B per room, less for stays of a week or more. Both have good facilities. Then on the right a little further is another hotel with one-bed rooms for 120B, two beds for 150B. They're clean and off the street a bit, so are probably quieter than the other two places.

You can also camp anywhere on the island without any hassle.

The town has several small restaurants, nothing special, but with all the Thai and Chinese standards.

Getting There

Buses to Si Racha leave the Eastern Bus Terminal in Bangkok every 25 minutes or so from 5 am to 7 pm. Ordinary bus is 28B, AC bus is 44B.

Getting Around

In Si Racha and on Si Chang Island there are fleets of huge motorcycle taxis, many powered by Nissan auto engines, that will take you anywhere in town or on the island for 10B. On Si Chang you can get a complete tour of the island for 70B to 80B. Although the distances aren't that far, you couldn't see everything by foot.

Getting to Koh Si Chang

Boats to Koh Si Chang leave regularly throughout the day from a pier in Si Racha at the end of Soi 14, Jermjompol Rd. The fare is 20B each way; first boat leaves about 8 am and the last at 6.30 pm. Last boat back to Si Racha from Si Chang is at 4.30 pm.

PATTAYA (population 35,000)
พัทยา

On the road through Pattaya city, before Pattaya Beach, the bus passes no less than five prosperous sign-making

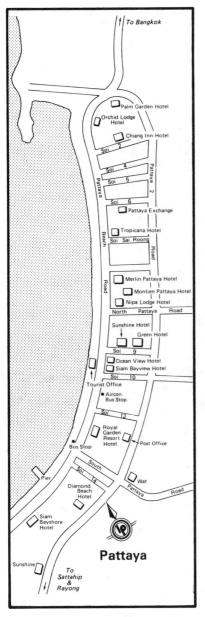

To Bangkok

Palm Garden Hotel

Orchid Lodge Hotel

Chiang Inn Hotel

Soi 2

Soi 4

Soi 5

Soi 6

Pattaya 2

Pattaya Exchange

Tropicana Hotel

Soi Sai Roong

Pattaya Beach Road

Merlin Pattaya Hotel

Montien Pattaya Hotel

Nipa Lodge Hotel

North Pattaya Road

Sunshine Hotel

Green Hotel

Soi 9

Ocean View Hotel

Siam Bayview Hotel

Soi 10

Tourist Office

● Aircon. Bus Stop

Soi 13

Royal Garden Resort Hotel

Post Office

● Bus Stop

Soi 14

South Pattaya Road

Pier

Wat

Diamond Beach Hotel

Siam Bayshore Hotel

Sunshine

To Sattahip & Rayong

Pattaya

businesses. Upon arrival at Pattaya Beach, the reason for their prosperity is immediately apparent – the place is lit up like Hollywood Boulevard at night. Most non-tourists will find Pattaya lacking in good taste as well as culture and would do well to preclude it from their itineraries. Pattaya Beach is not much of a beach to begin with and its biggest businesses, water sports and street sex, have driven prices for food and accommodation beyond Bangkok level.

It's a great place for a sailor on leave, I suppose. Pattaya in fact, got its start as a resort when there was an American base at nearby Sattaheep – nowadays there are still plenty of sailors about, both Thai and American. Food is good here, as claimed, but way over-priced. Lately that part of South Pattaya known as 'the village' has attracted a large number of *ka-toeys*, Thai transvestites, posing as hookers who ply their trade among the droves of well-heeled European tourists.

There are four or five nice islands off Pattaya's shore, expensive to get to, but if you're a snorkelling or scuba enthusiast, equipment can be booked at any of the several diving shops/schools at Pattaya Beach. **Koh Laan**, the most popular of the offshore islands, even has places to stay.

Information

To give you an idea of how expensive Pattaya is, TAT lists three categories of accommodation: 700B and over; 400B to 700B; 400B and under. 'Best seafood restaurants' are estimated to cost 800B for a meal for two including tax and service, but not including drinks. 'Economy places' are estimated at 200B for two and suggested restaurants in this category include *Mr Donut* and *Pizza Hut*. Don't say you weren't warned.

Places to Stay – bottom end

Cheapest places in town are along Pattaya 2 Rd (Pattaya Soi 2), the street parallel to Pattaya Beach Rd. Most are clustered near Sois 10, 11 and 12. The *Sea Horse Guest House* has 80B rooms, making it Pattaya's lowest price accommodation. The *Uthumphorn* and *Siam* guest houses have 100B rooms, while *Supin Guest House*, *Prompan Guest House* and the *Penpat Hotel* have rooms starting at 150B. The *Wang Thong* has fan-cooled rooms for 100B and AC rooms for 200B, but you may have to bargain for this. Finally, the *Drop Inn* has rooms for 180B.

Also on Pattaya 2 Rd, the *Diana Inn* has immaculate rooms with fan and bath (with hot water) for 175B, plus a pool with bar service – this is Pattaya's best deal. They also have more expensive AC rooms.

On Pattaya Sois 11 and 12, the *Pattaya 11* and the *Pattaya 12* have AC rooms for 200B and 250B respectively. On Soi 13, the *Malibu Guest House* has 180B rooms that include breakfast. The rest of the many guest houses on Soi 13 are in the 200B to 300B range, but rooms are usually cramped and without windows.

Just behind Soi 16 is hidden the *Top Thai Palace*, which rents passable AC rooms for 200B.

A German reader wrote to say 'Our impression of Pattaya wasn't as bad as yours' and recommended a place called *Garden Villa* on Naklua Rd (north Pattaya). It costs 200B for a double, is owned by Germans and has 'traditional German food and customs'. Another place that has been recommended is *In de Welkom*, doubles with fan cost 220B, AC 280B and AC singles at 250B.

Places to Stay – top end
Pattaya is really a resort for package tourists so the vast majority of its accommodation is in this bracket.

Asia Pattaya Beach Hotel (tel 418602-6), Cliff Rd, 314 rooms, 900B to 4500B
Hotel Chiang Inn Pattaya (tel 418718-20), Soi 2, Beach Rd, 121 rooms, singles/doubles 600B to 800B

Diamond Beach Hotel (tel 418071, 419885-6), Pattaya South, 120 rooms, 400B to 700B
Golden Beach Hotel, (tel 418891), 519/29 Pattaya 2nd Rd
Grand Palace Hotel (tel 418541, 418239), Beach Rd, 420 rooms, 1300B to 6000B
The Merlin Pattaya (tel 418755-9), Beach Rd, 360 rooms, singles/doubles 1000B to 3500B
The Montien Pattaya (tel 418155-6), Beach Rd, 320 rooms, singles/doubles 1050B to 8000B
Nina Lodge (tel 418321), Beach Rd, 139 rooms, singles/doubles 760B to 1800B
Ocean View Hotel (tel 418434), Beach Rd, 115 rooms, 660B to 1800B
The Orchid Lodge (tel 418175), Beach Rd, 236 rooms, singles/doubles 760B to 1550B
Palm Garden (tel 419386), Pattaya 2nd Rd, 119 rooms, 400B to 700B
Pattaya Palace Hotel (tel 418319), Beach Rd, 261 rooms, 1580B to 5400B
Pattaya Resort Hotel (tel 418065), North Pattaya Rd, 180 rooms, 750B
Prima Villa Hotel (tel 419398), Naklue Soi 18, 30 rooms, 400B to 700B
Regent Marina Hotel (tel 418015, 419298), North Pattaya Rd, 220 rooms, 800B to 2200B
Royal Cliff Beach Hotel (tel 418344, 418613-6), Cliff Rd, 700 rooms, 1100B to 5000B
Royal Garden Resort (tel 418126-7, 418122), Beach Rd, 192 rooms, 750B to 3000B
Sea View (tel 419189), Naklue Rd, 219 rooms, 700B to 2200B
Hotel Siam Bayshore (tel 418679-80), South Pattaya Rd, 275 rooms, 900B to 4000B
Siam Bayview Hotel (tel 418728), Beach Rd, 302 rooms, 600B to 3000B
Hotel Tropicana (tel 418645-8), Beach Rd, 200 rooms, singles/doubles 1075B to 2024B
Wongse Amatya Hotel (tel 418118-20), Naklue Rd, 207 rooms, singles/doubles 1139B to 1518B

Places to Eat
Most food in Pattaya is expensive, but good Thai food is available in shops along Pattaya's back street (Pattaya No 2 Rd), away from the beach. Also look for cheap rooms to rent here. The front signs outside the many snack bars reveal that 'bratwurst mit brot' is far more readily available than 'khao phat'.

Arabs and South Asians are coming to

Pattaya in droves these days, so there are an increasing number of Indian-Pakistani-Middle Eastern restaurants in town, some have fairly moderate prices.

Best seafood restaurants are in South Pattaya, where you pick out the sea creatures yourself and are charged by weight. Prices are sky-high.

Getting There

Ordinary non-AC buses from Bangkok cost 29B one-way and leave at 30-minute intervals from 6 am to 8 pm daily. Tour buses from the same station (Eastern Bus Terminal) leave at similar intervals for 53B between 6 am and 6 pm.

Several hotels and travel agencies in Bangkok also run thrice-daily AC tour buses to Pattaya for around 100B

From Si Racha you can catch a public bus on the Sukhumvit Highway to Pattaya for 10B.

Finally, if you've just flown into Don Muang and need to get to Pattaya right away (why?), there is an airport minibus that goes directly to Pattaya at 11 am and 9 pm daily for 190B or US$7.60 one-way.

Beyond Pattaya

Further south from Pattaya are more beaches and more resorts. In fact, the posher places are now located along **Jomtien Beach** and **Bang Saray**, while Pattaya's economy is restructuring itself toward more middle-class tourists and conventioneers. Jomtien has mostly bungalows while Bang Saray has hotels, apartments and condominiums.

Cobra Cabana (tel 418079) has bungalows for 380B at Jomtien – they may be less in the rainy season. In Bang Saray, *Bang Saray Villa* has AC rooms for 300B.

There are still some good seafood restaurants for local Thais in Bang Saray – something Pattaya hasn't seen for years.

Still further south is Sattahip, a vacation spot for the Thai military – some

of the best beaches in the area are reserved for their use. There are several Thai navy and air force bases in the vicinity.

RAYONG (population 28,000)
จังหวัดระยอง

Rayong is 220 km from Bangkok by the old highway (Route 3) or 185 km on Route 36. The province produces fine fruit (especially durian and pineapple) and *nam pla* (fish sauce). Rayong city itself is not really worth visiting but nearby beaches are fair and Koh Samet is beginning to attract travellers in search of a new Koh Samui. This area has not received many foreign visitors yet, although it has been popular with Thai tourists for several years now.

The beaches are all near **Ban Phe**, a seaside town a few km south-east of the provincial capital; this is also the departure point for Koh Samet. If sun and sand are what you've come to Rayong for, head straight for Ban Phe. Then pick out a beach or board a boat bound for Samet.

The **Suan Son Pine Park**, five km further down the highway from Ban Phe, is a popular place for Thai picnickers and has white sand beaches as well.

Suan Wang Kaew is 11 km south of Ban Phe and has more beaches and rather expensive bungalows. **Koh Talu**, across from Wang Kaew, is said to be a good diving area – the proprietors of Suan Wang Kaew, a private park, can arrange boats and gear.

Places to Stay & Eat

Rayong There are three hotels near the bus station off Sukhumvit Highway. The *Rayong*, 65/3 Sukhumvit and the *Otani*, 69 Sukhumvit, both have rooms from 100B. The latter has some AC rooms as well. The *Tawan Ok*, 52/3 Sukhumvit, has fan-cooled rooms for 50B without bath, 70B with.

For cheap eating check the market near the Thetsabanteung movie theatre or the noodle shop on Taksin Rd next to Wat

Lum Mahachaichunphon. There is a very good open-air restaurant along the river belonging to the Fishermen's Association (*Samaakhom Pramong* in Thai).

Ban Phe There are two hotels in Ban Phe, both near the central market. The new *Nuan Napa* has rooms from 150B with fan and bath while the *Queen* has rooms for 80B (no bath), 100B with bath and 150B AC.

The *Thale Thawng* restaurant, where the tour bus from Bangkok stops, has good Thai seafood dishes – especially recommended is the *kuaytiaw thale*, a seafood noodle soup for 10B. The shop across the street is a good place to stock up on food, mosquito coils, etc to take to Koh Samet. You'll most likely be spending some time in this spot, waiting either for the boat to leave the nearby pier for Koh Samet or for the bus to arrive from Bangkok.

KOH SAMET
เกาะเสม็ด

Formerly Koh Kaew Phitsadan ('vast jewel isle' – a reference to the abundant white sand), this island became known as Koh Samet or 'cajeput isle' after the cajeput tree which grows in abundance here and is very highly valued as firewood throughout South-East Asia. In the early '80s, the 131 square km Samet began receiving its first visitors interested in more than cajeput trees and sand – young Thais in search of a retreat from city life. At that time there were only about 40 houses on the island, built by fishermen and Ban Phe locals.

Rayong and Bangkok speculators saw the sudden interest in Samet as a chance to cash in on an up-and-coming Phuket and began buying up land along the beaches. No one bothered with the fact that Koh Samet, along with Cape Ya and other nearby islands were part of a National Park (one of seven marine parks now in Thailand) and had been since 1981.

When *farangs* started coming to Samet in greater and greater numbers, spurred on by rumors that Samet was similar to Koh Samui '10 years ago' (one always seems to miss it by a decade, eh?), the Park Service stepped in and built a visitor's office on the island, ordered that all bungalows be moved back behind the tree-line and started charging a 5B admission into the park.

Other rather recent changes have included the introduction of several more vehicles to the island, more frequent boat services from Ban Phe and a much improved water situation. Samet is a very dry island (which makes it an excellent place to visit during the rainy season). Before they started trucking water to the bungalows you had to bathe at sometimes muddy wells. Now most of the bungalow places have proper Thai-style bathrooms and as a result, Samet is a much more comfortable and convenient place to visit, though it may be in danger of becoming overcrowded, like other formerly idyllic isles in Thailand. For now, the bungalows are spread thinly over the north-east coast of the island and the beaches really are lovely, with the whitest, squeakiest sand in Thailand. There is even a little surf occasionally (best months are December to January). However, I still think the accommodation on Samui and Phangan Islands are better overall value, though of course they're much more expensive and time-consuming to reach from Bangkok.

A warning: Samet can be very crowded during Thai public holidays: early November (Loy Kratong); 5 December (King's birthday), 31 December-1 January (New Year's); mid-to-late February (Chinese New Year's). During these times there are people sleeping on the floors of beach restaurants, on the beach, everywhere.

Places to Stay
Haat Sai Kaew Samet's prettiest beach, 'Diamond Sand', is a km or so long and 25

to 30 metres wide. Here find *White Sand* and *Naga* bungalows, two of Samet's better operations. The former has 40B and 50B bungalows, the latter 50B up. There is another bungalow group a little north called *Diamond Beach*, not quite as good but similar prices. As with all beach bungalows here and elsewhere in Thailand, you can get lower rates for stays of a week or longer (except when they're really crowded). Naga is owned by a helpful Thai-British couple, Sue and Toss, who have a very good bar-restaurant. They also do glass-bottom boat tours of the coral reefs offshore for 10B per person.

Ao Phai Another nice spot. The bungalows here are *Niu's, Ao Phai, Charlee Villa* and *Seabreeze* all having huts in the 40B to 80B range. The new English name for this beach is 'Paradise Beach'. There is a place to rent windsurfing equipment and take lessons here.

Ao Thap Thim (Tubtim) The very popular *Tubtim* bungalows deserves its success: friendly management, good food and clean, comfortable huts for 40B to 50B. Nearby are *Pudsa Beach* and *Tup Tong* at similar rates.

Ao Tawan *Tantawon Villa* (also spelled Taratawan) has huts for 50B up and a pleasant restaurant overlooking the beach.

Ao Wong Deuan This area is now mostly given over to more expensive resort-type bungalows. The cheaper bungalows that were here a few years ago have nearly all disappeared and those that remain can't be recommended. It's a little crowded with buildings and people now, but if you want a 300B bungalow, complete with running water and flushing toilet, the best of the lot is *Wong Deuan Resort* with huts at 300B.

Ao Thian Better known by its English name, 'Candlelight Beach'. Far removed from the more active beaches to the north, this is the place to come for a little extra solitude, though the bungalow operations here, *Candlelight* and *Lung Dam* are no great shakes. Food is a definite minus here too. You can bring your own from the village on the northern tip of the island. Rates are 30B up.

Haat Ao Phrao 'Coconut Bay Beach' is one of the only beaches on the western side of the island. There is a restaurant here where East-West Tours brings tourists from Bangkok and Pattaya on weekends, but there are no bungalows as yet.

Camping Since this is a National Park, camping is allowed on any of the beaches, in spite of signs to the contrary posted by certain unscrupulous bungalow owners. In fact, this is a great island to camp on because it hardly ever rains. There is plenty of room; most of the island is uninhabited and tourism is pretty much restricted to the north-eastern beaches, at least so far.

Other Beaches There are many other small bays around the island, **Ao Wai, Ao Kiu, Na Nok, Ao Karang** on the eastern side, and **Ao Kiu Na Nai, Ao Phrao** and **Ao Kham** on the west; but none of them have bungalows so far. There are trails crossing the island at several points and the farthest you have to walk to reach the west coast is three km. Except for the lack of fresh water, these could make excellent camping spots.

Places to Eat

Best Thai food is at the *White Sand* at Haat Sai Kaew. Best western-style food is at *Seabreeze, Naga* and *Tubtim*. Naga has good homemade bread and a nice selection of cocktails with humorous names like Cubre Libra (Maekhong, Coke and lime) – most of the beach restaurants offer Maekhong fruit shakes.

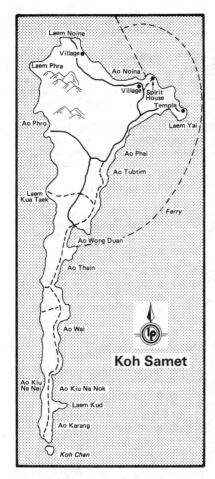

Koh Samet

Malaria on Samet

If you enter the park from the north end of the island near the village, you may notice a large English-language sign warning visitors that Koh Samet is highly malarious. If you're taking malarial prophylaxis you have little to worry about. If not, take a little extra care in avoiding mosquito bites at night. Malaria is not that easy to contract, even in malarious areas, unless you allow the mosquitos open season on your flesh. It's a good idea to take all precautions in order to minimise the chances of getting malaria – so make sure you cover your skin and use repellent, mosquito nets and coils at night time.

The locals claim that the danger of malaria on Samet is highly exaggerated, but the last time I was there, an Argentinian fellow came down with it and was taken to a hospital on the mainland. He had been on Samet for a month.

There is a public health clinic on the island, located halfway between the village harbour and the park entrance. Go there for a blood test if you develop a fever while on Samet, or for any other urgent health problems such as attacks from poisonous sea creatures or snakes.

Getting There

There are regular buses to Rayong throughout the day from the Eastern Bus Terminal but if your destination is Ban Phe (for Koh Samet), you'd do better to take one of the direct Ban Phe buses, which only cost 1B more; a *songthaew* to Ban Phe from Rayong is 10B. The Bangkok-Rayong bus is 69B, to Ban Phe 70B. You can also get a return (round trip) ticket to Ban Phe for 120B, a savings of 20B. The company that runs the Ban Phe bus, *DD Tours*, has a bad reputation for crummy service, often overbooking on the trip back to Bangkok. They also like to put all the *farangs* in the back of the bus, regardless of reserved seat numbers. Your only alternative is the ordinary non-AC bus which is 35B

Boats to Samet leave the Ban Phe pier at irregular intervals throughout the day. It mostly depends on whether they have enough passengers and/or cargo to make the trip profitable, so there are more frequent boats in the high season, November to February. Still, there are always at least two boats a day going. Two companies operate boats, one that goes to Wong Deuan and one that goes to Samet village (Na Dang). If you plan to stay at any beach other than Wong Deuan or Thap Thim, you should take the Na Dang boat. Either boat charges 20B per passenger one way.

Getting Around

If you take the boat from Ban Phe to the village harbour (Na Dang), you can easily walk to Sai Kaew Beach, Ao Phai or Ao Thap Thim. Don't believe the taxi operators who say these beaches are a long distance away. If you're going further down the island, or have a lot of luggage, you can take the taxi (a three-wheeled affair with a trailer) as far as Ao Wong Deuan. This will cost 20B per person for six to eight people, or 10B apiece to Ao Thap Thim. If they don't have enough people to fill the vehicle, they either won't go or passengers will have to pay more. If you want to go to Ao Thian (Candlelight Beach), you'll have to walk a short distance from Ao Wong Deuan.

CHANTHABURI (population 31,000)
จังหวัดจันทบุรี

Situated 330 km from Bangkok this is a busy gem mining centre, particularly noted for its star sapphires. Chanthaburi is also renowned for its tropical fruit and it has two pleasant waterfalls and the biggest church in Thailand.

Places to Stay

The *Kasemsam I* (tel 311100), 98/1 Benchamarachootit Rd has rooms from 125B or from 200B with air-con. The *Kiatkachorn* (tel 311212), 27/28 Ta Luang Rd is similarly priced.

Getting There

From Bangkok air-con buses cost 110B, regular buses 60B.

TRAT (population 13,000)
จังหวัดตราด

About 400 km from Bangkok, Trat is close to the border with Kampuchea. There are some, as yet little developed, islands off shore from here.

Places to Stay

The *Tung Nguan Seng* (tel 511028) at 66-77 Sukhumvit Rd has rooms from 80B to 150B. The *Thai Roong Roj* (tel 511141) at 296 Sukhumvit Rd has rooms from 100B or from 180B with air-con.

Getting There

Buses from Bangkok cost 135B air-con or 75B regular.

The first true Thai kingdoms (Sukhothai, Chiang Mai and Chiang Saen) arose in what is today northern Thailand, hence this region is dotted with great temple ruins. It is also the home of most of the Thai hill tribes whose cultures are dissolving fast in the face of Thai modernisation and foreign tourism. The scenic beauty of the north has been fairly well-preserved though, and Chiang Mai is still probably Thailand's most livable city.

The northern Thai people in general are known for their relaxed, easy-going manner, which shows up even in their speech – the northern dialect has a slower rhythm to it than Thailand's other three major dialects.

The north also contains the infamous Golden Triangle, the region where Burma, Laos and Thailand meet. This is the area where most of the world's illicit opium is grown. Aside from the air of adventure and mystery surrounding the Golden Triangle, it is simply a beautiful area through which to travel.

The Northern Loop

Although the straightforward way of travelling north is to simply head directly from Bangkok to Chiang Mai there are numerous interesting alternatives. The old 'Laotian Loop', which took you from Bangkok to Vientiane, Luang Prabang and Ban Houei Sai, then back into Thailand to Chiang Rai and eventually Chiang Mai, has been short-circuited by the government of Laos but you can still make an interesting northern loop from Bangkok through Chiang Mai and the north-east and back to Bangkok.

Starting north you could visit the ancient capitals of Ayuthaya, Lopburi and Sukhothai or you could take a longer and less 'beaten track' route by first heading west to Nakhon Pathom and

Kanchanaburi and then travelling north-east by bus to Lopburi via Suphanburi (backtracking to Ayuthaya if desired).

From Lopburi, you can either head straight north to Chiang Mai or stop off in Phitsanuloke for side trips to Sukhothai, Tak and Mae Sot.

Once you're in Chiang Mai, the usual route is to continue on to Fang for the Kok River boat ride to Chiang Rai, then from Chiang Rai into the Golden Triangle towns of Mae Sai and Chiang Saen. Travellers with more time might throw in the Chiang Mai-Pai-Mae Hong Son-Mae Sariang-Chiang Mai circle.

From the north you can proceed to the north-east via Phitsanuloke and Lom Sak, entering the north-east proper at either Loei or Khon Kaen. From there, Nong Khai, Udorn Thani and Khon Kaen are all on the rail line back to Bangkok, but there are a number of other places in the area worth exploring before heading back to the capital

CHIANG MAI (population 100,000)
จังหวัดเชียงใหม่

Over 700 km north-west of Bangkok, Chiang Mai has more than 300 temples – almost as many as in Bangkok – making it a striking city visually. Doi Suthep Mount rises 1676 metres above and behind the city, providing a nice setting for this fast-developing centre.

Historically, Chiang Mai became the successor to King Mengrai's Chiang Rai kingdom, after he had conquered the post-Dvaravati kingdom of Haripunchai (modern Lamphun) in 1281. Mengrai, originally a prince of Nan Chao, a Thai kingdom in south-west China, had the city of Chiang Mai ('new city') built from scratch at the foot of Doi Suthep in 1296. Chiang Mai later became a part of the larger Lan Na Thai ('million Thai rice-fields') kingdom, which extended as far

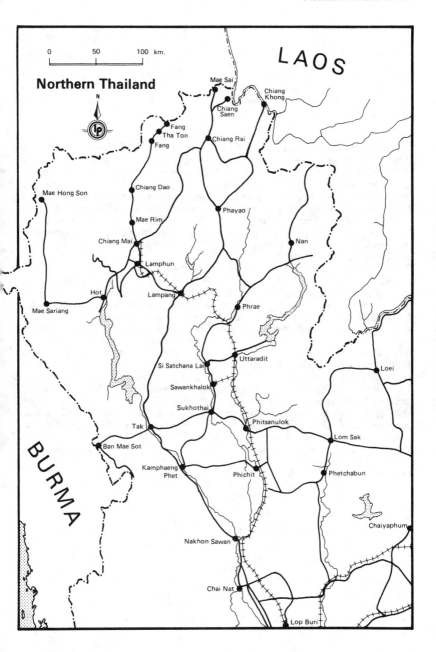

south as Kamphaeng Phet and as far north as Luang Prabang in Laos, until captured by the Burmese in 1556. This was the second time the Burmese had control of Chiang Mai province; before Mengrai came along, King Anuruddha of Pagan ruled the area during the 11th century. As a result, Chiang Mai architecture shows a great deal of Burmese influence.

Chiang Mai was recaptured by the Thais under King Taksin in 1775.

Today Chiang Mai has become a real tourist and world traveller centre. Many stay longer than originally planned because of the high quality of accommodation and food here, the cool nights (relative to central Thailand), the 'international' feel of the city and the friendliness of the Chiang Mai people. The city is also small enough to get around by bicycle. Chiang Mai residents often comment that living there has all the cultural advantages of being in Bangkok, but fewer of the disadvantages such as traffic jams and air pollution.

Information

Finding your way around Chiang Mai is fairly simple although a copy of Nancy Chandler's *Map Guide to Chiang Mai* is a worthwhile 60B investment. It shows all the main points of interest and innumerable oddities you'd be most unlikely to stumble upon by yourself. There are a number of bookshops in Chiang Mai, but the best are DK Books on Tha Phae Rd and the Suriwong Book Centre on Sri Dornchai Rd.

Chiang Mai has a friendly tourist office on Tha Phae Rd. Thai Airways (tel 211541) is within the city moat area on Phra Pokklao, behind Wat Chiang Man. Thai International (tel 233559) is outside the moat area on Chang Klan close to the intersection with Sri Dornchai. The Immigration Office (tel 235124) is on the highway to Mae Rim. One traveller has reported how easy it was to get a 14 day visa extension here by showing up with

two passport photos and 300B. There are Tourist Police (tel 235334, 235490) in Chiang Mai. To phone Bangkok from Chiang Mai dial 02 first. For Chiang Mai from Bangkok dial 053. Overseas calls can be made from the Telephone Office on Praisanee Rd from Monday to Friday from 8 am to 5 pm. After hours calls can be made from several locations including the New Chiang Mai Hotel.

The McCormick Hospital has been recommended over the Suandok as 'they are more geared up for foreigners, speak better English and won't keep you waiting for so long'. A consultation and treatment for something simple costs about 200B. Suandok Hospital has a malaria centre where you can get free Fansidar tablets.

Orientation

The old city of Chiang Mai is a neat square bounded by moats. Moon Muang Rd, along the east moat, is the centre for cheap accommodation and places to eat. Tha Phae Rd runs straight out from the middle of this side and crosses the Ping River where it changes name to Charoen Muang Rd.

The railway station and the GPO are further down Charoen Muang Rd, a fair distance from the centre. There are several bus stations around Chiang Mai so make certain you're going to the right one. Several of Chiang Mai's important temples are within the moat area but there are others to the north and west. Doi Suthep rises up to the west of the city and you have a fine view over the city from the temple.

Wat Chiang Man

The oldest *wat* in the city, founded by King Mengrai in 1296, features typical northern Thai architecture with massive teak columns inside the *bot*. Two important Buddha images are kept locked up in the smaller building to the right of the main bot. Try the door, it may be open with a monk on guard within. Or you may be able to see them on request although officially they're only on view on Sundays from 9 am to 5 pm.

The Buddha Sila is a marble bas-relief standing 20 cm to 30 cm high. It's supposed to have come from Sri Lanka or India 2500 years ago. The well-known Crystal Buddha, shuttled back and forth between Siam and Laos like the Emerald Buddha, is kept in the same glass cabinet. It's thought to have come from Lopburi, 1800 years ago and is a small image standing just 10 cm high.

Wat Phra Singh

Begun by King Pa Yo in 1345, the *wiharn* which houses the Phra Singh image was built between 1385 and 1400 and the *bot* was finished around 1600. The Phra Singh Buddha supposedly comes from Sri Lanka, but it is not particularly Sinhalese in style. Since it is identical to two images in Nakhon Si Thammarat and Bangkok and has quite a travel history behind it (Sukhothai, Ayuthaya, Chiang Rai, Luang Prabang – the usual itinerary for a travelling Buddha image, involving much royal trickery), no one really knows which image is the real one or can document its provenance. It's kept in the smaller building behind and to the left of the main bot. This wat has impressively well-kept grounds.

Wat Chedi Luang

This has a very large and venerable *chedi*, dated 1441. It's now in partial ruin either due to a 16th century earthquake, or according to others, because of the cannon-fire of King Taksin in 1775. It's said that the Emerald Buddha was placed in the eastern niche here in 1475. The *lak muang*, guardian deity-post for the city, is located within the wat compound in the small building just to the left of the main entrance.

Thailand's Fine Arts Department, with the financial support of the Japanese government, has plans to restore the great chedi within the next couple of years. Since no one knows for sure how the original spire looked, Thai artisans are designing a new spire for the chedi.

Adjacent to Wat Chedi Luang is **Wat Phan Tao** with a wooden *wiharn* and some interesting old monk's quarters. Just across Ratchadamnoen Rd from here, at the intersection with Phra Pokklao is an uninteresting monument marking the spot where King Mengrai was struck by lightning!

Wat Jet Yod

Out of town on the northern highway loop near the Chiang Mai museum. Built in the mid-15th century and based on the design of the Mahabodhi Temple in Bodh Gaya, India, the seven spires represent the seven weeks Buddha spent in Bodh Gaya after his enlightenment. The proportions for the Chiang Mai version are quite different than the Indian original, so it was probably modelled from a small votive tablet depicting the Mahabodhi in distorted perspective. There's an adjacent old stupa and a very glossy *wiharn* and the whole area is surrounded by well kept lawns. It's a pleasantly relaxing temple to visit although it's not a very 'busy' temple in terms of worship, curiously enough.

Wat Suan Dawk

Originally built in 1383, the large open *wiharn* was rebuilt in 1932. The *bot* contains a 500 year old bronze Buddha image and vivid Jataka murals. Amulets and Buddhist literature printed in English and Thai can be purchased at quite low prices in the wiharn.

There is an interesting group of whitewashed stupas in back, framed by Doi Suthep. The large central stupa contains a Buddha relic which supposedly self-multiplied. One relic was mounted on the back of a white elephant (commemorated by Chiang Mai's White Elephant gate) which was allowed to wander until it 'chose' a site on which to build a wat to shelter the relic. It stopped

Chiang Mai

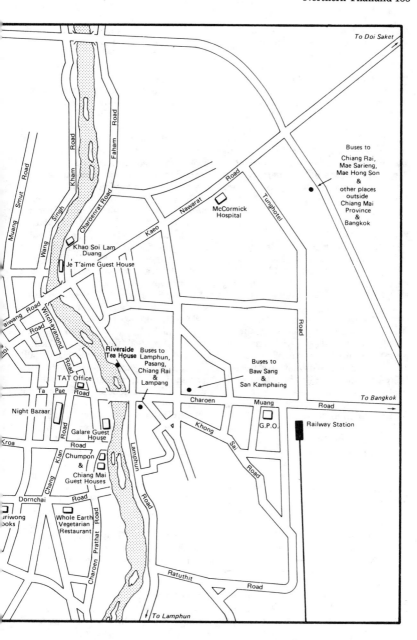

and died at a spot on Doi Suthep and Wat Phra That Doi Suthep was built.

Wat U Mong

U Mong is a forest *wat* which has been in use since Mengrai's rule in the 14th century. It is connected to another wat in Chaiya, South Thailand, by the influence of Achaan Buddhadasa, a well-known monk and teacher. There is a building here which contains modern artwork by various monks who have resided at U Mong, including a number of *farangs*. A marvellous grisly image of the fasting Buddha, ribs, veins and all can be seen here.

Wat Koo Tao

North of the moat, near the Sanam Kila sports stadium, Wat Koo Tao dates from 1613 and has a unique chedi like a pile of diminishing spheres. Note the amusing sculptures on the outer wall of the wat.

National Museum

A good selection of Buddha images are on display here, in all styles. A very large bronze Buddha head is displayed downstairs. Pottery is also displayed downstairs (note the 'failed' jar on the stairs) while upstairs there are household and work items. Look for the amusing wooden 'dog' used for spinning thread.

The museum is open 9 am to 12 noon and 1 pm to 4 pm, Wednesday to Sunday. Admission is 2B on Saturdays and Sundays, free on other days of the week. The museum is on Highway 11 which curves around the city, very near Wat Jet Yod.

Chiang Mai Jail

Near the centre of town, off Ratwithi, come here to see the dozens of *farangs* who have been incarcerated on drug charges. Chiang Mai is notorious for its *samlor* drivers who sell dope and then inform the police on their customers. Fines for even the smallest amounts of *ganja* are very high – 50,000B for a couple

of grams is not unusual. Those who cannot afford to buy out of this game go to jail.

Night Bazaar

An extensive night market sprawling over the area between Suriwong Rd and Tha Phae Rd, off Chang Klan Rd, just east of the Mae Kha canal, near the Chiang Inn. This market has an incredible variety of Thai and northern Thai goods at very low prices *if* you bargain well. Actually, many importers buy here, the prices are so good, especially when buying in quantity.

Good buys include Phrae-style *seua maw hawm* (the blue denim farmer's shirt), northern and north-eastern hand-woven fabrics, *yams* (Thai shoulder bags), hill-tribe crafts (many tribespeople set up their own concessions here), opium scales, hats, silver jewellery, lacquerware and many other items.

If you're in need of new travelling clothes, this is a good place to look – a light cotton dress or trousers, for example, can be picked up for 45B to 60B. Yams were 40B in 1986 (final price, not asking price), *maw hawm* shirts 45B to 50B depending on size. You must bargain patiently but mercilessly. There are so many different concessions selling the same kinds of items that competition effectively keeps prices low, if you haggle. Cover the whole bazaar if you can, before you begin buying. If you're not in the mood (or financial situation) to buy, it's worth a stroll anyway.

Nearby Kampaeng Din Rd, which follows an old earthern rampart between Loi Kroa and Tha Phae Rds, is a street of a thousand cut-rate prostitutes at night – strictly a Thai scene and probably dangerous. The Chiang Mai University Campus is also an interesting place to go in the evenings with a busy night bazaar of its own.

Other Attractions

Old Chiang Mai is a tourist 'instant hill tribes' centre. There are Thai and hill tribe dance performances here every night. The rather kitsch **Laddaland** also puts on a dance performance every morning. There's also a Chiang Mai zoo.

Festivals
The Winter Fair, for a week in late December to early January, is a great occasion in Chiang Mai. The April Songkran water festival is also celebrated with great enthusiasm.

Perhaps Chiang Mai's best celebrated festival is the Flower Festival, also called the Flower Carnival, which is held during the first week of February each year. The events occur over a three-day period and include displays of flower arrangement, a long parade of floats decorated with hundreds of thousands of flowers, folk music, cultural performances and the Queen of the Flower Festival contest. Most activities are centred at Buak Hat public park in the south-west corner of the city moats. People from all over the province and the rest of the country turn out for this occasion, so book in early if you want a room in town.

Places to Stay – bottom end
At any one time there are about 50 hotels and 35 guest houses in operation in Chiang Mai. The hotels range from 60B (Thai Charoen, Sri Rajawong) to 9680B (Chiang Mai Orchid) per room with an average room going from 100B to 300B. The guest houses range from 30B per person to 300B per room. A lot of cheap hotels have replaced the English word 'hotel' with the new flashword 'guest house', although the Thai still reads *rohng raem* ('hotel')!

Hotels *Roong Ruang Hotel*, also spelt Roong Raeng (tel 236746), 398 Tha Phae Rd, near Tha Phae gate, on the eastern side of the city moat. Good location, good service, clean, quiet rooms with fan and bath for 120B (one bed), 150B (two beds). There is also a hot water shower available.

Good place to stay for the Flower Festival in early February, as the Saturday parade passes right by the entrance. There is also an entrance on Chang Moi Kao Rd.

Thai Charoen (tel 236640), 165 Tha Phae Rd. Further out Tha Phae towards the river, between the moat and the TAT office – Seiko Tour has its office out front. Rooms with fan and bath for 60B up.

YMCA (tel 221819, 221820), 2/4 Mengrai-Rasni Rd, above north-west corner of the moat. Rooms with shared bath for 95B to 155B or dorm beds from 50B to 60B.

Sri Rajawong (tel 235864) at 103 Ratchawong Rd. Between east moat and the Ping River, 60B for rooms with a fan and bath, 40B without a bath.

Sri Santitham (tel 221585) 15 Chotana Soi 4. Near Bus Station Number 1 ('White Elephant' station). Rooms from 80B with fan and bath.

The well located *Muang Thong* (tel 211438) at 5 Ratchamankha Rd, inside the city moats has rooms from 80B with fan and bath.

The *New Chiang Mai* (tel 236561, 236766), 22 Chaiyaphum Rd, is pleasant, clean and well-located on the east moat and has spacious fan and bath rooms for 130B. Air-con rooms are available for 300B. Another reasonable hotel on Chaiyaphum is the *Miami*, with rooms for 100B. Similar but cheaper accommodation is available at the *Nakhorn Ping* (tel 236024) 43 Taiwang Rd, starting at 90B per room. Hotels bridging the gap from the bottom end to the top include, on the corner of Moon Muang and Ratchadamnoen, the *Montri* (tel 211069-70,) which costs 150B with fan and bath; 330B for deluxe AC. Similar rates and accommodation can be found at the *A & P* (tel 212309) which is also on Moon Muang Rd, next to Daret Restaurant. The *Anodard* (tel 211057) at 5 Ratchamankha, has the bonus of a swimming pool; rooms start at 170B. All three of the above hotels are within the city moat.

Guest Houses Guest houses are clustered together in several places: along Charoen Raj Rd east of the Ping River, far from the centre of the city but near buses to Chiang Rai, Lamphun and the railway station; along Moon Muang Rd (the inside of the east moat) and on *sois* off Moon Muang; along Charoen Prathet Rd, parallel to Charoen Raj, but west of the Ping River. Several others are scattered elsewhere around the west side of Chiang Mai.

All of the guest houses listed below, I've checked out and found adequate:

Lek House, 22 Chaiyaphum Rd, near Chang Moi Rd intersection on the soi to Wat Chompoo, has a nice garden and is quiet and clean. Rooms with fan and bath cost 60B single, 80B double. Discount is possible for long-term stay. Yves, the French owner, oversees the restaurant which specialises in homemade yoghurt, bread, muesli, and other western dishes, including a dinner of buffalo steak, potatoes and vegetables for 45B. Yves speaks Thai, English and of course, French.

In 1986 there was an imposter called Lek Guest House on Kotchasan Rd (between Tha Phae gate and the Aroon Rai Restaurant) which was snaring a lot of unwary travellers on the basis of Yves' Lek House reputation. The room rates were the same as the original but the service and food did not compare. There is only one Lek House.

Chiang Mai Youth Hostel (tel 212863) at 31 Prapakklao Rd inside the moat has dorm beds for 40B and rooms from 60B to 100B. An ISIC card is good for a 10B discount. It's clean, secure, friendly and their treks get good reviews.

Chiang Mai International Youth Hostel (tel 221180) at 302 Manee Noparat Rd, is across from the Tantraphan Department Store. It has one dorm with four beds, for 30B per person; singles with fan, shared bath, 40B student, 50B non-student; and doubles with fan, shared bath, 50B student, 60B non-student.

Students must have ISIC card for student rates. It's clean, secure and friendly, they even have video films every night.

Chumpol Guest House (tel 234526), 89 Charoen Prathet Rd, is next door to the Chiang Mai Guest House. Rooms here are 70B single with fan and shared bath or 120B double with fan and private bath. It also has motorcycles for rent.

At 91 Charoen Prathat Rd, *Chiang Mai Guest House* (tel 236501) has recently been expanded to 27 rooms. Rates range from 100B for a double with fan and shared bath, to 200B for a double with fan, private bath and a 'good view'. Hot water is available from 6 am to 10 am and 6 pm to 10 pm. Additional beds are only 30B more.

There's also *Gemini House* at 22 Ratchadamnoen Rd, an old teak house with a couple of dorms and several rooms. Dorm beds are 15B to 20B per person; rooms with shared bath are 50B a single or 60B a double; and rooms with fan and bath 80B.

Not far from the night bazaar is *Galare Guest House* at 7-7/1 Charoen Prathet Rd Soi 2. The quality here is similar to Chiang Mai Guest House for 90B single with fan and bath; 150B double with fan and bath and 220B with air-conditioning and bath. Several travellers have written to recommend this relatively new guest house. Another new place is *Happy House* at 11 Chiang Moi Kao Rd, near the Thapae Gate. Big clean rooms with fan and bathroom are 150B/180B. Opposite is the little *Pig Pen Pub*, with cheap beer!

The *Je T'aime Guest House* (tel 234912) at 247-9 Charoen Rat Rd is rather far removed from town, but favoured by many. It costs 50B a single or 60B a double, all rooms have fan and private shower. They'll arrange a free pickup from the railway or bus station if you phone. There have been recent reports that the staff has become rather unfriendly.

The *New Thai-German Guest House* at 19 Ratchamankha Rd Soi 2 has rooms for 40B single, 60B double while the nearby *Saitum*, 21 Ratchamankha Rd, Soi 2 offers the same for 30B/50B. Across the moat from Daret Restaurant is the *Garden House*, 2 Kotchasan Rd, an old Thai-style teak house with rooms from 50B to 80B.

The *Top North Guest House* at 31 Phrapokklao Rd Soi 7 is a friendly place to stay for 60B single, 70B double. All rooms have fan and bath. Another pleasant stand-by is the *Pao Come* at 9 Changmoi Kao Rd, not far from Lek House. Here singles are 50B, doubles 60B.

Manit's Guest House is a one-man show at 44 Ratchaphanikai Rd, where rooms are 60B single with bath, 70B double without bath, 80B double with bath. Manit handles every aspect of his business himself, in a large off-the-street house inside the city moat.

Chang Moi House (tel 251839) at 29 Changmoi Kao Rd is behind the New Chiang Mai Hotel. Rooms here are generally 70B but may be more during the high season, December to February, when it is usually full. Call for free transport from the railway or bus station. They also arrange hill treks. This guest house has perhaps suffered from too much notoriety and is not as good value as it was in years past, though the management try hard to please.

Out at 282/3 Charoenrat Rd is the popular *Gold Riverside* with rooms for 50B to 80B. Also on Charoenrat are the newer *Mee Guest House*, 193/1 Charoenrat, where they have double rooms with bath for 60B (they also serve magic mushroom omelettes) and the *Pun Pun* (tel 243362), 321 Charoenrat, where rooms start at a low 30B. All three of these guest houses are a bit far from the centre of town but are recommended for those seeking a quiet atmosphere; they are situated on the banks of the Ping River. The Pun Pun also has a few nice 50B bungalows right on the river – call them for a ride from the bus or train station.

Due to open sometime in 1986 is the *Teak House*, at 21/23 Tha Phae Soi 2, between Tha Phae and Changmoi Rds. As the name suggests, this is an old Thai-style teak house. The rates for large rooms furnished with local antiques were projected to be 65B.

There are plenty of other guest houses in Chiang Mai, especially in the Moon Muang and Tha Phae Rd areas, down the little side lanes. New ones are opening all the time, as there seems to be a shortage of rooms during January and February and during festivals such as Songkhran and the Flower Festival. Those guest houses that belong to the Chiang Mai Guest House Association are probably more secure in terms of theft than those which are not – the TAT office on Tha Phae Rd can give you an up-to-date list of the members – they pay government taxes so are more interested in long-term operations.

Just a word of warning, LP has received many letters from travellers who have left their valuable belongings in a guest house safe whilst they were trekking. Unfortunately upon their return, they have discovered that their property has actually been removed from the safe and some items have gone 'missing', for example, travellers cheques, Swiss army pocket knives, sunglasses, etc. One Australian traveller discovered that A$2500 had been spent on her Mastercard which had been left in a safe while she had been trekking. An Irish couple had £6000 worth of goods charged to their credit cards in Bangkok whilst on a three-day trek! If you leave your valuables in a safe, make sure you obtain a fully itemised receipt before leaving.

Places to Stay – top end

Chiang Mai has plenty of hotels in the more expensive categories including a number of places along Huay Kaew Rd, the road up to Doi Suthep. They include the following all air-con places with swimming pools:

Chiang Inn Hotel (tel 235655), 100 Chang Klan Rd, from 920B

Chiang Mai Hills (tel 221254), 18 Huay Kaew Rd, from 726B

Chiang Mai Orchid (tel 221625) 100 Huay Kaew Rd, from 1089B

Chiang Mai President (tel 235116), 226 Vitchayanon Rd, from 700B

Dusit Inn (formerly Chiang Mai Palace, tel 236835) 112 Chang Klan Rd, from 840B

Poy Luang Hotel (tel 242633), 146 Super Highway, from 886B

Rincome Hotel (tel 221044), 301 Huay Kaew Rd, from 1089B

Suriwongse Hotel (tel 236789), 110 Chang Klan Rd, from 847B

Hotels a notch down, some rooms air-con, some fan, include:

Chang Phuak Hotel (tel 221755), 133 Chotana Rd, from 190B to 400B

Chiang Come Hotel (tel 222237), 7/35 Suthep Rd, from 333B to 422B

Chiang Mai Phucome Hotel (tel 211026) 21 Huay Kaew, 500B to 1800B

Chom Doi House (tel 222249), 33/3 Huay Kaew Rd, from 250B to 300B

Diamond Hotel (tel 234155), 33/10 Charoenprathet, from 280B to 932B

Iyara Hotel (tel 222723), 126 Chotana Rd, from 490B to 1050B

Muang Mai Hotel (tel 221392) 502 Huay Kaew Rd, 532B to 1518B

New Asia Hotel (tel 235288), 55 Ratchawong Rd, from 200B to 1200B

Porn Ping Hotel (tel 235099), 46 Charoenprathet, from 633B to 1139B

Prince Hotel (tel 236396), Taiwang Rd, from 278B to 1518B

Rintr Hotel (tel 221483) 99/9 Huay Kaew Rd, 500B to 1800B

Sri Tokyo Hotel (tel 213899) 6 Boonruangrit Rd, 400B to 600B

Suan Erawan Hotel (tel 232450) 149/10 Chang Klan Rd, 500B to 2500B

Sumit Hotel (tel 211033), 198 Ratchaphanikai Rd, from 140B to 290B

Wiang Kaew Hotel (tel 221549), 7/9 Huay Kaew Rd, from 160B to 1090B

Places to Eat

Chiang Mai has the best variety of restaurants of any city in Thailand outside of Bangkok. Most travellers seem to have better luck here than in Bangkok, simply because it's so much easier to get around and experiment.

Travellers' Food *Daret Restaurant* (near Tha Phae Gate on Moon Muang Rd), *Thai German Dairy Restaurant* (corner of Moon Muang and Ratchadamnoen) and *Ban Rai Steakhouse* (Wiang Kaew Rd, next to Wat Chiang Man) are where all the travellers hang out to eat western food and drink fruit smoothies, although the Daret cooks up some pretty fair Thai dishes as well. Quite a few travellers have raved about the Ban Rai's steak and potatoes!

Lek House, 22 Chaiyaphum Rd (actually a short way down a soi off Chaiyaphum), has great food in this category, too. If you can't get a room in the place (it's often full), at least you can eat here. At New Year's Eve the place is packed out and owner/manager Yves sometimes gives out free champagne.

Thai Food Two good Thai restaurants are just across the moat from Daret, on Katchasan Rd, the big open-air *Aroon Rai*, specialising in northern Thai dishes and the smaller but better *Thanam Restaurant* (no English sign) between the new Chiang Mai Hotel and Tha Phae Gate. Specialities at the super-clean Thanam include *phak nam phrik* (fresh vegetables in pepper sauce), *pla duk phat phet* (spicy fried catfish), *kaeng som* (hot and sour vegetable ragout with shrimp), as well as local dishes like *khao soi* (Burmese chicken curry-soup with noodles) and *khanom jiin ngiaw* (Chinese noodles with spiced pureed fish and coconut milk).

Out on the road to San Kamphaeng, just before it crosses the superhighway (Route 11) east of the city, across from Poy Luang Hotel, is an excellent Thai restaurant specialising in seafood. The name is *Serimit* and there is no English sign.

Lung Thaworn, 'Uncle Eternity', on

Wiang Kaew not far from Wat Chiang Man and the Ban Rai restaurant, serves good Thai food and French food at very reasonable prices. Thaworn speaks French and was a cook at the French Embassy for 12 years.

Also good are the *Kai Yang* restaurants on Kotchasan Rd, just south of the Loi Kroa Rd intersection. North-eastern style food like *somtam*, *laap* and sticky rice are the specialties here, but other Thai foods are served as well. Another good place for north-eastern fare is *Phu Kradung*, a restaurant on the corner of Sam Larn and Bamrungburi Rds, at Suan Prung Gate. Order the *nam phrik num* to go with the *kai yang* – it's a northern Thai chilli sauce made of ground Thai eggplant, green chilli, salt and lime juice, very similar to a savoury Mexican salsa.

Chinese Food A recommended Chinese restaurant is *Ruam-mit Phochana*, across from the public playground on Sithiwong Rd. The owner-cooks are from China's Yunnan province so the specialities of the house are, of course, Yunnanese. The food here is better than anything you'll find in present-day Kunming. The menu includes *pla thawt nam daeng* (red-sauce fried fish, delicious whole fish cooked with large, semi-hot red peppers), *muu saam cham jim si-yu* (shredded white pork served with a chili-garlic-soy sauce), *muu tom khem* (salty-boiled pork or Yunnanese ham), and *tao hu phat phrik daeng* (braised bean curd and red peppers). Besides rice as an accompaniment you can order *mantou* – plain Chinese steamed buns, similar to the Thai *salabao* but without stuffing.

Another Yunnanese place is located across from the police box on Loi Kroa Rd, near Wat Pan Tong. Many of the Chinese living in Chiang Mai are Yunnanese immigrants or are direct descendants of Yunnanese immigrants who the Thais call *Jiin Haw*, or 'galloping Chinese'. It could be a reference to their migratory ways or to the fact that many bought pack horses from Yunnan.

Food Stalls Along Chaiyaphum Rd north of Lek House is a small but thriving night market where you can get everything from noodles and seafood to Yunnanese specialties at good prices.

The stalls across from the Thai-German Dairy restaurant on Ratchadamnoen Rd serve large 10B rice plates and they have an English menu.

Also good hunting grounds is the very large night market just west of Chiang Mai Gate on Bamrungburi Rd. This is a great place to make an evening of eating and drinking.

Good *khao man kai* (chicken rice) and *sate* are available along Intrawararot Rd, across from the south side of the old provincial office – also soups and dumplings.

The Somphet market on Moon Muang Rd just north of the Ratwithi intersection sells cheap take-away curries, *yam, laap, thawt man*, sweets, seafood, etc.

Noodles Noodles in Chiang Mai are wonderful and the variety astounding. For 'boat noodles' (rice noodles in a dark broth that contains that hunger-inducing herb *ganja*), try *Kolian* on the corner of Moon Muang and Ratchamankha.

For *khao soi*, a Burmese concoction of chicken, spicy curried broth and flat, squiggly, wheat noodles which bears a slight resemblance to Malaysian *laksa*, your best bet is *Khao Soi Lam Duang* on Charoen Rat Rd, not far from Je T'Aime Guest House. The cook here has prepared *khao soi* for no less a person than King Phumiphon (Bhumiphol). It only costs 8B per bowl. Also on the menu at Khao Soi Lam Duang are *kao lao* (soup without noodles), *muu sate* (grilled spiced pork on bamboo skewers), *khao soi* with beef or pork instead of chicken, beer, Maekhong rice whiskey and *khanom rang pheung* ('bee-hive pasty', a coconut-flavoured waffle).

Other noodle places serving khao soi can be found around the city – just look for the distinctive noodle shape. Great *kuaytiaw* can be bought in the night bazaar area at the 'all-night food' market (*ahaan toh rung*) – especially recommended is *laat naa thale*, rice noodles heaped with squid, shrimp and other seafoods. Another good night market is the small one on Chaiyaphum Rd, north of the intersection with Chang Moi Rd.

Vegetarian Food There are at least four vegetarian restaurants in Chiang Mai. Just west of town on the left side of the road to Wat Suan Dawk, is the *Vegetarian Restaurant (Raan Aahaan Mangsawirat)*, which makes excellent Thai vegetarian food using lots of bean curd, mushrooms and coconut milk. Prices are low – 7B to 8B per plate, with some large dishes 15B. Their desserts are good too – try the *kluay buat chee*, bananas in sweet coconut milk. They also have a good *khao soi*, made with wheat gluten instead of meat. Years ago this place was only open for lunch, but now has expanded hours from 8 am to 7 pm daily. They also have daily specials not listed on the standard bilingual menu – ask.

Another Thai veggie restaurant is *Ngam Nit*, at 107/1 Chang Moi Tat Mai, off Chang Moi Rd just after it crosses the canal, if you're walking from the city centre. This one's open Monday to Saturday only, 9 am to 5 pm. It's also quite good.

The new *Vegetarian* restaurant on Moon Muang Rd, south of Daret and the Thai-German, has irregular hours and rather indifferent food, but it's close to the centre of things.

Out Si Dornchai Rd, past the Chang Klan intersection, is *Whole Earth*, located in a Transcendental Meditation centre. The food is Thai and Indian and the atmosphere is suitably mellow, though the food may be a bit overpriced. Some Indian vegetarian dishes are served at the Indian-Pakistani-Middle Eastern *Al-*

Shiraz restaurant on Chang Klan Rd across from the Night Bazaar.

Other Possibilities If you like *suan ahaans*, garden restaurants, Chiang Mai has plenty. Several are along the super-highway near Wat Jet Yod and the National Museum. The food can be very good, but it is the *banyaakaat*, or atmosphere, that is most prized by Thais.

Finally, for a chuckle, check out the ostentatious *Nang Nual Seafood Restaurant* off the road to Lamphun, south of the city. This place, a branch of the Nang Nual in Pattaya, has large grounds with gardens, waterfalls, aviaries and attendants at every 10 steps along the path to the entrance who bow and *wai* as you approach. Inside the pretension doesn't stop, with more attendants in various costumes and a bored Thai classical orchestra. If you can bring yourself to sit down and look at the menu, you'll see that the prices are not as high as the surroundings would lead you to believe. Still, it is probably the most expensive place in Chiang Mai and unbearably stuffy.

Night Life

Anybody who's anybody makes the scene at *The Riverside (Rim Ping)*, a restaurant-cafe on Charoenrat Rd, right on the Ping River. Good food, fruit shakes, cocktails, live music every night and it's usually packed with *farangs* on weekends. Come early to get a table on the outdoor veranda overlooking the river.

For dancing, the hot spot is the 'disco' in the Porn Ping Hotel on Charoen Prathet Rd, where there is usually a good live band.

For real traditional Thai massage, contact *Rinkaew Povech* (tel 234565, 234567) at 183/4 Wualai Rd in Chiang Mai. If you call, they will provide free transportation to and from your hotel or guest house. Rates are 200B per hour in group or private rooms.

Getting There

Bus From Bangkok's Northern Terminal there are 13 ordinary buses daily to Chiang Mai, leaving between the hours of 5.25 am and 10 pm. The trip takes nine hours and costs 133B. Five public air-con buses leave between 9.10 am and 10.30 am and six buses between 8 pm and 9.35 pm. The AC bus takes about eight hours and costs 242B one way. (Note that the same bus back to Bangkok costs 150B, so a round trip passage on public AC bus is 392B.)

There are 11 private tour companies now running AC buses between Bangkok and Chiang Mai which leave from various points throughout both cities. Round trip tickets are always somewhat cheaper than one-ways. The least expensive tour bus is still the one that runs from the Boston Inn on Soi Si Bamphen, near Silom Rd in Bangkok, 290B return. Some other tour buses are:

Indra Tour 220B one way, 400B return; leaves Bangkok from beside the Indra Hotel on Ratchaprarop Rd in Pratunam at 9 pm. Leaves Chiang Mai from beside the Suriwong Hotel, Loi Kroa Rd, at 7.30 pm.

New Dusit 190B one way, 360B return; leaves Bangkok at 9 pm opposite the Mandarin Hotel on Rama IV Rd. Leaves Chiang Mai at 7.30 pm from 27 Charoen Rd.

Cosmos Tour 220B one way, 420B return; leaves Bangkok at 8.30 pm from 52/8 Suriwong Rd. Leaves Chiang Mai at 7 pm from the Porn Ping Hotel.

Public buses between Chiang Mai and other towns in the north and to Khon Kaen in the north-east have frequent departures throughout the day (at least every hour). Here are some fares and trip durations:

City	Fare	Duration
Chiang Rai	47B	4 hours
(air-con)	66B	3 hours
Fang*	32B	3 hours
Khon Kaen	153B	11 hours
Lampang	25B	1½ hours
(air-con)	50B	1 hour
Mae Hong Son (Route 108)	100B	9 hours
Mae Hong Son (Route 107/1095)	100B	9-10 hours
Mae Sariang	50B	5 hours
Nan	100B	6 hours
Pai	50B	4-5 hours
Phrae	80B	4 hours
Phetchabun (air-con)	235B	8 hours
Phitsanuloke	80B	5-6 hours
(air-con)	160B	5 hours
Tha Thon*	37B	4 hours

*Leaves from White Elephant (Chang Phuak) Bus Station, Chotana Rd. All other buses leave from the Chiang Mai Arcade Bus Station ('New Station'), off Kaew Nawarat Rd. For other buses out of Chiang Mai, remember that all buses to destinations within Chiang Mai province use the White Elephant Station while all buses outside the province use the Chiang Mai Arcade Station.

Train The Chiang Mai Express leaves Bangkok's Hualamphong Station daily at 6 pm, arriving in Chiang Mai at 7.40 am. The Rapid leaves at 3.45 pm and arrives at 6.35 am, not very rapid at all. The basic second class fare is 285B including express surcharge, add 150B for an upper berth and 180B lower in a sleeping car. Third class is 151B including express surcharge. Subtract 10B for the Rapid train fares.

Trains leave Lopburi for Chiang Mai at 6.12 pm (Rapid) and 8.26 pm (Express), arriving at the times listed above for the same trains from Bangkok. Fares are 245B second class, 130B third for the Express, 10B less for the Rapid.

Air Thai Airways has several daily flights between Bangkok and Chiang Mai for 1100B. There is also a special night fare available on Fridays and Sundays (departs 9.30 pm Bangkok-Chiang Mai and 11 pm Chiang Mai-Bangkok) for 880B. Flights take one hour.

Air fares between Chiang Mai and other cities in Thailand:

Chiang Rai	270B	Lampang	130B
Mae Hong Son	280B	Nan	330B

Mae Sot	360B	Phitsanuloke	440B
Phuket	2070B	Khon Kaen	1540B
Udon	1670B	Ubon	3340B
Surat Thani	1950B	Hat Yani	2240B

Getting Around

Songthaews go anywhere on their route for 5B. Large city buses are 2B – the TAT office in Chiang Mai has a map with bus routes. *Samlors* should be about 5B to 10B for most trips. Far and away the best way to get around Chiang Mai is by bicycle; the city is small enough that all is accessible by bike, including Chiang Mai University, Wat U Mong, Wat Suan Dawk and the National Museum on the outskirts of town.

Bikes can be rented for 20B to 25B per day from several of the guest houses – see Places to Stay – or from various places along the east moat. Motorcycles can also be rented there for 80B to 150B per day. Prices are very competitive in Chiang Mai because there's a real glut of motorcycles. For a couple of people it's cheaper to rent a small motorcycle for the day to visit Doi Suthep than to go up and back on a songthaew.

Airport You can get a taxi into the centre of Chiang Mai from the airport for less than 50B. A songthaew would be less again. It's a neat little airport with a bank, post office, tourist information counter, snack bar and another one out under the trees by the car park where you will also find a bar in an old air force transport aircraft. The airport is only two or three km from the city centre.

Immigration

The Immigration office is located near the airport off Highway 1141.

Things to Buy

There are numerous shops all over Chiang Mai selling hill tribe crafts and other local work. Thai Tribal Crafts at 208 Bamrung Rd near the McCormick Hospital is run by two church groups on a non-profit basis and has the 'best selection, quality and prices'. The Hilltribe Products Foundation near the Vegetarian Restaurant is also good – 'prices are much better than the night market' reported one traveller. You'll also find very competitive prices upcountry.

Although there are a lot of things to attract your money, Chiang Mai is at heart a very commercial and touristy place and a lot of junk is churned out for the undiscerning. So bargain hard and buy carefully!

Cotton & Silk Very attractive lengths of material can be made into all sorts of things. Go to Pasang, south of Lamphun, for cotton. For Thai silk, with its lush colours and pleasantly rough texture, try San Kamphaeng. It's cheaper up here than in Bangkok.

Ceramics Thai Celadon, about six km north of Chiang Mai, turns out ceramic-ware modelled on the Sawankhaloke pottery that used to be made at Sukhothai and exported all over the region, hundreds of years ago. With their deep, cracked, glazed finish some pieces are very beautiful and prices are often lower than in Bangkok. Other ceramics can be seen close to the Old Chiang Mai centre.

Woodcarving All sorts of carvings are available including countless elephants – but who would want a half life-size wooden elephant anyway? Teak salad bowls are good and very cheap.

Antiques You'll see lots of these around, including opium weights, the little animal-shaped weights supposedly used to measure out opium in the Golden Triangle. Check out prices in Bangkok first, Chiang Mai's shops are not always so cheap. And remember that anywhere in the world there are a lot more 'instant' antiques than real ones.

Lacquerware Decorated plates, containers,

utensils and other items are made by building up layers of lacquer over a wooden or woven bamboo base. You'll also see Burmese lacquerware in the north, smuggled across from Burma.

Silverwork A number of silverwork shops are located close to the south moat gate. The hill tribe jewellery, heavy chunky stuff, is very nice.

Clothes All sorts of shirts, blouses and dresses, plain and embroidered, are available at very low prices – but check the quality carefully.

Umbrellas Go out to Baw Sang, the umbrella village, where beautiful paper umbrellas are hand-painted. Leaf paintings, framed, are also made here and are very attractive.

AROUND CHIANG MAI
Doi Suthep
ดอยสุเทพ

Sixteen km north-west of Chiang Mai is Doi Suthep. Near the summit of Doi Suthep is **Wat Phra That Doi Suthep**, first established in 1383 under King Ku Na. A *naga* (dragon-headed serpent) staircase of 300 steps leads to the wat at the end of the winding road up the mountain. At the top you can get some fine aerial views of Chiang Mai if the weather is good. Inside the cloister is an intriguing copper-plated *chedi* topped by a five-tier gold umbrella.

Beyond Wat Phra That about five km is **Phu Ping Rajaniwat**, a royal palace, the gardens of which are open on weekends and holidays. The road that passes Phu Ping Rajaniwat splits off to the left, stopping at the peak of Doi Bui. From there a dirt road proceeds for two or three km to a nearby Meo hill tribe village, passable only by motorcycle/jeep or on foot. If you haven't already visited more remote villages, it's worth visiting even though very well-touristed. Some Meo handiwork can be purchased there and

traditional homes and costumes can be seen. 'Everyone knows some English' wrote one visitor, 'You buy', 'money' and 'I'll have no profit'. Tall *ganja* plants grow wild at the back of the village.

Getting There *Songthaews* to Doi Suthep leave throughout the day from Chang Phuak Gate, along Manee Noparat Rd, for 30B up. The same songthaew back from Suthep is 20B. Some travellers have been able to get lower fares by catching the songthaew further along the route but not at the white elephant gate or the zoo entrance.

Tribal Research Centre

This research centre is on Chiang Mai University campus, five km west of the city. A No 1 bus goes by the university. The centre features a small hill tribes museum and literature on hill tribes is available. It's open 8.30 am to 4.30 pm, Monday to Friday.

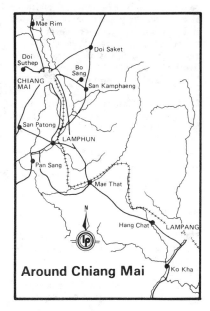

Around Chiang Mai

Baw Sang – San Kamphaeng
บ่อสร้าง — สันกำแพง

Baw Sang, nine km east of Chiang Mai on Highway 1006, is usually called the 'umbrella village' because of the many umbrella manufacturers there. Practically the entire village consists of craft shops of all types – painted umbrellas, fans, silverware, crafts made of straw, bamboo and teak, statuary, china, celadon, lacquerware, everything from the most tacky Chiang Mai-North Thailand souvenirs to pretty good stuff. The larger shops can also arrange overseas shipping at reasonable rates. As in Chiang Mai's night bazaar, discounts are offered for quantity purchases. Some of the places will pack and despatch parasols, apparently quite reliably.

Four or five km further down 1006 is **San Kamphaeng**, a town which flourishes on cotton and silk weaving. Stores offering finished products line the main street – the actual weaving is done in small factories down side streets. There are some deals to be had here, especially on silk. For cotton, you'd probably do better in Pasang village, a lesser known village near Lamphun (see Pasang below), though you may see shirt styles here not available in Pasang. A cotton shirt or blouse should cost around 40B to 60B.

Getting There Buses to Baw Sang (sometimes spelled Bo Sang or Bor Sang) and San Kamphaeng leave frequently during the day from the north side of Charoenmuang Rd, east of the Ping River towards the GPO and train station. Fare is 4B to Baw Sang and 5B to San Kamphaeng

Hang Dong
หางดง

Thirteen km south of Chiang Mai on Route 108, is Hang Dong, which could be called the 'basket village'. Catch a bus from the Chiang Mai Gate, 10B, to get to Hang Dong where anything made of straw, bamboo or rattan can be found:

hats, baskets, furniture, fishtraps, rice winnowers, coconut strainers, mats, brooms, rice and fish steamers, fighting-cock cages, bird cages, etc.

LAMPHUN (population 13,000)
จังหวัดลำพูน

Best seen on a day trip from Chiang Mai, along with Pasang, Lamphun was the centre of the small Haripunchai principality ruled originally by the Mon princess Chama Thevi. Long after Dvaravati, its progenitor, was vanquished by the Khmers, Haripunchai managed to remain independent of both the Khmers and the Chiang Mai Thais.

Wat Phra That Haripunchai
On the main road into Lamphun from Chiang Mai on the left is this wat which dates from 1157. It has some interesting post-Dvaravati architecture, a couple of fine Buddha images and two old *chedis* of the original Haripunchai style.

Wat Chama Thevi (Wat Kukut)
Another much larger Haripunchai chedi can be seen at Wat Chama Thevi (popularly called Wat Kukut), which is said to have been erected in the 9th century – as a Dvaravati monument – but has been restored many times so that it is a mixture of several schools.

Each of the four sides of the chedi has five rows of three Buddha figures, diminishing in size on each higher level. The stucco standing Buddhas are definitely of the Dvaravati style, but are probably not the original images.

Wat Kukut is on the opposite side of town from Wat Haripunchai; walk west down the narrow street perpendicular to the Chiang Mai-Lamphun Rd (opposite Wat Hari), passing over the town moat, passing the district government offices, until you come to Wat Chama Thevi on the left.

Getting There
Buses to Lamphun can be boarded in

Top: Flower festival, Chiang Mai (JC)
Bottom: Wat Phra Singh, Chiang Mai (JC)

Top: Akha house, Doi Tung (JC)
Left: Wat Phra That Doi Suthep, Chiang Mai (TW)
Right: Wat Chama Thevi (Wat Kukut), Lamphun (TW)

Chiang Mai on Lamphun Rd near the south side of Nawarat Bridge and they leave about every 20 minutes throughout the day. The 26 km bus ride, only 6B by bus or 8B by minibus, goes along a beautiful country road, some of it bordered with tall *yang* trees on both sides.

PASANG
อำเภอป่าซาง

Don't confuse this village, with Baw Sang, the 'umbrella village'. In Pasang, cotton-weaving is the cottage industry, The **Nantha Khwang shop**, one among many that weave and sell their own cotton, is on the right side of the main road going south – recommended for its selection and prices. A well-made cotton shirt of unique Pasang design can be purchased here for 50B to 60B. Pasang reputedly has the north's most beautiful women and I must say I can't disagree.

Getting There
A *songthaew* will take you from Lamphun to Pasang for a few baht. From Chiang Mai it's 12B by minibus.

Elephants
A daily 'elephants at work' show takes place near the 58 km marker on the Fang road. Arrive around 9 am or earlier to see bath time in the river. It's really just a tourist trap but probably worth the admission price. Once the spectators have gone the logs are all put back in place for tomorrow's show! It's a good idea to take a picture of an elephant to show the bus conductor or the word 'elephant' may get you to 'Fang', further north. There's a northern Thailand elephant meeting in November each year – hotel and food prices go up at that time.

Another place to see elephants is at the Elephant Training School (really) on the Lampang-Chiang Rai road. A big sign on the roadside in Thai and on the other side in English, indicates the location. You have to walk a couple of km up and down

hills to get to the well-hidden school – you might be able to find an elephant to follow.

The place is set up for tourists with seats and even toilets but nobody seems to know about it. When the trainer feels like it, sometime between 8 am and 12 noon, the elephants are put through their paces. They appreciate a few pieces of fruit – 'feels like feeding a vacuum cleaner with a wet nozzle' reported a visitor.

HILL TRIBE TREKS
For years now Chiang Mai has been a centre for treks into the mountainous northern areas inhabited by hill tribes. It used to be pretty exciting to knock about the dirt roads of rural Chiang Rai province, do the boat trip between Fang and Chiang Rai, and hike into the various villages of the Karen, Meo, Akha, and Yao tribes, and the Kuomintang settlements, spending the night in rustic surroundings, perhaps sharing some opium with the villagers.

Only a very few Thais living in Chiang Mai had the travel and linguistic knowledge necessary to lead adventurous foreigners through this area. Booking a trip usually meant waiting for optimum conditions and number of participants – sometimes quite a while. The trips began to get increasingly popular in the early 1970s and today virtually every hotel and guest house in Chiang Mai, books hill tribe tours for countless tour organisations.

Soon the word was out that the area north of the Kok River, in the Golden Triangle area, was being 'over-trekked', meaning that various treks were criss-crossing the area in such a fashion that the hill tribe villages were starting to become human zoos. When their only contact with the outside world and with foreigners is through a camera lens and a steady flow of sweets and cigarettes, it is no wonder that the villagers began to feel this way.

So the 'up-to-date' tours moved south

of the Kok River, around Chiang Dao and Wieng Papao, where most of them operate today. It's only a matter of time (not much) before this area suffers from the heavy traffic as well. Meanwhile hundreds of foreign travellers continue to take these treks every year, most of them still coming away with a sense of adventure and only a few disillusioned. What makes a good trek is most importantly, a good leader-organiser and, almost as important, a good group of trekkers. Some travellers finish a tour complaining more about the other trekkers than about the itinerary, food or trek leader.

This said, if you want to make a trek keep these things in mind: choose your trek operator carefully, try to meet the others in the group if you can – suggest a meeting or something; find out exactly what the tour includes and does not include – usually there are additional expenses beyond the basic rate. If everything works out, even an organised tour can be great. A useful checklist of questions to ask would be:

1. How many people will there be in the group, six is a good maximum reported one traveller although others have said that 10 is equally OK.
2. Can they guarantee no other tourists will visit the same village on the same day, especially overnight.
3. Can the guide speak the language of each village to be visited.
4. Exactly when does the tour begin and end – some companies' three-day treks turn out to be less than 48 hours.
5. Do they provide transport before and after the trek or is it just by public bus – often with long waits.

These days there are plenty of other places where you can arrange treks besides in Chiang Mai. In fact, these are often better alternatives to treks out of Chiang Mai since they may originate closer to the more remote and untrekked areas and are almost always less expensive.

Also, they are generally smaller, friendlier operations and the trekkers usually a more determined lot since they're not looking for a quick in and out trek. The treks are often informally arranged, usually involving discussions of duration, destinations, cost etc, (it used to be like that in Chiang Mai). You can easily arrange treks out of the following towns in the north: Chiang Rai, Mae Hong Son, Pai, Mae Sai and Tha Thon. With a little time to seek out the right people, you can also go on organised treks from Mae Sariang, Soppong (near Pai), Mae Sot, the Akha Guest House on the road to Doi Tung and other out-of-the-way guest houses which are springing up all over northern Thailand.

Alternatively, you might consider striking out on your own, either alone or in a small group, say two to four people. Gather as much information as you can about the area you'd like to trek in from the Tribal Research Centre on the Chiang Mai University campus – they have an informative pamphlet which they distribute at their library. Don't bother them with questions about trekking itself though, as they are quite non-committal about it, either from fear of liability or fear of retribution from the Chiang Mai trekking companies. There are maps around which pinpoint the locations of various hill-tribe areas in the north, most distributed by guest houses outside of Chiang Mai. DK Books in Chiang Mai sell two excellent maps on the Wawi area, just south of the Kok River and the Kok River area itself. Both lie in the Chiang Rai province and are considered safe areas for do-it-yourself treks. DK says they plan to bring out a whole series of trekking maps, based on Tribal Research Centre research. John Spies, an Australian who lives at the renowned Cave Lodge near Ban Tham, Mae Hong Son says that he thinks the trend in trekking in north Thailand is going the way of Himalayan treks in Nepal; where many people now do short treks on their own at the lower elevations, staying in villages along the way. An increasing number of travellers are doing the same thing in Thailand's hill tribe areas these days. It is not necessary to bring a lot of food or equipment, just money for food which can be bought along the way in small Thai towns and occasionally in the hill tribe settlements themselves.

Organised treks out of Chiang Mai average from 650B to 700B for a four-day, three-night trek to 2000B for a deluxe seven-day, six-night trek which includes elephant riding and/or rafting. Rates do vary quite a bit, so it pays to shop around. You can figure on an extra 1000B for elephants or other exotic additions to a basic trek. Don't choose a trek by price alone, it's better to talk to other travellers in town who have been on treks. Treks out of other towns in the north are usually about 100B to 150B per person per day.

In 1986, the companies in Chiang Mai that continued to get good reviews from trekkers were *Folkways Trekking*, (2-10 Changmoi Kao Rd, opposite Happy House or through Chang Moi House), *Northern Thailand Trekking* (next to the Oasis Bar on Moon Muang Rd) and *Summit Tour* (28 Tha Phae Rd). Newer companies also favourably received have been *Singha Travel* (275 Tha Phae Rd), *Seiko* (Thai Charoen Hotel, Tha Phar Rd) and *Youth's Tour* (operated out of the Chiang Mai Youth Hostel). There are at least 10 other companies doing treks in Chiang Mai, but with all the name changing and exchange of freelance guides (all the companies use them), it's quite difficult to make recommendations.

There is a Trekking Guide Association in Chiang Mai that meets once a month, sets prices for treks, discusses problems and issues regular, required reports to TAT about individual treks. All trekking guides and companies are supposed to be licenced by the government. As a result of these activities, a standard for trekking operators has emerged and you can expect the price you pay to include transport to and from the starting/ending points of a trek (if outside Chiang Mai), food (three meals a day) and accommodation in all villages visited, basic first aid, pre-departure valuables storage and sometimes the loan of specific equipment, like sleeping bags in cool weather or water bottles.

Not included are beverages besides drinking water or tea, the obligatory opium-smoking with the village headman (how many travellers have I heard say ' ... and then, oh wow, we actually smoked opium with the village headman!'), lunches on the first and last days and personal porters.

Probably the best time to trek is November to December. The weather is refreshing then – there should be little or no rain – and poppies are in bloom everywhere.

Finally, a warning – not necessarily against the particular organisation involved, but of possible trends to watch. In April 1981 a group of 10 travellers with *New Wave Treks*, doing a pretty well-worn route, were robbed while hiking between villages by a small band of armed robbers; everything of value was taken, cameras, watches, money and some clothes, plus there was an attempted rape and a few heads bashed. Some of the people in the group were stranded in northern Thailand until they could get money from home. The bandits were thought to be Karens who hightailed it across the border into Burma with their booty. Authorities in Chiang Mai consider it to be an isolated incident, but have stepped up hill-country patrols. The problem which remains, however, is that most people living in rural north Thailand believe that all foreigners are very rich (a fair assumption, relative to hill-tribe living standards). Most of these people have never been to Chiang Mai and, from what they have heard about it, they consider Bangkok to be a virtual paradise of wealth and luxury.

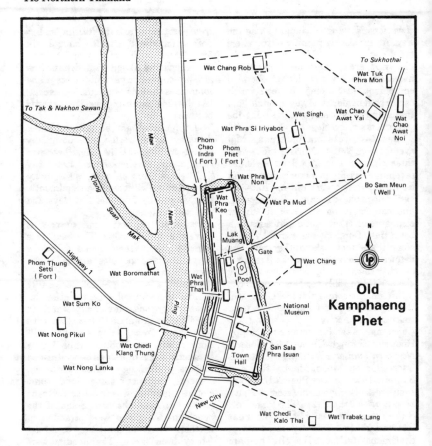

The map shows:

Wat Chang Rob

To Sukhothai

Wat Tuk Phra Mon

Wat Singh

Wat Chao Awat Yai

Wat Chao Awat Noi

To Tak & Nakhon Sawan

Mae

Wat Phra Si Iriyabot

Phom Chao Indra (Fort)

Phom Phet (Fort)

Wat Phra Non

Bo Sam Meun (Well)

Klong Suan Mak

Nam

Wat Phra Keo

Wat Pa Mud

Lak Muang

Gate

N

Phom Thung Setti (Fort)

Highway 1

Wat Boromathat

Wat Phra That

Pool

Wat Chang

Old Kamphaeng Phet

Wat Sum Ko

Ping

National Museum

Wat Nong Pikul

Wat Chedi Klang Thung

Town Hall

San Sala Phra Isuan

Wat Nong Lanka

New City

Wat Chedi Kalo Thai

Wat Trabak Lang

NAKHON SAWAN (population 86,000)
จังหวัดนครสวรรค์

This is a fairly large town on the way north from Bangkok. There is an excellent view from the hilltop **Wat Chom Kiri Nak Phrot**.

Places to Stay

If you stay here the *New White House* at 2 Matulee Rd and the *Irawan* at 1-5 Matulee Rd have reasonably priced rooms, the Irawan also has some with air-con. Or there's the *Nakkhon Sawan* at Tambol Pak Nam Po.

More expensive hotels include the *Vachara* (tel 213177, 214573) at 1016/9-12 Asia Rd with rooms from 100B or from 180B with air-con.

Getting There

Bus fare from Chiang Mai is 90B, from Bangkok 55B. Air-con buses from Bangkok are 100B.

KAMPHAENG PHET (population 20,000)
จังหวัดกำแพงเพชร

Only a couple of km off the Bangkok-Chiang Mai Rd there are a number of relics within the old city and very fine remains of the long city wall. Outside can be seen **Wat Phra Si Iriyabot** with the shattered remains of standing, sitting, walking and reclining Buddha images. **Wat Chang Rob** or 'temple surrounded by elephants' is just that, a temple with an elephant-buttressed wall.

Places to Stay

It can be a little difficult to find places since few signs are in English script. *Nitaya Pratapa* at 118/1 Tesa Rd is a little squalid and has rooms from 70B. It's on the main road leading to the river bridge.

There are night foodstalls opposite and the main ruins are around the corner beyond the foodstalls – further down the road away from the bridge towards Sukhothai. The *Chong Sawasdee* at 108 Tesa Rd is also hard to locate while the *Rajdamnoen* (tel 711022) at 892 Rajdamnoen Rd is more expensive at 70B to 90B and air-con from 120B.

Getting There

Bus fare from Chiang Mai is 72B, from Bangkok is 80B or 135B air-con.

PHITSANULOKE (population 73,000)
จังหวัดพิษณุโลก

Almost 390 km from Bangkok is Phitsanuloke where **Wat Phra Sri Ratana Mahathat** contains the Jinaraj Buddha, one of Thailand's most revered and copied images. Wat Mahathat is next to the bridge over the Nan River (on the right as you're heading out of Phit towards Sukhothai). The famous bronze image is in late Sukhothai style, but what makes it strikingly unique is the flame-like halo around the head and torso. The head is a little wider than standard Sukhothai, giving the statue a very solid feel. The walls of the *bot* are low, typical of northern-style temple architecture, so the image takes on larger proportions than it might in a central or north-eastern bot.

Wat Chulamani

Five km south of the city, a 2B bus trip down Borom Trilokanat Rd. The ruins here date from the Sukhothai period. The original buildings must have been pretty impressive, judging from what remains of the ornate Khmer-style *prang*. King Borom Trilokanat ordained as a monk here and there is an inscription to that effect on the ruined *wiharn*, in old Thai, from the reign of King Narai the Great.

The prang itself has little left of its original height but Khmer-style door lintels remain, including a very nice one with a Sukhothai walking Buddha and a *dhammachakka* in the background.

Besides the prang and the wiharn, the only original structures left are the remains of the monastery walls, but there is a peaceful, neglected atmosphere about the place.

Phitsanuloke is a good starting point for a tour of the north. Check out the markets by the river for bargains on upcountry craft.

Places to Stay & Eat

Near the railway station are several inexpensive hotels and places to eat. If you take a left out of the station and then your first right onto Sairuthat Rd you'll come to *Sombat Hotel* on the left side of the road. Clean rooms with shower are 70B with toilet down the hall or 80B with toilet. Further down towards the river are the *Sukkit* and the *Chokprasit*, not quite as good but similar rates.

On the next street south, Phayalithai Rd, are two old standbys, the *Haw Fa* and the *Unachak*. Both have adequate rooms with fan and bath for 80B up.

More expensive hotels include the *Thepnakhon* at 43/1 Sithamtripidok with AC rooms from 250B; the *Phailin* on Borom Trilokanat Rd, AC rooms from 600B and the *Amarin Nakhon* at 3/1 Chao Phraya Rd, AC rooms from 250B.

Excellent, low-priced Thai food can be had at the *Chuan Chim* (also called *Puun Sii*) restaurant across the street from the

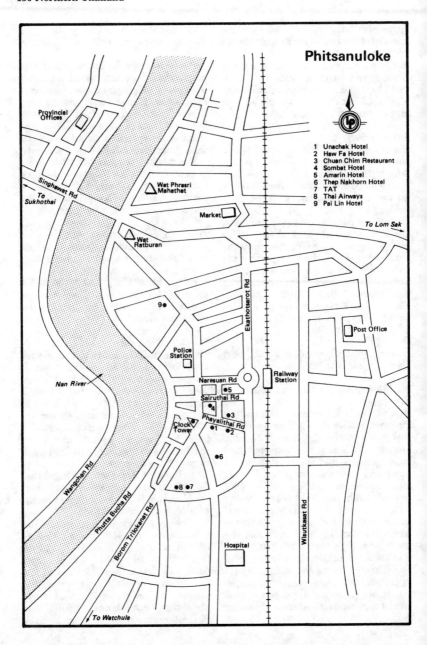

Phitsanuloke

1 Unachak Hotel
2 Haw Fa Hotel
3 Chuan Chim Restaurant
4 Sombat Hotel
5 Amarin Hotel
6 Thep Nakhorn Hotel
7 TAT
8 Thai Airways
9 Pai Lin Hotel

Haw Fa Hotel on Phayalithai Rd. There are plenty of other cheap Thai restaurants in this area as well. The markets along the Nan River have good food, particularly in the early mornings.

Getting There

Bus Ordinary buses leave for Phitsanuloke from Bangkok's Northern Bus Terminal at 8.10 am and 9.55 pm, arriving in seven hours, for 100B or 190B air-con. Buses to Khon Kaen are 34B. There are direct buses between Phitsanuloke and Loei via Dan Sai for 60B, the journey takes four hours.

Train The 3.45 pm Rapid (No 37) from Bangkok arrives in Phitsanuloke at 10.35 pm. Basic fare is 143B second class, 69B third class, plus 20B surcharge for Rapid service. If you're going straight on to Sukhothai from Phitsanuloke, the trishaw ride from the station to the bus station four km away is 15B. From there you can get a bus to Sukhothai. Or you can pick the bus up on Singhawat Rd, on the west side of the river, a 5B ride from the train station.

Air Thai Airways has a daily flight to Phitsanuloke which leaves Bangkok at 6.40 am and arrives at 7.15 am. On most other days of the week there is also a 4.10 pm flight that gets in at 4.45 pm. One-way fare is 630B if you fly on a Boeing 737 or 550B on a Shorts 330. Phitsanuloke's airport is just out of town, but *songthaews* come by every 20 minutes or so that go into town for 5B. The big hotels in town also run free buses from the airport.

SUKHOTHAI (population 22,000)
จังหวัดสุโขทัย

Thailand's first capital, Sukhothai, flourished from the mid-13th century to the late 14th century. The new town of Sukhothai, almost 450 km from Bangkok, is undistinguished except for its very good Municipal Market in the centre of town.

Old Sukhothai has quite an admirable spread of ruins 12 km outside of town, making an overnight stay in new Sukhothai worthwhile. The more remote ruins in the hills west of the old city walls (eg **Saphan Hin**) used to be considered a dangerous area, but since the UNESCO/Thai government development of the old city environs, all ruins are safe to visit with or without a guide. The Sukhothai ruins have been divided into five zones and there is a 20B admission fee into each zone.

Ramkhamhaeng National Museum

The museum provides a good starting point for an exploration of the ruins. Check the well-made miniature model of the old city and its environs for orientation and relative distances between sites. This will help in planning which sites to visit first and in what kind of order. A replica of the famous Ramkhamhaeng inscription is kept here amongst a good collection of Sukhothai artefacts. A guide to the ruins can be purchased here or at the entrance to the ruins of Wat Mahathat.

The museum is open 9 am to 12 noon and 1 pm to 4 pm, Wednesday to Sunday. Admission to the museum is 10B.

Sukhothai Historical Park

All of the ruins listed below are now part of the Sukhothai Historical Park.

Wat Mahathat The largest in the city, built in the 13th century. It is surrounded by brick walls (206 by 200 metres) and a moat. The spires feature the famous 'lotus-bud' motif of Sukhothai architecture. Some of the original stately Buddha figures still sit among the ruined columns of the old *wiharns*. There are 198 *chedis* within the monastery walls.

Wat Srisawai Just south of Wat Mahathat stands this 12th to 13th century shrine, featuring three corncob-like *prangs* and a picturesque moat. It was originally built by the Khmers as a Hindu temple.

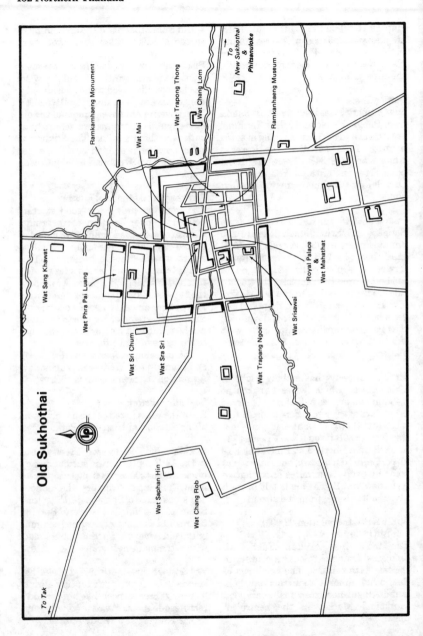

Wat Sra Sri This wat sits on an island west of the Ramkhamhaeng monument. It's a simple, classic Sukhothai style wat with one large Buddha, one *chedi* and the columns of the ruined *wiharn*.

Wat Trapang Thong Next to the museum, this small, still-inhabited wat is reached by a footbridge crossing the large lotus-filled pond which surrounds it. This reservoir, the original site of the Loy Krathong festival in Thailand, supplies the Sukhothai community with most of its water.

Wat Phra Pai Luang Outside the city walls to the north and somewhat isolated, this features three Khmer-style prangs, like at Srisawai but bigger, dating from the 12th century. This may have been the centre of Sukhothai when it was ruled by the Khmers of Angkor prior to the 13th century.

Wat Sri Chum This one is west of the old city and contains the impressive, much-photographed *mondop* with an 11-metre seated Buddha. A passage in the mondop wall leads to the top and Jataka inscriptions line the ceiling of the passageway – they can only be seen by candle or torch. A sign here warns you to report to the police before exploring remote ruins. A traveller reported that when he did this he got a police escort to some of the ruins and a ride on the back of the policeman's motorcycle.

Wat Chang Lom Off the main highway east of the old city, next to the 'Sukhothai Cultural Centre'. A large chedi here is 'supported' by 36 elephants sculpted into its base.

Wat Saphan Hin Saphan Hin is a couple of km to the west of the old city walls, on the crest of a hill that rises about 200 metres above the plain. The name of the wat, which means 'stone bridge', is a reference to the slate path/staircase leading to the temple, which is still in place. The site affords a good view of the Sukhothai ruins to the south-east and the mountains to the north and south. All that remains of the original temple are a few *chedis* and the ruined *wiharn* which has two rows of laterite columns flanking a 12.5-metre standing Buddha image on a brick terrace.

Wat Chang Rop Located on another hill west of the city, a bit south of Wat Saphan Hin. This site features an elephant-base stupa, much like Wat Chang Lom described above.

Places to Stay
There are five good hotels in Sukhothai:
Chinnawat (tel 311385) 1-3 Nikhorn Kasem Rd. Clean and comfortable rooms, friendly, helpful staff and a good restaurant downstairs. Rooms with fan and bath are 80B to 130B, depending on whether they are in the new or old wing – the old wing is cheaper and a bit quieter. There are air-con rooms available for 180B to 200B. They hand out an information sheet with bus schedules and maps of the new and old cities.
Kitimongkol (tel 611193) 43 Singhawat Rd. No complaints here either. Rooms are 80B up.
Sawatdipong (tel 611567) 56/2-5 Singhawat Rd. Across the street from the Kitimongkol and very similar in all respects, 100B up, including air-con 200B.
Sukhothai (tel 611133) 5/5 Singhawat Rd. A traveller's favourite with a decent restaurant and an informative staff. Lots of room to sit around downstairs. However LP has received one complaint regarding peepholes here. Fairly clean singles 60B, doubles 70B, air-con 160B to 200B.
River View A rather new hotel, across the street and down a bit from the Chinnawat Hotel on Nikhorn Kasem Rd, on the Yom River. Very clean rooms starting at 100B or 180B up for AC. Large lounge and restaurant downstairs.

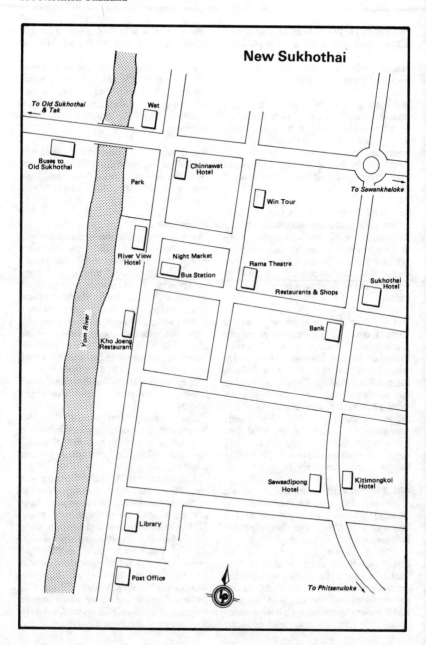

Places to Eat

The night market across from Win Tour and the municipal market near the town centre are good places to eat. Sukhothai Hotel and Chinnawat Hotel both have restaurants that try to prepare Thai and Chinese food oriented toward western tastes. The Chinnawat restaurant specialises in tasty bakery goods, fresh fruit and excellent steamed noodles and dumpling dishes like *kuaytiaw lawt* (wide stuffed rice noodles), *kuaytiaw laat naa thale* (seafood noodles) and *khanom jiip* (stuffed dumplings).

Nearby the Chinnawat and River View on Nikhorn Kasem Rd is the locally famous *Kho Joeng Hong* restaurant. This old, wooden Chinese restaurant serves delicious *pet phalo*, duck stewed in Chinese five-spice (star anise, coriander, ginger, etc) with boiled eggs, eaten with a sauce of vinegar, hot chillies and garlic. Equally tasty is the *kai phalo*, same as above with chicken instead of duck. Another popular dish here is *yam kraphaw plaa* or fish stomach salad. On the Chinnawat Hotel's map, this place is marked 'delicious ducks'.

In the Sukhothai Cultural Centre, near the old city, is the *Nam Kang Garden Restaurant*, a good outdoor Thai restaurant that looks expensive but is actually quite reasonable.

Getting There

From Phitsanuloke take a city bus (2B) to the *soon*, the 'centre', for buses out of town. If you're coming from the train station or airport you may have to take a minibus to a city bus at the market by the river, then a bus to the *soon*. The bus from the *soon* to Sukhothai is 14B, leaves regularly throughout the day, and takes about an hour. You could also catch this bus on the road to to Sukhothai out near the bridge over the Nan River, near Wat Mahathat.

Buses to Chiang Mai cost 72B, to Bangkok 90B or 165B air-con, to Chiang Rai 100B and to Khon Kaen 86B. The Chiang Rai bus now goes direct on a new road and takes about six hours. Buses to Sawankhaloke and Si Satchanalai leave regularly from the intersection across from the Sukhothai Hotel.

Getting Around

A *songthaew* to the old city *(muang kao)* from Sukhothai is 4B. It takes 20 minutes to half an hour. A *tuk-tuk* and driver can be hired for 20B to 50B an hour (depending on whether you hire them in town or at the old city) and this can save you much time and sore feet in touring the ruins. In addition, guides of varying ages and knowledge hang around hotels and markets in Sukhothai as well as around the ruins. If you have lots of time and stamina you can walk from site to site, though it might take two days to see it all.

Bicycles can be rented across from the National Museum in the old city for 20B a day. This is probably the best way to tour the ruins.

SI SATCHANALAI
อำเภอศรีสัชนาลัย

The Sukhothai period ruins in Si Satchanalai and Chaliang are in the same basic stylistic range as those in old Sukhothai, less well-cared for, but with some slightly larger sites. After getting off the bus at old Si Satch you'll have to follow the sign (in Thai and English) down a side road to the Yom River and cross by ferry near **Keng Luang** (Royal Rapids). The ruins are set among hills and are very picturesque, if somewhat neglected.

Sawankhaloke Pottery

Sukhothai was famous for its beautiful pottery much of which was exported. Particularly fine specimens can be seen in the National Museum in Jakarta, Indonesia as the Indonesians of the time were keen collectors. Much of the pottery was made in Si Satchanalai and rejects, buried in the fields, are still being found.

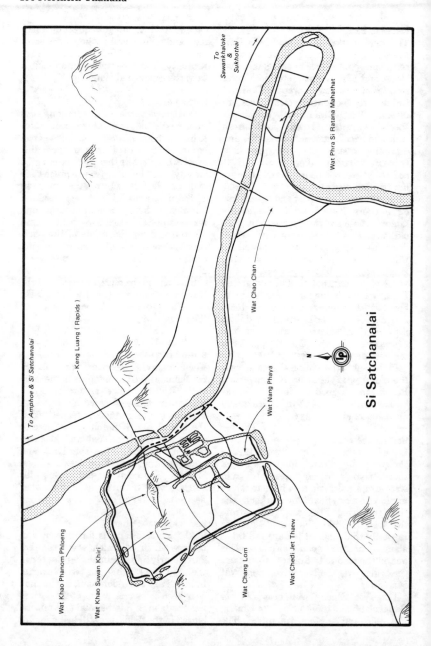

To Sawankhaloke & Sukhothai

Wat Phra Si Ratana Mahathat

To Amphoe & Si Satchanalai

Keng Luang (Rapids)

Wat Chao Chan

Wat Khao Phanom Phloeng

Wat Khao Suwan Khiri

Wat Nang Phaya

Wat Chang Lom

Wat Chedi Jet Thaew

N

Si Satchanalai

Shops have misfired, broken, warped and fused pieces at Sukhothai and Si Satchanalai. Thai Celadon in Chiang Mai is a modern interpretation of the old craft.

Wat Chang Lom

This is the first temple you'll come to after crossing the river. It has the same name and style as the one in Sukhothai – elephants surrounding a stupa – but somewhat better preserved.

Wat Khao Phanom Phloeng

On the hill overlooking Wat Chang Lom to the right are the remains of Wat Khao Phanom Phloeng – a large seated Buddha, a *chedi* and stone columns which once supported the roof of the *wiharn*. From this hill you can make out the general design of the once great city. The slightly higher hill west of Phanom Phloeng is capped by a large Sukhothai chedi, all that remains of **Wat Khao Suwan Khiri**.

Wat Chedi Jet Thaew

Next to Wat Chang Lom, these ruins contain seven rows of lotus-bud *chedis*, the largest of which is a copy of one at Wat Mahathat in old Sukhothai. There is also an interesting brick and plaster *wiharn* designed to look like a wooden structure (an ancient Indian technique used all over South-East Asia), with a *prasat* and chedi stacked on the roof.

Wat Nang Phaya

South of Wat Chang Lom and Wat Chedi Jet Thaew, this stupa is Sinhalese in style and was built in the 15th to 16th century, a bit later than other monuments at Si Satchanalai.

Places to Stay

In Sawankhaloke, the *Muang Indra* (tel 642722) at 21 Kasemrat Rd has rooms from 150B. Just outside Si Satchanalai is the *59 Bungalow* with similar rates.

Getting There

The Si Satchanalai ruins are off the road between new Si Satchanalai and Sawankhaloke. You can either take the Si Satch bus from Sawankhaloke all the way into the new city, and then hire a taxi or minibus back to the ruins, or ask to be let off the bus at the old city (*muang kao*), 12 km short of the new city. A bus from Sukhothai to Si Satchanalai will be about 16B.

CHALIANG

ชะเลียง

Two km back down Route 101 towards Sawankhaloke are the ruins of Wat Phra Si Ratana Mahathat and Wat Chao Chan. From the Si Satchanalai ruins, you can either walk there along a path following the left bank of the Yom River or cross the river again by ferry and follow the highway until you come to the turn-off on the right which crosses over a bridge to Chaliang. It's worth the walk – any *wat* called the Temple of the Great and Sacred Jewel Relic usually is.

Wat Phra Si Ratana Mahathat

These ruins consist of a large Sukhothai style *chedi* between two *wiharns*, one of which contains a large seated Sukhothai Buddha image, a smaller standing image and a bas-relief of the famous walking Buddha, so exemplary of the flowing 'boneless' Sukhothai style. The other wiharn contains less distinguished images.

Wat Chao Chan

These wat ruins are about 500 metres west of Wat Phra Si Ratana Mahathat. The central attraction here is a large Khmer style *prang* similar to later prangs in Lopburi, probably built during the Ayuthaya period. The prang has been restored and is in fairly good shape. The roofless *wiharn* on the right contains a large, ruined, standing Buddha.

TAK (population 20,000)
จังหวัดตาก

Tak, like Loei, Nan, Phetchabun, Krabi and certain other provinces, has traditionally been considered a 'remote' province, that is, one which the central Bangkok government has had little control over. In the '70s, the mountains of west Tak were a hotbed of Communist guerilla activity. Today, the former leader of the local CPT movement is involved in resort hotel development and Tak is open to outsiders, but the area still has an untamed feel about it.

Western Tak has always presented a distinct contrast with other parts of Thailand because of heavy Karenni and Burmese cultural influences. The Thai-Burmese border districts of Mae Ramat, Tha Song Yang and Mae Sot are dotted with Karen refugee camps, a recent development due to fighting between the Karen National Union and the Burmese government, which is driving Karenni civilians across the border. The main source of income for people living on both sides of the border is legal and illegal international trade. Black market dealings are estimated to account for at least 100 million baht per year in local income. The main smuggling gateways on the Thai side are Tha Song Yang, Mae Sarit, Mae Tan, Wangkha, Mae Sot and Waley. On the Burmese side, all of these gateways except Mae Sot are controlled by the KNU; only Myawaddy, across the Moei River from Mae Sot, is under full Burmese government control at this writing. One of the important contraband products is teak, which travels into Thailand from Burma on big tractor-trailers at night; around 125,000B in bribes per truckload is distributed among the local Thai authorities responsible for looking the other way.

The provincial capital of Tak itself is not very interesting except as a point from which to visit **Lang Sang National Park** to the west or **Phumiphon Yanhi Dam** to the north. Most of the province is in fact forested and mountainous so it is an excellent place for trekking; some organised trekking is going on in this area now – even out of Chiang Mai further north. There are Hmong (Meo), Musoe (Lahu), Lisu and White and Red Karen settlements throughout the west and north. A lot of Thais come to Tak to hunt, as the province is known for its abundance of wild animals, especially in the northern part of Tak province towards Mae Hong Son province. Much of the hunting is illegal, including tiger and elephant hunts in national wildlife preserves.

Places to Stay & Eat

Most of Tak's hotels are lined up on Mahat Thai Bamrung Rd in the centre of town. The biggest hotel in town is *Wiang Tak* (tel 511910) at 25/3 Mahat Tahi Bamrung Rd, with AC rooms from 410B.

Nearby on the same road, but less expensive, are the *Tak* (tel 511234), rooms with a fan and bath cost 90B up and the *Mae Ping* (tel 511807), with similar accommodation for 80B.

On the next street over is the *Sa-nguan Thai* (tel 511265) at 619 Taksin Rd. Rooms from 90B, restaurant downstairs.

Cheap food can be bought in the market across the street from the Mae Ping Hotel.

Getting There

Frequent buses go to Tak from Sukhothai for 20B. The trip takes about 50 minutes. Thai Airways flights are 700B from Bangkok.

The Tak bus station is just outside of town, but a motorised *samlor* will take you to the Tak Hotel (centre of town) for 10B.

MAE SOT
อำเภอแม่สอด

Several public billboards in Mae Sot carry the warning (in Thai): 'Have fun, but if you carry a gun, you go to jail', underscoring Mae Sot's reputation as a

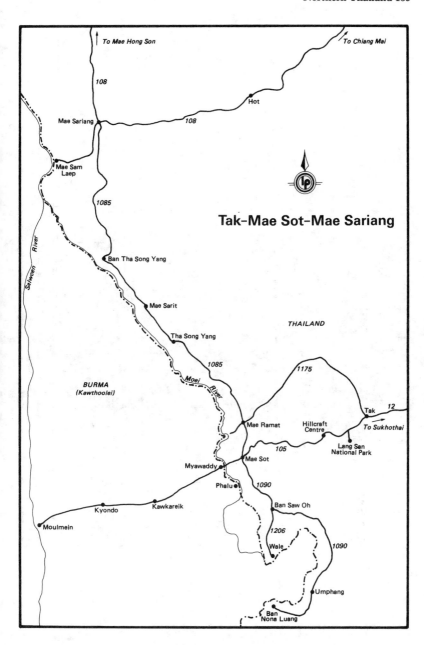

Tak-Mae Sot-Mae Sariang

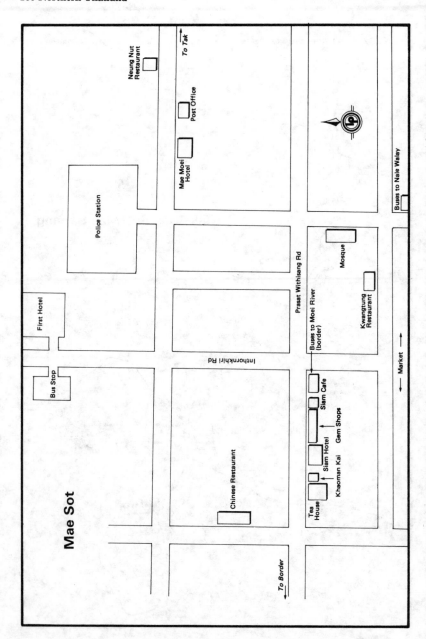

free-swinging, profiteering wild east town. Located 80 km from Tak city on the so-called Pan-Asian Highway (Asia Route 1, which would ostensibly link Istanbul and Singapore if only all the intervening countries allowed land crossings), Mae Sot is sort of a Burmese-Chinese-Karen-Thai trading outpost which is trying to become a tourist destination. Local opinion is divided on just how dangerous a town Mae Sot really is. Although a centralised Thai political presence dominates provincial politics, local economics is the sphere of a number of different factions that settle conflicts extra-legally, in some cases by violence. As elsewhere in Thailand where this situation exists, the local police are all powerful since they control the greatest number of armaments – business success often means cultivating 'special' connections with them. Outsiders face little danger as long as they stay out of the local trade in guns, narcotics, teak and gems.

The town itself is small but growing. Shop signs along the streets are in Thai, Burmese and Chinese; most of the local temple architecture is Burmese. The Burmese population in town is mostly Muslim, while the Karens are Christian. Walking down the streets of Mae Sot, you'll see an interesting mixture of ethnicity – Burmese men in their *longyis*, Hmong and Karen women in traditional hill tribe dress, bearded Indo-Burmese, Thai Army Rangers with M-16's and strings of opium poppies around their necks.

There are frequent *songthaews* out to the border, straight west from Mae Sot 16 km (5B); ask for *rim moei*, the Moei River bank. Here you can walk along the river and view the Socialist Republic of the Union of Burma's town, Myawaddy on the other side. Clearly visible are a school, Buddhist temple and compounds of thatched-roof houses. The border crossing here, which consists of a footbridge and a ferry service, has been closed since fighting broke out between the KNU and

the Burmese government in the early '80s. However, there is still a market legally selling Burmese goods on the Thai side, next to the river: dried fish and shrimp, dried bamboo shoots, mung beans, peanuts, woven straw products, teak carvings, lacquerware, jade and gems. Food is sold by the *pan*, that is, the pound, the Burmese/Karenni unit of weight measure, rather than by the kilogram, the usual measure in Thailand. Apparently, there are still some people crossing the border, as the Thai Immigration Office plainly entertains visitors from time to time.

Highway 1085 runs north out of Mae Sot towards Mae Hong Son province, stopping just 15 or so km from Mae Sariang. Soon, however, the Thai government will be completing a final section of highway that will make it possible to travel along the Burmese border from Mae Sot to Mae Sariang, passing through Mae Ramat, Mae Sarit, Tha Song Yang and Ban Sop Ngao. At this writing, you can only get public transport out of Mae Sot as far as Tha Song Yang.

Highway 1090 goes south from Mae Sot to Um Phang 150 km away. This road used to be called 'Death Highway' because of all the guerrilla activity in the area, which hindered highway development to say the least. Those days are past, but lives are still lost because of brake failure or treacherous turns on this steep, winding road which passes through incredible mountain scenery. Twenty six km from Mae Sot, route 1206 splits southwest off 1090 and terminates 15 km south at the border town of **Waley**, an important smuggling point. On the Burmese side is Phalu, one of the two major gateways to Kawthoolei, the Karenni nation, still under Karen control; since the Burmese began putting military pressure on the KNU (the other is Three Pagodas Pass, further south in Kanchanaburi province). Opium is cultivated extensively in this area. There are several daily *songthaews* to Waley from Mae Sot.

If you want to try to arrange a local hill trek out of Mae Sot, contact SP Tours (tel 531668) at 82/88 Asian Highway in town for information on local guides.

The village of **Mae Kit Saam Thaa**, 13 km north of Mae Sot, is a picturesque Thai village of peaceful corn-growers. The village temple abbot here is well known for his *metta* (loving-kindness) and the village seems to project a rural nirvana as you walk down its dirt roads. The Ban Ramat bus from Mae Sot stops here.

The big municipal market in Mae Sot, behind the Siam Hotel, sells a lot of interesting stuff, including Burmese clothing, Indian foods and cheap take-away eats.

Places to Stay & Eat

Best hotel in town at this writing is the *First*, on Inthornkhiri Rd, across from the Mae Sot bus station and behind the police station. Clean, comfortable rooms start at 140B with fan and bath or up to 300B AC. On the highway from Tak just before Mae Sot, the 120-room *Mae Sot Hills Hotel* is scheduled to open by the end of 1986 or early 1987. Rooms will go for 250B up, all air-con and the hotel will have a swimming pool.

For 100B, you can get an adequate room with bath at the *Siam Hotel* on Prasat Withithong Rd, Mae Sot's other main street. There are cheap restaurants and gem shops nearby.

Finally, there's the *Mae Moei Hotel* on the next street over, towards the east side of town near the post office. The adequate rooms in this old wooden hotel are 40B without bath and 50B with.

Outside of town towards Tak is *Thawiichailand*, a development of resort bungalows set off the highway and decorated with rather tasteless Thai and Chinese sculpture. The owner, Thawiichai, is a well-known right-winger and devotee of local-born Field Marshall Sarit (see History), a dictator who ruled Thailand on and off from 1951 to 1963. The centrepiece of the garden area is a statue

of the deceased Sarit. Bungalows here start at 300B but they don't seem to get a lot of business.

Still further afield is *Ban Ramat Village*, a jungle resort north of Mae Sot between the towns of Mae Ramat and Mae Sarit. Bungalows here start at a reasonable 100B per night and the staff arranges wildlife sighting for guests as this area is a natural habitat for wild deer, boar, tigers and other forest animals. Contact SP Tours or the Mae Sot Hills Hotel for more info.

In the vicinity of the Siam Hotel are several good places to eat. Just next door is a small *khao man kai* (chicken rice) place and next to that is a large tea house that serves exemplary *joke*, rice cingee with sliced ginger, as well as *pathongko*, fried Chinese pastries.

Down the road a bit from the Mae Moei Hotel is a nice garden restaurant called *Neung Nut*. The atmosphere is very pleasant, the service and food are of a high standard and the prices are quite reasonable. Especially good are the Thai *yam*s, very spicy meat or fish salads; try the *laap kai*, spicy chicken salad or the *yam plaa meuk*, squid salad. *Plaa bae sa*, whole fish steamed with Chinese plums, is also quite good here. The beer is ice-cold.

The best Chinese restaurant in town is the unassuming *Kwangtung*, which specialises in Cantonese cooking. It's located next to the big market which is on a sort of back street, behind the Siam Hotel.

For fried chicken, check out the many vendors in the market area.

Getting There

Buses to Mae Sot leave hourly from the Tak bus station from 6 am until 6 pm. Your choice of transport is AC minibus (*rot tuu*) for 25B or share taxi for 50B. The trip takes 1½ hours on a beautiful winding road through forested mountains and passes several hill-tribe villages.

Buses to Waley from Mae Sot depart

frequently from near the mosque. Buses to the Moei River (the border) leave from the corner of Prasat Withithong and Inthornkhiri Rds, next to the Siam Cafe (yellow awning).

By the time you read this, the road north to Mae Sariang should be finished and you should be able to get buses out of the Mae Sot bus station, if not all the way to Mae Sariang, at least to some point midway where you can pick up another bus.

UTTARADIT (population 33,000)
จังหวัดอุตรดิตถ์

You could continue north from Si Satchanalai and Sawankhaloke to Uttaradit on the railway line. The town is noted for fruit grown in the vicinity and the largest earth-filled dam in Thailand, the Sirikit Dam is 55 km away.

Places to Stay

Places to stay include *Pher Vanich 2* (tel 411499, 411749) by the river at 1 Sri Uttara Rd, within walking distance of the railway station. Rooms here are from 90B or from 200B with air-con. The *Uttaradit* at 24-28 Rasanarn Rd and the *Thanothai* at 149-153 Kasemraj are similarly priced.

Getting There

Buses from Bangkok cost 110B or 200B air-con.

LAMPANG (population 44,000)
จังหวัดลำปาง

One hundred km from Chiang Mai is the city of Lampang, which was inhabited as far back as 7th century Dvaravati and played an important part in the history of Haripunchai. Many rich Thais have retired here so the *wats* of Lampang are well endowed. Two typical, well cared for northern-style temples, **Wat Phra Saeng** and **Wat Phra Keo Don Tao** (which once housed the Emerald Buddha for 32 years) can be seen on opposite sides of the Wang River in the northern end of town.

Wat Phra That Lampang Luang
วัดพระธาตุลำปางหลวง

Out of town this is a fantastic walled temple originally constructed during the Haripunchai period (10th to 11th century) but restored in the 16th century. It is unique in overall design, inside and out.

Getting There To get to Wat Lampang Luang, you must catch a *songthaew* along Lampang's Praisani Rd to the small town of Koh Ka, about 20 km southwest of Lampang city. The fare should be about 10B.

Places to Stay & Eat

There are a couple of choices here. The *Asia Lampang* (tel 217844) at 229 Boonyawat Rd costs from 150B up for rooms with fan and bath or from 225B with air-con. *Sri Sanga* (tel 217070, 217811) at 213-15/1-5 Boonyawat Rd is cheaper from 70B.

Others include the *Aroon Sak* (tel 217344) at 90/9 Boonyawat Rd with rooms from 130B or 225B with air-con. The *Suan Dok* (tel 217588, 217721) at 168 on the same road is similarly priced. Right up at the top end the *Thipchang Garnet Lampang* (tel 218450, 218337) at 54/22 Tarkrao Noi Rd has air-con rooms from 300B and up.

There are several good foodstalls near the train station. The *Jamthewi* restaurant, across from the slaughterhouse, has northern specialities like *laap* and *naem* as well as fresh pig and calf brains, if you like that sort of thing.

Getting There

There is an 8.30 am and 1.30 pm bus to Lampang from Phitsanuloke's main bus station. From Chiang Mai, the best departure point for Lampang by bus is from the 'new' bus station just north of Chang Puak Gate. Fare is 25B.

The bus station in Lampang is some way out of town – 5B to 10B by *samlor* if you arrive late at night. You can get air-con buses to Bangkok or Chiang Mai from

Lampang. The air-con buses have offices in town, you don't have to go out to the bus station.

CHOM (JAWM) THONG – DOI INTHANON
อำเภอจอมทอง – คอยอินทนนท์

A nice day trip (or overnight, if you stay in Chom Thong or Hot, or continue on to Mae Sariang) can be made from Chiang Mai to Doi Inthanon via Chom Thong, or you could do this on the way to Mae Sariang.

Doi Inthanon & Waterfalls
Doi Inthanon is Thailand's highest peak (2595 metres) and there are three impressive waterfalls cascading down its slopes. Starting from the bottom, these are **Mae Klang Falls, Wachiratan Falls** and **Siriphum Falls**. The first two have picnic areas and food vendors. Mae Klang is the largest fall and easiest to get to, since you have to stop there anyway to get a bus to the top of Doi Inthanon. Mae Klang Falls can also be 'climbed' on near the top, as there is a footbridge leading to massive rock formations over which the water falls. Wachiratan is also very nice and less crowded.

The views from Inthanon are best in the cool-dry season of November to February. You can expect the air to be quite chilly towards the top – bring a jacket or sweater. Most of the year there is a constant mist around the topmost peak formed by the condensation of warm humid air from below. Along the 47 km road to the top are many terraced rice fields, tremendous valleys and a few small hill tribe villages. The entire mountain is a National Park, despite agriculture and human habitation.

Chom Thong
Chom Thong (pronounced *jawm thawng*) is another necessary stop between Chiang Mai and Doi Inthanon. If you have time, you might walk down Chom Thong's main street to **Wat Phra That Si Chom Thong**. The gilded Burmese *chedi* in the compound was built in 1451. The Burmese-style *bot*, built in 1516, is one of the most beautiful in northern Thailand. Inside and out it is an integrated work of art that deserves admiration and it is well-cared for by the local Thais. Fine wood carving can be seen along the eaves of the roof and inside on the ceiling, which is supported by massive teak columns. The impressive altar is designed like a small *prasat* and is said to contain a relic of the right side of the Buddha's skull. The abbot here is a very serene old guy, softly-spoken and radiant.

Behind the prasat-altar is a room containing religious antiques. More interesting is a glass case along one wall of the bot which contains ancient Thai weaponry – even if it is a little out of place in a wat.

Wat Phra Nawn Yai
วัดพระนอนใหญ่
About half-way between Chiang Mai and Chom Thong you may see Wat Phra Nawn Yai off to the side of the highway (on the right heading towards Chom Thong) with its distinctive Disney-like Buddha figures, standing, sitting, reclining and sculptured scenes from selected Jatakas. The statuary is incredibly garish and cartoon-like – watch for it.

Getting There
Buses to Chom Thong leave regularly from the Chiang Mai Gate, south moat in Chiang Mai. Some buses go directly to Mae Klang Falls, if you prefer, and some terminate in Hot, though the latter will let you off in Chom Thong. The fare to Chom Thong, 50 km away, is only 11B. From Chom Thong there are regular *songthaews* to Mae Klang, about five km north, for 3B. Songthaews from Mae Klang to Doi Inthanon leave about once an hour until late afternoon and cost 25B to 30B per person. Most of the passengers are locals who get off at various points along the road up, allowing a few stationary views of the valleys below.

For another 10B you can go from Chom Thong to Hot, where you can get buses on to Mae Sariang or Mae Hong Son. However, if you've gone to Doi Inthanon and the waterfalls, you probably won't have time to make it all the way to Mae Sariang or Mae Hong Son in one day, so you may want to overnight in Chom Thong. Ask at the wat for a place to sleep. There's probably a hotel somewhere in town.

MAE HONG SON (population 6000)
จังหวัดแม่ฮ่องสอน

This is 368 km by the southern road from Chiang Mai through Mae Sariang on Route 108, or 270 km by the northern road through Pai on Route 1095. Thailand's most north-western province is a real crossroads for hill tribes (mostly Karen, some Hmong, Lisu, Lahu), Burmese immigrants and opium traders living in and around the forested Pai River valley. As the province is so far from the influence of seawinds and is thickly forested and mountainous, the temperature seldom rises above 40°C, while in January the temperature can drop to 2°C. The air is often misty with ground fog in the winter and smoke from slash-and-burn agriculture in the hot season.

The provincial capital is still peaceful – boring to some – after all these years, despite daily flights from Chiang Mai. Climb the hill west of town called Doi Kong Mu (1500 metres) for a nice view of the valley from Burmese-built Wat Phra That Doi Kong Mu. A lot of Burma-watching journalists and hill tribe-watching linguists/anthropologists hang out in Mae Hong Son these days. Look for the khaki safari jackets.

In town there are a couple of semi-interesting Burmese-style wats, Wat Jong Kham and Wat Jong Klang, next to a large pond in the southern part of town. Jong Kham was built nearly two hundred years ago by Thai Yai or Shan people, who make up about 50% of the population of Mae Hong Son province. Jong Klang houses some 100-year-old glass paintings and wood carvings from Burma which depict the various lives of the Buddha, but you have to ask to see them as they are kept locked up.

Trekking out of Mae Hong Son can be arranged at either of the two guest houses in town. There is a nearby Karen village which can be visited without a guide by walking one or two hours outside of town. Raft trips on the Pai River to Pai and beyond are gaining in popularity, as are boat trips into the Karen state (or nation, depending on your political alliances) of Burma. The Pai River raft trips can be good if the raft holds up (it's not uncommon for them to fall apart and/or sink), but the Burma trip, which attracts travellers who want to see the Padaung or 'long-necked' people, is a bit of a rip-off, costing around 700B for a four-hour trip through unspectacular scenery to see maybe four Padaung people who are practically captives of the Karen operators involved. If you must do this trip, don't pay more than 350B to 400B

One of the best day trips you can do out of the provincial capital is to Mae Aw แม่แอ๋ว north of Mae Hong Son on a mountain peak at the Burmese border. A songthaew there costs 100B round-trip during the dry season or 200B in the rainy season and leaves from Singhanat Bamrung Rd near the telephone office – get there around 8 am. The trip takes two hours and passes Shan, Karen and Meo villages, the Pang Tong Summer Palace and waterfalls. Mae Aw itself is a settlement of Hmong (Meo) and KMT peoples, one of the last true KMT outposts in Thailand.

You can also walk from Mae Hong Son to Chiang Mai if you're up to it. A very high, steep, mountain path begins in the mountains on the southeast side of town; the trip is said to take seven days and is supposed to be pretty safe. There are only a few villages along the route, but the scenery is incredible. Food must be carried part of the way – a trek for the

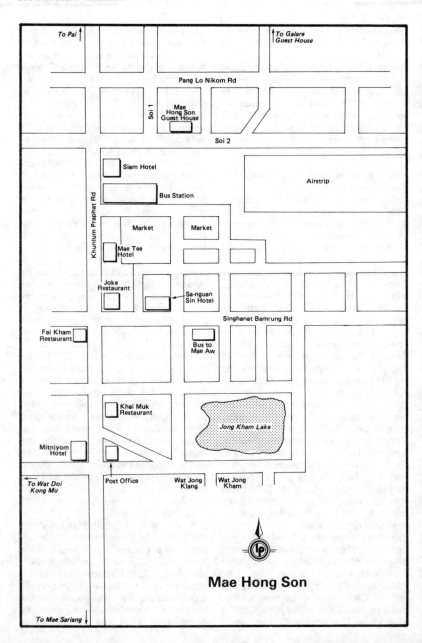

Mae Hong Son

hardy and experienced. Ask at the Mae Hong Son Guest House about details.

Mae Hong Son is best visited between November and March, when its beauty is at its peak. During the rainy season, June to October, travel in the province can be difficult because there are few paved roads. During the hot season the Pai valley fills with smoke from swidden agriculture. The only problem with going there in the cool season is that the nights are downright cold – you'll need at least one thick sweater and a good pair of socks for mornings and evenings and a sleeping bag or several blankets for sleeping. If you're caught short, you might consider buying a blanket in a market (the made-in-China acrylic blankets are cheap) and cutting a hole in the middle for use as a poncho.

Places to Stay & Eat

Most of the hotels in Mae Hong Son are along the main north-south street, Khunlum Praphat. The *Siam Hotel*, next to the bus station, has decent rooms for 100B up. Down the street are the *Methi (Mae Tee)* and the *Mitniyom*, both with very clean rooms from 100B. The Mae Tee also has AC rooms for 220B.

The *Sa-nguan Sin Hotel* on Singhanat Bamrung Rd, which runs east-west, is an old wooden hotel with fairly clean rooms for 50B shared bath, 70B with bath. Every room has two beds, which seems to be a tradition among old wooden hotels in the north.

There are two guest houses in town, the *Mae Hong Son Guest House*, on Khunlum Praphat Soi 2 and the *Garlare Guest House*, further north off Pang Lo Nikom Rd. Both advertise at the bus station, so you shouldn't have any trouble finding them. The Garlare Guest House is 50B per person while the Mae Hong Son is 30B per person in shared rooms. Both have very friendly staff; the Mae Hong Son is a particularly good source of information and has a little more atmosphere. Both serve food.

The *Khai Muk* and the *Fai Kham* are two of the better Thai-Chinese restaurants on Khunlum Praphat. There is also a *joke* (broken-rice soup) place that does 'American breakfasts' for 20B to 25B, near the Mae Tee Hotel.

The morning market behind the Mae Tee Hotel is a good place to pick up food for trekking. Get there before 8 am.

Getting There

From Chiang Mai you can either fly or take a bus to Mae Hong Son. The bus trip is rather gruelling over the northern route through Pai – probably the only reason to go this way is if you plan to stop over in Pai and/or Soppong. The southern route through Mae Sariang is much more manageable, not only because it's over paved roads but because the bus stops every two hours for a 10 to 15 minute break. Either way the trip takes eight to nine hours and costs 100B. The Pai road will probably be completely paved within the next couple of years.

The Pai bus leaves Chiang Mai (Arcade Bus Station) three times a day, at 8.30 am, 10.30 am and 2 pm. You must change buses in Pai. Departure times may change as the government paves more of the Chiang Mai-Pai-Mae Hong Son road. The Mae Sariang bus leaves the same station at 6.30 am, 8 am, 11 am, 8 pm and 9 pm.

Thai Airways flies to Mae Hong Son from Chiang Mai twice a day for 280B and the flight takes 35 minutes. From Bangkok it's 1240B and requires a change of plane in Chiang Mai. Two years ago flights to Mae Hong Son were once a day rather than twice; two years before that they were twice a week. Look for this town to change rapidly in the next few years.

A Hill Tribe Primer

The term 'hill tribe' refers to ethnic minorities living in the mountainous regions of north and west Thailand. Each hill tribe has its own language, customs, mode of dress and spiritual beliefs. Most are of semi-nomadic origins,

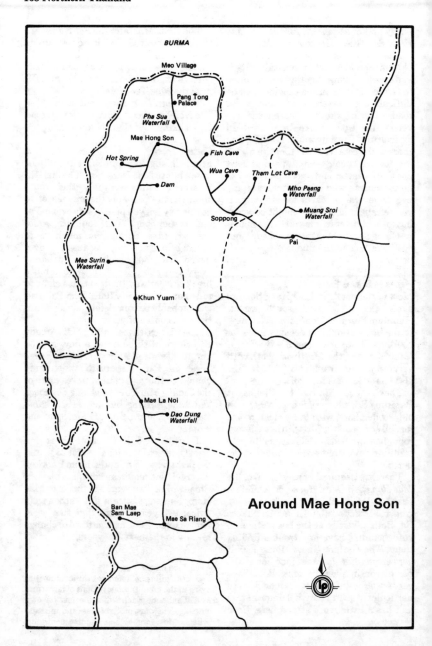

Around Mae Hong Son

having migrated to Thailand from Tibet, Burma, China and Laos during the last 200 years or so, although some groups may have been in Thailand much longer. They are 'fourth world' peoples in the sense that they belong neither to the major aligned powers nor to the third world nations – they have crossed and continue to cross national borders without regard for recent nationhood. Language and culture constitute the borders of their world as some groups are caught between the 6th and 20th centuries while others are gradually being assimilated into modern Thai life.

The Tribal Research Institute in Chiang Mai recognizes 10 different hill tribes but there may be up to 20 living in Thailand. The TRI's 1985 estimate of the total population was 457,234. The following descriptions cover the largest tribes and they are also the groups most likely to be encountered on hill-tribe treks. The comments on ethnic dress refer mostly to the female members of each group as hill-tribe men tend to dress like rural Thais.

The Shan (Thai *Thai Yai*) are not included here since they are not a hill tribe group per se; they live in permanent locations, practice Theravada Buddhism and speak a language very similar to Thai. Thai scholars, in fact consider them to have been the original inhabitants (*Thai Yai* means 'larger' or 'majority' Thais) of the area. Nevertheless, Shan villages are common stops on hill-tribe trekking itineraries.

Akha Thai – *I-kaw*
Origins: Tibet
Present day locations: Thailand, Laos, Burma, Yunnan
Economy: rice, corn, opium
Belief system: animism, with emphasis on ancestor worship
Distinctive characteristics: headresses of beads, feathers and dangling silver ornaments. Villages are located along mountain ridges or on steep slopes from 1000 to 1400 metres in altitude. The Akha are amongst the poorest of Thailand's ethnic minorities and tend to resist assimilation into the Thai mainstream. Like the Lahu, they often cultivate opium for their own consumption.

Karen Thai – *Yang* or *Kariang*
Origins: Burma
Present day locations: Thailand, Burma
Economy: rice, vegetables, livestock
Belief system: animism, Buddhism,

Christianity – depending on the group
Distinctive characteristics: Thickly woven V-neck tunics of various colours, (unmarried women wear white). Kinship is matrilineal and marriage is endogamous. They tend to live in lowland valleys.

There are four distinct Karen groups – the White Karen, Red Karen, Pa-o and Kayah. These groups combined are the largest hill tribe in Thailand, numbering nearly a quarter of a million or half of all hill tribe people. Many Karen continue to migrate into Thailand from Burma, fleeing Burmese government persecution.

Hmong Thai – *Meo* or *Maew*
Origins: south China
Present day locations: south China, Thailand, Laos, Vietnam
Economy: rice, opium
Belief system: animism
Distinctive characteristics: Simple black jackets and trousers with striped borders, silver jewellery. Most women wear their hair in a large bun on top of their head. They usually live on mountain peaks or plateaus. They are Thailand's second largest hill tribe group, especially numerous in Chiang Mai province.

Lahu Thai – *Musoe*
Origins: Tibet
Present day locations: south China, Thailand, Burma
Economy: rice, opium, corn
Belief system: 'theistic' animism, some groups are Christian
Distinctive characteristics: Black and red jackets with narrow skirts for women. They live in mountainous areas at about 1,000 metres. Their intricately woven *yaam*s or shoulder bags are prized by collectors.
There are four groups – Red Lahu, Black Lahu, Yellow Lahu and Lahu Sheleh.

Lisu Thai – *Lisaw*
Origins: Tibet
Present day locations: Thailand, Yunnan
Economy: rice, opium, corn, livestock
Belief system: animism with ancestor worship, spirit possession
Distinctive characteristics: Women wear long multi-coloured tunics over their trousers and sometimes black turbans with tassles. Men wear baggy green or blue pants pegged in at the ankles. They wear lots of bright colours. Premarital sex is said to be common, along

with freedom in choosing marital partners. Their villages are usually high in the mountains.

Mien Thai – *Yao*
Origins: central China
Present day locations: Thailand, south China, Laos, Burma, Vietnam
Economy: rice, opium, corn
Belief system: animism with ancestor worship and Taoism
Distinctive characteristics: Women wear black jackets and trousers decorated with intricately embroidered patches and red fur-like collars, along with large dark blue or black turbans. They have been heavily influenced by Chinese traditions – use Chinese characters to write Mien language. They tend to settle near mountain springs at 1000 to 1200 metres.

PAI
อำเภอปาย

At first it appears there's not a lot to see in Pai, a peaceful two-street town about halfway between Chiang Mai and Mae Hong Son on route 1095. But if you stick around a few days and talk to some of the locals, you may discover some beautiful out-of-town spots in the surrounding hills. At the Pai Guest House there is information on local trekking (there are several hill tribe villages nearby) and they even do some guided treks for about 100B per day.

Wat Phra That Mae Yen (or simply Wat Mae Yen) is a new temple built on a hill overlooking the valley with a good view. Walk one km east from the main intersection in town, across a stream and through a village, to get to the stairs which lead to the top – 353 steps. The monks here are vegetarian, uncommon in Thai Buddhist temples. Six km further down the same road is a waterfall.

Places to Stay
The *Pai Guest House* only has three rooms with two beds each, so they can't take a lot of people. It's back towards Chiang Mai, where the bus from Chiang Mai stops on the main street. Rates are

30B per person. Good place for info – part of an informal 'chain' of guest houses throughout the north, recognisable by the water buffalo skull hanging out the front. They're not actually owned by any one group but they all know each other.

More comfortable perhaps is the *Wiang Pai Hotel*, a traditional wooden hotel with 15 rooms a little further down the street in the same direction. Two can sleep in one bed for 50B, or 40B for one person alone. A two bed room is 80B.

There is another guest house (no name) at the end of the street in the Mae Hong Son direction, on the corner. A cinder block dorm with four beds is located behind the low-ceilinged restaurant; rates are 30B per person.

There are several fair restaurants near the no-name guest house, two of which serve *khao sawy*.

Getting There

From Chiang Mai you can either fly or take a bus to Mae Hong Son. The bus trip is rather grueling over the northern route through Pai – probably the only reason to go this way is if you plan to stop over in Pai and/or Soppong. The southern route through Mae Sariang is much more manageable, not only because it's over paved road but because the bus stops every two hours for a 10 to 15 minute break. Either way the trip takes eight to nine hours and costs 100B. The old Pai road, built by the Japanese in WW II, will probably be completely paved and restructured within the next couple of years.

SOPPONG

สบปอง

Soppong is a relatively prosperous Thai and Shan market village a couple of hours north-west of Pai and about 70 km from Mae Hong Son. Some of Mae Hong Son's most beautiful scenery is within a day's walk of Soppong, including **Tham Lot**, a large limestone cave with a stream running through it. It is possible to hike all the way through the cave by following the stream, though it requires some wading back and forth. Tham Lot is one of two local caves which happen to be the longest known caves in mainland South-East Asia, (though some as yet unexplored caves in south Thailand may be even longer) and there are many other caves in the area as well, some of which contain 2000-year old wooden coffins.

Accommodation is sparse in the Soppong area. The *Lisu Lodge*, a few km east of Soppong off Highway 1095 in Ban Namrin, is run by a very friendly and helpful Lisu family. A bed is 30B per night and large meals are 20B. The popular *Cave Lodge*, run by Diu, a former trekking guide who was very much in demand in Chiang Mai a few years ago, is quite near Tham Lot. Diu's Australian husband John is a mine of information on local hill tribes and caves. Follow signs in

Soppong to get to either of the guest houses, it's about an hour and a half walk to Ban Tham, the village closest to the Cave Lodge. Beds are 30B, meals 20B to 30B. Keep in mind that this area has only recently opened up to independent travel and can't really support great numbers of travellers.

Getting There

Pai-Mae Hong Son buses stop in Soppong – there are two or three each day in either direction. The bus trip between Pai and Soppong costs 20B and takes 1½ to two hours.

MAE SARIANG – KHUN YUAM

อำเภอแม่สะเรียง – อำเภอขุนยวม

Many of the hill-tribe settlements in Mae Hong Son province are concentrated in the districts of Khun Yuam, Mae La Noi and Mae Sariang, so these are good departure points for treks. Of these three small towns, Mae Sariang is the largest and offers the most facilities for use as a base. Nearby **Ban Mae Sam Laep**, straight west on the Burmese border, is easily reached by *songthaew* and from there one can hire boats for trips down the scenic Salween River.

There is little to see in Mae Sariang town itself besides the two Burmese/Shan temples – **Wat Jong Sung (Utthayarom)** and **Wat Si Boonruang** – just off Mae Sariang's main street, not far from the bus station and the hotel.

Places to Stay & Eat

Mae Sariang's one hotel is the *Mitaree*, near the bus station, with rooms from 80B. There is also a guest house near the bus station that charges 30B per person and organises treks. The *Inthara* restaurant, on the left as you enter town from Chiang Mai, serves what is considered some of Thailand's best *kai phat bai kaphrao*, chicken fried in holy basil and chillies. The Inthara is also well known for its batter-fried frogs.

In Khun Yuam, the *Mit Khun Yuam*

Hotel on the main street has rooms for 40B up.

Getting There

Buses to Mae Sariang leave Chiang Mai three times a day (see Mae Hong Son above for departure times) and cost 50B. To Khun Yuam it's 80B.

FANG - THA THON

ฝาง — ท่าถอน

The present city of Fang was founded by King Mengrai in the 13th century, though as a human settlement and trading centre the locale dates back at least 1000 years. There are Yao and Karen villages nearby which you can visit on your own but for most people, Fang is just a road marker on the way to Tha Thon. Tha Thon is the starting point for Kok River trips to Chiang Rai (and other points along the river between Tha Thon and Chiang Rai), and for guided or on-your-own treks to the many hill-tribe settlements in the region.

About 10 km west of Fang at Ban Muang Chom is a system of hot springs, near the Agricultural Station. Just ask for the *baw nam rawn* ('hot water springs'), *baw nam hawn* in northern Thai.

On the way north to Fang/Tha Thon, you can visit the **Chiang Dao** caves, five km off the road and 72 km north of Chiang Mai. Entrance into Tham Chiang Dao is 3B, the cave is said to extend some 10 to 14 km into Chiang Dao mountain but the lighting system only runs in about half a km or so.

Places to Stay

Places to stay in Fang include the *Fang* and *Si Sukit* hotels, for around 70B a room. Or you can stay near the pier in Tha Thon at *Phanga's House* or in the *Lisu Village* for 30B per person. Also in Tha Thon is *Thip's Travellers House* which has received favourable reports from travellers, doubles are 50B, singles 40B.

Getting There

Buses to Fang leave from the new bus station north of White Elephant (Chang Puak) Gate in Chiang Mai. The three-hour trip costs 32B by ordinary bus, 40B by minibus. If you stop at Chiang Dao the fare is 17B. From Fang a *songthaew* will take you to Tha Ton for 6B

RIVER TRIP TO CHIANG RAI

From Tha Ton you can get a boat to Chiang Rai down the Kok River; the trip takes at least five hours, leaves around noon and costs 160B per person or so, depending on the boat. You can also charter a boat, between eight or 10 people it works out at much the same cost per person but does give you more room. The trip is a bit of a tourist trap these days – the villages along the way sell coke and there are lots of TV aerials – but it's still fun. To catch a boat on the same day from Chiang Mai you'd have to leave by 7 am or 7.30 am at the latest and make no stops on the way. The 6 am bus is the best bet.

The travel time downriver depends to some extent on the river height. It usually takes three or four hours. You get an armed guard on the boat but he seems to spend most of the time asleep with his machine gun in a plastic sack. You could actually make this trip in a day from Chiang Mai, catching a bus back from Chiang Rai as soon as you arrive, but it's far better to stay in Fang or Tha Ton, then Chiang Rai or Chiang Saen and travelling on. You may sometimes have to get off and walk and it's also possible to make the trip (much more slowly) upriver, despite the rapids.

These days some travellers take the boat to Chiang Rai in two stages, stopping first in Mae Salak, a large Lahu village which is about a third of the distance. Boat fare to Mae Salak is 40B. From here they trek in the vicinity of the river to other Shan, Thai and hill tribe villages, or do longer treks south to Wawi, a large multi-ethnic community of Jiin Haw (Chinese refugees), Lahu, Lisu, Akha,

Shan, Karen, Yao and Thai peoples. In the Wawi area there are dozens of hill tribe villages of various ethnicities, including the largest Akha community in Thailand (Saen Charoen) and the oldest Lisu settlement (Doi Chang). If this kind of trip appeals to you, pick up the Wawi or Kok River trekking maps at DK Books in Chiang Mai, which marks trails and village locations.

Another alternative is to trek south from Mae Salak all the way to the town of Mae Suai, where you can catch a bus on to Chiang Rai or back to Chiang Mai.

CHIANG RAI (population 41,000)
จังหวัดเชียงราย

Just over 100 km from Chiang Mai, there's nothing really to see here unless you want to do a hill-tribe trek out of Chiang Rai – check with the Chiang Rai Guest House. The town is a bus junction for proceeding on to Mae Chan, Fang, Chiang Saen and Mae Sai.

Wat Phra Keo once housed the Emerald Buddha during its circuitous travels which eventually ended up at the wat of the same name in Bangkok. It now houses a replica of the Chiang Mai Wat Phra Singh Buddha image. Wat Jet Yot and Wat Klang Muang are other temples of interest in Chiang Rai.

Places to Stay

The Chiang Rai Guest House at 717/2 Srikerd Rd is the typical (in this case, the original) northern guest house with a water buffalo skull out front, although it's a bit run-down these days. Rooms are 50B or 30B per person. It's near the bus station but a bit away from everything else in Chiang Rai.

The Porn House at 503 Ratanaket Rd is better located and better value with clean rooms for 50B, also the food here is good.

Near the Kok River boat pier for boats from Tha Thon, at 445 Singhakai Rd is Mae Kok Villa which has dorm accommodation for 30B, single rooms for 40B,

doubles for 60B and a room with hot water bath for 120B single, 160B double.

Another nice place is Chat House at 1 Trailat Rd near the Kok River pier. It's an old Thai house with 50B rooms and a friendly staff.

Or there's the Rama Hotel (tel 311344) at 331/4 Traimit Rd, in the centre of town, a couple of blocks from the clock tower, next to Wat Moon Muang. The Rama has clean rooms from 180B or from 275B with air-con. Restaurants, night clubs and theatres are nearby.

On Suksathit Rd near the clock tower and district government building is the Chiang Rai Hotel (tel 311266). Rooms here cost from 80B with fan.

Another option is the tidy Sukniran (tel 311055) at 424/1 Banphaprakan Rd. It's between the clock tower and Wat Ming Muang, around the corner from the Chiang Rai Hotel, rooms from 140B up.

Similar to the Sukniran but cheaper is the Siam at 531/6-8 Banphaprakan, rates from 110B.

Four people can get a room with bath for 200B at the Ruang Nakhorn, 25 Ruang Nakhorn Rd, near the hospital. Bungalows here are 120B, doubles 180B and AC from 220B.

If you favour the old Thai-Chinese type of hotel, check out the Areepracharat at 541 Phahonyothin, 80B up, or the Paowattana at 150 Thanarai Rd, with 50B rooms.

Near the top of the Chiang Rai price scale is the Wiang Inn (tel 311543) at 893 Phahonyothin Rd with rooms, all air-con, from 350B, a swimming pool and other luxuries. Chiang Rai's newest hotel, the Wiang Come, in the Chiang Rai Trade Centre (tel 311800, 869/90 Pemawibhata Rd) is an international class hotel with AC rooms from 500B to 800B, there's a television and refrigerator in every room.

Just outside of town at 330 Soi 18 Mithuna, Phahonyothin Rd, is a private house called Ban Thai, owned by a friendly Thai woman who teaches English and who takes farang guests.

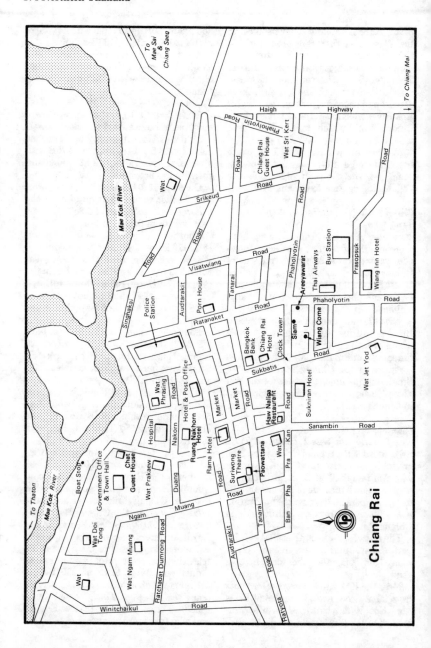

Places to Eat

There are plenty of restaurants in Chiang Rai, especially along Trairat Rd. Near the bus station are the usual food stalls, cheap and tasty.

Haw Naliga or the 'clock tower' restaurant has good Thai-Chinese food at reasonable prices. The locals say you haven't been to Chiang Rai if you haven't eaten at this place (near the clock tower in the centre of the city on Banphaprakan Rd). Especially good are the baked and steamed dishes *pla neua awn pae sa*, moist and tender whole butterfish steamed in a spicy-sour broth with mushrooms, *tao hu maw din*, bean curd stew baked in a clay pot and *pla nin thawt krathiam phrik Thai*, blue 'Nile' fish fried in garlic and black pepper. They've recently opened an outdoor garden section.

Large open-air restaurants on either side of Phahonyothin Rd near the Areepracharat Hotel make especially good rice dishes for 10B – one is open days, the other nights.

Getting There

Bus Buses to Chiang Rai can be boarded at two places in Chiang Mai: the bus stop on Lamphun Rd, down a few metres from the Lamphun bus stop near Nawarat Bridge; and the new Bus Station No 2 (*Baw Kaw Saw*) out on the 'superhighway', north-east of the city. To get to the latter, take a city bus No 3 or No 4.

There are two different bus routes to Chiang Rai from Chiang Mai – the 'old route' and the 'new route'. The old route (Thai: *sai kao*) heads south from Chiang Mai to Lampang before heading north through Ngao, Phayao, Mae Chai and finally Chiang Rai. If you want to stop off in any of these cities, this is the bus to take; if not, you can count on the trip taking up to nine hours. This bus leaves from the station near the Nawarat Bridge.

The new route (*sai mai*) heads north-east along Route 1019 to Chiang Rai, stopping in Doi Saket and Wiang Papao.

This one takes about four hours. The fare to Chiang Rai is 47B ordinary, 66B air-con. New-route buses as well as the more expensive AC buses leave from Bus Station No 2. Chiang Mai-Chiang Rai buses are sometimes stopped by the police for drug searches.

Air Thai Airways has daily flights to Chiang Rai from Chiang Mai International Airport at 8.50 am and 1.15 pm. The flight takes 40 minutes and cost 270B.

Boat One of the most popular ways of getting to Chiang Rai is the river trip from Tha Thon, see River Trip to Chiang Rai for details.

CHIANG KHONG

อำเภอเชียงของ

Across the river from Ban Houei Sai in Laos, this was the place where you began or finished the old 'Laotian Loop'. There's no real reason to go there now but there are a number of cheap hotels along the main street.

CHIANG SAEN – SOP RUAK

เชียงแสน — สบรวก

Just over 30 km from Chiang Rai, Chiang Saen is a wonderful little one-street town on the banks of the Maekhong (Mekong) River. The ruins of numerous temples from the Chiang Saen kingdom; stupas, images of the Buddha, earthen ramparts and a small museum are there to be admired. The museum is open from 9 am to 12 noon and 1 pm to 4 pm, closed on Mondays and Tuesdays. Entry is 2B on weekends, free on other days. The archaeological station behind the museum has a large detailed wall map of Chiang Saen and the surrounding area. Some of the villagers, Lao immigrants, speak French.

The Laotian side of the mighty Maekhong looks deserted but Lao boats flying Pathet Lao flags do occasionally float by. Hill-tribe crafts can be bought at

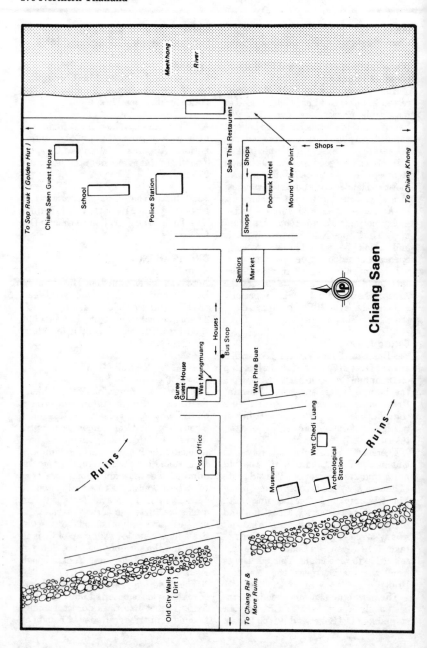

Top: Wat Maha That, Sukhothai (DC)
Left: Wat Sri Chum, Sukhothai (BP)
Right: Sukhothai (DC)

Top: Sculpture at Phutthamamakasamakhom, Nong Khai (JC)
Bottom: Farang monks on alms round, Wat Ba Nanachat (JC)

the Chiang Saen Guest House which is along the river a few hundred metres up from the police station.

Further north, 11 km up the road which runs alongside the river, is **Sop Ruak**, the official apex of the Golden Triangle. This is where the borders of Burma, Thailand and Laos meet, at the confluence of the Sop Ruak River and the Maekhong.

A good way to see the Golden Triangle area is by motorcycle and they can be rented either in Chiang Saen or in Mae Sai. There is a better choice of machines in Mae Sai, but either town could serve as a base for covering the territory.

Places to Stay

Sop Ruak There are now a couple of places to stay for the traveller who makes it this far. In Sop Ruak there is the isolated *Golden Hut*, your typical tropical bungalow but a bit run-down. Rates are 30B to 40B. Also in Sop Ruak is the relatively new *Golden Triangle Guest House* with clean bungalows overlooking the Maekhong. It has electricity, good swimming, is well run and costs 40B per bed or 60B per bungalow.

Chiang Saen If you aren't able to get to Sop Ruak, there is the *Chiang Saen Guest House* in Chiang Saen, on the road to Sop Ruak. Chiang Saen Guest House and the Golden Hut are run by the same family and have similar rates, though the man who runs the guest house is known to be a bit moody. Bicycles can be rented at the Chiang Saen Guest House for 25B per day and you can make some interesting bike trips in the vicinity; they also have a couple of beaten-up motorcycles for rent. Both sell Burmese and Laotian handicrafts.

Also in town is the *Suree Guest House*, about 100 metres off the main road in Chiang Saen near Wat Mungmuang. A big house run by friendly folks, 40B per person.

If these two are full, the only other choice is the *Poonsuk Hotel*, a bright blue ramshackle building near the end of Chiang Saen's main street, towards the river. A double is 40B to 70B and mosquito nets are provided. Hill tribes passing through Chiang Saen sometimes stay at this hotel, as well as Laotian refugees, so staying here can be an interesting experience.

Another interesting place to stay is the *Thammachat Village Centre* in the Si Don Mun district between Chiang Saen and Mae Sai. This place is within walking distance of Yao and Akha villages, for do-it-yourself trekkers. Accommodation is provided for 30B per person and food is also available – the kitchen specialises in northern Thai dishes. To get there you'll have to take a *tuk-tuk* from Mae Sai or Chiang Saen; ask for Si Don Mun. The address is 166 Ban Wiang Keo, Si Don Mun, Chiang Saen.

There are a few small restaurants in Chiang Saen and a very good garden restaurant outside of town five km towards Mae Chan – the *Yonok*. It's 1.3 km off the highway next to Chiang Saen Lake. They specialise in fresh water seafood – try the *plaa nin thawt*, fresh fried Nile fish. No English menu, so bring your eating guide if your Thai isn't up to it.

Getting There

There are frequent buses from Chiang Rai to Chiang Saen for 15B, the trip takes about 40 minutes to 1½ hours. On to Sop Ruak a share-taxi costs 10B and they leave several times a day. One bus a day goes to Sop Ruak. It leaves in the early morning from the Chiang Saen bus stop. You can also hitch-hike from the front of the Sala Thai Restaurant or you can get there by hiring a long-tail boat.

Returning from Chiang Saen, don't take a Chiang Mai bus (out of Chiang Saen directly) unless you want to travel along the old road, which means passing through Pham, Payao, Ngao, Lampang and Lamphun before arriving in Chiang Mai, a nine-hour trip. First go to Chiang

Rai (on a Chiang Rai bus of course) then changing to a Chiang Mai bus which goes along the new road (*sai mai*) makes for a trip of about 4½ hours.

MAE SAI
อำเภอแม่สาย

The northernmost point in Thailand. This is a good place from which to explore the Golden Triangle, Doi Tung and Mae Salong – also to observe border life – as Mae Sai is the only official land crossing open between Burma and Thailand. At this writing, only Burmese and Thai nationals are allowed to cross the bridge which spans the Sai River border though there is talk of letting foreigners cross over for the day at some point in the future. Burmese lacquerware, gems, jade and other stuff from Laos and Burma are sold in shops along the main street, though the trade is mainly a tourist scene nowadays.

Many Burmese come over during the daytime from Tachilek to work or do business locally, hurrying back by sunset. Take the steps up the hill near the border to Wat Phra Thai Doi Wao west of the main street for superb views over Burma and Mae Sai. There are also some interesting trails in the cliffs and hills over-looking the Mae Sai Guest House and the river.

Wat Tham Pha Jom
วัดถ้ำผาจอม

South of Mae Sai a few km, just off Highway 110, in the village of **Ban Tham**, is a cave wat called Wat Tham Pha Jom. Bring a flashlight if you want to explore the cave as there are no lights. The real attraction here though, is the very unique Khmer-style *chedi* in front of the cave entrance, a very large, multi-tiered structure that is unlike any other chedi in Thailand.

Doi Tung
ดอยตุง

About halfway between Mae Chan and Mae Sai on Highway 110 is the turn-off west for Doi Tung. Highway 1149 is mostly paved all the way to the peak of Doi Tung, but the road is winding, steep, and narrow: if you're riding a motorcycle, take it slowly. Along the way are Shan, Akha and Musoe (Lahu) villages. Opium is cultivated in the vicinity of Doi Tung and is readily available in nearby Akha villages. Burma is a short trek from the peak and many travellers have crossed over to view the very large poppy fields guarded by hill tribespeople and KMT refugees. It is probably not safe to trek in this area without a Thai or hill tribe guide simply because you may be mistaken for a USDEA agent (by the opium traders) or drug dealer (by the Thai Army Rangers, who patrol the area). In fact, you may hear gunfire from time to time – Rangers in pursuit of SUA, Karen rebels and others caught between two hostile governments.

At the peak, 1512 metres above sea level, is **Wat Phra That Doi Tung**, which is nothing special as wats go but you can't beat the setting. From here you can get an aerial view of the snaky road you have just climbed.

Places to Stay

The *Mae Sai Guest House* is often full due to its scenic and restful location right on the river across from Burma. It's about a km walk from the end of Mae Sai's main road and thus very quiet. Bungalows are 40B single, 60B double and there is a good restaurant. They also rent motorcycles and arrange treks. The only drawback to staying here is that it's a long dark walk into town if you want to eat out or see a movie in the evening.

Nearly as good is *Chad Guest House*, off the street near the town entrance. The family that runs the place is very friendly and helpful, also the food here is particularly good. There is a garden with tables for evening repasts and a talking *nok wiang phao* bird from Burma that speaks Shan dialect. They also rent motorcycles. Rates are 30B per person in shared rooms.

There are a couple of hotels in town as well, the *Top North Hotel* on Phahonyothin Rd (the main road) with rooms at 70B single, 100B double and the *Mae Sai Hotel*, off Phahonyothin on the other side, same price. The Top North is cleaner but the Mae Sai is somewhat quieter. There's also the *Northern Guest House* at 40B per night.

Out on Highway 1149, the road to Doi Tung, is the *Akha Guest House*, which is located in the Akha village of **Ban Pakha**. This is the place to stay if you want to trek in the Doi Tung area. There is no electricity or running water here and the food is not that good, but there are nice views and two grades of opium. Bungalows are 50B per night. Guides hire out for as little as 50B per person for a day trek. About three or four hours walk south-west of Ban Pakha is the *Chiang Rai Mountain Guest House* on the Mae Kham River near Samakhee Mai village. From here you could trek on to Mae Salong.

Getting There
Buses to Mae Sai leave frequently from Chiang Rai for 15B, the trip takes 1½ hours. You can also bus to Mae Sai from Chiang Saen for 14B.

Buses to the turnoff for Doi Tung are 7B from either Mae Chan or Mae Sai. From Ban Huai Khrai, the village at this intersection, a *songthaew* is 10B to the Akha Guest House or 30B all the way to Doi Tung, 18 km from Ban Huai Khrai.

MAE SALONG (SANTIKHIRI)
แมสะลอง (สันติคีรี)
The village of Mae Salong was originally settled by the renegade Kuomintang 93rd Regiment, who fled to Burma from China after the Chinese 1949 revolution. They were again forced to flee in 1961 when the Burmese government decided they wouldn't allow the KMT to remain legally in northern Burma (some still hide out in the hills). Ever since the Thai

government granted them refugee status in the '60s, the Thais have been trying to incorporate the Yunnanese KMT and their families into the Thai nation. Before now they weren't having much success, as the KMT persisted in involving themselves in the Golden Triangle opium trade, along with opium warlord Khun Sa and the Shan United Army (SUA). Thereby ignoring attempts by Thai authorities to suppress opium activity and tame the area. The area is very mountainous and there are few paved roads, so the outside world has always been somewhat cut off from the goings-on in Mae Salong. Khun Sa, in fact, made his home in nearby Ban Hin Taek (now Ban Thoet Thai) until the early '80s, when he was finally routed out by the Thai military. Khun Sa's retreat to Burma seemed to signal a change in local attitudes and the Thai government finally began making progress in the 'pacification' of Mae Salong and the surrounding area. For more detailed information see the section 'Opium & the Golden Triangle' in Facts about the Country.

The Thai government has officially changed the name of the village from Mae Salong to Santikhiri meaning 'Hill of Peace'. The 36-km road has been paved from Basang, near Mae Chan, to Santikhiri, (before it was paved, pack horses were used to move goods up the mountain to Mae Salong), and a Thai language elementary school has been established. There are also evening classes for adults in Thai language. Most of the people in the area still speak Yunnanese, except of course for the local hill tribes, who are mainly Akha and speak hill tribe dialects. Like other villages throughout rural Thailand undergoing similar pacification programmes, Mae Salong or Santikhiri is wired with a loudspeaker system that broadcasts official programming in the streets starting at 6 am. A sign in Thai near the local police headquarters reads:

Don't pull the sky down;
Don't break rocks;
Don't divide the land.

What this admonition means is not altogether clear, but the second line, *yaa tham hin taek*, seems to be an overt reference to Ban Hin Taek ('broken-rock village'), Khun Sa's former head-quarters, while the last is perhaps a plea for Thai nationalism. The locals are reluctant to speak of their KMT past and in fact, deny that there are any KMT regulars left in the area. To the Thais, they are simply the *Jiin haw* or 'galloping Chinese', a reference either to their use of horses or their migratory status.

One of the most important local government programmes is the crop substitution plan to encourage local hill tribes to cultivate tea, coffee, corn and fruit trees. This seems to be somewhat successful, as there are plenty of these products for sale in the town markets and tea and corn are abundant in the surrounding fields. There is a tea factory in town where you can taste the fragrant Mae Salong teas (originally from Taiwan), and there are many fruit wines and liquors for sale in the markets. The local illicit corn whiskey is much in demand – perhaps an all too obvious substitution for the poppy.

Another current local specialty is Chinese herbs, particularly the kind that are mixed with liquor, called *yaa dong* in Thai. Thai and Chinese tourists who come to Mae Salong always take back a bag or two of assorted Chinese herbs.

Mae Salong/Santikhiri is unlike any other town in Thailand; the combination of pack horses, hill tribes (Akha, Lisu, Mien, Yao) and southern Chinese style houses conjures up the picture of a small town or village in Yunnan province in China.

It is possible to walk south from Mae Salong to Chiang Rai, following trails which pass through hill tribe villages in three or four days.

Places to Stay & Eat

The *Mae Salong Guest House* is at the high end of town and the couple who run it are very friendly. Clean rooms are 50B without a bath for one bed, 70B for the same with two beds and 100B for a room with bath, single or double. Good Yunnanese food is served here and they also sell several varieties of local fruit spirits, Mae Salong tea and Chinese herbal medicines. The owners can arrange treks on horse-back for 100B per person per day or advise you on making treks on your own.

Then there is the *Chin Sae Hotel*, Mae Salong's original hotel, a wooden Chinese affair around the corner from the guest house, where rooms are 50B. Top end is the *Sakura Resort* above the town with rooms in the 200B to 300B range.

For eating, don't miss the many street noodle vendors who sell *khanom jiin nam ngiaw*, a delicious Yunnanese rice noodle concoction topped with spicy chicken curry, Mae Salong's most famous local dish. A gourmet bargain at 5B per bowl.

Getting There

To get to Mae Salong by public transport, you have to take a bus from Mae Sai or Chiang Rai to Ban Basang บ้านป่าซาง , which is about two km north of Mae Chan. From Ban Basang, there are *songthaews* to Mae Salong (Santikhiri) for 40B per person up the mountain; from Mae Salong back down the mountain it's 30B. The trip takes about an hour.

Bus fare from Chiang Rai to Ban Basang is 10B.

NAN (population 23,000)
น่าน

Just over 340 km from Chiang Mai and 295 km from Sukhothai, the main attraction to Nan is getting there. Nan, one of Thailand's 'remote provinces' (an official Thai government designation), was formerly so choked with bandits and PLAT insurgents that travellers were

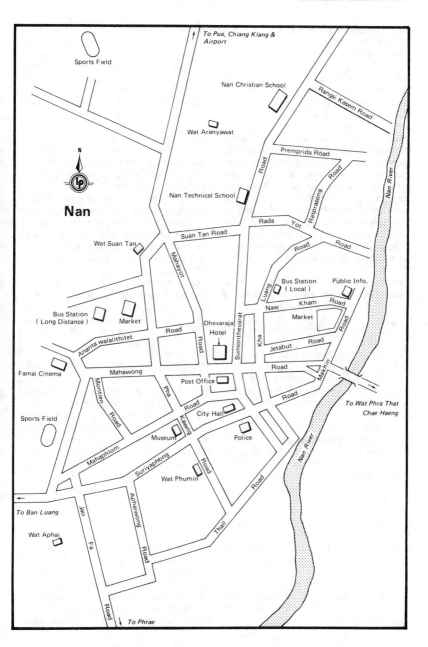

discouraged from going there. The Thai government couldn't get any roads built in the province because guerrillas would periodically destroy highway department equipment at night.

With the successes of the Thai army and a slightly more stable political machine in Bangkok during the last few years, Nan has been opening up and more roads are being built. The roads that link the provincial capital with the nearby provinces of Chiang Rai, Phrae, Uttaradit, etc, pass through exquisite scenery of rich river valleys and rice fields. Like Loei province in the north-east, this is a province to be explored for its natural beauty and likeable people – people living close to traditional rural rhythms.

There are a couple of historic temples to see in *amphoe muang* Nan.

Wat Phumin

Near the municipal buildings off Suriyaphong Rd, the *bot*, like many northern temples, was built in 1496 on a cruciform plan with carved doors and ceilings. The altar in the centre has four sides with Sukhothai-style sitting Buddhas in *marawichai* ('victory over Mara', one hand touching the ground) poses facing each direction.

Wat Phra That Chae Haeng

Two km past the bridge which spans the Nan River, heading west out of town. A very old temple, dating from 1355, Wat Phra That is the most sacred wat in Nan province. It is set on a hill with a view of Nan and the valley. The bot features a five-level roof with carved wooden eaves. A gilded Lao-style chedi sits on a large square base; each side is 22.5 metres long and the entire chedi is 55.5 metres high.

Boat Races

During *thawt kathin*, mid-October to

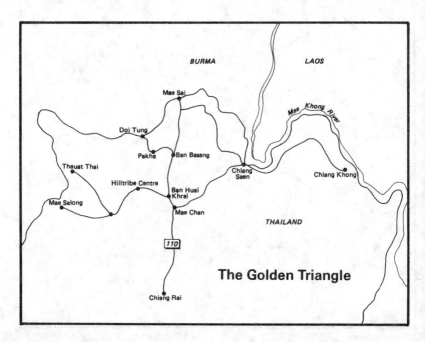

The Golden Triangle

mid-November, the city of Nan holds boat races (*khaeng reua*) on the river. The all-wooden 30-metre-long boats display sculpted *naga* heads and tails and hold up to 50 rowers.

Places to Stay

If you want to stay in Nan you could try the basic *Amorn Si* at 97 Mahayot Rd or the *Nan Fah* (tel 710284) at 438-440 Samundhevaraj, both with rooms at around 80B. The *Sukkasem* (tel 710141) at 29/31 Anantavoraritdet Rd is more expensive with rooms from 100B or 160B with air-con.

The *Dhevaraj Hotel* (tel 710094) at 466 Sumonthewarat Rd has rooms with fan and bath from 160B or from 250B with AC.

Getting There

Bus At the present time, buses run from Chiang Mai and Sukhothai to Nan. In the near future there should also be buses from Chiang Rai – ask at the Chiang Rai bus station. The fare from either Chiang Mai or Sukhothai should be about 60B and the trip takes nine hours. Eventually you should be able to bus from Nan to Nakhon Thai and connect with the Phitsanuloke-Loei route.

Air You can also fly to Nan from Chiang Mai, Chiang Rai or Phitsanuloke, though all flights require connections in other northern cities. Fares are 330B from Chiang Mai, 370B from Chiang Rai and 380B from Phitsanuloke.

In many ways the north-eastern region of Thailand is the Kingdom's 'heart-land'. The older Thai customs remain more intact here than elsewhere in the country; partly as a function of the general non-development of the area, the north-east has hosted less tourism. Sites of historical and archaeological significance abound in the north-east, several of which have been restored or excavated recently, so that visitors are finally beginning to 'discover' north-eastern travel. The pace here is slower, the people friendlier and inflation less effective in the provinces, known collectively as *Isaan*, than in Thailand's other major regions.

The term *Isaan* is also used to classify the local people (*khon isaan*) and the local food (*aahaan isaan*). It comes from the Sanskrit name for the Mon-Khmer kingdom Isana, which flourished in the area of (what is now) north-eastern Thailand and pre-Angkor Kampuchea. A mixture of Lao and Khmer influence is a mark of Isaan culture and language. The Khmers have left behind several Angkor Wat-like monuments near Surin, Khorat, Buriram and other north-eastern towns. Near the Maekhong River/Lao border in the town of That Phanom is the famous Lao-style temple Wat That Phanom. Many of the people living in this area speak Lao or a Thai dialect which is very close to Lao.

Isaan food is famous for its pungency and choice of ingredients. Well-known dishes include *kai yang*, roast spiced chicken and *som tam*, a spicy salad made with grated unripe papaya, lime juice, garlic, fish sauce and fresh hot pepper. North-easterners eat glutinous rice with their meals, rolling the almost translucent grains into balls with the hands.

The music of the north-east is also highly distinctive in its folk tradition, using instruments like the *khaen*, a reed instrument with two long rows of bamboo pipes strung together, the *pong lang*, a xylophone-like instrument made of short wooden logs and the *pin*, a small three-stringed lute of sorts played with a large plectrum. The most popular song forms are of the *luuk tung* ('children of the fields') type, a very rhythmic style in comparison to the classical music of central Thailand.

The best silk in Thailand is said to come from the north-east, around Khorat (Nakhon Ratchasima) and Roi Et. A visit to north-eastern silk-weaving towns can produce bargains as well as an education in Thai weaving techniques for those interested.

For real antiquity, Udorn province offers prehistoric cave drawings at Ban Phu, north of Udorn Thani and the recently discovered ancient ceramic and bronze culture at Ban Chiang to the east. This latter site, excavated by the late Chester Gorman and his team of University of Pennsylvania anthropologists, may prove to be the remains of the world's oldest agricultural society and first bronze metallurgy, predating developments in the Tigris-Euphrates valley and in China by centuries.

Main transportation lines (train and bus) in the north-east are along the routes between Bangkok and Nong Khai and between Bangkok and Ubon Ratchathani. The north-east can also be reached from north Thailand by bus or plane from Phitsanuloke, with Khon Kaen as the 'gateway', as travel agents put it.

If you proceed to the north-east from Bangkok, the first principal stop should be Khorat.

NAKHORN RATCHASIMA (KHORAT)
จังหวัดนครราชสีมา
(population 89,000)
Exactly 250 km from Bangkok, this town

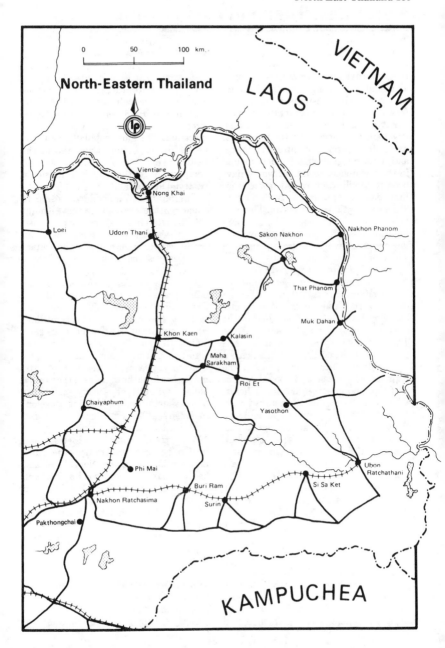

is often cited as only a train or bus stop from which to visit the nearby Phimai ruins, but it is a fairly interesting town in itself. Up until the mid-Ayuthaya period it was actually two towns, Sema and Khorakpura, which were merged under the reign of King Narai. To this day, Khorat has a split personality of sorts, with the older, less commercial half to the west, and the newer, 'downtown' half inside the city moats to the east, though neither town was originally located here. You can watch beautiful pottery being made at the village of **Lan Kwian**, a few km from Khorat.

Information

The TAT office on Mitthaphap Rd (west edge of town) is worth a visit since they have plenty of information on the northeast. To get there, walk straight across from the entrance to the Nakhon Ratchasima railway station to Mukkhamontri Rd, turn left and walk (or catch a No 2 bus) west until you reach the highway to Bangkok – Mitthaphap Rd. TAT is just across the road, on the northwest corner.

Mahawirong Museum

In the grounds of Wat Sutchinda, directly across from the government buildings off

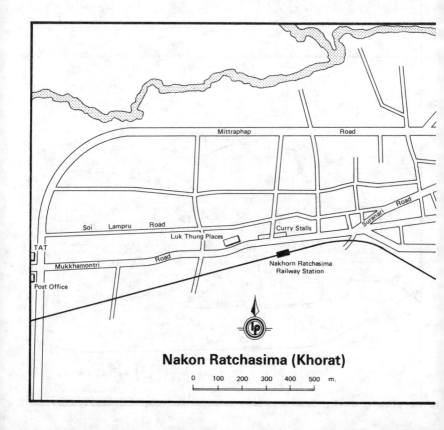

Mittraphap Road

Soi Lampru Road

Luk Thung Places

Curry Stalls

Suranari Road

TAT

Mukkhamontri Road

Nakhorn Ratchasima Railway Station

Post Office

Nakon Ratchasima (Khorat)

0 100 200 300 400 500 m.

Ratchadamnoen Rd, just outside the city moat, this museum has a good collection of Khmer art objects, especially door lintels, as well as objects from other periods. Open 9 am to 12 noon and 1 pm to 4 pm, Wednesday to Sunday.

Thao Suranari Shrine

At the Chumphon gate to downtown Khorat, on the west side, is this much-worshipped shrine to Khun Ying Mo, a courageous Thai woman who led the local citizens in a battle against Lao invaders from Vientiane during the rule of Rama III. There is a curious miniature model of a bus at the shrine, donated by local bus drivers, perhaps, in hope that they will be protected from danger by Khun Ying Mo's spirit.

If you are interested in *luuk tung* music or *likhee* theatre, note that Khorat is the north-east's centre for both – check out the establishments on Mukkhamontri Rd, near the Nakhon Ratchasima railway station. There are a few places to see or buy silk in Khorat but to see it made go to Pakthongchai.

Wat Sala Loi (Temple of the Floating Pavilion)

This distinctive modern temple is 400 metres east from the north-east corner of

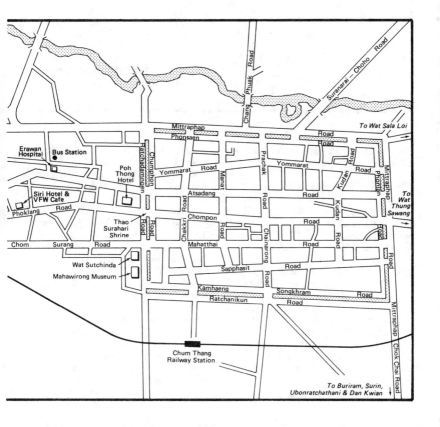

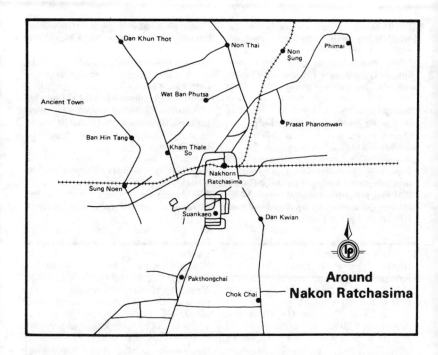

Around Nakon Ratchasima

the city moat. The *bot* is shaped like a Chinese junk.

Places to Stay - bottom end
Visit the TAT office in Khorat – they not only give you a map and complete list of hotels, but names of night clubs, restaurants, theatres and 'Turkish baths'. Some recommended hotels:

Fah Sang, 68-70 Mukkhamontri Rd, not far from the railroad station. This place has clean rooms and friendly staff, singles 75B, doubles 150B.

Poh Thong, 658 Ratdamnoen Rd, has rooms for 80B to 100B. Noisy but livable, near Ratchadamnoen Rd.

The *Siri Hotel*, is at 167-8 Poh Klang Rd, a couple of blocks west of the city moats. Good location, quiet and friendly. Rooms begin at 70B.

Damrongrak, 120 Chumphon Rd, inside the city moats, has 90B singles, 150B doubles.

Thai Pokaphan, 104-6 Atsadang Rd, is also inside the city moats, across the street from the expensive Khorat Hotel, CP Turkish Bath, near Charoen Rath Theatre and the post office. Same rates as the Damrongrak.

Cathay, 3692/5-6 Ratchadamnoen Rd. Reasonable (90B to 160B) but a bit out of the way. *Khorat Hotel* (tel 242260), 191 Atsadang Rd, has rooms for 100B to 150B single, 300B double.

Places to Stay - top end
The *Sri Pattana* (tel 242944) on Suranari Rd has air-con rooms from 250B. The *Chom Surang* (tel 242940) has rooms from 350B, again all with air-con. The newer *Muangmai Chao Phraya* (tel 244906) ranges from 400B to 500B.

Places to Eat

Khorat has many excellent Thai and Chinese restaurants, especially along the western gates to downtown Khorat, near the Thao Surinari Shrine. The curry shops across from the railway station are also very good and cheap. The best pineapple curry I've eaten in Thailand I bought in one of these latter stalls.

Getting There

Bus Ordinary buses leave the Northern Bus Terminal in Bangkok every 15 or 20 minutes from 5 am to 9.40 pm. The fare is 55B and the trip takes four hours. There are also AC buses for 92B. Buses between Khorat and Khon Kaen cost 39B.

Train Two Express trains leave Bangkok's Hualamphong station bound for Nong Khai (departs 9 pm) and Ubon Ratchathani (8.30 pm), arriving in Khorat at 2.09 am and 1.26 am – hardly the best time to look for a hotel.

The Rapid train on the Ubon line departs at 6.50 am and arrives at 11.47 am. This gives you a more convenient arrival time and leaves plenty of daylight in which to explore the town. There are also ordinary diesel trains at 9.05 am (third class seating only), 11.45 am (third class only) and 1.30 pm (second and third class only) on the Nong Khai line, all arrive in Khorat about six hours after departure. First class fare is 207B, second class is 104B, third class 50B. Add 20B for the rapid train. The train passes through some great scenery on the Khorat plateau, including a view of the enormous white Buddha figure of **Wat Theppitak**, situated on a thickly forested hillside.

Air Thai Airways does not fly to Khorat, but a new domestic airline, Bangkok Airways, has plans to begin flying there – check with any Bangkok travel agency.

PAKTHONGCHAI
อำเภอปักธงชัย

Twenty-eight km south of Nakhon Ratchasima on route 304 is Pakthongchai. Several varieties and prices of silk are available here and most weavers sell directly to the public.

Places to Stay

The *Achaan Pan* and the *Pak Thong Chai* hotels are both on the main road through town. Both have rooms from 60B.

Getting There

A bus to Pakthongchai leaves the bus station in Khorat every 30 minutes, last bus at 4 pm; the fare is 6B.

PHIMAI
อำเภอพิมาย

The 12th century Khmer shrine called **Prasat Hin Phimai**, 60 km north-east of Khorat, is really worth a visit. Built by King Jayavarman VII as a Mahayana Buddhist temple, the monument projects a majesty that transcends its size. The main shrine, of cruciform design, is made of white sandstone, while the adjunct shrines are of pink sandstone and laterite. The lintel sculpture over the doorways to the main shrine are particularly impressive.

The reconstruction work undertaken by the Fine Arts Department has been completed. Despite the fact that now all the pieces do not quite fit together as they must have originally done, it only seems to add to the monument's somewhat eerie quality. Admission to the complex is 20B. Between the main entrance and the main street of the small town is a ruined palace and, further on, an open-air museum featuring Khmer sculpture.

The small town of Phimai itself is nothing much but staying the night here seems rather pleasant anyway. Outside the town entrance, a couple of km down route 206, is Thailand's largest banyan tree, spread over an island in a state irrigation reservoir. The locals call it *sai ngam*, meaning 'beautiful banyan'.

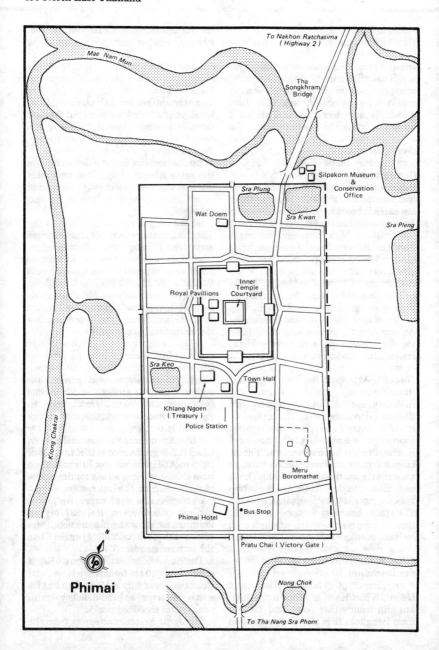

Phimai

Places to Stay & Eat

Only one hotel in town, right around the corner from the bus terminal – *Phimai Hotel*. A very clean and comfortable room is 80B to 130B without bath, 120B to 170B with or 200B to 260B with air-con. A recent letter however, indicated that standards may have taken a plunge – 'maybe they need some competition', the letter concluded. The restaurant next door is very good.

Getting There

Buses to Phimai from Khorat leave every half an hour during the day from the main bus station behind the Erawan Hospital on Suranari Rd. Take the No 2 city bus (2B) east on Mukkhamontri Rd (right from the railway station) and get off at the hospital; then walk around back by a side street to the bus station.

The trip to Phimai takes one to 1½ hours, depending on the number of passengers that have to be picked up along the way. The 'terminal' in Phimai is right around the corner from the Phimai Hotel and just down the street from Prasat Hin Phimai. Fare is 14B.

PRASAT PHANOMWAN

ปราสาทพนมวัน

Although not as large as Prasat Hin Phimai, Phanomwan is equally impressive. It's off highway 2 about half-way between Phimai and Khorat – ask to be let off the Khorat-Phimai bus at Ban Long Thong. Hop a local *songthaew*, hitch-hike, or walk the six km through Ban Long Thong and Ban Makha, both knife-making villages, to get to Prasat Phanomwan. Though basically not restored, Phanomwan is an in-worship temple with resident monks.

KHON KAEN (population 90,000)

จังหวัดขอนแก่น

A stopping-off place between Khorat and Udorn, Khon Kaen is about a 2½ hour bus trip from either point and 450 km from Bangkok. It is also the gateway to the north-east if you are coming from Phitsanuloke in northern Thailand by bus or plane.

Khon Kaen, a medium-sized town, has a university and a very good provincial branch of the National Museum. The museum features some Dvaravati objects, *sema* stones from Kalasin and bronze/ceramic artefacts from Ban Chiang. It's open Wednesday to Sunday from 9 am to 12 noon and 1 pm to 5 pm.

On the banks of Khon Kaen's large (in the rainy season) lake, is a venerable north-eastern style wat, with elongated spires on the *prasat* – typical for this area.

Khon Kaen is also well-known as the principal place where 'Thai sticks' are assembled. That portion of the product that does not leave town for bigger markets is reputed to be the very best available, in other words, the locals keep the best for themselves – old Thai hands call it 'Khon Kaen Crippler'.

Chonabot, 11 km from Ban Phai, is a centre for good quality silk.

Places to Stay & Eat

The *Roma Hotel* (tel 236276), 50/2 Klang Muang Rd costs from 100B or from 200B with air-con. *Sawatdi*, 177-9 Na Muang Rd, same rates. *King's Hotel*, near the market, has rooms from 80B to 100B with fan and bath.

Khon Kaen Bungalow (tel 236220), Sri Chan Rd, is good value at 80B to 120B or 140B to 200B with air-con. It's just down from the fancy Kosa so ask for directions to the Kosa from the bus station.

There are also more expensive places like the *Khon Kaen* (tel 237711) on Phimphasut Rd with air-con rooms from 350B or the *Kosa* (tel 236711) on Sri Chan Rd with rooms from 375B.

The *Ban Phai*, 396 Chan Prasit Rd, is at Ban Phai, 40 km from Khon Kaen, and has rooms from 80B to 150B. Ban Phai is worth a stop for the local delicacy – *muu yang* (roast shredded pork).

The *Jerat Restaurant* across from the

municipal market on Klang Muang Rd has good *isaan* food. Khon Kaen has lively night markets with plenty of good food stalls.

Getting There

Bus The Phitsanuloke-Khon Khaen road runs through spectacular scenery, including a couple of National Parks. Check at the main bus station in Phitsanuloke for departures and fares, which vary according to type of bus and routing.

Buses leave Khorat for Khon Kaen several times daily, arriving 2½ hours later for 39B. From Khon Kaen it requires a change of bus to get to Phimai. The first bus costs 30B, the second 4B.

An air-con bus from Bangkok's Northern Bus Terminal costs 153B; departures are every half hour between 8 am and midnight. Ordinary buses are less frequent, only seven departures a day between 7.35 am and midnight. Fare is 85B.

Train The departure times for trains to Khon Kaen from Bangkok are the same as those noted for the Nong Khai line to Khorat in the Khorat section. The trip takes about eight hours regardless of which train you take. Note that only the Express has first class service. The basic fare is 333B first class, 162B second, 77B third, plus appropriate charges for Rapid or Express service.

Trains from Khorat leave daily at 6.10 am, 8.20 am and 3.36 pm, arriving in Khon Kaen at 9.33 am, 12.15 pm and 7.09 pm. Third class fare is 35B.

Air At this writing there is no longer a Thai Airways flight between Phitsanuloke and Khon Kaen. However, there are direct flights daily from Bangkok at 7 am and 2.20 pm. The fare is 710B when flying Boeing aircraft, 610B on Shorts.

UDORN THANI - BAN CHIANG
จังหวัดอุดรธานี - บ้านเชียง
(population 80,000)

Just over 560 km from Bangkok, Udorn is one of three north-eastern cities (including Ubon and Khorat) that boomed virtually overnight when an American military base was established in each during the US-Vietnam war (there were seven US bases in Thailand during that period – since 1976 there have been none). Except for nearby Ban Chiang, Udorn has nothing much to offer unless you've spent a long time already in the north-east and seek 'western' amenities like air-conditioned coffee houses, flashy ice cream and massage parlours (no, not together), or *farang* food. However, Udorn, apart from Si Saket, possibly has the best *kai yang* in the north-east.

Ban Chiang
บ้านเชียง

The little village of Ban Chiang, 50 km east of Udorn, now plays host to a steady trickle of tourists from all over Thailand and a few from beyond. Besides the original excavation at **Wat Pho Si Nai** at the village edge, now open to the public, there is also a recently constructed museum with extensive Ban Chiang exhibits. This is worth a trip if you're at all interested in the historic Ban Chiang culture, which goes back at least 5000 years and quite possibly 7000. The museum may not be open on Mondays and Tuesdays, so check if you are going there.

This agricultural society, which once thrived in north-east Thailand, is known for its early bronze metallurgy and clay pottery, especially pots and vases with distinctive burnt-ochre 'swirl' designs, most of which were associated with burial sites. The local villagers attempt to sell Ban Chiang artefacts, real and fake, but neither type will be allowed out of the country so don't buy them. Some of the local handicrafts, like thick hand-woven cotton fabrics, are good buys.

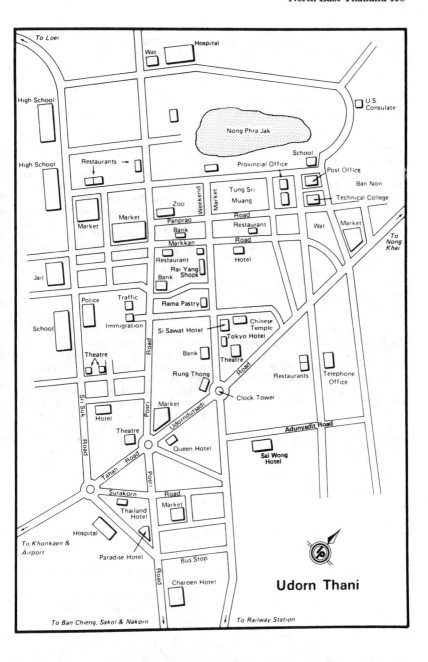

Udorn Thani

Getting There There is a regular bus between Udorn and Ban Chiang for 20B. Buses leave in either direction several times a day, but the last leaves Bang Chiang in the late afternoon.

Places to Stay – bottom end

Some recommended Udorn hotels are:

Queen Hotel, 6-8 Udorn-dutsadi Rd, which has rooms from 80B with fan and bath. It's a 5B *samlor* ride from the railway station.

Tokyo, 147 Prachak Rd, in the centre of town, with 60B rooms that have fan and bath. You can also get air-conditioned rooms for 280B.

Srisawat, at 123 Prachak Rd, near the Tokyo Hotel, costs 50B for a room with fan and shared bath in the old building, or 70B for a room with fan and bath in the new building.

Paradise Hotel, 44/29 Pho Si Rd, near the bus station and the fancy Charoen Hotel, at 150B to 200B for air-con rooms with bath and hot water.

Thailand, 4/5 Surakorn Rd, near the bus station, is 80B up for rooms with fan and bath.

Saiwong at 39 Adulyadet Rd, off Udorn-dutsadi Rd near the Chinese temple, is a small wooden Chinese hotel with rooms for 50B with fan and shared bath.

Places to Stay – top end

The *Charoen* (tel 221331) at 549 Pho Sri Rd has air-con rooms from 290B. The *Chaiyaporn* (tel 221913, 222144) at 209-211 Mak Khaeng Rd has rooms from 140B or from 200B with air-con.

Places to Eat

There is plenty of good food in Udorn, especially *isaan* fare. Best *kai yang* shops are along Prachak Rd west of the clock tower, just before Prachak crosses Makkan Rd. Try *Khun Phaen* beer, a brand mostly available in the north-east and east of Thailand – very similar in taste to Singha, but 5B to 10B cheaper.

The *Rung Thong* sells excellent Thai curries at the west side of the clock tower traffic circle and is also cheap.

There's also the *Rama Pastry*, an air-con pastry and coffee shop with good pastries, on Prachak Rd between Adunyadet (Adulyadet) and Makkan Rds, a few blocks towards the clock tower from the kai yang shops.

Six km north of Udorn on the road to Nong Khai is a very good (and inexpensive) seafood-*isaan* restaurant-park called *Suan Kaset Rang San*. The restaurant is situated on an island among several small lakes – great food in a rustic atmosphere. Many varieties of fish served here are caught in the lakes, which are owned by the *Suan Kaset*, including *pla nin* ('Nile' fish or Tilapia), *pla taphian* (carp), *pla nai* ('wheel' fish), *pla yisok* (Probarbus carp) and *pla jiin* (freshwater catfish).

Recommended dishes include: *plan nin phao* (grilled Nile fish), *tom yam pla* (seafood soup seasoned with lemon grass, mushrooms and a few chillies), and *pla nai jian puay* (a fantastic dish of steamed whole *pla nai* smothered in coriander, ginger and *puay*, a salty-sour Chinese plum). They also have good *isaan* food. An English menu is available. Fishing in the lakes during the day is allowed. You are charged a flat rate of 10B per day fishing fee, plus 20B per kg for any fish you catch. However, you are welcome to enjoy the surroundings, without a fishing rod, for free.

For somewhere to go at night the *Charoen Hotel* has a very dark 'cafe' with live music – quite a scene. The other big night-spot in Udorn is the *Tibet* club.

Getting There

Bus Buses for Udorn leave Bangkok's Northern Bus Terminal throughout the day from 9 am to 11.30 pm. The trip takes 11 to 12 hours and the fare is 106B, air-con buses are 191B.

From Khorat, buses leave the main bus station for Udorn every half hour during the day, arriving in five hours, for 60B.

Train The 9 pm Nong Khai Express from Bangkok arrives in Udorn at 6.50 am the next day. First class fare is 413B, second class 198B, third class 95B, plus applicable charges for sleeper and Express service. There is a special third class fare on Rapid trains to Udorn for 110B inclusive. Rapid trains leave Bangkok on the Nong Khai line at 6.10 am and 6.30 pm, arriving in Udorn at 4.17 pm and 4.55 am. The Express to Bangkok leaves Udorn at 8.02 pm and arrives at Hualamphong station at 5.58 am. There are also Rapid trains which leave Udorn at 7.32 am and 7.01 pm, arriving in Bangkok at 5.45 pm and 5.32 am.

Air Thai Airways flies to Udorn from Bangkok daily by way of Khon Kaen, see Khon Kaen for departure times. The flight takes 1½ hours and costs 870B by Boeing 737 (flying upcountry), 750B by Shorts 330 (flying back to Bangkok).

NONG KHAI (population 25,000)
จังหวัดหนองคาย
Over 620 km from Bangkok and 55 km from Udorn, Nong Khai is where Route 2, the Friendship Highway ends, right at the Maekhong River. Across the river is Laos. Nong Khai is the only point open along the Thai-Lao border – when the border is open between infrequent skirmishes. Check with the Lao embassy in Bangkok for the possibility (remote) of getting a visa for a visit to Vientiane, 20 km north-west of Nong Khai. You could also try the Immigration Office in Nong Khai. You can take a ferry across to Tha Deua in Laos if your visit is approved and then catch a taxi to Vientiane.

Nong Khai province is long and narrow, with 300 km of its length along the Maekhong River. It's only 50 km across at its widest point. Even if you can't cross into Laos, Nong Khai is a fascinating province to explore. It has long, open views of the Maekhong River and Laos on the other side. There are touches of Lao-French influence on local culture which

has made for good food and interesting wats.

The city itself has a row of old buildings of French-Chinese architecture along the east stretch of Meechai Rd, parallel to the river. Sit in the restaurant next to the Immigration Office/pier and watch the small ferry boats flying Pathet Lao flags cross back and forth between Thailand and the People's Democratic Republic of Laos. Obviously some travel is allowed between shores, as the boats always have passengers.

Out there in the river is **Phra That Nong Khai**, a Lao *chedi* which can be seen in the dry season when the Maekhong goes down some 30 metres. The chedi slipped into the river in 1847; it continues to slide and is near the middle now.

In the second week of March there is the Nong Kai Show, lots of festivities if you are in town, reported one traveller.

Wat Phra That Bang Phuan
วัดพระธาตุบางพวน
Twelve km south of Nong Khai city on Route 2 to Route 211 west through Ban Nong Hong Song, is one of the most sacred sites in the north-east because of the Indian-style stupa originally found here. It's similar to the original Phra Pathom Chedi in Nakhorn Pathom, no-one knows when either chedi was built, but it must have been in the early centuries AD or possibly even earlier.

In 1559 King Jayachettha of Chantaburi (not the current Chantaburi in Thailand but Wieng Chan – known as Vientiane – in Laos) extended his capital across the Maekhong and built a newer, taller, Lao-style chedi over the original as a demonstration of faith; just as King Mongkut did in Nakhorn Pathom. Vientiane is the French spelling of the Lao name Wieng Chan, which like the Thai Chantaburi, means 'City of the Moon'. Rain caused the chedi to lean precariously and in 1970 it fell over. The Fine Arts Department restored it in 1978 with the Sangharaja, Thailand's Supreme

Buddhist Patriarch, presiding over the re-dedication.

Actually, it's the remaining 16th century Lao chedis in the compound that have not been restored which give the wat its charm. These two chedis contain semi-intact Buddha images in their niches. There's also a roofless *wiharn* with a large Buddha image and a massive, round, brick base that must have supported another large chedi at one stage.

Getting There To get to Wat Phra That

Bang Phuan, get a *songthaew* or bus anywhere along Route 2 south of the city hall and say Ban Nong Hong Song or the name of the wat. Fare should be about 10B to the road leading off Route 211 to the wat, an easy walk from that point.

Wat Hin Maak Peng
วัดหินหมากเปง
Sixty km north-west of Nong Khai between Si Chiengmai and Sang Khom, Wat Hin is worth a trip just for the scenery along Route 211 from Nong Khai

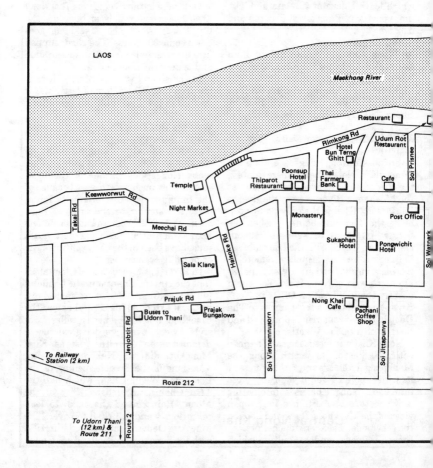

town. This monastery is locally known for its *thutong* (Pali: *dhutanga*) monks, men who have taken ascetic vows in addition to the standard 227 precepts. These include eating only once a day, wearing only 'forest' robes made of discarded cloth and a strong emphasis on meditation. There are also several *mae chee*, Buddhist nuns (not actually ordained *bhikkhunis*) living here.

The place is very quiet and peaceful, set in a cool forest with lots of bamboo groves overlooking the Maekhong. The monastic *kutis* are built amongst giant boulders that form a cliff high above the river. Below the cliff is a sandy beach and more rock formations. Directly across the river a Lao forest temple can be seen. Fishermen occasionally drift by on house-rafts. Very atmospheric.

Getting There To get there take a *songthaew* from Nong Khai to Si Chiengmai (20B) and ask for songthaews directly to Wat Hin (there are a few) or to Sang Khom, which is just past the

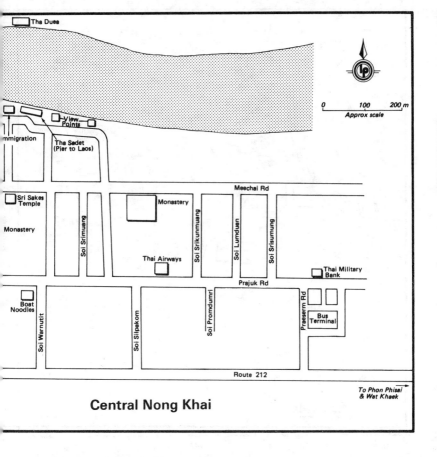

Central Nong Khai

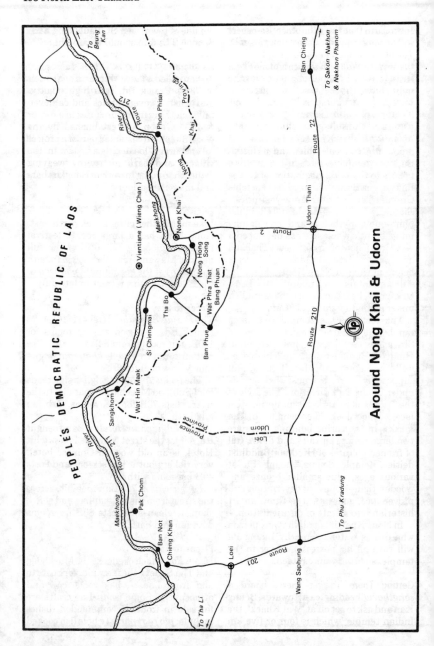

Around Nong Khai & Udorn

entrance to Wat Hin – the other passengers will let you know when the truck passes it. The second songthaew is 10B to 15B. On the way to Wat Hin you might notice a large topiary in **Ban Phran Phrao** on the right side of the highway.

Phutthamamakasamakhom
พุทธมามกะสมาคม

Also called Wat Khaek (a lot easier to pronounce) by locals, this strange Hindu-Buddhist temple, established in 1978, is a tribute to the wild imagination of Luang Pu Bunleua Surirat. Luang Pu (Venerable Grandfather) is a Brahminic yogi-priest-shaman who merges Hindu and Buddhist philosophy, mythology and iconography into a cryptic whole. He has developed a very large following in north-east Thailand and Laos, where he lived for many years before moving to Nong Khai; in fact, he still maintains a temple in Laos. Originally, he is supposed to have studied under a Hindu *rishi* in Vietnam.

The focus of the temple is a large number of bizarre cement statues of Shiva, Vishnu, Buddha and every other Hindu or Buddhist deity imaginable, as well as many secular figures, all supposedly cast by unskilled artists under Luang Pu's direction. The style of the figures is remarkably uniform, with faces which look like benign African masks. In the shrine building there are two large rooms, upstairs and down, full of framed pictures of Hindu or Buddhist deities, temple donors, Luang Pu at various ages, plus smaller bronze and wooden figures of every description and provenance, guaranteed to throw an art historian into a state of disorientation.

In Nong Khai, it is said that any person who drinks water offered by Luang Pu will turn all his possessions over to the temple, so bring your canteen.

Getting There To get there, board a *songthaew* heading east towards Beung Kan and ask to get off at 'Wat Khaek', the Indian temple, which is four or five km

outside of town, near St. Paul Nong Khai School. The fare should be around 8B.

Handicrafts

A shop called *Village Weaver Handicrafts* at 786/1 Prajak Rd, sells high quality, inexpensive woven fabrics and can even tailor clothing from purchases in a day or two. The shop was established by the Good Shepherd Sisters as part of a project to encourage local girls to stay in the villages and earn money by weaving rather than going to work in Bangkok bars and massage parlours.

Festivals

Like many other cities in the north-east, Nong Khai has a large rocket festival (*ngaan bun bong fai*) during the full moon of May and a candle festival (*ngaan hae thian*) at the beginning of *phansaa* or the Buddhist rains retreat in late July.

Places to Stay

The *Prajak Bungalows* (tel 411116), 1178 Prajak Rd, has good air-con rooms for 150B, fan rooms from 80B to 100B. The restaurant in front sells *khao raat kaeng* (curry and rice) for 6B.

The *Poonsup Hotel* (English sign reads Pool Sub), on Meechai Rd, parallel to the river, costs 70B for OK rooms with fan and bath.

The *Sukhaphan Hotel* on Bamtoengjit Rd, across the street from the Pongwichit Hotel, is an old wooden Chinese hotel, very rickety but it has screens and costs 40B per room with fan.

Pongwichit at 723 Bamtoengjit, across the street from the Sukhaphan and coffee shop, is clean and costs 80B for rooms with fan and bath.

Places to Eat

Udom Rot, which overlooks the Maekhong and Tha Sadet – the ferry pier for boats to and from Laos – has good food and atmosphere. Some *isaan*-Lao crafts are for sale in front. Recommended dishes include: *pla raat phrik* (whole fish cooked in garlic and chillies), *paw pia yuan* (Vietnamese spring rolls), *laap kai* (spicy mint chicken salad), *po taek* ('broken fishtrap' savoury seafood soup), and especially *kai lao daeng* – the local favourite – chicken cooked in red wine, Lao-style. Medium-priced.

Thiparot, next to the Pool Sub Hotel on Meechai Rd, serves excellent Chinese, Thai and Lao food. The specialty of the house is *pla beuk*, the giant Maekhong catfish *(Pangasianodon gigas)*; this species is the largest fish in the Maekhong River, sometimes reaching 200 kg. Locals reckon this fish must swim all the way from Qinghai province in China where the Maekhong originates. The texture is very meaty but it has a delicate flavour, similar to tuna or swordfish, but whiter in colour. Best prepared as *pla beuk phat phet*, chunks of *pla beuk* fried in fresh basil-laced curry paste. Also good at Thiparot are the *pla sa-nguang sa-nguan*, a tender-fleshed freshwater fish fried in garlic and black pepper, and the *kai lao daeng*, described above. Reasonably priced.

The cheap and tasty Loet Rot coffee shop has left the scene, leaving only the *Pachani Coffee House*, air-con and not so cheap, near Prajak Bungalows on Prajak Rd.

Getting There

Bus Buses to Nong Khai leave Udorn approximately every 30 minutes throughout the day from the Udorn bus station. The trip takes just over 1¼ hours and costs 20B.

Buses to Nong Khai from Bangkok's Northern Bus Terminal leave during the early morning hours from 4 am to 9 am and in the evening between 7.30 pm and 9 pm. The trip is a long nine to 10 hours and costs 120B for an ordinary (non air-con) bus. Air-con buses are 209B and leave three times a day, at 9 am, 9 pm and 9.30 pm. Most people take the train.

Buses from Khorat start running in the afternoon and into the early evening. The

fare is 75B and the trip takes six to seven hours.

If you're coming from Loei province you can get buses from Chiang Khan or Pak Chom, without having to double back to Udorn. It's 65B from Chiang Khan, 50B from Pak Chom.

Train From Bangkok, the Nong Khai Express leaves Hualamphong daily at 9 pm, arriving in Nong Khai at 7.40 am. Two Rapid trains leave daily at 6.10 am and 6.30 pm, arriving at 5 pm and 5.40 am. Basic one-way fares are 450B first class, 215B second class, 103B third class, not including surcharges for Express or Rapid service (30B and 20B) or sleeping berths. The State Railway runs a third class special on Rapid trains for 115B inclusive, a savings of 8B.

LOM SAK
หลมสัก
It's a scenic trip from Phitsanuloke to this small town on the way to Loei and Udorn Thani. It's also a pleasant trip from here to Khon Kaen. There are several places to stay near the bus stop including the *Sawang Hotel* which also has good Chinese food in the restaurant.

LOEI (population 15,000)
จังหวัดเลย
Nearly 560 km from Bangkok; 150 km from Udorn; 287 km from Phitsanuloke via Lom Sak, 200 km via Nakhon Thai, Loei is one of Thailand's most beautiful and unspoiled provinces. The geography is mountainous and the temperature ranges from one extreme to the other, that is the weather is hotter here than elsewhere in Thailand during the hot season and colder during the cold season. This is the only province in Thailand where temperatures occasionally drop to 0°C. The culture is an unusual mix of northern and north-eastern influences which have produced a large number of local dialects. The rural life of Loei outside of the provincial capital has

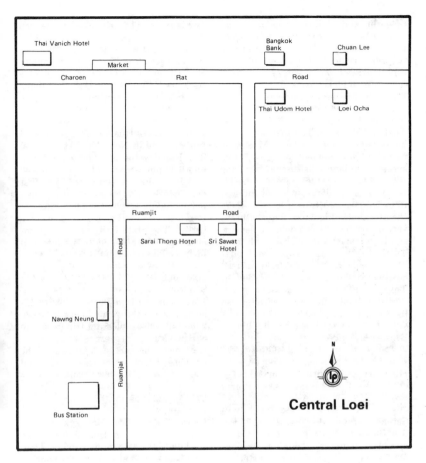

Thai Vanich Hotel

Market

Charoen

Rat

Road

Bangkok Bank

Chuan Lee

Thai Udom Hotel

Loei Ocha

Ruamjit

Road

Road

Sarai Thong Hotel

Sri Sawat Hotel

Nawng Neung

Ruamjai

N

Central Loei

Bus Station

retained more of a traditional village flavour than you'll find elsewhere in Thailand, with the possible exceptions of Nan and Phetchabun, also once classified as 'remote' or 'closed' provinces.

Places to Stay

The *Sarai Thong* on Ruamjit Rd has 56 rooms in three buildings, ranging from 50B to 120B. All rooms have fan and bath. It's off the street and is quiet and clean.

Thai Wanit (Vanich) has changed its name to *Phu Luang Hotel* (tel 811532,

811570) at 55 Charoen Rat Rd, near the market, costs 100B up for rooms with fan and bath, 220B up for air-con. It also has a night club.

At 122/1 Charoen Rat Rd, across from the Bangkok Bank, is the *Thai Udom* (tel 811763). Rooms with fan and bath cost 100B and rooms with air-con are 180B to 200B.

The *Srisawat* on Ruamjit, near Sarai Thong, is 50B and similar in facilities to Sarai Thong.

Places to Eat

The market at the intersection of Ruamjai and Charoen Rat has cheap eats and other items of local provenance. Look for the local specialty, *kai ping*, eggs-in-the-shell toasted on skewers.

Chuan Lee and *Loei Ocha* are two pastry-coffee shops on opposite sides of Charoen Rat Rd, not far from the Thai Udom Hotel and Bangkok Bank.

Nawng Neung, on the west side of Ruamjai Rd around the corner from the bus station, has great *khao man kai* (sliced chicken over marinated rice) and *kuaytiaw pet* (duck noodles). *Nam cha yen* is served in engraved aluminium cups and the soup in Chinese porcelain, yet most dishes are 10B or less.

Getting There

Buses to Loei leave Udorn regularly until late afternoon for 31B. The 150 km trip takes about four hours.

Loei can also be approached from Phitsanuloke by bus via Lom Sak. The Phit-Lom Sak leg takes 2½ hours and costs 34B. Lom Sak-Loei costs 45B and takes 3½ hours. The road from Nakhon Thai to Dan Sai may be open now, in which case you could bus to Nakhon Thai from Phit and from Nakhon Thai to Loei, saving some time since this route is more direct. There are direct buses from Phit to Loei via Dan Sai, the cost is 60B and the trip takes four hours.

Air-con buses from Bangkok's Northern Terminal cost 191B and leave at 9 am, 8 pm, 9 pm, 9.30 pm and 10 pm, arriving in Loei about 10 hours later. Ordinary buses are 106B and leave at 4.30 am, 5.30 am, 2 pm, 8.30 pm and 9.30 pm.

PHU KRADUNG

ภูกระดึง

Phu Kradung, a national park, is the highest point in Loei at 1500 metres. The top of the mountain is a large plateau with a network of marked trails and government-owned cabins. The main trail scaling Phu Kradung is five km long and takes about four hours to climb, or rather, walk – it's not really that challenging since the most difficult parts have bamboo ladders and stairs for support. it's a further three km to park headquarters. The climb is quite scenic. Phu Kradung is also a habitat for various forest animals, including deer and tigers.

It can get quite cold here at night in February and March, 5°C, it is possible to hire blankets though. Phu Kradung is closed to visitors during the rainy season from mid-July to mid-October because it is considered too hazardous then – very slippery and subject to mudslides.

Places to Stay

Lots of young Thai campers at the site here, mainly college students and friendly. There are tents already set up for 40B a night and boards for the bottom of the tents. Blankets and pillows cost extra. The cabins have water and electricity, but food must be brought along from the villages below. The park gates open at 8 am.

Getting There

Buses to Phu Kradung leave the Loei bus station in the morning for the 75 km trip.

THA LI

ท่าลี่

Perhaps the most beautiful part of Loei is the area which borders Laos from Dan Sai district in the west to Pak Chom in the east, including the districts of Tha Li and Chiang Khan.

Tha Li is 50 km from *amphoe muang* Loei on Route 2115, and the village is only about eight km from the Lao border, formed here by the Heuang River, a tributary of the Maekhong (which joins the border east of here towards Chiang Khan). Much of *amphoe* Tha Li is the Thai half of a valley surrounded by the Khao Noi, Khao Laem and Khao Ngu mountains on the Thai side, and Phu

Lane, Phu Hat Sone and Phu Nam Kieng on the Lao side.

When relations between Laos and Thailand were normal there was undoubtedly much local commerce back and forth across the Mae Heuang. Today, the Thai villages of Ban A Hi and Ban Nong Pheu, perched on the border, thrive on black market trade. Hand-made products like cotton fabrics and straw mats, as well as contraband like *ganja* and *lao khao* ('white liquor'), come across from Laos in exchange for finished goods from Thailand like medicine and machine parts. These are 'wild west' villages, where travellers go at their own risk. The local border police fish in the Heuang River using hand grenades. The village brothels offer young Lao refugees.

The village men are prodigious drinkers but rarely touch beer or Maekhong whiskey, instead they drink *lao khao*, a clear, colourless, fiery liquid with a very high alcohol content distilled from glutinous rice. In a pun referring to Thailand's famous Maekhong whiskey, they call it Mae Heuang after the local tributary. Inside every bottle (20B per litre) is inserted a thick black medicinal root called *ya dong*, which is said to dissolve away the aches and pains of the day's work and prevent hangovers. It does seem to mellow the flavour of the *lao khao*, which has a taste somewhere in between high-proof rum and tequila.

In vivid contrast to the villages described above are several 'model villages' (*muu baan tua yang*) organised by government officials as showcases for counter-insurgency in Loei province. You'll know if you've stumbled upon one of these by the fenced-in houses with name-tags on the doors. They also seem to be mostly empty of people – all hard at work in the fields, say officials. Some model villages even have model families (only one per village) which you are invited to visit. Walk right in and see Model Dad and Model Mum.

Getting There
See the Chiang Khan section below for details of transport from Loei.

CHIANG KHAN
อำเภอเชียงคาน

Chiang Khan is also about 50 km from Loei town, right on the Maekhong River. Like Tha Li, the town is situated in a large valley surrounded by mountains; unlike Tha Li, Chiang Khan has a hotel and a few restaurants. The place has a bit of the frontier atmosphere and nice Maekhong views. Downstream about four km is the **Kaeng Khut Ku**, a stretch of rapids (best in the dry/hot season) with a park on the Thai side and a village on the Lao side. You can hire a boat to reach the rapids. The park has a viewing tower and roofed picnic areas. Vendors sell delicious isaan food – *kai yang, somtan* and *khao niaw* – as well as *kung ten* or 'dancing shrimp' (fresh river prawns served *live* in a light sauce of *nam pla*, lime juice and chillies), and *kung thawt* (same fried whole in batter) and drinks. A nice place to spend a few hours.

If you want to see one of Loei's 'model villages', catch a *songthaew* east on Route 211 to Ban Noi (very near Kaeng Khut Ku).

Wat Tha Khaek is a 600 to 700 year old temple two km outside of Chiang Khan on the way to Ban Noi and Kaeng Khut Khu. The seated Buddha image in the *bot* is very sacred and it is said, that holy water prepared before the image, has the power to cure any ailing person who drinks or bathes in it.

Ban Winai
บ้านวินัย

About 40 km east of Chiang Khan, near the small town of Pak Chom, is a very large (over 30,000) Lao refugee camp called Ban Winai (sometimes spelled Ban Vinai). Over 40 national and international volunteer agencies are involved with the camp. This means that any *farang* who arrives at the camp is likely to be admitted, though recent reports say that the camp is becoming stricter about checking passes at the gate. Some people have been fined for entering without a pass. Like many refugee camps in the north and north-east, Ban Winai looks like a large, densely-populated, but prosperous hill-tribe village from a distance, with thatched roofs and dirt roads. As you get closer, tank trucks and basket-ball courts tell the tale. Most of the refugees are Lao hill tribespeople, especially Hmong (also called Meo), but there are also some low-land Lao, Khmer and Vietnamese.

Getting There There are *songthaews* to Ban Winai from Chiang Khan and Pak Chom. The latter are easier to get, as there are regular songthaews stationed along the route. A songthaew from Chiang Khan to Pak Chom is 15B; from Pak Chom songthaews leave in the morning for Ban Winai – the fare varies.

Places to Stay
If you want to overnight in Chiang Khan try the *Suksamboon* on the Maekhong side of town. It's 60B with fan and shared bath; an extra 70B with own bath. There are two more hotels on the same road, the *Amnatsiri* and the *Poonsawat*, with similar rates.

Getting There
Songthaews for Chiang Khan and Tha Li leave about once an hour from Loei's bus station – 15B to either destination (different routes), about a two-hour ride either way. There is no regular transport between Tha Li and Chiang Khan, though a dirt road does run along the border.

BEUNG KAN
บึงกาฬ
A small dusty town on the Maekhong 185 km from *amphoe muang* Nong Khai by Route 212. If you are working your way

around the north-eastern border from Nong Khai to Nakhon Phanom (as opposed to the easier but less interesting Udorn-Sakon Nakhon-Nakhon Phanom route) you may want to break your journey here. There are a couple of cheap hotels and several eating places.

The bus from Nong Khai to Beung Khan is 40B. The closer you get to Nakhon Phanom province, the more Vietnamese you will see working in the rice fields or herding cows along the road. All the farmers in this area, whether ethnic Vietnamese or Thais, wear a simple Vietnamese-style straw hat to fend off the sun and rain.

Wat Phu Thawk
วัดพูทอก
Those travellers interested in north-eastern forest *wats* can visit nearby Wat Phu Thawk. Phu Thawk is a massive sandstone outcropping in the middle of a rather arid plain, a real hermit's delight. The entire outcropping with its amazing network of caves and breathtaking views belong to the wat. The wat-mountain is climbed by a seven-level series of stairs representing the seven levels of enlightenment in Buddhist philosophy. Monastic *kutis* are scattered around the mountain, in caves, on cliffs, etc. As you make the strenuous climb, each level is cooler than the one before. It is the cool and quiet isolation of Wat Phu Thawk that entices monks and *mae chees* from all over the north-east to come and practice meditation here.

This wat used to be the domain of the famous meditation master Achaan Juan – a disciple of the fierce Achaan Mun who disappeared many years ago. Achaan Juan died in a plane crash a few years ago, along with several other monks who were flying to Bangkok for Queen Sirikhit's birthday celebration. The plane went down just outside Don Muang. Many north-easterners have taken this incident as proof that the current Queen is a source of misfortune.

Getting There To get to Wat Phu Thawk, you'll have to take an early morning *songthaew* south on Route 222 to Ban Siwilai (25 km, 10B), then another songthaew east (left) on a dirt road, 20 km to the wat (also 10B). This songthaew to Wat Phu Thawk leaves only in the morning, carrying merit-makers. Hitching might be possible if you miss the truck.

NAKHON PHANOM (population 33,000)
จังหวัดนครพนม

Nakhon Phanom is 242 km from Udorn; 296 km from Nong Kai. A dull city in itself, which just happens to have a really panoramic view of the Maekhong River and the craggy mountains of Laos beyond. Nakhon Phanom province has a large Lao and Vietnamese presence, though the capital is in the hands of ethnic Chinese. If you've come to see That Phanom, you'll probably have to stop here first to change buses, unless you go directly to That Phanom from Sakon Nakhon *via* Route 223. **Wat Sri Thep** in town on the street with the same name as the wat, has a display of murals. One traveller reported that they were as good as those in the Sistine Chapel! There is a fair selection of hotels and eating places in Nakhon Phanom.

Places to Stay
The top end in town is the *Nakhon Phanom Hotel* at 403 Aphiban Bancha Rd, (tel 511455) with rooms with fan and bath for 120B. Air-con rooms cost 220B up.

Pong, on the corner of Pon Keo and Bamrung Muang, is 60B per room with fan and bath, but it is run down and not very clean.

Charoensuk, at 692/45 Bamrung Muang Rd, is adequate for 70B with fan and bath.

Then there's the *Si Thep* (tel 511036), 708/11 Si Thep Rd, which costs 60B for a bungalow, 120B for a room with fan and bath and 180B for air-con.

A good bet is the *First Hotel*, 370 Si

Thep, which has clean rooms with fan and bath for 80B up. Recommended.

Also good is the *Windsor*, 692/19 Bamrung Muang Rd, which has very nice rooms for 90B with fan and bath, but is not as quiet as the First Hotel.

Behind the Windsor, on the corner of Si Thep and Ruamjit, is the *Grand* which has similar rooms for 60B.

Another one is the *River Inn* on the Maekhong River. Here rooms with fan and bath cost 100B up, some air-con rooms are available. It also has a terrace restaurant that overlooks the river – nice atmosphere.

Places to Eat
There are several good, inexpensive restaurants serving noodles, curry and rice, etc along Bamrung Muang Rd near the Windsor Hotel. Hottest nightspot in town is the *Tatiya Club* on the corner of Fuang Nakhon and Bamrung Muang. A real variety show with glittery Thai pop singers. Adjacent to the Tatiya Club is a good, small Thai restaurant.

Getting There
There are regular buses from Nong Khai to Nakhon Phanom through Sakon Nakhon for 50B. There is a direct bus at 9.30 am (starts in Udorn around 8 am), the price is 70B and takes 7½ hours. If you want to come through Beung Kan, you must get a bus to Beung Kan first, then change.

THAT PHANOM
ท่านครธาตุพนม

Fifty-three km from Nakhon Phanom; 107 km from Sakon Nakhon, the centre of activity in the small town of That Phanom is **Wat That Phanom**, a Lao-style wat that is very similar to Wat That Luang in Wieng Chan (Vientiane), Laos. The impressive *chedi*, which caved in during heavy rains in 1975 and was restored in 1978, is a talismanic symbol of *isaan* and highly revered by Buddhists all over Thailand. The dating of the wat is disputed but some archaeologists set its age at around 1500 years. The chedi is 52 metres high and the spire is decorated with 10 kg of gold. Surrounding the famous chedi is a cloister filled with Buddha images and behind the wat is a shady park.

The short road between Wat That Phanom and the old town on the Maekhong passes under a large Lao 'arch of victory' almost identical to the arch at the end of Lane Sang Rd in Wieng Chan (which also leads to Wieng Chan's Wat That). This section of That Phanom is interesting, with French-Chinese architecture reminiscent of old Vientiane or Saigon. There are hotels and restaurants here, so it is not necessary to backtrack to Nakhon Phanom for accommodation.

In mid-February there is an annual Phra That Phanom fair and the little town gets very crowded.

If you need to change money, go to the Thai Military Bank, on the road to Nakhon Phanom.

Places to Stay

There are two hotels in the old town: *Sang Thong*, turn right on Phanom Panarak Rd as you pass under the arch and it's on the left side of the street 30 metres down. The price here is 60B for an adequate room with fan and shared bath. A real funky place with an inner courtyard and lots of characters. Looks about 100 years old.

Chai Won, opposite side of Phanom Panarak Rd, to the north of the arch (turn left as you pass under the arch) is similar to Sang Thong, also costs 50B.

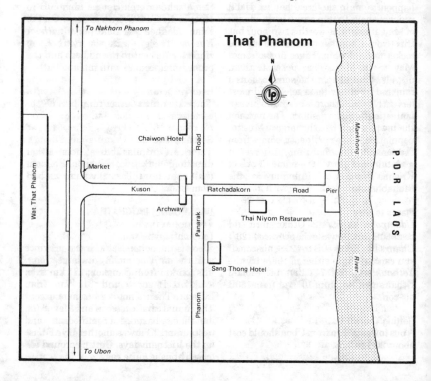

To Nakhorn Phanom

That Phanom

N

Chaiwon Hotel

Market

Kuson

Archway

Ratchadakorn Road

Pier

Thai Niyom Restaurant

Sang Thong Hotel

Wat That Phanom

Panarak

Phanom

Road

Maekhong

River

P. D. R   L A O S

To Ubon

Places to Eat

There are plenty of noodle shops along Kuson Ratchadamnoen, the road leading from Phra That Phanom to the river. Nicest restaurant is *Thai Niyom*, about half-way down on the right.

Getting There

Songthaews to That Phanom leave regularly from the intersection near the Nakhon Phanom Hotel in Nakhon Phanom for 125B; stay on until you see the chedi on the right. The trip takes about 1½ hours. From the Sakon Nakhon bus station, buses take three hours and cost 45B.

YASOTHORN (population 19,000)
จังหวัดยโสธร

This town is difficult to get to, but if you happen to be in the area (say, in Ubon which is about 100 km away) in the month of May, it might be worth a two-hour bus trip (from Ubon) to witness the annual rocket festival which takes place from 8 May to 10 May. The rocket festival, prevalent throughout the north-east as a rain and fertility rite, is celebrated most fervently in Yasothorn where it involves a fantastic fireworks display. The name of the town, which has the largest Muslim population in the north-east, comes from the sanskrit *Yasodhara* for 'preserver or maintainer of glory', the name of one of Krishna's sons by Rukmini in the Mahabharata.

Places to Stay

Udomporn at 80/1-2 Uthairamrit Rd costs 60B to 80B, while the *Surawit*, 128/1 Changsanit Rd, is 50B to 120B, air-con. If you can't get into either of these try the *Yothnakhorn* (tel 711122), 141-143/1-3 Uthairamrit Rd, from 100B or from 150B air-con.

Getting There

A bus to Yasothorn from Ubon should cost about 25B to 30B.

MUKHDAHAN (population 90,000)
มุกดาหาร

Exactly 55 km south of That Phanom; 170 km north of Ubon Ratchathani, Mukhdahan was formerly part of Nakhon Phanom and Ubon. Created in September 1982 it's Thailand's newest province. The *amphoe muang* is known for its beautiful Maekhong scenery and as a current centre of Thai-Lao trade – directly opposite is the city of Suwannakhet in Laos. This might make a nice stopover between Nakhon Phanom or That Phanom and Ubon.

For a view of town, climb the 353-metre **Phu Muu**, or 'Pig Hill' (named for the wild pigs that used to live there).

Places to Stay & Eat

The *Hua Nam* (tel 611137) at 20 Samutsakdarak has rooms from 60B to 125B or from 220B with air-con. On the same road is the cheaper *Banthom Kasem*. There is also the *Hong Kong Hotel* for 70B with fan and bath and the *Siam Hotel* for 90B with fan and bath.

A good place to eat and relax on the river is *Suan Malakaw*, the 'Papaya Garden', which sells fruit and north-eastern food.

Getting There

There are regular buses from either direction, 40B from Nakhon Phanom (half that from That Phanom) or 50B from Ubon.

UBON (UBOL) RATCHATHANI
จังหวัดอุบลราชธานี
(population 49,000)

Ubon is the north-east's largest province and the *amphoe muang* its largest city. It's 557 km from Bangkok; 271 km from Nakhon Phanom and 311 km from Khorat. There's not a lot to here except the annual candle festival and a few *wats*, but the city has good accommodation and restaurants as it was another USAF base in the Vietnam days. Getting around the city by bus is quite easy.

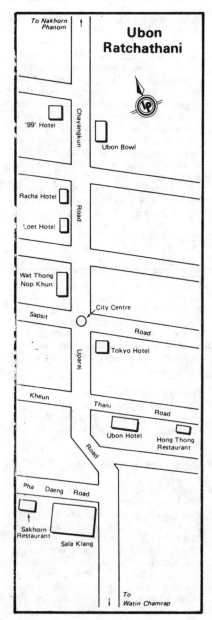

The candle festival is most grandly celebrated in Ubon, with music, parades, floats, enormous carved candles of all shapes – human, animal, divine, and abstract – beauty contests, etc. The night time processions are impressive. The festival begins around *khao phansaa*, the first day of the Buddhist rains retreat in late July and lasts five days. Spirits are high and hotels are full. It's worth the trip.

Nearby Si Saket (63 km west) is famous for its *kai yang* (roast spiced chicken). Vendors line the road outside of town and people in Bangkok ask friends from Ubon to bring Si Saket kai yang with them when they come to visit.

Wat Thung Sri Muang
Off Luang Rd, near the centre of town, this wat was originally built during the reign of Rama III (1824 to 1851). Note the *haw trai*, or Tripitaka library, which is in good shape. It rests on high angled stilts in the middle of a small pond. Nearby is an old *mondop* with a Buddha footprint symbol.

Wat Phra That Nong Bua
This one is on the road to Nakhon Phanom on the outskirts of town – take a white city bus for 2B. It is centred around an almost exact copy of the Mahabodhi stupa in Bodh Gaya, India, much better than Wat Jet Yod in Chiang Mai, which is purported to be a Mahabodhi reproduction designed by people who never saw the real thing. The *jataka* reliefs on the outside of the *chedi* are very good. There are two groups of four niches on each side of the four-sided chedi which contain Buddhas in different standing postures. The stances look like stylised Gupta or Dvaravati 'closed-robe' poses.

Wat Ba Pong – Wat Ba Nanachat Beung Wai
วัดป่าพง — วัดป่านานาชาติ บุงหวาย
South of Ubon in Warin Chamrap district, about 10 km past the train station, is Wat

Top: Auspicious chest tattoo (JC)
Bottom: Water buffalo (DC)

Top: Prasat Hin Phimai (JC)
Left: Wat That Phanom, That Phanom (JC)
Right: Chedi at Ban Tham, near Mae Sai (JC)

Ba Pong, also known as Wat Nong Pa Phong. This very famous forest wat is in the care of Achaan Cha, who has many other branch temples in Ubon province and one in Sussex, England. All of these temples are known for their quiet discipline and daily routine of work and meditation. Dozens of westerners have studied here during the past 20 years and many now live here or in branch temples as ordained monks. Achaan Cha, a former disciple of the most famous north-eastern teacher of them all, Achaan Mun (who disappeared from sight some years ago), is known for his simple and direct teaching method which seems to cross all international barriers.

At nearby Wat Ba Nanachat Beung Wai (Beung Wai International Forest Monastery) the abbot is Canadian, the vice-abbot Japanese and most of the monks are European. As Achaan Cha is quite old now and has been very ill in recent years, Wat Ba Nanachat is where you should go if you are interested in more than sightseeing. The wat is very clean, cool and quiet.

Getting There To get to Wat Ba Nanachat, take an Ubon city bus south down Uparaj Rd, cross the bridge over Mun River, and get off as the bus turns right in Warin Chamrap for the train station. From there catch any *songthaew* heading south (actually heading west, eventually, towards Si Saket) and ask to be let off at Wat Nanachat – everybody knows it. You can also get there by catching a Si Saket bus from Ubon for 3B to Beung Wai, the village across the road from Wat Nanachat. There is a sign in English at the edge of the road – the wat is back in the forest behind the rice fields.

Places to Stay
There are a number of places to stay here. Among them are: *Ratchathani Hotel*, 229 Kheun Thani Rd, the biggest hotel in Ubon, which has tourist info. Rooms with fan and bath are 150B or 250 with AC.

Racha Hotel at 149/21 Chayangkun Rd, north of the city centre, is 110B for clean rooms with fan and bath. Friendly staff.

At 224/5 Chayangkun, north of the Racha Hotel and municipal market and next to the flashy Pathumrat Hotel, is the *99 Hotel (Ubon Rat)*. All rooms have air-con and bath and cost 160B. Ask for their business card (*nam bat*) first and then present it to them for a 20% discount.

The *Tokyo* is at 178 Uparaj Rd, where it meets Chayangkun Rd, near the city centre. It's very nice and well-kept, but usually full near the end of July before the Candle Festival. Rooms with fan and bath cost 100B or 140B with air-con.

The *Pathumrat* (tel 254417, 254547, 255054) at 173 Chayangkun is probably the best hotel in Ubon with air-con rooms from 250B up.

Places to Eat
The *Loet Rot* at 147/13 Chayangkun, near the Racha Hotel, has excellent noodle dishes. Or there's the *Raan Khao Tom Hong Thong*, a Chinese-Thai restaurant on Kheun Thani Rd (not far from the Ratchathani Hotel, same side of the street) that has the largest selection of dishes on display that I have ever seen in a restaurant of its size. Goose and duck dishes are house specialties (try *khao naa pet* or *khao naa haan* – roast duck or goose on rice, cheap and delicious). Also good are the crab claw curry, *hawy jaw* (fried crab rolls), *khreuang naikai phat bai kaphrao* (chicken giblets fried in holy basil) and *kai phat khing* (chicken fried in ginger).

The *Sakhon* restaurant on Pha Daeng Rd near the provincial offices has the best *isaan* food in Ubon, according to the locals. The restaurant is family-run and their version of the local specialty *laap pet* (spicy duck salad) is a knock-out. Other great local dishes served here are *yam makheua yao, yam makheua thet, yam hawy khraeng* (spicy eggplant, tomato and cockle salads) and seven other yams. There's more – *kawy kai*, a soupy, hot chicken salad, *pla lai phat phet* (eel fried in fresh curry paste), *pla lai tom pret* (tangy eel soup served in a fire-pot) and *kiat thawt krawp* (tiny crisp-fried frogs). Most dishes are around 15B.

There are two *suan ahaans* (outdoor garden restaurants) on Route 23 at the outskirts of the city toward Nakhon Phanom. Best is *Khun Biak*, which has good *laap pet* and serves *kaeng baa* ('forest curries') that will tear your head off. The restaurant is built over a pond, but mosquitoes are not a problem.

The Fern Bakery near the teacher's college (Thai: *withayalai khruu*) sells good cakes and other baked goods. Take a city bus north and get off near the clock tower.

Getting There
Bus There are two tour buses a day to Ubon from Nakhon Phanom at 7 am and 2 pm, leaving from the intersection of Bamrung Muang and Ratsadorn Uthit Rds near the Windsor Hotel. It will cost you 96B. Ordinary buses from the *Baw Kaw Saw* station leave regularly from morning until late afternoon for 60B. The trip takes 5½ hours on the tour bus, six to seven hours on the *rot thammada*.

Buses for Ubon leave the Northern Bus Terminal in Bangkok up to 15 times a day from 4.30 am right through to nearly midnight. They cost 135B or 240B air-con, but the AC buses only run between 7.30 pm and 9.30 pm.

Train Rapid trains from Khorat leave at 12.07 pm and 11.54 pm, arriving in Ubon at 5.05 pm and 5.15 am. Basic fares are 121B second class, 58B third.

The Ubon Ratchathani Express leaves Bangkok daily at 8.30 pm, arriving in Ubon at 6.25 am the next day. Basic first class fare is 416B, second class 200B, third class 95B, not including surcharges for express service or sleeping berth. Rapid trains leave at 6.50 am and 6.45

pm, arriving in Ubon about 11 hours later. There is no first class on Rapid trains.

The Express back to Bangkok leaves Ubon at 7.35 pm, arriving at Hualamphong station at 5.46 am. There are Rapid trains at 6.35 am and 6.20 pm, arriving in Bangkok at 5 pm and 5.12 am respectively. Ordinary trains only take an hour longer; there are departures at 7 am, 3.10 pm and 11.20 pm.

Air Thai Airways flies daily to Ubon from Bangkok, Tuesday to Saturday at 7 am and on Sunday and Monday at 2.20 pm. The fare is 870B.

SURIN (population 34,000)
จังหวัดสุรินทร์
452 km from Bangkok. A forgettable town except during the 'Elephant Round-up' in late November each year. At that time a carnival atmosphere reigns with elephants providing the entertainment. If ever you wanted to see a lot of elephants in one place (there are more elephants now in Thailand than in India), this is your chance.

Places to Stay
Hotel rates may increase during the elephant round-up and hotels may fill up, but *Krung Si* (tel 511037), 15/11-4 Krung Si Nai Rd, is 70B to 90B. The *New Hotel* (tel 511341, 511322) at 22 Tanasarn Rd, is 90B to 220B, with some air-con rooms from 180B. Or there's the *Amarin* (tel 511407), Tesaban 1 Rd which costs 80B to 140B or from 160B with air-con. Not far from the Amarin is a cheaper place, the *Tanachai*.

Cheaper still are three hotels near the railway station, the *Nimit Thong, Hom Saat* and *Saeng Charoen*, all small places with 80B rooms.

Getting There
Bus Surin buses leave several times a day from Bangkok's Northern Bus Terminal between 6 am and 10.15 pm for 86B one way. During the 'round-up' time there are

also many special air-con buses to Surin from major hotels and tour companies. The regular government-run AC bus costs 155B and leaves the Northern Terminal daily at 11 am, 9.30 pm and 10 pm.

Train Most people travel to Surin by Rapid train No 31, which leaves Bangkok at 6.50 am, arriving in Surin at 2.47 pm. The fares are 173B second, 90B third, including the Rapid surcharge. Book your seats at least two weeks in advance for travel during November. Faster is the ordinary diesel No 931 to Surin at 10.55 am, arriving at 5.05 pm for 20B less.

Although under Thai political domination for several centuries, the south has always remained culturally apart from the other regions of Thailand. Historically the peninsular has been linked to cultures in ancient Indonesia, particularly the Srivijaya empire, which ruled a string of principalities in what is today Malaysia, southern Thailand and Indonesia. The Srivijaya dynasty was based in Sumatra and lasted nearly 500 years (from the 8th to the 13th centuries). The influence of Malay-Indonesian culture is still apparent in the ethnicity, religion, art and language of the *Thai pak tai*, the southern Thais.

The Thai pak tai dress differently, build their houses differently and eat differently from their countrymen in the north. Many are followers of Islam, so there are quite a few mosques in southern cities; men often cover their heads and the long *sarong* is favoured over the shorter *phaakamaa* worn in the northern, central and north-eastern regions. There are also a good many Chinese living in the south – the influence of whom can be seen in the old architecture and in the baggy Chinese pants worn by non-Muslims. All speak a dialect common among southern Thais that confounds even visitors from other Thai regions – diction is short and fast: *pai nai* (where are you going?) becomes *p'nai, tam arai* (what are you doing?) *tam'rai* and the clipped tones fly into the outer regions of intelligibility, giving the aural impression of a tape played at the wrong speed. In the provinces nearest Malaysia, Yala, Pattani, Narathiwat and Satun, many Thai Muslims speak Yawi, an old Malay dialect with some similarities to modern Bahasa Malaysia and Bahasa Indonesia.

Southern Thais are stereotypically regarded as rebellious folk, considering themselves reluctant subjects of Bangkok rule and Thai (central Thai) custom. Indeed, Thai Muslims (ethnically Malay) living in the provinces bordering on Malaysia complain of persecution by Thai government troops who police the area for insurgent activity. There has even been some talk of these provinces seceding from Thailand, an event that is unlikely to occur in the near future.

Bounded by water on two sides, the people of south Thailand are by and large a seafaring lot. One consequence of this natural affinity with the ocean is the availability of an abundance of delectable seafood, prepared southern-style. Brightly painted fishing boats, hanging nets and neat thatched huts add to the *pak tai* setting; the traveller who does a stint in south Thailand is likely to come face to face with more than a few visions of 'tropical paradise', whatever his/her expectations might be.

Three of Thailand's most important exports – rubber, tin and coconut – are produced in the south so that the standard of living is a bit higher here than in other provincial regions. However, southern Thais claim that most of the wealth is in the hands of ethnic Chinese. In any of the truly 'southern Thai' provinces (from Chumphon south), it is obvious that the Chinese are concentrated in the urban provincial capitals while the poorer Muslims live in the rural areas. Actually, the urban concentration of Chinese is a fact of life throughout South-East Asia which becomes more noticeable in south Thailand, Indonesia and the Islamic state of Malaysia because of religious-cultural differences.

RATCHABURI (population 43,000)
จังหวัดราชบุรี

Just a town on the way south from Nakhon Pathom, well before you get to the coast and Hua Hin.

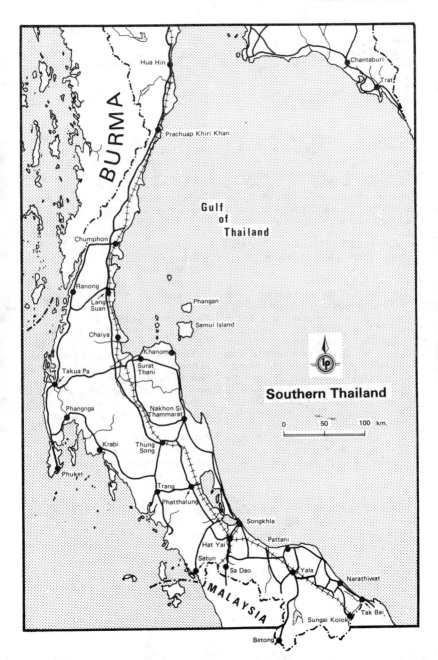

BURMA

Hua Hin

Chantaburi

Trat

Prachuap Khiri Khan

Gulf
of
Thailand

Chumphon

Ranong

Lang
Suan

Phangan

Chaiya

Samui Island

Khanom

Takua Pa

Surat
Thani

Phangnga

Nakhon Si
Thammarat

Southern Thailand

0   50   100 km.

Krabi

Thung
Song

Phuket

Trang

Phatthalung

Songkhla

Hat Yai

Pattani

Satun

Sa Dao

Yala

Narathiwat

MALAYSIA

Tak Bai

Sungai Kolok

Betong

Places to Stay

The *Zin Zin Hotel* on Railway Rd is cheap. Others include the *Araya* (tel 337781-2) with rooms from 100B or from 175B with air-con.

PHETBURI (population 35,000)
เพชรบุรี

Situated 160 km south of Bangkok, Phetburi (or Phetchaburi) is worth a stopover for its many old temples which span several centuries. Six or seven of them can be seen while taking a circular walk of two or three hours through the city. Also noteworthy is **Khao Wang**, just west of the city, which has the remains of a King Mongkut palace and several wats, plus a good aerial view of the city. The underground Buddhist shrine at the **Khao Luang Caves** is also worth seeing.

Information & Orientation

If you arrive at the train station, follow the road parallel to the tracks until you come to Route 4, then turn right. Follow Route 4 to the second major intersection and turn left towards downtown Phetburi to begin the walk. Or take a *samlor* from the station to Chomrut Bridge *(Saphan Chomrut)* over the Phetburi River, for 8B. If you've come by bus, you'll be getting off very near the Chomrut Bridge. This is the centre of Phetburi, more or less – from here you can check out hotels if you're spending the night, or, if you're not, stow your gear at the Anglican Church next to the bus station.

Things to See & Do

Cross the bridge to begin a long walk that passes **Wat Yai Suwannaram, Wat Trailok, Wat Kamphaeng Laeng, Wat Phra Suang, Wat Ko Keo Sutharam** and **Wat Mahathat**. These temples have made very few concessions to the 20th century and thus provide a glimpse of the traditional Siamese urban wat.

Wat Yai Suwannaram

After you've crossed the Phetburi River

by Chomrut Bridge (the second northern-most bridge in Phetburi) and passed the Chom Klao and Nam Chai Hotels on the left, walk a little further until you see a big temple on the right. This is Wat Yai, dating from the reign of King Chulalongkorn (1851 to 1868). The main *bot* is surrounded by a cloister filled with sober Buddha images. The murals inside the bot are in good condition. Next to the bot is a beautifully-designed old *haw trai*, a Tripitaka (Buddhist scripture) library.

Wat Borom – Wat Trailok

These two wats are next to one another on the opposite side of the road from Wat Yai, a little east. They are distinctive for their monastic halls and long, graceful wooden 'dormitories' on stilts.

Turn right onto the road heading south from Wat Trai Lok and follow this road down past a bamboo fence on the right to the entrance for Wat Kamphaeng.

Wat Kamphaeng Laeng

This is a very old Khmer site with four Khmer *prangs* and part of the original wall still standing. One prang is situated in front of the other three and contains a Buddha footprint. Of the three in the back, two contain images dedicated to famous Luang Po's (venerable elderly monks) and the third one is in ruins.

Wat Phra Suang & Wat Raj

Follow the road next to Wat Kamphaeng, heading west back towards the river until you pass Wat Phra Suang on the left, undistinguished except for one very nice Ayuthaya-style *prasat*. Turn left immediately after this wat, heading south again until you come to the clock tower at the south edge of town. You'll have passed Wat Raj on the left side of the street along the way, not worth breaking your momentum for; this is a long walk.

Wat Ko Keo Sutharam

Turn right at the clock tower and look for signs leading to Wat Ko; two different *sois*

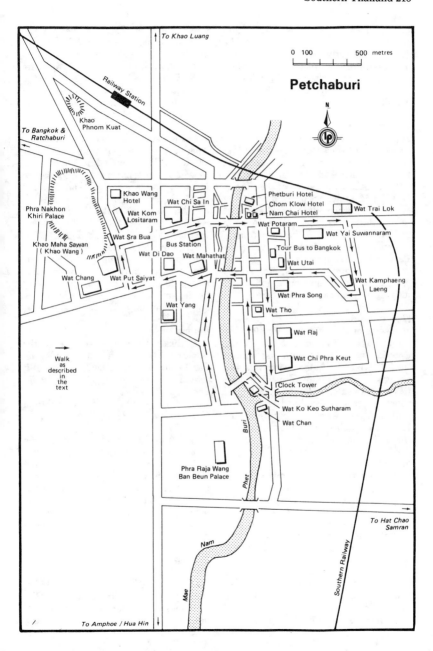

To Khao Luang

Railway Station

Khao Phnom Kuat

To Bangkok & Ratchaburi

0   100   500 metres

Petchaburi

N

Phra Nakhon Khiri Palace

Khao Maha Sawan (Khao Wang)

Khao Wang Hotel

Wat Kom Lositaram

Wat Chi Sa In

Phetburi Hotel
Chom Klow Hotel
Nam Chai Hotel

Wat Trai Lok

Wat Potaram

Wat Yai Suwannaram

Wat Sra Bua

Bus Station

Wat Di Dao

Wat Mahathat

Tour Bus to Bangkok

Wat Utai

Wat Chang

Wat Put Saiyat

Wat Kamphaeng Laeng

Wat Phra Song

Wat Yang

Wat Tho

Wat Raj

Wat Chi Phra Keut

Walk as described in the text

Clock Tower

Wat Ko Keo Sutharam

Wat Chan

Buri

Phet

Phra Raja Wang Ban Beun Palace

To Hat Chao Samran

Southern Railway

Nam

Mae

To Amphoe / Hua Hin

on the left lead to the wat, which is behind the shops along the curving street. The *bot* features early 18th century murals. There is also a large wooden monastic hall on stilts similar to the one at Wat Borom-Wat Trailok, but in much better condition.

Wat Mahathat

Follow the street in front of Wat Ko north (back towards downtown Phetburi) and walk over the first bridge you come to on the left, which leads to Wat Mahathat. (Alternatively, you can cross the river at Wat Ko, near the clock tower and take the street on the other side of the river around to Wat Mahathat). The large white *prang* of Wat Mahathat can be seen from a distance – a typical late Ayuthaya-early Rattanakosin adaptation of the Khmer prangs of Lopburi, Phimai, etc. This is obviously an important temple in Phetburi, judging from all the activity here.

Khao Wang

Just west of the city, a 5B *samlor* ride from the bus station is Khao Wang. Cobblestone paths lead up and around the hill, which is studded with wats and various components of Mongkut's **Phra Nakhon Khiri** palace (Holy City Hill). The views are great, especially at sunset. The walk up looks easy but is fairly strenuous. Fat monkeys loll about in the trees and on the walls along the main paths.

Places to Stay

Of the variety of places to stay here, the following are recommended. On the east side of Chomrut Bridge, right bank of Phetburi River, is the *Chom Klao*, an ordinary semi-clean Chinese hotel with friendly staff. It costs 50B for rooms with fan and shared bath, or 60B with private bath.

The *Nam Chai* is a block further east from Chomrut Bridge and the Chom Klao Hotel and has rooms for 50B to 70B, but is not such good value as Chom Klao.

Then there's the *Phetburi* on the next

street north of Chomrut, behind the Chom Klao, with rooms for 60B with fan and bath.

The *Khao Wang* (tel 425167), opposite Khao Wang, the hill palace, is by far the best hotel in Phetburi at 70B to 100B for a fairly clean room with fan and bath. Air-con rooms are 120B to 160B.

Places to Eat

There are several good restaurants near the Khao Wang hotel. The *Khao Wang Restaurant* in front of the hotel specialises in various kinds of vegetable and seafood *yam* – squid, oyster, eggplant, catfish, etc. An enormous plate of shrimp fried rice is 10B.

Other good eating can be found downtown along the main street to the clocktower. Across from Wat Mahathat, *Lamiet* sells really good *khanom maw kaeng* (egg custard) and *foi thawng* (sweet shredded egg yolk) – which they ship to Bangkok.

Getting There

Bus Buses leave regularly from the Southern Bus Terminal on Charan Sanitwong Rd in Thonburi for 29B ordinary, or 54B air-con. The bus takes about 2½ hours.

There are also buses to Phetburi from Cha-am and Hua Hin (9B and 15B).

Train Trains leave Hualamphong station in Bangkok at 9 am, 12.10 pm (rapid), 1.40 pm, 2.30 pm (express), 4.10 pm (express), 5.30 pm (rapid) and 6.25 pm (rapid). All trains take about 3½ hours to reach Phetburi so it's not worth the surcharges for rapid or express service – take a *rot thammada*. Third class fare is 34B.

CHA-AM
ชะอำ

A tiny town 178 km from Bangkok; 18 km from Phetburi; 25 km from Hua Hin. Cha-am is known for its casuarina-lined beaches, good seafood and party atmosphere – sort of a Palm Beach or Fort Lauderdale for Thai students. On weekends, things really get wild. However, rather expensive accommodation makes it unattractive to the budgeteer, unless you come here on a day trip from Phetburi. There are public bath-houses where you can bathe in fresh water for 4B.

Places to Stay & Eat

Every place on the beach is way overpriced except *Arunthip*, near the south end of the beach across from the tourist office. A room here is 120B with fan and bath. Very friendly people run this place and on the ground floor of the hotel is a coffee shop with live music nightly from 9 pm to 3 am.

The next cheapest places are *Jitravee Bungalow* and *Cha-am Villa* (tel 471010, 471241), which will let you have a room for 150B mid-week (300B on weekends). Next up in price is *Santisuk Bungalows*, which has a few rooms for 250B and *Kaen Chan Bungalow* at 300B. The rest of the places are 500B and over.

Out of town a bit is the *Regent Cha-am* for 400B up. One traveller said he stayed in a dormitory here for 50B.

Vendors on the beach sell fair chow. Opposite the beach are several good seafood restaurants which, unlike the bungalows, are reasonably priced.

Getting There

Bus Buses from Phetburi are 9B, buses from Hua Hin are 12B (from Hua Hin, take a Phetburi-bound bus). Ask to be let off at Haat Cha-am (Cha-am Beach).

Buses from Bangkok to Cha-am cost 38B for a *rot thammada* or 55B for air-con. Buses leave from the Southern Bus Terminal.

HUA HIN (population 31,000)
อำเภอหัวหิน

A favourite beach resort for Thais, Hua Hin is 230 km from Bangkok, but the Thais seem to want to keep this one for themselves, since it is seldom mentioned in any of the TAT literature. I don't blame them, Hua Hin is a nice, quiet place to get away from it all and yet is a convenient distance from Bangkok.

Rama VII had a summer residence built here, right on the beach, which is still used by the royal family. Just north of the palace are Hua Hin's rickety piers, bustling with activity in the early morning when the fishing boats go out and in the evening when they return. A few of the piers are used exclusively for drying squid – thousands of them – and this part of town exudes a powerful aroma.

The main swimming beach, not Thailand's best, has thatched umbrellas and long chairs. Vendors from the nearby food stalls will bring loungers steamed crab, mussels, beer, etc, and there are pony rides for the kids.

Thirteen km south of Hua Hin are the slightly more secluded beaches of Sai Yai and Sai Noi (Big Sand and Little Sand).

Places to Stay – bottom end

Hua Hin Ramluk (Raluk) at 16 Damnoen Kasem, has rooms with fan and bath for 100B up. It also has a pleasant outdoor restaurant.

Several hotels clustered in and around Phetkasem Rd include: *Chaat Chai* at 59/1 Phetkasem Rd with rooms with fan and bath for 100B. Just off Phetkasem, behind the bank, is *Suphamit* (tel 511208, 511487) with very clean rooms with fan and bath for 100B. Just past the market at 46 Phetkasem is *Damrong* (tel 511574), also 100B for rooms with fan and bath, there are also more expensive air-con rooms.

Then there's the *Meechai*, across from Damrong and a little further north, with double rooms for 80B up with fan and bath. On the corner of Phetkasem and Chonsin Rd (the road to Tha Thiap Pier) is the *New Hotel*. This costs 80B for rooms without a bath.

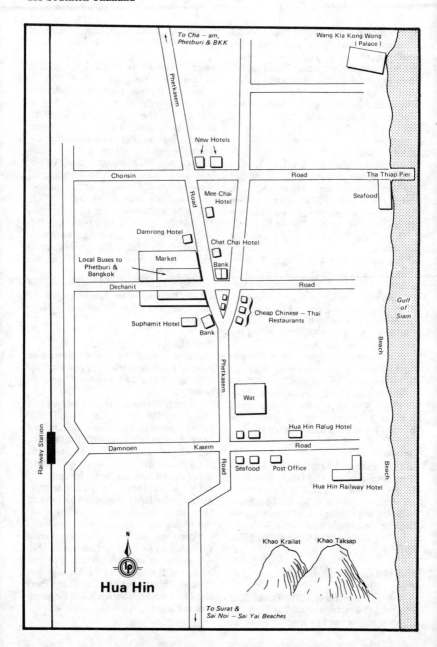

Hua Hin

Places to Stay - top end
Formerly the Hua Hin Railway Hotel, it is now the *Central Hua Hin Resort Hotel* (tel 511012-5), just off the beach on Damnoen Kasem Rd. This old 'colonial-style' hotel (despite the fact that Thailand never was a colony) and restaurant with real tablecloths on the tables, was renovated in early 1986. In 1983 this hotel was used as 'Hotel Le Phnom' for the filming of the *Killing Fields*. Reports from travellers suggest that this is an expensive place to stay but the hotel also has a separate Guest House with rates starting at 300B. If you want to make an advance reservation from Bangkok, phone 235 4430, 235 4424 or 235 4473.

Places to Eat
The best seafood in Hua Hin is concentrated in three main areas: Firstly, along Damnoen Kasem Rd near the Central Hua Hin Resort Hotel and Raluk Hotel - medium-priced; secondly, there's excellent and inexpensive food in the market off Phetkasem at Dechanit Rd and also at *Tha Thiap Reua Pramong*, the big fishing pier at the end of Chonsin Rd. The fish here, of course, is fresh off the boats and quite cheap. The smell may overpower some eaters, however. There is also a night market at Chonsin Rd.

The best seafood to order in Hua Hin is *pla samlee* (cotton fish or kingfish), *pla kapong* (perch), *pla meuk* (squid), *hawy maleng phu* (mussels), and *pu* (crab) in any of several forms: *phat* (sliced, filleted and fried), *yang* (roast, squid only), *phao* (grilled), *neung* (steamed), *tom yam* (in a hot and tangy broth), *raat phrik* (smothered in garlic and chillies), *thawt* (fried whole) and *dip* (raw).

The central market is excellent for Thai breakfast - they sell very good *jok* and *khao tom* (rice soups). Fresh-fried *pathong-ko*, Hua Hin-style (small and crispy, not oily), are 1B for four. A few vendors also serve hot soy milk in bowls (2B) - break a few *pathong-ko* into the soy milk and drink free *nam cha* - a very tasty

and filling breakfast for 5B if you can eat 12 *pathong-ko*.

Getting There
Bus Buses from Bangkok's Southern Bus Terminal are 70B air-con, 41B ordinary. The trip takes about four hours.

Buses for Hua Hin leave Phetburi regularly for 15B. The same bus can be picked up in Cha-am for 9B.

Train Same trains south as described under Getting There - Phetburi. The train trip takes 4½ hours, first class fare is 182B (Express only), second class 92B (Rapid and Express only), third class is 44B.

There is also a special day excursion fare to Hua Hin for 70B round trip, only on weekends. The train leaves Hualamphong at 6.15 am, arriving in Hua Hin at 11.30 am, then departs Hua Hin the same day at 4.10 pm, arriving back in Bangkok at 8.20 pm.

PRACHUAP KHIRI KHAN
จังหวัดประจวบคีรีขันธ์
(population 14,000)
Further south from Hua Hin - there is a row of bungalows on the seafront and some fine seafood can be found here.

Places to Stay
The *Indira Hotel* has rooms in the 50B to 75B range. The *King Hotel* (tel 611170) has fan-cooled rooms at 70B to 120B. On the beach, the *Suksan* has rooms from 70B and bungalows from 150B.

CHUMPHON (population 15,000)
จังหวัดชุมพร
Nearly 500 km south of Bangkok this is the junction town where you turn west to Ranong and Phuket or continue south on the newer road to Surat Thani, Nakhon Si Thammarat and Songkhla. It's a busy place but of no particular interest except that this is where south Thailand really begins in terms of ethnic markers like dialect and religion. The port of Chumphon

is 10 km from the junction town. A little south there's a big Buddha on a hillside beside the road.

Places to Stay

There are a number of hotels in Chumphon including cheaper places along Sala Daeng Rd like the *Namtai* (tel 511412) at 130/5 Sala Daeng Rd with rooms from 100B. A traveller has reported that next door to the Namtai above the Kawasaki shop, rooms are available for 50B with a fan. Also the *Sri Taifa* has been recommended, it's about one km from the railway station and rooms cost 80B. There's also the *Thai Prasert*, 202-204 Sala Daeng, 40B to 80B, and the *Suriya*, 125/24-26 Sala Daeng, 50B to 80B. Much more expensive is the *Paradorn Inn* (tel 511598) at 180/12 Paradorn Rd where rooms cost from 400B to 1600B. There's another expensive resort hotel at the coast, *Porn Sawan Home Beach Resort* with similar rates to the Paradorn.

RANONG (population 15,000)
จังหวัดระนอง

This small port is only separated from Burma by the Chan River. Burmese from nearby Kawthaung (Victoria Point) hop across to shop in Thailand and Ranong does very nicely out of supplying Burmese needs. Although there is nothing of great interest in the towns the houses are architecturally interesting. Ranong is about 600 km south of Bangkok, 300 km north of Phuket. It is also a departure point for the Surin Islands – see section on Phangnga below.

Places to Stay

Up on the main road the expensive *Thara Hotel* (tel 811509) is very pleasant with rooms at 100B to 160B with fan, 275B to 400B with air-con.

There's also some cheaper places in the town including the *Asia*, the *Sin Ranong* and the *Suriyanon* along Ruangrat Rd. The Asia (tel 811113, 811177) has rooms from 80B to 200B.

CHAIYA
อำเภอไชยา

About 640 km from Bangkok, just north of Surat, Chaiya is best visited as a day trip from Surat Thani. Chaiya is one of the oldest cities in Thailand, dating back to the Srivijaya empire. In fact, the name may be a contraction of Siwichaiya, the Thai pronunciation, as Chaiya was a regional capital between the 8th and 10th centuries. Previous to this time the area was on the Indian trade route in South-East Asia. Many Srivijaya artefacts at the National Museum in Bangkok were found in Chaiya, including the Avalokitesvara Bodhisattva bronze, considered to be a masterpiece of Buddhist art.

The restored **Borom That Chaiya** stupa at **Wat Phra Mahathat**, just outside of town, is a fine example of Srivijaya architecture and strongly resembles the *candis* of central Java. A ruined stupa at nearby **Wat Kaew**, also from the Srivijaya period, again shows central Javanese influence (or perhaps vice versa) as well as Cham (9th century South Vietnam) characteristics.

Another attraction for visitors to Chaiya is **Wat Suanmoke**, west of Wat Kaew, a modern forest wat founded by Buddhadasa Bhikkhu (Thai: *Phutthathat*), Thailand's most famous monk. Buddhadasa, a rotund octogenarian, ordained as a monk when he was 21 years old, spent many years studying the Pali scriptures and then retired to the forest for six years of solitary meditation. Returning to ecclesiastical society, he was made abbot of Wat Phra Mahathat, a high distinction, but conceived of Suanmoke ('garden of liberation') as an alternative to orthodox Thai temples.

The philosophy that has guided Buddhadasa is ecumenical in nature, comprising Zen, Taoist and Christian elements, as well as the traditional Theravada schemata. Today the hermitage is spread over 60 hectares of wooded hillside and features huts for 40 monks, a museum-library, and a 'spiritual theatre'. This latter building has bas-reliefs on the outer walls which are facsimiles of sculpture at Sanchi, Bharhut and Amaravati in India. The interior walls feature modern Buddhist painting, eclectic to say the least, executed by the resident monks. An interesting and peaceful place.

Places to Stay

Stay in Surat for visits to Chaiya or request permission to stay in the guest quarters at Wat Suanmoke. One traveller reported that there's a 'nice, old Chinese hotel' which costs 60B.

Getting There

If you're going to Surat by train, you can get off at the small Chaiya railway station, then later grab another train on to Surat. From Surat you can either hire a taxi or get a train going north from Surat's train station at Phun Phin. Taxis are best hired from Phun Phin, too. The trains between Surat and Chaiya may be full but you can always stand or squat in a third-class car for the short trip.

The ordinary train costs 7B third class from Phun Phin to Chaiya and takes about an hour to get there. Until late afternoon there are *songthaews* from the Chaiya train station to Wat Suanmoke for 5B per passenger. There are also buses (bound for Surat) from the front of the movie theatre on Chaiya's main street. Turn right on the road in front of the railway station. The fare to Wat Suanmoke is 3B. Suanmoke is about seven km outside of town on the highway to Surat and Chumphon. If buses aren't running you can hire a motorcycle (and driver) for 10B to 15B anywhere along Chaiya's main street.

Coming from Surat Thani it isn't necessary to go to Chaiya at all if you're heading for Wat Suanmoke. Buses run there frequently and directly from Surat Thani bus station. The trip takes about 45 minutes and costs 10B.

SURAT THANI/BAN DON
จังหวัดสุราษฎร์ธานี / บ้านดอน
(population 36,000)

There's little of historical interest at Surat, a busy commercial centre and port dealing in rubber and coconut, but the town has character nonetheless. It's 651 km from Bangkok and the first point in a southbound journey towards Malaysia that really feels and looks like south Thailand. For most, Surat is only a stop on the way to Koh Samui, a luscious island 32 km off the coast, so that Ban Don, a Surat *amphoe* on the east, becomes the centre of attention.

The daily boats to Koh Samui leave from Ban Don, proceeding into the Gulf of Thailand from the River Tapi for the three-hour trip. Actually, Ban Don is a great place to wander about while waiting for a boat to Samui. There is a fabulous fruit market along the waterfront and several good all-purpose 'general stores' and pharmacies on the street opposite the pier – good deals on *phaakamaas* and Thai work shirts, as well as a place to pick up some mosquito repellent for Samui. Lots of good restaurants can be found in Surat/Ban Don, too. See Places to Stay & Eat.

During the low seasons (anytime besides January to February or August) Thai girls throng the Ban Don pier around departure time for the Koh Samui express boat, inviting *farangs* to stay at this or that bungalow. This same tactic is employed at the Na Thawn pier upon arrival at Koh Samui. During high tourist season this isn't necessary as every place is just about booked out.

Places to Stay – bottom end

Many of Surat Thani's cheaper hotels devote a lot of their energy to pursuing the 'short time' trade. This doesn't make them any less suitable as a regular hotel, it's just that there's likely to be rather more noise as guests arrive and depart with some frequency. In fact, in many ways it's better to zip straight through

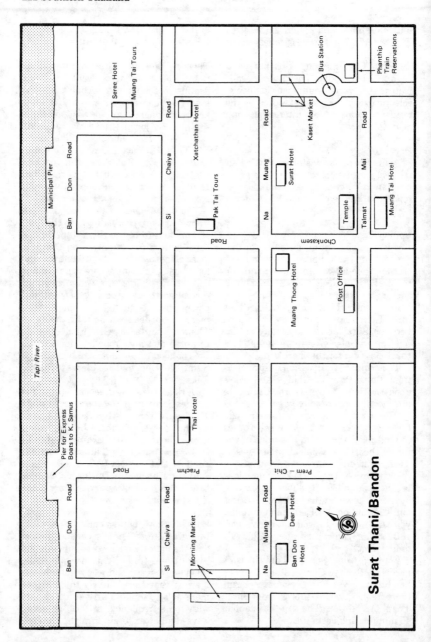

Surat Thani/Bandon

Surat Thani since there's nothing of interest to hold you. You're quite likely to sleep better on the night boat than in a noisy hotel. All of the following are within walking distance (or *samlor*) of the Koh Samui boat pier.

Off Ban Don Rd, near the municipal pier on a fairly quiet street, Si Chaiya Rd, is *Seree*. You get clean rooms with fan and bath for 100B here. They also have AC rooms for 200B.

The *Surat* (tel 272243) on Na Muang Rd, between Muang Thong Hotel and the market/bus station, is 80B to 100B for rooms with fan and bath, there are some renovated rooms which are quiet to stay in, reported one traveller.

The *Muang Thong* (tel 272560) at 428 Na Muang Rd is clean, comfortable and costs from 120B with fan and bath. There are also more expensive air-con rooms. It has a restaurant, night club and travel agency in the complex.

One block from the express boat pier on Si Chaiya Rd is the *Thai* which is 80B for adequate rooms with fan and bath.

The best bargain in Surat is the *Ban Don* on Na Muang Rd, towards the morning market. Enter through a Chinese restaurant, rooms with fan and bath cost 70B.

On the corner of Si Chaiya and the road between the river and Kaset Market (and bus station) is *Ratchathani* (tel 272972, 272143), 120B and up for rooms with fan and bath, more expensive with air-con. The *Lipa Guest House* is a brand new place at the bus station with rooms for 80B.

Another alternative is to stay near the railway station in Phun Phin – see Train below.

Places to Stay – top end

Surat Thani also has a number of more expensive hotels including the *Wang Tai* (tel 273410-1) at 1 Talaat Mai Rd. It's a big hotel with nearly 300 rooms, a swimming pool and prices from 400B. The *Siam Thani* (tel 391 0280) at 180

Surat Thani-Phun Phin Rd costs 480B but during the low season they offer 50% discount. They have a good restaurant reported one traveller.

The *Ta Pee* (tel 272575) at 100 Chon Kasem Rd has air-con rooms from 300B, fan cooled rooms from 200B. The *Muang Tai* (tel 272367) at 390-392 Talaat Mai Rd has air-con rooms from 225B, fan rooms from 175B.

Places to Eat

The Kaset Market area next to the bus terminal and the morning market between Na Muang and Si Chaiya are good food-hunting places. Many stalls near the bus station specialise in *khao kai op*, a marinated baked chicken on rice which is very tasty.

While waiting for the morning express boat to Koh Samui you can eat *pathong-ko* (1B each – tourist price) and tea at little tables set up near the pier.

Getting There

Bus Air-con buses leave the Southern Bus Terminal in Thonburi daily at 9 am, 8 pm and 8.30 pm, arriving in Surat 11 hours later; the fare is 225B. Ordinary buses leave the same terminal at 8 am, 8 pm and 9.30 pm for 125B.

Several private tour companies run buses to Surat from Bangkok for 300B or more.

There are buses to Surat from Phuket for 80B. The trip takes six to seven hours.

For tour bus tickets to Bangkok, Phuket or Hat Yai try *Muang Tai Tour*, next door to the Seree Hotel.

From Nakhon Si Thammarat you can take an air-con bus to Surat for 60B which includes a substantial Thai meal – check Muang Tai Tours at 1487/9 Jamroenwithi Rd in Nakhon Si Thammarat. Ordinary buses from the *Baw Kaw Saw* station are about half that fare.

Train Trains for Surat, which don't really stop in Surat town but in Phun Phin, 14 km west of town, leave Bangkok's Hualamphong station daily at 10.30 am (Rapid), 12.10 pm (Rapid), 2.30 pm (Express), 4.10 pm (Express), 5.30 pm (Rapid) and 6.25 pm (Rapid), arriving 12 to 13 hours later. The 6.25 pm train (Rapid No 41) is the most convenient, arriving at 6.50 am, plenty of time to catch a boat to Samui – if that's your destination. Fares are 470B in first class (available only on the 4.10 pm Express), 224B in second, 107B in third, not including Rapid/Express surcharges or berths.

It can be difficult to book a train out of Surat (Phun Phin) – it is better to book a bus, especially if proceeding south. The trains are very often full and it's a drag to take the bus 14 km from town to the Phun Phin train station and be turned away. The railway will sell you 'standing room only' third class tickets however, and this is a reasonable alternative if you can tolerate standing for an hour or two until someone vacates a seat down the line.

Advance train reservations can be made without going all the way out to Phun Phin station, at Phanthip travel agency on Talaat Mai Rd in Ban Don, near the market/bus station. You might try making a reservation *before* boarding a boat for Samui. The Songserm Travel Service on Samui also does reservations.

Places to Stay – Phun Phin

You may find yourself needing accommodation in Phun Phin, either because you've become stranded there due to booked-out trains or because you've come in from Samui in the evening and plan to get an early morning train out of Surat before the Surat-Phun Phin bus service starts. If so, there are several good places to stay.

Right across from the railway station are several cheap but adequate hotels. The best is probably the *Tai Fah*. The family that runs it is very helpful to travellers and they allow people to sleep on the floor of the restaurant downstairs if

they're full, no charge. Rooms are 60B without a bath. Another satisfactory place in the same location is the *Sri Thani*, with rooms for 50B.

Around the corner on the road to Surat, also quite close to the train station, are the *Kaew Fah* for 70B and the nicer *Queen* for 100B.

Across from the Queen and Kaew Fah is a good night market with cheap eats. The Tai Fah does Thai, Chinese and *farang* food at reasonable prices.

Getting Around

Phun Phin to Ban Don Buses to Ban Don from Phun Phin railway station leave every five minutes from 6 am to 8 pm for 5B per person. Some buses drive straight to the pier (if they have enough tourists on the bus), while others will terminate at the Ban Don bus station, from where you can walk to the pier. If you arrive in Phun Phin on one of the night trains, you can get a free bus from the train station to the pier, courtesy of the boat service, for the 8 am or 10 am boat departures. If your train arrives in Phun Phin when the buses aren't running (which includes all trains except No 41 and No 47, the 5.30 pm and 6.25 pm trains), you're out of luck and will have to hire a taxi to Ban Don, about 60B to 70B. Or hang out in one of the Phun Phin street cafes until buses start running.

Buses from the Ban Don bus station to the Phun Phin railway station run every five minutes from 5 am to 7.30 pm. Empty buses also wait at the Ban Don pier for passengers arriving from Koh Samui on the express boat, ready to drive them directly to the train station.

KOH SAMUI (population 32,000)
เกาะสมุย

Samui Island long ago attained a somewhat legendary status among Asian travellers, yet until recently it never really escalated to the touristic proportions of other similar getaways found between Goa and Bali. With the advent of the Don Sak

Top: Floods in Bangkok (TW)
Bottom: Chao Phraya River, Bangkok (TW)

Top: Fortune telling in Nakhon Pathom (JC)
Bottom: Bang Pa In (TW)

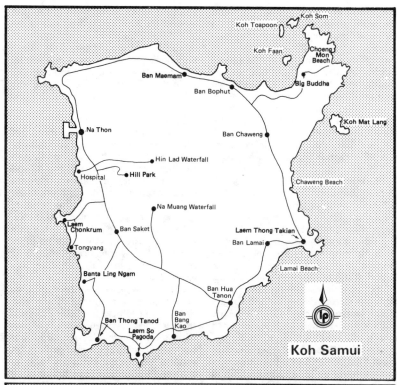

Koh Samui

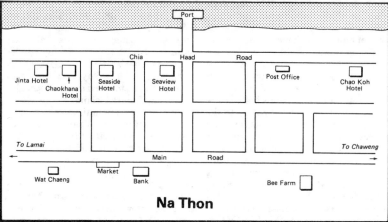

Na Thon

auto/bus ferry a couple of years ago and the pending airport construction, things are now changing. During the high seasons, January to February and July to August, it can be difficult to find a place to stay, even though most beaches are crowded with bungalows. The port town teems with *farangs* getting on and off the ferry boats, booking tickets onward, collecting mail at the post office. When the airport is finished, Bangkok Airways will be flying regular flights in as well as accepting charter flights from Malaysia and Singapore.

This is not to say that Samui is not still an enjoyable place to spend some time. It still has some of the best accommodation values in Thailand and a laid-back atmosphere that makes it quite relaxing. If Samui survives its current identity crisis, it may yet escape the fate of Pattaya and Phuket. Airport or no airport, it still has the advantage of being off the mainland and far away from Bangkok. Coconuts are still the mainstay of the local economy and in fact, two million are shipped to Bangkok each month.

Samui is different from other islands in south Thailand and its inhabitants refer to themselves as *chao samui* – 'Samui folk' – rather than Thais. They are even friendlier than the average upcountry Thai, in my opinion, and have a great sense of humour, although those who are in constant contact with tourists may be a bit jaded. The island also has a distinctive cuisine, influenced by the omnipresent coconut, the main source of income for chao samui. Coconut palms blanket the island, from the hillocks right up to the beaches. The durian, rambutan and langsat fruits are also cultivated on Samui. The main island of the Samui group, Koh Samui, is Thailand's third largest, it's 247 square km and is surrounded by 80 smaller islands. Six of these, Phangan, Ta Loy, Tao, Tan, Ma Koh and Ta Pao are inhabited as well.

The population of Samui Island is for the most part concentrated in the port town of **Na Thon**, on the west side of the island facing the mainland and in 10 or 11 small villages scattered around the island. One road encircles the island with several side roads poking into the interior; this main road is now paved all the way around.

Information

The best time to visit the Samui group of islands is during the hot and dry season, February to late June. From July to October it can be raining on and off and between October and January there are sometimes heavy winds. However, many travellers have reported fine weather (and fewer crowds) in September/October. November tends to get some of the rain which also affects the east coast of Malaysia at this time. Prices tend to soar from February to July, whatever the weather.

Some travellers have been able to extend their tourist visas at the Koh Samui post office for 300B. Several travellers have written to say take care with local agents for train and bus bookings. Bookings sometimes don't get made at all, the bus turns out to be far inferior to what was expected or other hassles develop.

Great 45-minute massages for 40B are often available at the *sala* opposite the post office – male masseurs. Take care with local boat trips to nearby islands reported one visitor. His boat nearly swamped on a windy day and they eventually had to spend the night stranded on an uninhabited island.

In Surat or on Samui, you can pick up TAT's helpful Surat Thani map, which has maps of Surat city, the province, Ang Thong Marine Park and Samui Island, along with travel info.

Waterfalls

Besides the beaches and rustic, thatched roof bungalows, Samui has a couple of waterfalls. **Hin Lad** waterfall is about three km from Na Thon and is a worthwhile visit if you're waiting in town for a boat back to the mainland. You can get there on foot – walk 100 metres or so south of town on the main road, turning left at the road by the hospital. Go straight along this road about two km to arrive at the entrance to the falls. From here, it's about a half hour walk along a trail to the top of the falls. Near the parking lot at the entrance is another trail left to **Suan Dharmapala**, a meditation temple. **Na Muang** waterfall, in the centre of the island 10 km from Na Thon, is more scenic and less frequented. A *songthaew* from Na Thon to these latter falls should be about 20B. Songthaews can also be hired at Chaweng and Lamai Beaches.

Temples

For temple enthusiasts there is, at the southern end of the island, near the village of Bang Kao, **Wat Laem Saw** with an interesting old *chedi*. At the northern end, on a small rocky island joined to Samui by a causeway, is the so-called **Temple of the Big Buddha**. The modern image, about 12 metres in height, makes a nice silhouette against the tropical sky and sea behind it. The image is surrounded by *kutis*, or meditation huts, mostly unoccupied. The monks like receiving visitors there, though a sign in English requests that proper attire (no shorts) be worn on the temple premises. There is also an old semi-abandoned wat near the north end of Chaweng Beach where 10-day *vipassana* courses are occasionally held for farangs, led by Phra Khit (Keith), an Australian monk from Wat Suanmoke in Chaiya.

Beaches

There are plenty of beaches to choose from with bungalows appearing at more small bays all the time. Transportation has also improved so getting from beach to beach is no problem. The two main beaches at which most travellers rent bungalows are **Chaweng** and **Lamai**. The former has more bungalow 'villages', over 30 at the last count. Chaweng also is the longest beach, over twice the size of Lamai and has the island of **Mat Lang** opposite. Both beaches have clear blue-green waters; Lamai is a little quieter, though neither place is particularly lively. There is a coral reef for snorkelling and underwater sightseeing.

For more peace and quiet, try **Bo Phut**, **Big Buddha** or **Thong Yang** beaches. The first two are part of a bay that holds Koh Faan (the island with the 'big Buddha'), separated by a small headland. The water here is not quite as clear as at Chaweng or Lamai but the feeling of seclusion is greater, although it is becoming a little more travelled these days. Thong Yang Beach is located on the west side of the island and is even more secluded (only a few sets of bungalows there), but the beach isn't that great by Samui standards. There is also **Ang Thong Beach**, just north of Na Thon, very rocky but with more local colour (eg fishing boats) than the others. The south end of the island now has a few bungalows as well, set in little out-of-the-way coves – worth seeking out.

Places to Stay & Eat

Everyone has his or her own idea of what the perfect beach bungalow is. At Koh Samui, the search could take a week or two, with nearly 70 bungalow operations to choose from. Most offer roughly the same services and accommodation for 40B to 50B, though some are quite a bit more. The best thing to do is to go to the beach you think you want to stay at and pick one you like – look inside the huts, check out the restaurant, the menu, the guests. I prefer the smaller, four to eight bungalow sites, some of which are only 30B per night. They don't have the Singha-bottle porch bannisters and stained wooden frames of the larger sites, but can be just as comfortable. Food is touch and go at all the beaches – one meal can be great, the next at the very same place not so great. Fresh seafood is usually what they do best and the cheapest way to eat it is to catch it yourself and have the bungalow cooks prepare it for you, or buy it in one of the many fishing villages around the island, direct from the fishermen themselves or in the village markets. Good places to buy are in the relatively large Muslim fishing villages of Mae Nam, Bo Phut and Hua Thanon.

The island has changed so much in the years between editions of this book (not to mention the way it has changed since 1971, when the first tourists arrived), that I hesitate to name favourites. Cooks come and go, bungalows flourish and go bankrupt, owners die (my favourite, Niyom, in 1981) – you never can tell from season to season. Fortunately though, prices have remained fairly stable here in recent years, unlike at Phuket. It's easy to get from one beach to another, so you can always change bungalows. The jet set seem to be discovering Samui but thank goodness, Club Med decided to build on Phuket rather than here.

Here are some general comments on staying at Samui's various beaches, moving clockwise around the island from Na Thon:

Haat Mae Nam Fourteen km from Na Thon and is expanding rapidly in terms of bungalow development. Recommended is *Friendly*, which has clean, well-kept huts for 40B per person. Good food too. Also good are *LaPaz Villa* and *Silent*.

At the north-west end of Mae Nam Bay are the *Holiday, Golden Hut* and *Shangri-La*, all new enough that the staff try hard to please, yet experienced enough to know what they're doing.

At the headland, Laem Na Phra Laan, where Mae Nam ends before Bang Baw Bay begins is *Plant Inn*, also spelt *Phalarn*, with bungalows from 30B to 80B. Fair snorkelling and swimming here, a good site.

Bo Phut Beach This is fast becoming a favourite beach for peace and quiet. *World* and *Peace* each have huts ranging from 40B to 100B. The former has friendly staff and a good restaurant; the latter sells the biggest mushrooms I've ever seen. Food at the Peace is good but also expensive. *Calm* bungalows are nice, but *Neat* is anything but neat.

Boon Bungalows is a small operation in the fishing village of Bo Phut, east of World and the rest, close to the Bo Phut departure point for boats to Koh Phangan. Boon hasn't changed her 30B rate in several years and manages to stay full. Her specialties are gold-topped mushrooms and herb cookies.

There are a couple of cheap local-style restaurants in the village of Bo Phut itself.

Big Buddha Beach (Haat Phra Yai) This now has four bungalow operations, including the very expensive air-con *Nara Bungalows. Big Buddha Bungalows* is still your best bet – Niyom's wife carries on – for 40B up. It's still quiet and peaceful here. *Sunset* is not bad either with bungalows from 30B to 80B.

Chaweng Chaweng, Samui's longest beach, also has the island's highest concentration of bungalows. Instead of holding prices down to remain competitive as you might expect, many proprietors charge 60B and up per night; but then, many different 'villages' are owned by the same families. If there are a lot of vacant huts (there usually are during the low season) you can sometimes talk them down to 40B or even 30B. The beach is beautiful here, but lack of planning on the part of bungalow developers has led to trashy areas behind the bungalows.

Chaweng is where the night scene is with amplified music, fish roasts and impromptu beach parties. *Joy* bungalows now has a disco and bar girls. If you like quieter evenings, this might not be the beach for you.

There are km after km of beach and bungalows at Chaweng, so have a look around before deciding on a hut. Those currently in favour include *Munchies* (there are two; one was formerly Viking, one formerly Moon), *Maeo, Chaweng Villa* (which has a few 40B huts) and *Tawee*. Chaweng is a pretty good place to learn windsurfing as the hourly costs are comparatively low.

Thong Ta Khian Just between Chaweng and Lamai is a beautiful little fishing bay banked by huge boulders called Ao Tong Tha Khian. There is one small set of bungalows there at this writing, rather new, the name as yet uncertain (tentatively *Jom Thong*). The huts overlook the bay and cost 50B. There are a couple of good seafood restaurants down on the bay.

A little north of this bay is another small bay where the *Coral Cove* (or Coral Park) rents huts for 50B – very secluded.

Lamai After Chaweng, this is Samui's most popular beach for *farangs*. Lamai Beach rates are about the same as Chaweng. Overall it's a quieter beach, though the *Lanai Inn* does have a disco now. Recommended for cleanliness and friendliness are *White Sand* or *Palm*, but there are 10 others to chose from, most 50B to 80B for a small hut. For those in search of all-mod-cons the *Weekender* bungalows have more of them than most.

Away from the Lamai 'scene' further down at the north end of Lamai are the *Comfort, Silver Cliff* and *Tong Kaid Garden* bungalows.

There is good seafood at the fishermen's restaurant on the north end of Lamai, towards Chaweng. The *Vineyard Haven* in the centre of Lamai, has a popular happy hour.

South End Bungalow development is underway in some of the smaller bays and coves on Samui's south end. At **Ao Phang Ka** is the secluded *Emerald Cove* with 40B

rates – nice setting and perfectly quiet. Even more exclusive is the *Laem Set Inn* in Samui's south-eastern corner. In fact, it's supposedly a members-only place, but the proprietor, an Englishman, will occasionally take on new guests if there is room. Well-designed bungalows, quiet, scenic, near reefs and a good bar. Rates average 200B.

Thong Yang The car ferry jetty is here in Thong Yang Bay. Near the pier are *Sunflower, Coco Cabana Beach Club* and the *Samui Ferry Inn* all with huts in the 60B to 80B range. The Coco Cabana is the best of the lot.

Better are the *Lipa Lodge* and *Plern Guest House*. The Lipa Lodge is especially nice, with a good site on Laem Din Bay, just north of Thong Yang on the way to Na Thon. Rates start at 40B, most huts are about 80B, with a few as high as 350B. Good restaurant and bar here, very classy for a beach bungalow actually. The upscale Plern bungalows are 100B and 150B during high season weekends, 80B to 90B at other times.

Na Thon (the port town) If you want or need to stay in Samui's largest settlement, (pronounced Naa Thawn) there are seven places to chose from. The *Seaview Hotel* is Samui's oldest, a wooden building overlooking the water; safe, clean and friendly. Rooms are 60B with shared bath, 70B including fan. Downstairs is a Thai-Chinese restaurant specialising in *khao man kai*.

The Seaside Hotel has changed its name to *Palace Hotel* and has been remodeled inside and out. Clean, spacious rooms start at 100B and they have a restaurant downstairs. Next door to the Palace is a dark wooden building with no sign that happens to be Na Thom's cheapest hotel at 40B to 45B per room.

Chao Koh Bungalow, a bit north of town is 300B to 600B. *Samui Bungalow*, near the post office, is 120B up for rather small rooms with fan and bath. South of town are the *Chokana*, 100B single or double, 150B for a room that sleeps four and the *Jinta*, 150B.

There are several good places to eat in Na Thon. On the road facing the harbour are *King's Cafe*, *Darin*, *Siriroad* and *Bamboo House*, all serving seafood and traveller's specialties. The shark steak dinner at Bamboo House is an especially good deal, 30B for a substantial serving of fish, potatoes and veggies. Farther down the road towards Thong Yang is the *Sri Samui*, a Thai seafood garden restaurant, also quite good. During the high season, these restaurants fill up at night with travellers waiting for the night ferry.

Getting There

Express Boats Three express boats go to Samui daily from Ban Don and each takes two to 2½ hours to reach the island. The departure times are usually 8 am, 10 am and 1 pm, though these change from time to time. Passage is 60B one way, 100B round trip. The express ferry boats have two decks, one with seats below and an upper deck that is really just a big luggage rack – but it is good for sunbathing.

From Samui back to Surat, there are departures at 7.15 am, noon and 2.30 pm. The 7.15 am boat includes a bus ride to the train station in Phun Phin; the 2.30 pm boat includes a bus to the train station and to the bus station.

Night Ferry There is also a slow boat for Samui that leaves the Ban Don pier each night at 9 pm, reaching Na Thon around 3 am. This one costs 40B for the upper deck, 50B down below. Not recommended unless you arrive in Surat too late for the fast boat and don't want to stay in Ban Don. Some travellers have reported however, that a night on the boat is preferable to a night in a noisy Surat Thani short-time hotel. It does give you more sun time on Samui, after all. The night ferry back to Samui leaves Na Thon at 9 pm, arriving at 3 am.

Car Ferry Tour buses run directly from Bangkok to Koh Samui, via the car-ferry from Don Sak in Surat Thani province, for around 220B. Check with the big tour bus companies or any travel agency. Pedestrians or people in private vehicles can also take the Don Sak ferry, which costs 40B, leaves at 9 am, 3.40 pm and 4 pm, and takes 1½ hours. Don Sak is about 60 km from Surat and a bus from the Surat bus station is 10B and takes 45 minutes to an hour to arrive there. If you're coming north from Nakhorn Si Thammarat, this might be the ferry to take, though from Surat the Ban Don ferry is definitely more convenient.

From Koh Samui an air-con bus to Bangkok leaves at 2.30 pm daily, arriving at 5 am. Another leaves at 8 am for Hat Yai, arriving at 2.30 pm. Tickets are 220B and 180B and are sold through several travel agencies in Na Thon.

One problem with this ferry service is that it has opened the island up to bus loads of day trippers. 'I counted 40 bus loads of day trippers from Surat Thani descending on the Big Buddha temple one Sunday', reported a visitor.

Train The State Railway also does rail/bus/ferry tickets straight through to Samui from Bangkok. The fares are 369B for a second class upper berth, 399B second class lower berth, 299B second class seat and 142B third class seat. This is 10B cheaper than doing the connections yourself.

Getting Around

It's quite possible to hitch around the island, despite the fact that anyone on the island with a car is likely to want to boost their income by charging for rides. The official *songthaew* fares are 10B from Na Thon to Lamai, Mae Nam or Bo Phut, 15B to Big Buddha or Chaweng. These minibuses run regularly all day.

Several places rent motorcycles in Na Thon. The going rate is 150B per day, but on longer rents you can get the price down (say 280B for two days, 400B for three days). Take it easy on the bikes; several *farangs* die or are seriously injured in motorcycle accidents every year on Samui and besides, the locals really don't like seeing their roads become race tracks.

KOH PHANGAN
เกาะพะงัน
Nearby Koh Phangan, about a half hour's boat ride north of Koh Samui, is worth a visit for its deserted beaches and, if you like snorkelling, for its live coral formations. In the interior of this somewhat smaller island are the **Than Sadet** and **Phaeng** waterfalls. There's an interesting meditation temple, **Wat Khao Tham**, beautifully situated on top of a hill near the little village of Ban Khrai. Some travellers are already looking for islands even further off the beaten track. **Koh Tae**, directly across from the Thong Sala pier, even has a few bungalows now, as does **Koh Tao** to the north.

Places to Stay
Bungalow operations on Phangan are mainly located along the west coast just north of the island's biggest town, **Thong Sala**, and around the south-eastern tip on or near **Haat Rin** beach. This island definitely deserves its word-of-mouth billing as 'like Samui 10 years ago', with a much lower concentration of bungalows, many deserted beaches and coves and an overall less 'spoiled' atmosphere, though things are of course changing quickly. Phangan afficionados say the seafood is fresher and cheaper than on Samui's beaches, but it really varies from place to place. Bungalows go for 30B to 40B a night on average; many do not have electricity or running water. A few have generators which are only on for limited hours in the evening – the lights dim when they make a fruit shake. For many people, this actually adds to Phangan's appeal.

Between Hat Rin in the south and Ban Khrai village a little north, there are several scattered bungalow villages and the locals also rent rooms to travellers, especially from December to February when just about everything is filled up. You can get a hut for a month at very low rates here. There are also a few bungalows on the north end of the island near Ban Chalok Lam.

Above Thong Sala are *OK*, *Thanong*, *Windward* and *Phangan* bungalows. Just south of Thong Sala are *Anna's Huts*, *Sundance*, *Mr Good* and *Boon* bungalows. The beaches in the Thong Sala area are really rather disappointing in comparison with beaches further south and especially in contrast to Haat Rin on the lower east coast.

On Haat Rin, a long, beautiful, quiet beach are the *Paradise*, *Haad Rin*, *Sunrise* and *Seaview*. All offer about the same type of accommodation. The Paradise and the Haad Rin are very popular eating places. Across the ridge from east Haat Rin is the lower west coast, also called Haat Rin. Here find *Sunset*, *Mac's* and *Palm Beach*. On both sides of Haat Rin busy hammers and saws are putting together new huts, so there are probably quite a few more places by now. The west side of course has the sunset but the beach isn't quite as nice as the one on the east side; however, just a short walk north of west Haat Rin is a string of secluded coves that are quite nice.

A few foreigners have stayed at Wat Khao Tham – there's plenty of room there if you don't mind very basic accommodation. You'll have to walk down the steep hill every day for food. An American monk lived here for over a decade and his ashes are interred on a cliff overlooking a field of palms below the wat.

Getting Around
A couple of roads branch out over the island from Thong Sala, primarily in north-south directions. There are no roads (only footpaths) in the very southern part of the island. So if you stay down

there and need to go into Thong Sala (eg to change money at one of the several money-changers), you must walk first to **Ban Khrai**, which is five km north on the windward side (west coast). In Ban Khrai, there begins a road that goes to Thong Sala, passing through the market village of **Ban Tai**. You can get a motorcycle taxi in Ban Khrai all the way to Thong Sala, seven km north, for 15B. If motorcycles are scarce in Ban Khrai, you can walk another km north to Ban Tai, where they are more frequent.

There is a road which goes north-west from Thong Sala a few km along the shoreline to the villages of **Ban Hin Kong** and **Ban Si Thanu**. Another road travels straight north across the island to **Ban Chalok Lam**. A motorcycle taxi from Thong Sala to Ban Chalok Lam is 15B. A little way beyond the village is a beach called **Mae Haat** where there are a few huts for rent.

You can also rent motorcycles in Thong Sala for 150B to 200B a day.

Getting There

Boats to Koh Phangan leave Na Thon, Koh Samui every day at 3.45 pm. The trip takes 30 minutes and costs 30B one-way. You also have to pay another 5B to reach the shore by long boat as the boat can't dock on the island. Boats back to Samui leave Phangan's pier at 6.15 am daily. You can also get a small boat direct from Samui's Bo Phut village to Haat Rin on Koh Phangan for 50B. The boat leaves just about every day, depending on the weather, around 9.30 am and takes 40 to 45 minutes to reach the bay at Haat Rin. Sometimes there is also an afternoon boat. As more and more people choose this route to Koh Phangan, service will probably get more regular. This is the boat to take if you want to stay on Haat Rin.

There is also a night boat to Thong Sala from Ban Don for 60B one-way which leaves at 11 pm and a daily ferry at 8 am which costs 60B to Koh Samui and 75B to

Koh Phangan or 25B from Samui to Koh Phangan.

ANG THONG NATIONAL MARINE PARK
สวนสัตว์ทะเลอ่างทองแห่งชาติ

From Koh Samui, a couple of tour operators run day trips out to the Ang Thong archipelago, 31 km north-west. A typical tour costs 150B per person, leaves Na Thon at 8.30 am and returns at 5 pm. Lunch is included, along with snorkelling in a sort of lagoon formed by one of the islands, from whence Ang Thong gets its name ('Golden Tub'), and a climb to the top of a 240-metre hill to view the whole island group. Departures are usually only twice a week. At least once a month there's also an overnight tour, as there are bungalows on **Koh Wua Ta Lap**. You may be able to book passage alone to the Ang Thong islands; inquire at Songserm Travel Service or Koh Samui Travel Centre in Na Thon.

NAKHON SI THAMMARAT
จังหวัดนครศรีธรรมราช

This city is 814 km from Bangkok. Centuries before the 8th century Srivijaya empire subjugated the peninsula, there was a city called Ligor or Lagor, capital of the Tambralinga kingdom, which was well-known throughout Oceania. Later, when Ceylonese-ordained monks established a cloister at the city, the name was changed to the Sanskrit *Nagara Sri Dhammaraja* ('City of the Sacred Dharma-King'), rendered in Thai phonetics as Nakhon Si Thammarat. Thai shadow-play (*nang*) and classical dance-drama (*lakhorn*, Thai pronunciation of Lagor) are supposed to have been developed in Nakhon Si Thammarat; buffalo-hide shadow puppets and dance masks are still made here.

Today Nakhon Si Thammarat is known for its neilloware, a silver and black alloy/enamel jewellery technique borrowed from China many centuries ago. It is also, oddly enough, known for its 'gangsters'. Yes, the best hoodlums in Thailand

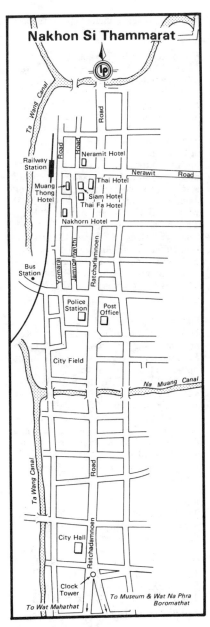

Nakhon Si Thammarat

supposedly come from here, although I can't say I've ever met one.

The new centre of Nakhon Si Thammarat is north of the clock tower where Ratchadamnoen Rd splits. The new city has all the hotels and most of the restaurants, as well as more movie theatres per square km than any other city in Thailand.

Wat Mahathat

This is the city's most historic site, reputed to be over a thousand years old. Reconstructed in the mid-13th century, it features a 78-metre *chedi*, crowned by a solid gold spire weighing several 100 kg. The temple's *bot* contains one of Thailand's three identical Phra Singh Buddhas, one of which is supposed to have been originally cast in Ceylon before being brought to Sukhothai (through Nakhon Si Thammarat), Chiang Mai, and later, Ayuthaya. The other images are at Wat Phra Singh in Chiang Mai and the National Museum in Bangkok – each is claimed to be the original.

Besides the distinctive bot and chedi there are many intricately designed *wiharns* surrounding the chedi, several of which contain crowned Nakhon Si Thammarat-Ayuthaya style Buddhas in glass cabinets. One *wiharn* houses a museum with carved wooden kruts (*garudas*, Vishnu's mythical bird-mount), old Siwichai votive tablets, Buddha figures of every description including a standing Dvaravati figure and a Siwichai *naga* Buddha, pearl-inlaid alms bowls and other oddities. It would really be good if the artefacts were labelled – no labels in Thai or English. This is the biggest wat in the south, comparable to Wat Po and other large Bangkok wats. Well worth a trip, if you like wats.

Wat Na Phra Boromathat

Across the road from Wat Mahathat, this is where monks who serve at Mahathat live. There is a nice Gandhara-style fasting Buddha in front of the *bot* here.

Nakhon Si Thammarat National Museum

This is past the principal wats on Ratchadamnoen Rd heading south, across from Wat Thao Khot and Wat Phet Jarik, on the left – 1B by city bus or 2B by *songthaew*. Since the Tampaling (or Tambralinga) kingdom traded with Indian, Arabic, Dvaravati and Champa states, much art from these places found its way to the Nakhon Si Thammarat area, and some is now on display in the National Museum here. Notable are Dong-Son bronze drums, Dvaravati Buddha images and Pallava (south Indian) Hindu sculpture. Locally-produced art is also on display.

Go straight to the 'Art of Southern Thailand' exhibit in a room on the left of the foyer, if you've already had your fill of the usual Thai art history surveys from Ban Chiang to Ayuthaya. This room has many fine images of Nakhon Si Thammarat provenance, including Phutthasihing, U Thong and late Ayuthaya styles. The Nakhon Si Thammarat-produced Ayuthaya style seems to be the most common, with distinctive, almost comical, crowned faces. The so-called Phutthasihing-style Buddha looks a little like the Palla-influenced Chiang Saen Buddha but is shorter and more 'pneumatic'.

Hindu Temples

There are also three Hindu temples in Nakhon Si Thammarat, along Ratchadamnoen, inside the city walls. Brahmin priests from these temples take part each year in the royal ploughing ceremony in Bangkok. One temple houses a locally famous Shivalingam (phallic shrine) which is worshipped amongst others, by women hoping to bear children.

Other

Every year in mid-October there is a southern Thai festival called **Chaak Phra Pak Tai** held in Songkhla, Surat Thani and Nakhon Si Thammarat. In Nakhon Si Thammarat the festival is centred around Wat Mahathat and includes performances of *nang thalung*, *lakhorn*, etc.

Places to Stay – bottom end

Most of Nakhon Si Thammarat's hotels are near the train and bus stations.

On Yomaraj Rd, across from the railway station, is the *Si Thong*, with adequate rooms for 70B with fan and bath. Also on Yomaraj are the *Nakhon* and *Yaowarat*, same rates and facilities as Si Thong.

On Jamroenwithi Rd (walk straight down Neramit Rd opposite the train station two blocks; make a right on Jamroenwithi) is the *Siam*, a large hotel with rooms with fan and bath for 80B up. This hotel also has buses to Hat Yai, Surat and Bangkok. Across the street is the *Muang Thong*, 70B for rooms with fan and bath. Near the Siam, on the same side of the street, is the *Thai Fa*, which, at 60B, has better rooms than either Nakhon or Si Thong.

Places to Stay – top end

Nakhon Si Thammarat's flashiest hotels are the *Thai* (tel 356505, 356451) on Ratchadamnoen Rd, two blocks from the railway station, and the *Taksin* (tel 356788-90) on Si Prat Rd. Both have fan and air-con rooms. Fan rooms cost from 250B, air-con from 350B to 500B.

Other places are the *Neramit* (tel 356514), on the corner of Neramit and Jamroenwithi Rds, which has rooms starting at 90B. The Neramit has a dark, sleazy coffee shop downstairs. Others are the *Seree* and the *Saen Suk*.

Places to Eat

There are lots of funky old Chinese restaurants along Yomaraj and Jamroenwithi. Two very good, inexpensive Chinese restaurants are located between the Neramit and Thai Fa hotels on Jamroenwithi Rd – *Bo Seng* and *Yong Seng* (no English signs). Nearby is a small Thai *kaeng* shop with excellent *kaeng som* and *tom kha kai*.

Getting There

Bus Air-con buses bound for Nakhon Si Thammarat leave Bangkok's Southern Bus Terminal daily at 7.40 pm and 8.05 pm, arriving 12 hours later, fare 200B. Non air-con buses leave at 8 pm and 9 pm for about 50B less. Private tour bus companies do trips to Nakhon Si Thammarat for around 220B.

From Surat Thani there are daily buses to Nakhon. Check with the tour bus companies on Na Muang Rd. A tour bus from Surat to Nakhon should cost about 65B one-way. Buses run from Songkhla to Hat Yai to Nakhon. From Songkhla to Nakhom, you cross the river by ferry – there can be long delays here. Check with the Choke Dee Hotel in Songkhla or at one of the tour bus companies on Niphat-U-Thit 2 Rd in Hat Yai. *Muang Tai Tours* on Jamroenwithi Rd in Nakhon Si Thammarat does a 60B trip to Surat that includes a good meal and a video movie.

Train Southbound trains stop at the junction of Khao Chum Thong, about 30 km west of Nakhon Si Thammarat, from where you must take a bus or taxi to the coast. One train actually goes all the way to Nakhon Si Thammarat (there is a branch line from Khao Chum Thong to Nakhon Si Thammarat): the Rapid No 47, which leaves Bangkok's Hualamphong station at 5.30 pm, arriving in Nakhon Si Thammarat at 10.15 am. Most travellers will not be booking a train directly to Nakhon Si Thammarat, but if you want to, first class fare is 590B, second class 279B, third class 133B, not including surcharges for Rapid service or sleeping berths.

AROUND NAKHON SI THAMMARAT

Laem Talumpuk

แหลมตะลุมพุก

This is a small scenic cape not far from the *amphoe muang*. Take a bus from Neramit Rd going east to Pak Nakhon for 8B, then cross the inlet by ferry to Laem Talumpuk.

Haat Sa Bua

หาดสระบัว

Sixteen km north of the *amphoe muang* in the Tha Sala district, about 9B by *songthaew*, off Route 401 to Surat, are some semi-deserted white sand beaches – no tourists. There are some very reasonably priced restaurants here and there are also vendors selling prawn-cakes, reported one traveller.

Haat Hin Ngam

หาดหินงาม

Haat Hin Ngam is a stunning beach 60 km north of Nakhon Si Thammarat in Sichon district. Get the bus for Haat Hin Ngam or Sichon from the *Baw Kaw Saw* bus station, 15B. There are some bungalows for rent here.

PHATTALUNG (population 21,000)

จังหวัดพัทลุง

Over 860 km from Bangkok and 110 km from Hat Yai, Phattalung is one of the south's only rice-growing provinces and it has prospered as a result. The *amphoe muang* is fairly small, you can walk around the perimeter of downtown Phattalung in an hour, even stopping for rice, but it is unique among southern Thai towns. Judging from the number of *hang thong* – gold dealers – on Poh Saat Rd, there must be a large Chinese population.

Phattalung is also famous for the original *nang thalung*, Thai shadow-play named most likely for Phattalung – *nang* means hide (untanned leather), thalung from Phattalung. The Thai shadow-play tradition remains only in Nakhon Si Thammarat and Phattalung, though the best performances are seen in the latter. A typical performance begins at midnight and lasts four to five hours. Usually they take place during *ngaan wat* or temple fairs.

The town is situated between two picturesque foliage-trimmed limestone peaks, **Khao Ok Thalu** (punctured-chest mountain) and **Khao Hua Taek** (broken-head mountain). Local myth has it that

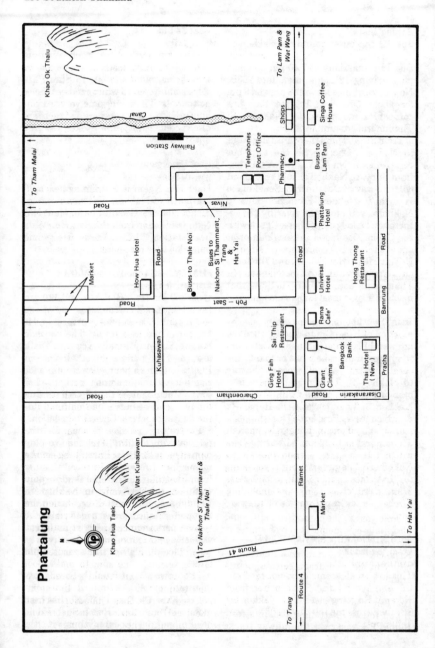

Phattalung

these two mountains were the wife and mistress of a third mountain to the north, **Khao Muang**, who fought a fierce battle over the adulterous husband, leaving them with their 'wounds'. The names refer to their geographic peculiarities – Ok Thalu has a tunnel through its upper peak, while Hua Taek is sort of split at the top. Like most Thai towns, Phattalung's street plan is laid out in a grid pattern. Most of the local sights are nearby. To change money it's best to go to the Thai Farmer's Bank on Ramet Rd.

Wat Wang

Over 100 years old, this is the oldest *wat* in Phattalung. Originally the palace of a Thai prince was located just east of the wat (*wang* means palace), but only the wall remains. The original *chedi* is in front of the wat. A closed *bot* has a decaying set of murals with Buddhist and Ramayana themes. You have to open the doors and windows to see them. Wat Wang is four to five km east of Phattalung town on the road to Lam Bam. Take a *songthaew* next to the PO for the 3B ride to Wat Wang.

Wat Kuhasawan

On the west side of town – Kuhasawan Rd from the train station leads right to it – this comprises one large cave with rather ugly statues, but the cave is high and cool. A tall passageway leads deeper into the cave – lights can be switched on by the monks. Steps lead around the cave to the top of the mountain for a nice view of rice fields and mountains further west.

To the right of the main cave is an old hermit's cave – the monk died in 1973 and his form is commemorated by a statue at the second level of stairs. Good views of Khao Ok Thalu and most of Phattalung city can be had from certain points around this cave.

Lam Pam

If you follow Phattalung's main street, Ramet Rd, east over the railway tracks past Wat Wang, you'll come to Lam Pam on the banks of the Thale Luang, the upper part of the south's inland sea. For 5B you can ride a *songthaew* from next to the post office out to Lam Pam in 15 minutes, or hire a motorcycle for 10B.

Under shady trees next to the sea (which is fresh water here), are beach chairs and tables where you can relax, enjoy the breeze and order food – crab, mussels, other shellfish, squid, plus beer, soda, etc. Although the inland sea itself is not at all spectacular, this is a nice spot to while away a few hours drinking beer and eating the fabulous *pla meuk kluay yaang* ('banana' squid – egg-carrying squid, roasted over charcoal), along with *mieng kham*, that unique do-it-yourself concoction of dried shrimp, peanuts, lime, garlic, ginger, chilli, toasted coconut and salty-sweet sauce wrapped in wild tea leaves. Cheap, too.

Thale Noi Waterbird Sanctuary
แหล่งพิทักษ์นกน้ำทะเลน้อย

Thale Noi is a small inland sea or lake 32 km north-east of Phattalung which is a waterbird sanctuary protected by the Forestry Department. There are 182 species of waterbird here, most prominently the *nok i kong* with its long funny feet which quiver like malfunctioning landing gear as the bird takes flight, and the *nok pet daeng*, a small, red-headed 'duck bird', related to the whistling teal, that skitters along the water.

The sea itself is sort of a large swamp similar to the Everglades in the southern US. The major forms of vegetation are water vines and *don kok*, a reed which the nok i kong use to build large 'platforms' over the water for nesting purposes. The local Thais use these same reeds, after drying them in the sun, to make floor mats which are sold throughout Phattalung.

To get there, take a Thale Noi bus from the local bus stop on Poh-Saat Rd in Phattalung. The bus stops at the sanctuary after about an hour's journey and costs 8B. Long boats can be hired at the pier to take passengers out and around the Thale Noi for two hours for 150B.

Tham Malai
ถ้ำมาลัย

Three km north of Phattalung near the railway is a hill with a large cave, Tham Malai, at its base. On the top of the hill are some Chinese shrines, though a Thai Theravada monk resides there. There are excellent views of Phattalung and surrounding mountains from the top.

The cave itself is more interesting than the shrines. Bring a torch (flashlight) and you can explore the various rooms within the cavern. The cave is more or less in its natural state, stalagmites and stalactites intact. Even without a light, it's worth exploring a bit – when the cave reaches its darkest point, you'll come upon an opening leading back around to daylight.

If the canal running parallel to the railway has enough water, you can get a boat for 5B as far as Tham Malai – easiest in December and January. If the water is too low, walk along the tracks until you come to a footbridge which will take you over the canal onto a path leading to the cave.

Places to Stay

Ramet Rd is the main drag where you will find all but one of Phattalung's five hotels.

At 43 Ramet Rd, the *Phattalung* is dingy and costs 50B with fan and bath. The *Sakon* (English sign reads 'Universal Hotel') is a short distance west of the Phattalung Hotel on Ramet Rd, at the intersection with Poh-Saat Rd. It's clean and has adequate rooms with fan and bath for 65B.

Across from the Grant cinema, corner of Ramet and Charoentham, is the *Ging Fah* (tel 611055). Similar to the Universal for 70B.

The *Thai Hotel* is a new, large hotel on Disara-Nakarin Rd, off Ramet near the Rama Cafe and Bangkok Bank. It should be open by the time you read this and should cost about 90B up with fan and bath.

The *How Hua* on the corner of Poh-Saat and Kuhasawan has rooms with fan and bath for 100B, air-con rooms for 200B. It's also very clean.

Places to Eat

Most cheap restaurants in Phattalung are on the grubby side, but *Sai Thip*, a clean, airy place on Ramet Rd across from Disara-Nakarin Rd, has great *khao man kai*, *khao naa pet*, *kuaytiaw*, etc for 10B a plate.

The best restaurant in town is the well-known *Hong Thong* on Pracha Bamrung Rd – turn left off Disara-Nakarin Rd just past the new Thai Hotel. This is a family-run Chinese place and the seafood is excellent since Phattalung is only a few km from the Thale Luang. *Hawy jaw*, crab sausage served with sliced pineapple on the side, is very nice. Also excellent are *pla kao neung puay* (whole fish steamed in a broth of onions, peppers, Chinese mushrooms and tangy plums), *pla tuk phat phet* (catfish fried in chilli and fresh holy basil), *yam ma-muang* (spicy mango salad), *kai manao raat nam krewi* (chicken in lime sauce), *pla kapong khao thawt* (fresh-water perch fried whole) and *kung nam jeud phao* (grilled fresh-water shrimp). Prices are not high.

The market off Poh-Saat Rd is a good place for cheap take-aways (take-outs). For breakfast, try the local specialty *khao yam*, dry rice mixed with coconut, peanuts, lime leaves, and shrimp – delicious. About three km west of town there is a market. It's where Route 4 meets Route 41 and there are several food stalls selling Muslim food like *khao mok kai* (chicken biryani) and the southern Thai version of *kai yang*.

Getting There

Bus Buses from the *Baw Kaw Saw* station

in Nakhon Si Thammarat take 1 ½ hours and cost 30B. Buses from Hat Yai are also 30B and take about the same time.

Buses from Trang are 25B and take 1 ½ hours.

Train Express trains from Bangkok leave Hualamphong at 2.30 pm and 4.10 pm, arriving in Phattalung at 6.55 am and 8.38 am. Basic fares are 611B first class, 288B second class, 137B third class, plus appropriate surcharges.

SONGKHLA (population 73;000)
จังหวัดสงขลา

1320 km from Bangkok. Another former Srivijaya satellite on the east coast, not much is known about the pre-8th century history of Songkhla, called Singora by the Malays. The city, small in area and population, is on a peninsula between the **Thale Sap Songkhla** (an 'inland sea') and the South China Sea (or Gulf of Thailand, depending on how you look at it). The inhabitants are a colourful mixture of Thais, Chinese and Muslims (ethnic Malays), and the local architecture and cuisine reflect the combination. The seafood served along the white **Samila Beach** is excellent, though the beach itself is not that great for swimming, especially if you've just come from Koh Samui. However, beaches are not Songkhla's main attraction, even if the TAT so promotes them – the town has plenty of other curiosities to offer. The evergreen trees along Samila Beach do give it a rather nice visual effect.

The Waterfront
The waterfront on the inland sea is buzzing with activity most of the time. Ice is loaded onto fishing boats on their way out to sea, baskets and baskets of fish are unloaded onto the pier from boats just arrived, fish markets are setting up and disassembling, long boats doing taxi business between islands and mainland are tooling about. The fish smell along the piers is pretty powerful – be warned.

Around Town
For interesting Songkhla architecture, walk along the back street parallel to the inland sea waterfront – Nakhon Nawk Rd. Many of the buildings here are very old and show Chinese, Portuguese and Malay influence. South of Samila Beach is a quaint Muslim fishing village – here is where the tourist photos of gaily painted fishing vessels are taken.

National Museum
This is in a 100-year-old building of southern Sino-Portuguese architecture, between Rong Muang Rd and Jana Rd (off Vichianchom Rd), next to Songkhla's bus station. Admission is free and there are exhibits from all national art-style periods, especially Srivijaya.

Wat Matchimawat
On Saiburi Rd towards Hat Yai, this has an old marble Buddha image and a small museum. There is also an old *chedi* at the top of **Khao Noi**, a hill rising up at the north end of the peninsula.

Koh Yaw
เกาะยอ

An island on the inland sea, Koh Yaw (or Kaw Yaw) is worth visiting just to see the cotton-weaving cottage industry there. The good-quality, distinctive *phaa kaw yaw* is hand-woven on rustic looms and available on the spot at 'wholesale' prices – meaning you still have to bargain but have a chance of undercutting the market price. Many different households around this thickly forested, sultry island are engaged in cotton-weaving, so it is best to go from place to place comparing prices and fabric quality. There are also a couple of wats, **Khao Bo** and **Thai Yaw**, to visit.

Getting There Boat taxis to Koh Yaw are available from the Songkhla inlet near the canal which feeds into the inland sea. The trip is 5B per person and boats are easiest to get in the morning around 7 am to 8 am. An entire long boat to Koh Yaw,

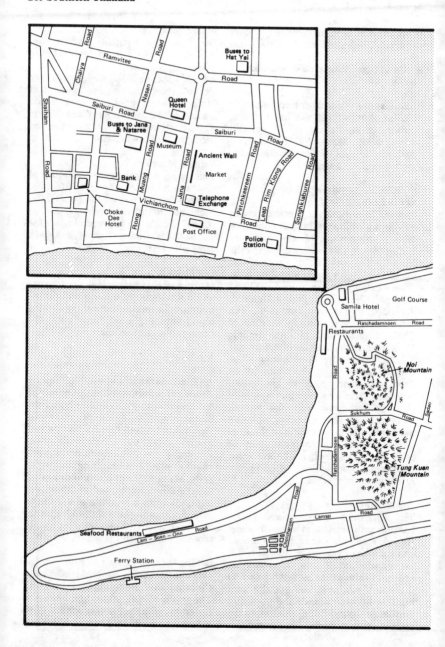

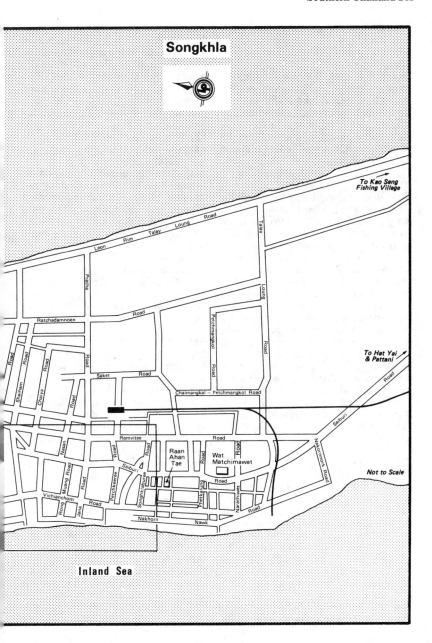

Songkhla

To Kao Seng
Fishing Village

Leon Rim Talay Loung Road

Pratha

Road

Talay

Loung

Road

Ratchadamnoen

Road

Petchmangkol Road

To Hat Yai
& Pattani

Road

Road

Road

Road

Saket Road

Chaimangkal — Petchmangkol Road

Saiburi

Road

Shaiham

Chava

Road

Road

Nasin

Road

Ramvitee Road

Saiburi

Road

Road

Road

Raan
Ahan
Tae

Wat
Matchimawat

Road

Nakornmork Road

Not to Scale

Muang Road

Petchkeere

Songkhlaburee

Phetklung

Narathiwes

Road

Vichianchom

Rong Jana Road

Nakhorn Nawk Road

Inland Sea

with pilot, can be rented for 70B to 100B, anytime of day.

Other
Songkhla is south Thailand's educational centre; there is one university, several colleges, technical schools and research institutes, a nursing college and a military training camp, all in or near the town. **Suan Tun**, a topiary park across from the Samila Hotel, has yew hedges trimmed into animal shapes.

Places to Stay - bottom end
Best deal in Songkhla is the *Songkhla Hotel*, on Vichianchom Rd across from the Fishing Station. The 90B rooms are very clean and comfortable; towels and purified water go with the room. Also good, but less quiet, is the *Choke Dee* (tel 311158), just down the road from the Songkhla. Similar rooms there are 120B per double (all rooms are doubles here).

The *Suk Somboon II* on Saiburi Rd, near the museum, is not bad for 100B a double although they're just wooden rooms, off a large central area, and you have to ask for that price – posted rates start at 130B. There's also a more expensive *Suk Somboon I* on the same road a block south, 150B up. The *Wiang Sawan*, in the middle of the block between Saiburi and Ramwithi Rds not far from Wat Matchimawat, has rooms from 140B.

Places to Stay - top end
The *Samila Hotel* (tel 311310-4) on the beachfront has rooms starting from 700B – all air-con, there's a swimming pool and other luxuries. Other expensive hotels include the *Queen* (tel 311138) at 20 Sai Buri Rd, next door to the Suksomboon 2, with air-con rooms from 240B. The similarly priced *Charn* (tel 311903) is on the same road but on the outskirts of the downtown area on the way to Hat Yai.

Places to Eat
There are lots of good restaurants in

Songkhla but a few tend to overcharge foreign tourists. The Chinese restaurant on the corner opposite the Choke Dee Hotel is a rip-off, it looks good but walk on by unless you think 25B for fried rice is reasonable. The best seafood place, according to the locals, is the *Raan Aahaan Tae* on Nang Ngam Rd (off Songkhlaburi Rd and parallel to Saiburi Rd). The seafood on the beach is pretty good too – try the curried crab claws or spicy fried squid.

A great day and night market off Vichianchom Rd offers excellent market fare – a couple of stalls feature tasty Muslim food in addition to the usual Thai-Chinese selections. The local Muslim speciality is *khao mok kai*, it's like a chicken biryani.

The *Black Gold Pub* on Sadao Rd towards Samila Beach, next door to the Khao Noi Palace, is a hang-out of sorts for people who work on off-shore oil rigs. Look for the water buffalo skull out the front.

Getting There
Bus A *Pak Tai Company* tour bus from Surat to Songkhla/Hat Yai costs 130B one-way and leaves the Muang Thong Hotel in Surat at 4.45 am.

Air-con state-run buses leave Bangkok's Southern Bus Terminal daily at 6.30 pm, 7 pm and 7.35 pm, arriving 19 hours later, for 319B. Non air-con buses are 182B or 187B to Hat Yai. The privately-owned tour buses out of Bangkok (and there are several available) are quicker but cost around 350B.

See the Hat Yai section for details of transport between Hat Yai and Songkhla.

Train For trains see Hat Yai below.

Getting Around
For getting around in town, *songthaews* circulate Songkhla and take passengers for 2B to any point on their route.

HAT YAI (population 130,000)

อำเภอหาดใหญ่

Hat Yai, 1298 km from Bangkok, is south Thailand's commercial centre and one of the kingdom's largest cities, though it is only a district of Songkhla province. A steady stream of customers from Malaysia keep Hat Yai's downtown business district booming. Everything from dried fruit to stereos are sold in the shops along Niphat-U-Thit Rds Nos 1, 2 and 3, not far from the railway station. Many travellers stay in Hat Yai, taking side trips to Songkhla, but I would recommend the opposite.

Information & Orientation

The TAT Tourist Office (tel 243747) is at 1/1 Soi 2 Niphat Uthit 3 Rd. The Tourist Police can also be found here. Thai Airways (tel 243711) and Malaysian Airlines System (tel 243729, 245443) are both on Niphat Uthit 2 Rd.

Four of Hat Yai's six cinemas have sound rooms where the original English soundtrack of English-language films can be heard while watching films that have been dubbed in Thai for the rest of the theatre; *Siam* (Phetkasem Rd), *Coliseum* (Pratchathipat Rd), *Chalerm Thai* (Suppasamongsan Rd) and the *Haadyai Rama* (Phetkasem Rd).

Wat Hat Yai Nai

West of town a few km, off Phetkasem Rd towards the airport, is Wat Hat Yai Nai. A very large (35 metres) reclining Buddha on the premises (Phra Phut Mahatamongkon) is currently being restored along with the *wiharn* to house it. Inside the image's gigantic base is a curious little museum/souvenir shop/mausoleum. The old abbot likes receiving visitors. To get there, hop on a *songthaew* near the intersection of Niphat-U-Thit 1 Rd and Phetkasem, get off after crossing the U Thapao Bridge.

Bullfights

Bullfighting, involving two bulls in opposition rather than man and bull, takes place as a spectator sport twice monthly in Hat Yai. On the first Sunday of each month it's at an arena next to the Nora Hotel off Thamnoonwithi Rd (the same road which leads to the railway station), and on the second Sunday it is at the Hat Yai Arena on Route 4, near the airport. Matches take place continuously all day from 10.30 am until 6 pm and admission is 10B to 30B – although many hundred times that amount changes hands during the non-stop betting by Thai spectators.

Places to Stay – bottom end

Hat Yai has dozens of hotels within walking distance of the railway station. Very popular with Malaysian visitors is the *King's Hotel* on Niphat-U-Thit 3 Rd. Rooms start at 120B.

Cheaper hotels nearby include the *Cathay Guest House* on the corner of Thamnoonwithi and Niphat-U-Thit 2, three blocks from the station, with rooms ranging from 80B to 150B; there is also a 50B dorm. The Cathay has become a traveller's centre in Hat Yai because of its good location, helpful staff and plentiful travel info for trips onward, including tips on travel in Malaysia. They serve food (and also don't mind if you bring takeways in and eat in the lounge). There is a bus ticket agency downstairs. The *Saeng Fa*, off Niphat-U-Thit 3 Rd, has clean 140B rooms with fan and bath or 240B for air-con. Also on Niphat-U-Thit 3 Rd are the *Tong Nam* and the *Rung Fah*, both rather basic Chinese hotels with 80B/100B rooms, single/double. *Kim Hua*, further south on the same road, is 130B for fan and bath.

The *Savoy*, 3½ blocks from the station on Niphat-U-Thit 2 Rd, has good 80B rooms although doubles are often 120B or more.

On Niphat-U-Thit 1 Rd is the *Mandarin*, with adequate rooms for 100B with fan and bath.

The *Thai Hotel* on Raj-U-Thit Rd

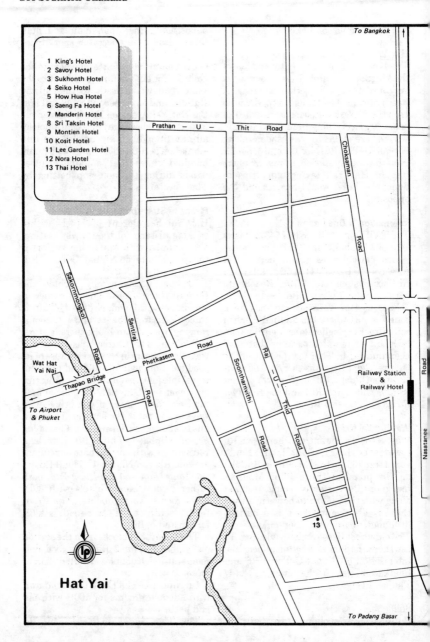

1 King's Hotel
2 Savoy Hotel
3 Sukhonth Hotel
4 Seiko Hotel
5 How Hua Hotel
6 Saeng Fa Hotel
7 Manderin Hotel
8 Sri Taksin Hotel
9 Montien Hotel
10 Kosit Hotel
11 Lee Garden Hotel
12 Nora Hotel
13 Thai Hotel

Hat Yai

south-west of the train station has fan rooms from 110B and AC rooms from 180B. They also have cheaper 70B rooms on the top floor. *Seiko* is not bad, five blocks from the station on the corner of Thamnoonwithi and Sanchanusorn – 100B rooms with fan and bath. The *Aun-Aun* and the *Hok Jeen Hin* are two Chinese hotels on opposite sides of Niphat-U-Thit Rd 1 between Thamnoonwithi and Prachathipat Rd with rooms for 60B.

Places to Stay – top end

There are also lots of hotels in this category, mainly catering to those Malaysian weekenders. All of the following are air-con:

Hat Yai Inter (tel 24474), Duang Chan Rd, 210 rooms, doubles from 440B

Kosit (tel 244711), Niphat-U-Thit 2 Rd, 192 rooms, doubles from 506B

Lee Gardens Hotel (tel 245888), 1 Lee Pattana Rd, doubles from 751B

Montien (tel 245593), Niphat-U-Thit 1 Rd, 180 rooms, doubles from 506B

Nora Hotel (tel 244944, 244982), Thamoonvithi Rd, 160 rooms, doubles from 506B

Rama of Haadyai (tel 244477), 420 Phetchkasem Rd, 110 rooms, doubles from 620B

Rajathani (tel 232288), Railway Station, doubles from 580B

The Regent (tel 245454, 231021) Prachatiphat Rd, 189 rooms, doubles from 751B

Sukhontha (tel 243999), Sanehanusom Rd, 204 rooms, doubles from 400B

Places to Eat

Lots of good, cheap restaurants can be found along the three Niphat-U-Thit Rds and in the markets off side streets between them, also near the railway station. *Muslim-O-Cha*, a Muslim restaurant (no pork) across from the King's Hotel, is cheap and has a good reputation among Malaysian customers.

Very good and very cheap take-away curries, rice, fried fishcakes, *haw mok* and many other Thai foods can be bought from street vendors along Ratakarn Rd, across the street from the Post Office near the railway station.

Jeng Nguan is a very good, inexpensive Chinese restaurant one block before the south end of Niphat-U-Thit 1 Rd (turn right from the station, it's on a corner on the left-hand side). Try the *tao hu thawt krawp* (fried bean curd), *huu chalaam* (shark fin soup), *bami pla phat* (fried noodles with fish), or *kiaw pla* (fish wonton). It's open from 5 am until late at night.

On the south end of Niphat-U-Thit 3 near the Dianna Club are two or three places specialising in *isaan* food.

Another good restaurant in Hat Yai is *Niyom Rot* in front of the expensive Nora Hotel on Phanfa, next to an import liquor store. The *pla krabawk thawt*, whole sea mullet fried with eggs intact, is particularly good.

On Thamnoonwithi Rd between Niphat-U-Thit Rds 1 and 2 are the *Thanad Sri Number 1* and *Thanad Sri Number 2* noodle shops, which serve very tasty and inexpensive noodle and rice dishes. They close about 6 pm.

There is an excellent Thai vegetarian restaurant down Niphat-U-Thit Rd, two blocks south of Thamoonwithi Rd on the right side. Rice plates with two choices of curry or whatever are 10B. Unfortunately, it's only open between 10.30 am and 2 pm.

Nightlife

Most of the many clubs and coffeeshops in town cater almost exclusively to Malaysian clientele. The bigger hotels like The Regent and Sukhontha have discos. The *Post Laserdisc* on Thamnoonwithi Rd near the Indra Hotel is a music video/laserdisc bar with an excellent sound system and well-placed monitors, they change programmes nightly and their music selection is fairly up to date – mostly Thais and farangs come here.

Getting There

Bus From Songkhla big green buses leave every 15 minutes from Rongmuang Rd, across from the Songkhla National Museum, around the corner from the Songkhla Hotel, or they can be flagged down anywhere along Vichianchom Rd or Saiburi Rd, towards Hat Yai. The fare for these buses is 7B. There are also share taxis for 12B.

Back to Songkhla from Hat Yai the green buses start from the Municipal Market. Share taxis also start from the market and from the corner of Supphasan Rangsan Rd. For buses from Bangkok to Hat Yai, see the section on Songkhla, above.

Tour buses from Bangkok are 319B and they leave the Southern Bus Terminal at 1.30 pm and 5 pm. The trip takes 14 hours. Ordinary buses cost 187B and they leave Bangkok at 7.30 am, 2 pm and 4 pm.

From Padang Besar at the Malaysian border, buses are 13B and take an hour to reach Hat Yai. Bus service is between 6 am and 4 pm.

There are also buses running between Phuket and Hat Yai; ordinary buses are 94B and AC is 154B. The trip takes six hours.

Train Trains from Bangkok to Hat Yai leave Hualamphong daily at 2.30 pm (Express No 19), 4.10 pm (Express 11/15) and 12.10 pm (Rapid No 43), arriving in Hat Yai at 8.23 am, 10.15 am and 7.05 am. The basic fare is 664B first class (Express only), 313B second class or 149B third class.

Surat Thani to Hat Yai costs 75B, third class.

Air Thai Airways flies to Hat Yai from Bangkok daily at 7.15 pm; there are also other flights at different times, depending on the day of the week (eg, on Monday there are three flights and on Tuesday there are four flights). Flights take an hour and 15 minutes, except for the few flights that stop in Phuket first, which adds another hour onto the trip. Fare is 1530B one way except for the 9.30 pm

flights on Friday and Sunday, which are only 1225B.

There are also flights to Hat Yai from Phuket for 510B and from Hat Yai to Penang for 760B. Thai Airways and MAS fly to Penang.

Getting Around
Songthaews around Hat Yai cost 4B per person.

PHUKET (population 45,000)
จังหวัดภูเก็ต

Exactly 885 km from Bangkok, the 'Pearl of the South', as the tourist industry has dubbed it, is Thailand's largest island (810 square km) and a province in itself. Tin and tourism are Phuket's major moneymakers, yet the island is big enough to accommodate escapists of nearly all budget levels. Formerly called Koh Thalang ('Phuket' and 'Thalang' are both Malay names), Phuket has a culture all of its own, combining Chinese and Portuguese influences, like Songkhla, with that of the indigenous ocean-going people. In the Andaman Sea off south Thailand's west coast, the island's terrain is incredibly varied, with rocky beaches, long, broad, sandy beaches, limestone cliffs, forested hills and tropical vegetation of all kinds. Great seafood is available all over the island and several off-shore islands are known for good snorkelling and scuba-diving.

Comparisons with Koh Samui, off the east coast, as well as with other Thai islands, are inevitable of course. All in all, there is more to do in Phuket, but that means more to spend your money on, too. There are more tourists in Phuket but they are concentrated at certain beaches – Patong and Kata, for example. Beaches like Nai Harn and Karon are quiet, in spite of major tourist development at both. Koh Samui is nowhere near as developed as Phuket yet. The feel of the islands is different – Samui is much further out in the sea and as such gives one more a feeling of adventure than

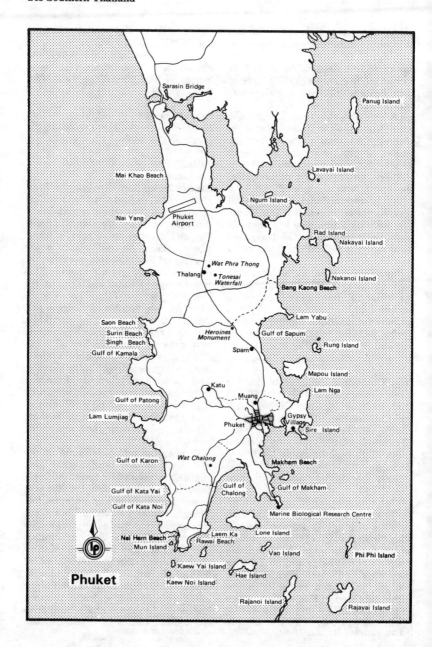

Phuket

Phuket, which is connected to the mainland by a bridge. The geography of Phuket is more varied than any other island in Thailand. One reason for this is its size, which has allowed micro-climates to develop in different areas of the island. Ultimately it's a matter of personal preference. Try them all if you have time.

Development on Phuket has been influenced by the fact that Phuket is Thailand's richest province (on a per capita basis) and so there has always been a lot of money available for investment. The turning point in alternative directions was probably reached when a Club Mediteranee was established at Kata Beach, followed by the more recent construction of the lavish Phuket Yacht Club on Nai Harn. This marked an end to an era of cheap bungalows which started in the early '70s and lasted a decade. Now the cheapies have just about all been bought out. However, Phuket still has a few secluded and undeveloped beaches, at least for the time being.

PHUKET TOWN
เมืองภูเก็ต

At the south-eastern end of the island is Phuket town. There's some interesting markets, many decent restaurants and several cinemas, but little else of interest. Rather than stay in town it's best to rent a bungalow at one of the island's beaches. Walk up **Khao Rang**, sometimes called Phuket Hill, south-west of town, for a nice view of the city, jungle and sea. Twenty km north of town is the **Ton Sai Waterfall National Park**; take Thep Kasatri Rd to the district of Thalang, turn right at the intersection for Ton Sai falls, three km down the road.

Also in Thalang district, just north of the crossroads near Thalang village, is **Wat Phra Thong**, Phuket's 'Temple of the Gold Buddha'. The image is half buried – those who have tried to excavate it have met with unfortunate consequences.

The island of **Koh Sire**, four km east of Phuket town and separated from the bigger island by a canal, has a sea gypsy village and a hill-top reclining Buddha.

At some time in October or November, there is a festival to celebrate the end of the Taoist Lent.

Information

The TAT Tourist Office (tel 212213, 211036) on Phuket Rd has a list of the standard *songthaew* charges out to the various beaches and also the recommended charter costs for a complete vehicle. Thai Airways (tel 211195) are on Ranong Rd. The Post Office is on Montri Rd.

Places to Stay – bottom end

In the centre of town at 81 Phangnga Rd is the *Sin Tawee* (tel 212153) with very comfortable rooms from 100B to 200B or more for doubles and triples with shower and fan. The Sin Tawee also has a few rooms for 80B – ask.

Also near the centre of town is the *Charoensuk*, 136 Thalang Rd, one of Phuket's cheapest, singles for 40B, doubles for 50B, with fan.

Rates at the *On On* 19 Phangnga Rd, (not far from the Sin Tawee) are 80B and up, and it's a hotel with real character – old Sino-Portuguese architecture. One traveller reports that there is lots of short-time trade here. The *Koh Sawan* (19/8 Poonpol Rd) is now 80B and over – the latter is out towards the waterfront, the former near the market and songthaew terminal for most outlying beaches. The *Pengmin* at 69 Phangnga Rd costs 60B with fan and bath, but is not too special. The *Thara* on Thep Kasatri Rd is 70B with fan and bath. The *Siam*, 13-15 Phuket Rd has rooms with fan and bath for 80B, but there is a tape vendor downstairs that plays very loud pop music most of the day and evening.

A notch higher are *Sukchai*, 17/1 Komarapat Rd, at 100B with fan and bath and *Taweekit* at 7/3 Chao Fa Rd which costs the same.

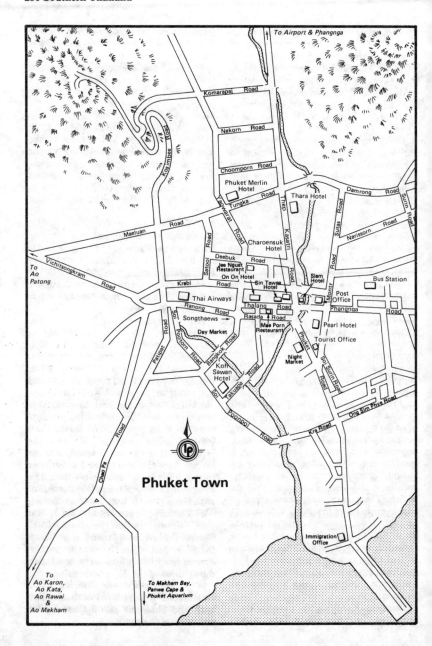

Phuket Town

Places to Stay – top end

The *Pearl Hotel* (tel 211091-3) at 42 Montri Rd has 221 rooms from 500B, a roof top restaurant, swimming pool and so on. The *Phuket Merlin* (tel 211618) at 158/1 Yaowarat Rd has 185 rooms from 590B, again there's a swimming pool.

Places to Eat

There are a couple of local restaurants worth mentioning. One is *Raan Jee Nguat*, a Phuket-style restaurant run by Hokkien Chinese, across the street from the now defunct Siam Cinema on the corner of Yawoarat and Deebuk Rds. Here they have delicious 5B *khanom jeen nam ya phuket*, Chinese noodles in a pureed fish and curry sauce, Phuket-style, with fresh cucumbers, long green beans and other fresh vegetables on the side. Also good are *khai pla mok*, a Phuket version of *haw mok*, eggs, fish and curry paste steamed in banana leaves and the *kari mai fan*, similar to Malaysian *laksa*, but using rice noodles. Their curries are highly esteemed as well. This is one of many Phuket restaurants that have won the *Chuan Chim* or 'Invitation to Taste' designation by a panel of Thai connoiseurs sponsored by Shell Oil Thailand – similar to the Michelin rating in France – look for the yellow Shell symbol over the doorway.

At Ao Chalong, just past Wat Chalong (on the left past the five-road intersection, *haa yaek Wat Chalong*) is *Kan Aeng*, a good fresh seafood place. You order by weight, choosing from squid, oysters, cockles, crab, mussels and several kinds of fish, Then you specify the method of cooking, whether grilled (*phao*), steamed (*neung*), fried (*thawt*), parboiled (*luak* – for squid), or in soup (*tom yam*). Large grilled crabs are about 40B to 50B apiece. It used to be out on a pier over the bay itself, but is now housed in a new enclosed restaurant, not as cheap as the old location.

Thungka Kafae is an outdoor restaurant at the top of Khao Rang, which has a nice atmosphere and good food. Try *tom kha kai* (chicken coconut soup) or *khai jiaw hawy nang rom* (oyster omelette). They're open 11 am to 11 pm daily.

Very popular with Thais and farangs alike and deservedly so, is the *Mae Porn*, a restaurant with everything, at the corner of Phangnga and Soi Pradit, close to the On On and Sin Tawee hotels. There's an air-con room and an open-air room and they sell curries, seafood, fruit shakes, you name it and Mae Porn has it.

Another popular spot in town is *Kanda Bakery* on Ratsada Rd. They're open early in the morning with fresh-baked whole wheat bread, baguettes, croissants and real brewed coffee.

Finally, there's the ever dependable and ever tasty night market on Phuket Rd near the Ratsada Rd intersection, fast and cheap. If there's one thing the town of Phuket has, it's good food.

Getting There

Bus From Bangkok, one air-con bus leaves the Southern Bus Terminal at 8 am, and then nine buses leave at 15-minute intervals between 6.30 pm and 8.30 pm. The trip takes 13 to 14 hours and the one-way fare is 299B. Non air-con buses leave seven times a day from 7.30 am until 10.30 pm for 165B, no advance booking.

Several private tour buses run to Phuket regularly with fares of 299B one-way or 540B round-trip. Most have one bus a day which leaves at 6 pm or 7 pm. Try *Thai Transport* on Ratchadamnoen Klang near the Benz showroom. The ride along the west coast between Ranong and Phuket can be hair-raising if you are awake, so it is fortunate that this part of the trip takes place during the wee hours of the morning.

From Phuket, most tour buses to Bangkok leave at 3 pm. Several agencies have their offices on Ratsada and Phangnga Rds downtown.

Here are fares and trip durations for local bus trips to and from Phuket:

city	fare	hours
Surat Thani	61B	6
Trang	62B	6
Hat Yai	91B/154B*	8
Nakhon Si Thammarat	75B	8
Krabi	38B	3½
Phangnga	22B	1¾

* air-conditioning

There are also share taxis between Phuket and other provincial capitals in the south; taxi fares are generally about double the fare of an ordinary bus. The taxi stand for Nakhorn Si Thammarat, Surat Thani, Krabi, Trang and Hat Yai is on Phangnga near the Pearl Cinema.

Air Thai Airways has several daily flights from Bangkok. The flight takes just over an hour, except for departures which have a half-hour stopover in Surat. One-way fare Bangkok-Phuket is 1340B. On Mondays and Tuesdays there are special night flight fares at 1040B.

There are also regular flights to and from Hat Yai (510B), Penang (1030B) and Kuala Lumpur (1700B).

Getting Around
Songthaews *Songthaews* run regularly from Phuket town to the various Phuket beaches, see the Phuket Beach section below for details. Beware of tales about the tourist office being five km away or the only way to reach the beaches is by taxi or even that you'll need a taxi to get from the bus station to the town centre. Bus station rip-offs are a way of life in Phuket!

Songthaews or *tuk-tuks* around town cost a standard 5B. Songthaews to the beaches depart from close to the town centre and the tourist office is also central. Officially the songthaews all stop running at 5 pm so after that time the 'official' fares are likely to suffer an increase. You can charter your own songthaew for about 100B to most of the beaches.

Motorcycles You can hire motorcycles (usually 80 to 125cc Japanese bikes) from various places at the beaches or in Phuket town. Costs are in the 150B to 250B per day range. Take care riding a bike – if you have an accident you're unlikely to find medical attention is as good as you get back home. People who ride around in shorts and T-shirt and a pair of thongs are asking for trouble. A minor spill whilst wearing reasonable clothes would leave you bruised and shaken but for somebody clad in shorts, it could result in enough skin loss, to end their travels right there. It's also said that riding after dark in Phuket is not safe due to robberies.

Airport To get from the airport (11 km from the town) to Phuket town, you can take one of the rather infrequent *songthaews* for 15B or the Thai Airways limousine service for 40B. Try to avoid having to go to the airport by taxi, especially from the beach, even from the town it's expensive.

PHUKET BEACHES
Patong
ปาตอง
Directly west of Phuket town, Patong is a large curved beach around **Ao Patong**, Patong Bay. In the last few years, Patong Beach has been rapidly turning into another Pattaya in all respects. It is now a strip of hotels, up-scale bungalows, German restaurants, expensive seafood places, night clubs and coffee houses.

Places to Stay The cheapest bungalows are the *Bangla*, 100B to 200B and the *Seven Seas* at 150B. From May to October these two will rent some huts for as low as 50B. In the 200B to 300B range are *Happy Heart, Paradise, Royal Palm, Sunshine Garden* and *Sala Thai* bungalows. They all will discount their bungalows 30% to 40% in the low season, May to October.

At the other end of the price range the *Patong Beach Hotel* (tel 321301) has rooms from 560B. *Patong Beach Bungalows* (tel 321213) start at 380B, *Club Andaman* (tel 211451) has bungalows from 580B and the *Phuket Cabana* (tel 321135) starts at 900B and goes up to 3600B. At the very pinnacle of expense, perched on a cliff over Patong Beach, is the *Coral Beach Hotel* (tel 321106) with rooms from 1610B to 4040B – not really within the budget range of most backpackers.

Getting There *Songthaews* to Patong leave from Ranong Rd, near the day market and Fountain Circle, fare is 10B.

Karon
กะรน

A long, gently curving beach with small sand dunes and a few evergreen trees. Karon used to be quite a spot for budget travellers, but now there are nine sets of bungalows, of which only three offer any rooms or huts for under 150B. Not much shade here, suntan guaranteed. It is still a quiet peaceful beach where fishermen cast nets and where you can buy fresh seafood from their boats, though the rice fields between the beach and the surrounding hills have been abandoned. See Kata (below) for details on transport to Karon.

Places to Stay The *Dream Hut* has 12 huts for 80B and 100B. *My Friend* ranges from 60B to 250B and *Karon Bungalow* is the lowest with 70B and 80B bungalows – they will most likely be bought out soon. *Karon-on-Sea, Karon Bay Resort, Karon Inn, Karon Villa, Kampong Karon* and the *Golden Sand* are all 200B and over, averaging 300B to 500B. Food in these places is not too cheap, but there are still a couple of thatched-roof places right on the beach that do fresh seafood at good prices (eg a fresh whole tuna as long as your forearm for 30B, grilled).

Kata
กะตะ

Just around a headland from Karon, Kata is more interesting as a beach and is divided into two – Big Kata Bay and Little Kata Bay, **Ao Kata Yai** and **Ao Kata Noi**. The small island of **Koh Pu** is within swimming distance of the shore and on the way are some pretty nice coral reefs. The water here is very clear and snorkelling gear can be rented from several of the bungalow groups. With 11 sets of bungalows and a Club Med it can get a bit crowded, but stays quiet just the same. There has been a bit of friction between Club Med and local residents, firstly because Club Med tried to make the beach area private and secondly they tried to bar people from using the road to that end of Kata. Club Med is now trying to win local approval by offering discount memberships to local residents and by building a computer lab at the local public school.

Places to Stay Bungalow rates have really gone up in Kata in recent years; only eight years ago there was only one bungalow village, with bungalows for 10B. Now the crowd ranges from 50B at the *Kata Tropicana* and the *Kata Villa* (certain huts only, others are 70B with toilet and shower) to 2900B at the *Club Mediteranee*. The *Kata Shangrila* is now 150B to 350B, the *Kata Guest House* 130B up and the *Friendship* 100B. *Kampong Kata* has bungalows for 300B and 450B, the *Kata Noi Resort* is 150B to 250B. A night at Club Med (tel 212901) is only 2200B single, 2900B double.

All of the bungalows except for Club Med will give discounts during the low season, May to October.

Getting There *Songthaews* to both Kata and Karon leave frequently from the Ranong Rd market in Phuket town for 10B per person.

Nai Harn
นายหาญ

A few km south of Kata, on a small bay, this one is similar to Kata and Karon. It used to be less frequented as there was not much room for bungalow development until they started cutting away the forests on the hillsides overlooking the beach. Now every inch of space is developed and Nai Harn bay somehow looks twice as big as it did a decade ago. The opening of the Phuket Yacht Club in early 1986 has changed the atmosphere of this beach considerably – this used to be the bottom end place to hang out. The TAT says Nai Harn beach is a dangerous place to swim during the monsoon season (May to October) but it really varies according to daily or weekly weather changes.

Places to Stay There are still some budget-priced bungalow operations here for around 40B to 50B per night: *Ao Saen* is off the beach but has huts from 50B to 150B; *Coconut* is the lowest with some 30B and 40B huts; *Jongdee* huts are all 50B; the *Sunset* and *Grandpa's* rent places for 40B to 150B. The Sunset is nicely situated on a hillside along the south end of the beach, opposite the Phuket Yacht Club, which occupies the north end. The *Phuket Yacht Club* is in a class by itself, built at a cost of 145 million baht. It sits on the northern end of Nai Harn, with 120 'state rooms' and suites catering to the world yachting community. There are plans to construct a mobile pier that will swing back and forth in front of the Club to transport yachties from boat to landing. Nightly rates start at 1950B for a double room and reach 5850B for the better suites.

Getting There Nai Harn is 18 km from town and a *songthaew* (leaving from the intersection of Bangkok Rd and Fountain Circle) costs 20B per person.

Rawai
ราไวย์

Rawai was one of the first coastal areas on Phuket to be developed, simply because it was near Phuket town and there was already a rather large fishing community there. Once other nicer beach areas like Patong and Karon were 'discovered', Rawai began gradually losing popularity and today it is a rather spiritless place. The big 88-room Rawai Resort Hotel, as well as other Rawai hotel and bungalow operations, are in danger of going out of business. The beach is not so great but there is a lot happening in or near Rawai – a local sea gypsy village; **Laem Ka Beach** (better than Rawai) to the north; boats to the nearby islands of **Koh Lone, Koh Hae, Koh Hew, Koh Phi Phi** and others; and good snorkelling off **Laem Phromthep** at the southern tip of the island, easy to approach from Rawai. In fact, most of the visitors who stay at Rawai these days are divers who want to be near Phromthep and/or boat facilities for off-island diving trips.

The diving around the offshore islands is great, especially at **Kaew Yai/Kaew Noi**, off Phromthep and at **Koh Hae**. Shop around for boat trips to these islands for the least expensive passage – the larger the group, the cheaper the cost per person.

Places to Stay *Pornmae Bungalow*, 58/1 Wiset Rd, has bungalows for 100B to 200B and the *Salaloi* has 100B to 250B rates.

Moving upscale here, the *Rawai Resort Hotel* (tel 212943) has rooms from 350B to 530B. The *Rawai Garden Resort* has eight rooms for 200B to 300B. Round at Laem Ka the big *Phuket Island Resort* (tel 212676, 212910) has rooms from 700B, all air-con, swimming pool and all mod-cons. The *Promthep Palace* (tel 212980) at Laem Phromthep goes for 300B to 350B.

Getting There Rawai is about 16 km from town and getting there costs 10B by *songthaew* from the circle at Bangkok Rd.

Surin - Cape Singh - Kamala
สุรินทร์ — แหลมสิงห์ — กมลา

North of Patong Bay, 24 km from Phuket town, Surin has a long beach and sometimes fairly heavy surf. Surin is a popular place for local Thais to come and nibble at seafood snacks and *mieng kham* sold by vendors along the beach. A very nice place to come and spend a few peaceful hours swimming and eating Thai food.

There is a golf course nearby and a resort hotel on the north end, the *Pansea*, with rooms from 950B.

Just south of Surin Beach is **Laem Singh** (Cape Singh), a beautiful little rock-dominated beach. You could camp here and eat on Surin beach or in Ban Kamala, a village further south.

Kamala Beach is a lovely stretch of sand and sea south of Surin and Laem Singh. There is one set of very well-designed screened bungalows down a road at the north end that go for 200B, including maid service and there is a restaurant/bar at the south end next to Ban Kamala village.

If you're renting a motorbike, this is a nice little trip down Route 4025 and then over dirt roads from Surin to Kamala. Just before Surin, in Ban Thao village number 2, is one of south Thailand's most beautiful mosques, a large whitewashed, immaculate structure with lacquered wooden doors.

Getting There A *songthaew* from Ranong Rd costs 10B.

Nai Yang - Mai Khao
นายยาง — ไม้ขาว

This one is near the Phuket airport, about 30 km from town. Nai Yang is a fairly secluded beach favoured by Thais, actually a National Park with one set of government-run bungalows. It's about five km further north along Route 402

(Thep Kasatri Rd) and is Phuket's longest beach, **Hat Mai Khao**, where sea turtles lay their eggs between November and February each year. Camping is allowed on both Nai Yang and Mai Khao beaches.

Getting There A *songthaew* to NaiYang costs 15B.

PHANGNGA (population 8000)
จังหวัดพังงา

Over 94 km from Phuket town, the area around Phangnga Bay is quite scenic – lots of limestone cliffs, odd rock formations, islands that rise out of the sea like inverted mountains, not to mention caves and quaint fishing villages. Phangnga would make a good motorcycle trip from Phuket, or, if you have time, one could spend a few days in Phangnga.

On the way to the town of Phangnga, turn left off Route 4 just five km past the small town of Takua Thung, to get to **Tham Suwan Kuha**, a cave temple full of Buddha images. Between Takua Thung and Phangnga town is the road to **Tha Don**, the Phangnga customs pier. It is at this pier that boats can be hired to tour Phangnga Bay, visiting a Muslim fishing village on stilts, half-submerged caves, strangely-shaped islands (yes, including those filmed in the 007 flick, *Man with the Golden Gun*) and other local oddities. Worthwhile if you have the bread – say 350B for five hours for a whole boat. Tours from Phuket cost around 300B per person but one traveller related how he bargained a seat down to 50B by explaining that he didn't really care about air-con buses or seafood lunches! A postman from Panyi Island named Sayan has been doing overnight tours of Phangnga Bay from Tha Don for several years now. They have received good reviews from travellers. The tour is 200B per person and includes a boat tour of **Tham Lot**, a large water cave, **Koh Phing Kan** ('Leaning Island'), **Koh Khao Tapu** ('Nail Mountain Island') and **Koh Panyi**, plus dinner, breakfast and accommodation in a Muslim fishing village on Koh Panyi. Look for him at Tha Don or in front of the market on the main street of Phangnga town – he has his own bus and is usually there every morning around 8.30 or 9 am. You can also take a ferry to Koh Panyi on your own for 20B.

Phangnga's best beach areas are on the west coast facing the Andaman Sea. Between Thai Muang in the south and Takua Pa in the north are **Hat Thai Muang** and **Bang Sak** beaches.

Similan & Surin Islands
สิมิลัน + หมูเกาะสุรินทร์

The Similan Islands, 65 km from Thai Muang and the Surin Islands, 70 km from Khuraburi, are world-renowned for good diving. The Similans are also sometimes called Koh Kao, or Nine Islands because there are nine of them – each has a number for a name.

There are expensive tours to Similan from Phuket or you can try to book passage on a boat from the Thai Coast Guard station at Thap Lamu, about 20 km north of Thai Muang. There are some government bungalows on Surin and occasional boats there from Khuraburi. Both Similan and Surin are designated National Marine Parks in Thailand so you are free to camp anywhere. Few *farangs* have made it to these islands.

Places to Stay & Eat
There are several small hotels in Phangnga town. The *Thawisuk* is right in the middle of town, a bright blue building with the English sign 'Hotel'; fairly clean, quiet rooms upstairs go for 80B, with fan, bath, towel, soap and boiled water – Phangnga's best value. On the rooftop of Thawisuk you can sit and have a beer while watching the sun set over Phangnga's rooftops and the limestone cliffs surrounding the town. The *Lak Muang* (tel 411125, 411288), on Phetkasem Rd just outside of town towards Krabi, has rooms from 100B and a restaurant. The *Rak Phang-nga*, across the street from

Thawisuk toward Phuket, is 80B but somewhat dirty and noisy. Further down the road towards Phuket is the *Muang Thong*, with adequate rooms for 100B single, 150B double. Outside of town even further towards Phuket is *Lak Muang II* with all AC rooms from 230B. The *Phangnga Bay Resort* (tel 411067-70) near the customs pier is beyond the means of most budget travellers (500B to 1000B) but has a swimming pool and a decent restaurant.

There are several food stalls on the main street selling cheap and delicious *khanom jiin* with chicken curry, *nam yaa*, or *nam phrik*. Plus the usual Chinese *khao man kai* places.

Getting There
Buses for Phangnga leave from the Phuket bus terminal on Phangnga Rd, near the Thep Kasatri Rd intersection, hourly between 6.20 am and 6 pm. The trip to Phangnga town takes 1¾ hours and the one-way fare is 22B. Or rent a motorcycle from Phuket. From Krabi a bus is 25B and takes 1½ hours. *Songthaews* between Phangnga and Tha Don (the Customs Pier) are 7B.

KRABI (population 13,000)
จังหวัดกระบี่

Nearly 1000 km from Bangkok and 180 km from Phuket town, this fast-developing provincial capital has good beaches nearby, friendly townspeople and good food. Accommodation here is cheap and there are regular boats to **Koh Phi Phi** 42 km west. Boats to Koh Phi Phi do not sail though during the monsoon season which begins in late May. The beaches of Krabi are nearly deserted and there is some excellent snorkelling offshore and among the 130 islands in the province. This part of Krabi is just being 'discovered' by travellers and the beach bungalows are expanding their operations. The interior, noted for its tropical forests and the Phanom Bencha mountain range, has barely been explored.

Top: Pattani market (JC)
Bottom: Cotton weaving at Koh Yaw, Songkhla (JC)

Top: Koh Phi Phi (Don Sai Beach) (JC)
Bottom: Rama VI's Palace, Nakhon Pathom (TW)

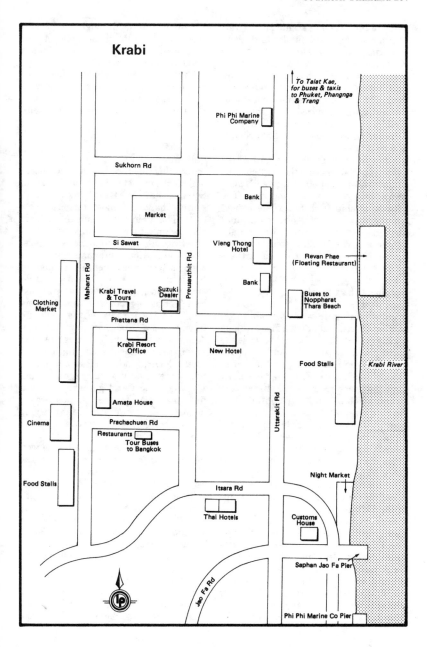

Krabi province has scenic karst formations near the coast, similar to those in Phangnga, even in the middle of the Krabi River. Krabi town itself sits on the banks of the river right before it empties into the Andaman. Near town you can see Bird, Cat and Mouse Islands, named for their shapes. Hundreds of years ago, Krabi's waters were a favourite hideout for Asian pirates because of all the islands and water caves.

Krabi has a nearly new but hardly used deep-sea port financed by local speculators in tin, rubber and palm oil, Krabi's most important sources of income. The occasional ship from Singapore (sometimes even a Singapore or Penang junk) anchors here and if you know the right people you can buy tax-free cigarettes and other luxury items while one of these boats is in port.

Noppharat Thara Beach
หาดธารนพรัตน์

Eighteen km north-west of Krabi town, this beach used to be called Haat Khlong Haeng or 'Dry Canal Beach' because the canal that flows into the Andaman Sea here is dry except during and just after the monsoon season. Field Marshall Sarit gave the beach its current Pali-Sanskrit name, which means 'Beach of the Nine-Gemmed Stream', as a tribute to its beauty. The two km-long beach is part of Noppharat Thara Beach – Phi Phi Islands National Marine Park and is a favourite spot for Thai picnickers. Good place for shell-hunting. There are some government bungalows for rent here and a visitors centre of sorts, with wall maps of the Marine Park.

Ao Phra Nang or Phra Nang Bay is a lovely spot where limestone cliffs and caves drop right into the sea. The water here is quite clear and there are some coral reefs in the shallows. Plenty of cheap places to stay, too. Nearby **Pai Pong** and **Rai Lae** beaches are accessible only by hiking in over head-land cliffs or by boat from the pier in Phra Nang Bay (10B).

Worth the effort, although word has it that Rai Lae Beach is going to be developed soon into resort condominiums for artists and the wealthy.

Nineteen km west of town on Laem Pho is the so-called **Shell Fossil Museum**, a shell 'graveyard' where 75-million-year-old shell fossils have formed giant slabs jutting into the sea.

Wat Tham Seua
วัดถ้ำเสือ

In the other direction, about six km north and eight km east of town, is Wat Tham Seua, or the 'Tiger Cave Temple', one of south Thailand's most famous forest *wats*. The main *bot* is built into a long, shallow limestone cave, on either side of which are dozens of *kutis*, monastic cells, built into various cliffs and caves. The abbot is Achaan Jamnien, a Thai monk in his forties who has allowed a rather obvious personality cult to develop around him. The usual pictures of split cadavers and decaying corpses on the walls are interspersed with large portraits of Achaan Jamnien, who is well-known as a teacher of *vipassana*, insight meditation and *metta*, loving-kindness. It is said that he was apprenticed at an early age to a blind lay priest and astrologer who practiced folk medicine and that he has been a celibate his entire life. Many young women come here to practice as eight-precept nuns.

The best part of the temple grounds can be found in a little valley behind the ridge where the bot is located. Follow the path past the main wat buildings, through a little village with nuns quarters, until you come to some steep stairways on the left. The first leads to an arduous climb to the top of a karst hill with a good view of the area. The second stairway leads over a gap in the ridge and into a valley of tall trees and limestone caves. Enter the caves on your left and look for light switches on the walls; the network of caves is wired so that you can light your way chamber by chamber through the labyrinth until you come out on the other side. There are several *kutis* in and around the caves, and it's interesting to see the differences in interior decorating – some are very spare and others are outfitted like oriental bachelor pads. A path winds through a grove of trees surrounded by tall limestone cliffs covered with a patchwork of foliage. If you continue to follow the path you'll eventually end up where you started, at the bottom of the stair-case.

Than Bokkharani Botanical Gardens
สวนพฤกษชาติแท่นโบกขรณี
This place looks like a Disney fantasy but it's real and entirely natural. Emerald green waters flow out of a cave cleft in a tall cliff and into a large lotus pool which overflows steadily into a wide stream which divides itself into many smaller streams in several stages. At each stage there's a pool and a little water-fall. Tall trees spread over 40 *rai* provide plenty of cool shade. Thais from Ao Luk come to bathe here on weekends and then it's full of laughing people playing in the streams and pools. During the week there are only a few people about, mostly kids doing a little fishing. There are vendors selling noodles, roast chicken, delicious batter-fried squid and *som-tam* under the trees. Than-Bok, as the locals call it, is off Highway 4 between Krabi and Phangnga near the town of Ao Luk, one km south-west toward Laem Sak. To get there, take a *songthaew* from Krabi to Ao Luk for 12B; from there it's an easy walk down Route 4039 to the park entrance on the left.

Koh Lanta
เกาะลันตา
Koh Lanta is an island district south of the provincial capital that consists of 52 islands. Twelve of those islands are inhabited and of these, three are large enough to be worth exploring, **Koh Klang** เกาะกลาง , **Koh Lanta Noi** เกาะลันตานอย and **Koh Lanta Yai**

เกาะลันตาใหญ่ . At present you have to get there by ferry from either Nam Thaw, on the mainland across from Koh Klang, or from Baw Muang further south. The boats from Baw Muang are larger, holding about 80 people and sail for an hour (30B fare) before reaching Lanta Yai, the largest of the three islands – also where the district offices are. The west sides of all the islands have beaches, but the best are along the south-west end of Lanta Yai. The people in this district are a mixture of Muslim Thais and Chao Le or 'sea gypsies' who settled here long ago. No one will mind if you camp on the beaches; probably within the next year or two some bungalows will be built by the locals as more and more travellers discover Lanta. The village of **Ban Sangka-U** on Lanta Yai's southern tip is a traditional Muslim fishing village and the people are friendly.

There is also a nice beach on the little island between Koh Lanta Noi and Koh Klang called **Haat Thung Thale** – hire a boat from Koh Klang and walk around to the west side.

To get to Koh Lanta *amphoe*, get a bus south from Krabi towards Trang on Highway 4, getting off either at Nam Thaw (Route 4043) about 50 km away (12B), or a little further south at Baw Muang (Route 4042). From either point it's about 14 km down a dirt road to the piers for boat departures to the islands. There are also occasional boats to Lanta from the Saphan Jao Fa pier in Krabi – ask at Phi Phi Marine Transport on Uttarakit Rd or at Krabi Tours & Travel. Rumour has it that a road from Ban Huay Nam Khao, about 15 km north of Ban Nam Thaw, will eventually connect with a bridge to Koh Klang. From there it would be only be two short boat rides to Koh Lanta Noi and Lanta Yai.

Places to Stay & Eat
Cheapest hotels in town are the *New Hotel* (tel 611318), on Phattana Rd, and the old wing of the *Thai Hotel* on Itsara

Rd, both of which have rooms from 90B. The new *Thai Hotel* on the right has very nice rooms for 120B with fan and bath, plus more expensive AC rooms.

The *Vieng Thong* (tel 611188, 611288) was the best place in town before the construction of the new Thai Hotel; it's at 155 Uttarakit Rd and has air-con rooms from 275B, fan cooled from 100B. Both the Vieng Thong and the Thai have rather expensive coffeeshops.

Max Guest House is scheduled to open in late '86 and will be located on Jao Fa Rd near the court house in a quiet, breezy neighbourhood. Rates will be 30B per person or 50B per room. Max is a young Thai who speaks good English and has an amazing knowledge of pop music, from country and western to heavy metal.

At *Thara Park*, just outside of town at the mouth of the river, are a few province-owned bungalows which rent for 100B to 200B. The area is a sort of municipal park, very shady and quiet.

There are lots of good eating places in town. Forget the expensive and not-so-tasty *Reuan Phae*, a floating restaurant on the river in front of town (though this might be a nice place to have a beer or rice whiskey and watch the river rise and fall with the tide); next to it is a row of food stalls with cheap rice plates and noodles, including Muslim food like *khao mok kai*. Further south down Uttarakit Rd there is a night market next to the big pier (called *Saphan Jao Fa*) with great seafood at low prices. For cheap breakfasts, the morning market off Si Sawat Rd in the middle of town is good. There are also food stalls next to the movie theatre on Maharat Rd and across the street from the theatre. In the midst of these latter places is the *Amata House*, a thatched-roof cafe/bar favoured by young Thais and travellers. Amata House is open from 11 am until after midnight and is a great place for info on what to see and do in Krabi; in fact, you might consider making this your first stop if you really plan to have a look around Krabi province. They serve beer,

coffee, tea, fruit shakes and a few snacks and baked goods.

Best restaurant in town for Thai standards and local cuisine is the *Kotung* on Prachachuen Rd, around the corner from Amata House. The *tom yam kung* is especially good here, as is anything else made with fresh seafood. One of the specialties of the house is *hawy lawt*, a tube-like shellfish something like 'squid-in-a-shell', quickly steamed/stir-fried in a sauce of basil and garlic – delectable. Two can order three dishes, rice, and a large Singha here for about 90B, a bargain when you remember the beer costs half that.

Out of Town

The *Krabi Resort* (tel 611300, 611198) is at the north end of Phra Nang Bay and has bungalows that cost 600B on the water, 500B off. They also have a clean dorm for 50B per person. Most of the guests here are with package tours or conferences. There are the usual resort amenities, including a swimming pool, bar and restaurant. Bookings can be made at the Krabi Resort office in town on Phattana Rd. They'll provide free transport out to the resort for guests.

Also along Phra Nang Bay are several other bungalow operations, though in a different class. The *Ao Nang, Ao Phra Nang* and *Coconut Garden* bungalows all go for 50B or 60B a night. They are still in the trial-and-error stage when it comes to food service, etc.

Just over the headland at the south end of the beach is *Pai Pong Bungalows*, a well-run operation that has no running water or electricity and no plans to install some. Amata House in Krabi town can give you information on this one, as well as free transport out to look at the place before you decide whether you want to stay there or not – the same folks own both. Huts here are 50B and 70B and food is generally good. To get here on your own, you'll have to get out to Phra Nang Bay first (the Krabi Resort has a mini-bus or

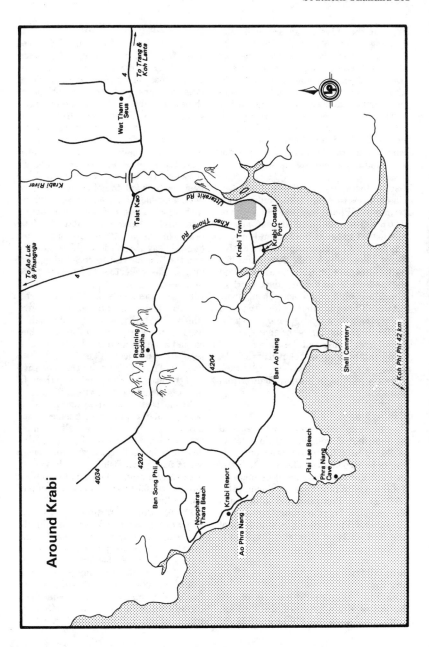

Around Krabi

To Trang & Koh Lanta

Wat Tham Seua

4

Krabi River

Talat Kao

To Ao Luk & Phangnga

4

Utarakit Rd

Khao Thong Rd

Krabi Town

Krabi Coastal Port

Reclining Buddha

4204

Ban Ao Nang

Shell Cemetery

4034

4202

Ban Song Phli

Nopparat Thara Beach

Krabi Resort

Ao Phra Nang

Rai Lee Beach

Phra Nang Cave

Koh Phi Phi 42 km

two out there every day and will take passengers for 15B). From Phra Nang, you can either take a boat from the pier there for 10B or walk down the beach and over the steep headland onto the beach, about a 15 to 20 minute walk. The only problem is finding the trail, as it's rather hidden in the vegetation covering the cliffs. As in the case of the Cave Lodge in north Thailand, Pai Pong's owners are committed to keeping the natural surroundings as natural as possible.

Getting There
Catch buses to Krabi from Phuket's bus terminal on Phang-nga Rd at 12.50 pm or 2.30 pm. The price is 38B. Buses for Krabi also leave Phangnga town several times a day for 22B. There are now direct Krabi-Surat buses which take four hours for 50B. Buses to or from Krabi arrive at and depart from **Talaat Kao**, a village north of Krabi a couple of km on the highway between Phangnga and Trang. To get to the centre of Krabi, catch a *songthaew* for 2B. There are also buses and share taxis to Krabi from Trang and Satun.

When the current renovation of the Krabi airport is finished, Bangkok Airways will begin regular flights from Bangkok

Getting Around
Any place in town can easily be reached on foot, but if you plan to do a lot of exploring out of town, renting a motorcycle might be a good idea. The Suzuki dealer on Phattana Rd rents some good bikes for 150B a day. Krabi Tours & Travel (611-507) at 36 Phattana Rd also rents motorcycles. There are *songthaews* out to Noppharat Thara Beach from in front of the food stalls on Uttarakit Rd. Fare is 15B.

KOH PHI PHI
เกาะพีพี
Koh Phi Phi actually consists of two islands in Krabi province about 40 km from Krabi town, Phi Phi Le and Phi Phi

Don. **Phi Phi Le** พีพีเล is almost all sheer cliffs, with a few caves and a sea lake formed by a cleft between two cliffs that allows water to enter into a bowl-shaped canyon. The so-called **Viking Cave** contains prehistoric paintings of ships and is also a collection point for sea swallow nests. The swallows like to build their nests high up in the caves in rocky hollows which can be very difficult to reach. Agile collectors build bamboo scaffolding to get at the nests but are occasionally injured or killed in falls. People who want to collect sea swallow nests must bid for a license in competition with other collectors which gives them a franchise to harvest the nests for four years. In one year there are only three harvests, as the birds build seasonally and the first harvest fetches the highest prices. The collectors sell the nests to middle-men who then sell them to Chinese restaurants in Thailand and abroad. The nests are made of saliva which the birds secrete – the saliva hardens when exposed to the air. When cooked in chicken broth, they soften and separate and look like bean thread noodles. The Chinese value the expensive bird secretions highly, believing them to be a medicinal food that imparts vigor.

No one is allowed to stay on Phi Phi Le because of the bird nest business, but boats can be hired from Phi Phi Don for the short jaunt over to see the caves and to do a little snorkelling at the coral reefs in **Ma-Ya Bay**. Spear-fishing here is so easy it's nearly a crime. The usual rate for a day trip is 100B per person in a group of four or five.

Phi Phi Don พีพีดอน is the larger of the two islands, sort of a dumbbell shaped island with scenic hills, awesome cliffs, long beaches, emerald waters and remarkable bird and sea life. The 'handle' in the middle has long white-sand beaches on either side, only a few hundred metres apart. The beach on the south side curves around **Ao Don Sai**, where boats from Phuket and Krabi dock.

There is also a Thai Muslim village here. The uninhabited western section of the island is called Koh Nawk, or 'outer island' and the eastern section, which is much larger, is Koh Nai or 'inner island'. At the east end is **Laem Tong**, where the island's *chao le* population lives. **Haat Yao**, or 'Long Beach', faces east and has some of Phi Phi Don's best coral reefs. Both Don Sai and Haat Yao have beach bungalows. Over a ridge north-west from Long Beach is another very beautiful beach with good surf, but the locals won't allow any bungalows here out of respect for the large village mosque situated in a coconut grove above the beach. The number of sea gypsies here varies from time to time, as they are still a somewhat nomadic people, sailing from island to island, stopping off to repair their boats or fishing nets, but there are generally about a hundred. Like Pacific islanders of perhaps 100 or so years ago, they tend to be very warm and friendly horizon-gazers.

Only parts of Phi Phi Don are actually under the administration of the Park Division of the Royal Thai Forestry Department. Phi Phi Le and the western cliffs of Phi Phi Don are left to the nest collectors and the part of Phi Phi Don where the *chao le* live is also not included in the Park.

Places to Stay

At Don Sai, there are three places to stay. The *Pee Pee Islands Cabana* has the greatest capacity and variety of accommodation, with quite nice one-bed bungalows for 100B, two-bed bungalows with bath for 400B and a nine-person bungalow for 630B. There is also dorm accommodation for 70B per person and tents for 50B. The restaurant here, *Ma-Yah Kitchen*, is a bit on the expensive side. To book in advance, contact the Phi Phi Marine Travel Co in Krabi.

Also at Don Sai are *Pee Pee Paradise*, up against the cliffs to the west and *Phi Don Beach Bungalows*, to the east of the pier and village. The Paradise has clean, airy bungalows for 70B and is especially quiet because of the lack of electricity. Each room comes with a mirror, comb, tissues, oil lantern and matches. The kitchen is rather so-so and in fact in all of the bungalow kitchens on the island (except for Pee Pee Cabana, which has its own fleet of boats), food varies according to how recently a boat delivery of food has been made. Seafood is always abundant, but vegetables scarce. The Phi Don Bungalow does the best cooking of all the budget places. Their bungalows are 70B for the small ones, 90B for the large, and they have electricity.

Further east a bit, away from Don Sai, is a rocky peninsula where *Laem Hin Bungalows* is located. Here huts are built rather close together, though secluded from the rest of the island and go for 60B. Around the peninsula on the other side is *Long Beach Bungalow*. The best way to get here is to walk along the trail through the centre of the island over the hills to Hat Yao, where the bungalows are located, although it is possible to walk along the shoreline all the way. Huts are 50B and there is no electricity. Nearby snorkelling is good.

Getting There

Koh Phi Phi is equidistant from Phuket and Krabi, but Krabi is your most economical point of departure. From either place, boats only travel during the dry season, from late November to May, as the seas are too rough during the monsoons. Two different companies run boats between Krabi and Phi Phi, so there is at least one boat a day and sometimes two, leaving in the morning. The Phi Phi Marine Co boats, owned by Pee Pee Islands Cabana, leave from the pier near the customs house, while the company associated with Krabi Tours and Travel leaves from the main pier in town, Saphan Jao Fa. On either boat, round-trip fare is 200B. Pee Pee Islands Cabana also does package deals that include accommodation and a tour of Phi Phi Le.

From Phuket you'll have to pay 350B to 450B for a day-trip that includes round-trip transport, lunch and a tour. If you want to stay overnight and catch another tour boat back, you have to pay another 100B. Your only other alternative from Phuket is to pay a one-way fare of 250B to the tour companies for straight transport to the island, more than twice the cost of a ticket from Krabi, though travellers have been known to get passage for less by haggling. If demand for cheap transport to Phi Phi increases, a regular ferry boat service from Phuket with reasonable fares may start up.

See Getting There section on Krabi for transport to Krabi.

TRANG (population 44,000)
จังหวัดตรัง

The province of Trang has a geography similar to that of Krabi and Phangnga but is much less frequented by tourists. Historically, Trang has played an important role as a centre of trade since at least the 1st century AD and was especially important between the 7th and 12th centuries when it was a sea port for ocean-going sampans sailing between Trang and the Malacca Straits. Nakhorn Si Thammarat and Surat Thani were major commercial and cultural centres for the Srivijaya empire at this time and Trang served as a relay point for communications between the east coast of the Thai peninsula and Palembang, Sumatra. Trang was then known as Krung Thani and later as Trangkhapura, 'City of Waves', until the name was shortened during the early years of the Rattanakosin period. During the Ayuthaya period, Trang was a common port of entry for seafaring western visitors who continued by land to Nakhorn Si Thammarat or Ayuthaya. The town was then located right at the mouth of the Trang River, but later King Mongkut gave orders to move the city to its present location inland because of frequent flooding.

Today Trang is still an important point of exit for rubber from the province's many plantations. Trang's main attractions are its beaches and islands, plus the fact that it can be reached by rail. However, there is not much in the way of facilities for travellers, so potential visitors should be willing to rough it a bit. The provincial capital itself doesn't offer much, but 20 km north there is a 3500 *rai* National Park which preserves a tropical forest in its original state. In the park there are three waterfalls and government rest houses. Between Trang and Huay Yot to the north is **Thale Song Hong** or 'Sea of Two Rooms', a large lake surrounded with limestone hills. The hills in the middle of the lake nearly divide it in half, hence the name.

Haat Samran
หาดสำราญ

A beautiful white-sand beach in Palian district about 40 km south-west of Trang city. From the customs pier at nearby Yong Sata you should be able to get a boat to Koh Sukon (also called Koh Muu), where there are more beaches.

Haat Jao Mai
หาดเจ้าไหม่

In *amphoe* Kantang about 35 km from Trang. The wide white-sand beach is five km long and gets some of Thailand's biggest surf (probably the source of the city's original unshortened name, City of Waves). Haat Jao Mai is backed by pine trees and hills with caves, some of which contain prehistoric human skeletal remains. Off the coast here is Koh Lipong, for which there are occasional boats from Kantang.

Haat Pak Meng
หาดปากเม็ง

Thirty-nine km from Trang, north of Haat Jao Mai in Sikao district, is another long, fine sand beach, actually a

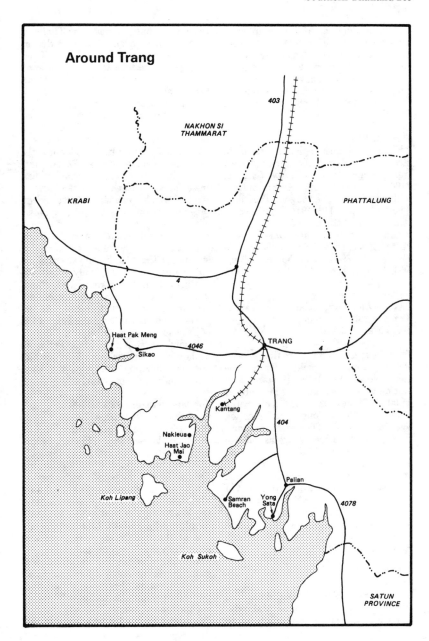

Around Trang

403

NAKHON SI THAMMARAT

KRABI

PHATTALUNG

4

Haat Pak Meng

Sikao

4046

TRANG

4

Kantang

Nakleua

Haat Jao Mai

404

Koh Lipang

Palian

Samran Beach

Yong Sata

4078

Koh Sukoh

SATUN PROVINCE

continuation of Jao Mai interrupted by the village of Ban Khlong Meng. A couple of hundred metres offshore are several limestone rock formations, including a very large one with caves. To get there, take a bus to Sikao from Trang and then a *songthaew* to Ban Khlong Meng. Total fare should be about 20B.

Places to Stay
There are a number of places on the main street, Phra Ram 6 Rd, running down from the clock tower. The *Koh Teng* (tel 218622) has rooms from 70B or from 160B with air-con and also has good Thai food. The *Wattana* (tel 218184) is on the same stretch and a little more expensive.

On Visetkul Rd are *Queen's* (tel 218522), with rooms from 130B and the *Trang* (tel 218944), near the clock tower, with AC rooms from 150B.

Getting There
Bus Bus from Satun, Hat Yai or Krabi to Trang is 35B. Share taxi from the same cities is around 70B.

Train There is only one train that goes all the way from Bangkok to Trang, the Rapid No 41, which leaves Hualamphong station at 6.25 pm, arriving in Trang at 11.30 am the next day. You can also catch a train in Thung Song, a rail junction town in Nakhorn Si Thammarat province. From here, there are two trains daily to Trang, leaving at 9.05 am and 3.30 pm, arriving an hour and 45 minutes later. If you want to continue on to Kantang on the coast, there is one daily train out of Trang at 5.15 pm which arrives in Kantang at 5.55 pm. The Bangkok-Trang fare is 302B second class, 155B third including the Rapid surcharge. Trang-Kantang is 4B in third class.

SATUN (SATUL)
จังหวัดสตูล
Satun is Thailand's southern most province on the west coast, bordering Malaysia. There is absolutely nothing of interest to

see in town, but you may enter Thailand here by boat from Kuala Perlis in Malaysia. North of Satun 60 km is the small port of **Pak Bara**, the departure point for boats to **Koh Tarutao National Marine Park**, Satun's big attraction. Eighty percent of Satun's population is Muslim; in fact, throughout the entire province there are only 11 or 12 Buddhist temples, in contrast to 117 mosques. As in Thailand's other three predominantly Muslim provinces, (Yala, Pattan and Narathiwat) the Thai government has installed a loudspeaker system in the streets which broadcasts government programmes from 6 am to 6 pm (beginning with wake-up call to work and ending with the Thai national anthem, for which everyone must stop and stand in the streets), either to instill a sense of nationalism in the typically rebellious southern Thais, or perhaps to try and drown out the prayer calls and amplified sermons from local mosques. As in Pattani and Narathiwat, one hears a lot of Yawi spoken in the streets.

If you are going to Kuala Perlis in Malaysia, remember that banks are not open on Thursday afternoons or Friday due to observance of Islam.

Koh Tarutao Marine Park
สวนสัตว์ทะเลเกาะตะรุเตา
The park is actually a large archipelago of 61 islands located approximately 30 km from Pak Bara in La-ngu district, which is 50 km from *amphoe muang* Satun. Tarutao Island, the biggest of the group, is only five km from Langkawi Island in Malaysia. Only five of the islands have any kind of regular boat service to them, Tarutao, Adang, Rawi, Lipe and Klang, and of these, only the first three are generally visited by tourists.

Tarutao ตะรุเตา is about 151 square km in size and features waterfalls, inland streams, beaches, caves and protected wildlife that includes dolphins, sea turtles and lobster. Nobody lives on this island except for employees of the

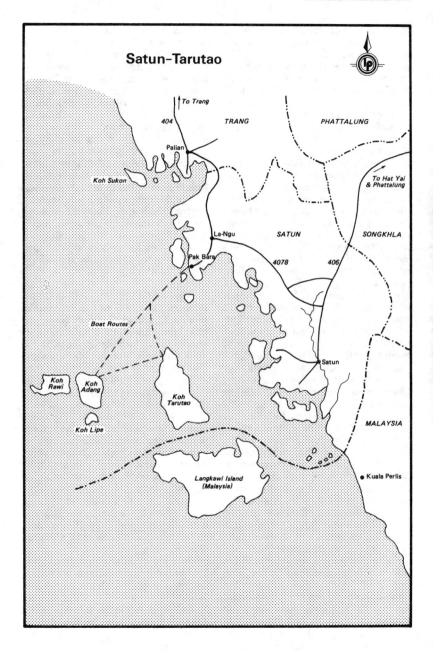

Royal Forest Department. The island was a place of exile for political prisoners between 1939 and 1947 and remains of the prisons can be seen near **Talo Udang Bay** on the southern tip of the island and at **Talo Wao Bay** on the east coast in the middle of the island, including a graveyard, charcoal furnaces and fermentation tanks for making fish sauce. Tarutao's largest stream, Khlong Phante Malacca, enters the sea at the north-west tip of the island at Phante Bay; the brackish waters flow out of Tham Jara-Khe or Crocodile Cave (the stream was once inhabited by ferocious crocodiles which seem to have disappeared), which extends for at least a km under a limestone mountain – no one has yet followed the stream to the cave's end. The mangrove-lined watercourse should not be navigated at high tide, when the mouth of the cave fills. The Park pier, headquarters and bungalows are also here at **Phante Bay**. Best camping is at **Ao Jak** beach, a little south of Park headquarters. For a view of the bay, climb Topu Hill, 500 metres north of the Park office. There is also camping at **Ao Makham**, or Tamarind Bay, at the south-west end of the island about 2½ km from another Park office at Talo Udang Bay. There is a road between Phante Bay in the north and Talo Udang Bay in the south, of which 11 km were constructed by the political prisoners in the '40s and 12 km were more recently constructed by the Park Division. The road is for the most part overgrown but Park personnel have kept a path open to make it easier to get from north to south without having to climb over rocky headlands along the shore. Koh Rang Nok ('Bird Nest Island'), in Talo Udang Bay, is another collection place for the expensive swallow nests craved by Chinese throughout the world.

Adang อาดัง island is 43 km west of Tarutao and about 80 km from Pak Bara. Adang's 30 square km are covered with forests and fresh-water streams which fortunately supply water year-round. There is a Park office here as well as a few bungalows. Camping is allowed. **Rawi** ราวี island is just east of Adang and a bit smaller. Off the west coast of Adang and the south-east coast of Rawi are coral reefs with many live species of coral and tropical fish. **Lipa** ลิปะใหญ่ island is immediately south of Adang and is inhabited by about 500 'sea gypsies', whom the Thai call *chao le* and the Malays *orang rawot*. They subsist on fishing and some cultivation of vegetables and rice on the flatter parts of the island. They are said to have originated from the Lanta islands in Krabi province. One could probably camp here or rent a hut from the *chao le*. There is a coral reef along the south side of the small island.

The nightly rate for bungalows in Tarutao National Park is 60B and they may be booked in advance at the Park pier in Pak Bara.

Getting There

Boats to Tarutao leave the Park pier in Pak Bara regularly between November and April. There are always boats on weekends and occasionally during the week, but there is no iron-clad schedule. Best thing to do is show up at the Park office early on a Friday morning and let them know you want to go out to Tarutao. Sometimes on a Friday morning or early afternoon, there will be two boat departures: one to Koh Tarutao and one to Koh Adang. Saturday the Tarutao boat returns to Pak Bara while the Adang boat continues on to Tarutao, returning to Pak Bara on Sunday. So your length of stay is generally limited to either a weekend or a full week, unless there happens to be a boat mid-week. The fare for the Park boat is 100B per person. From the main commercial pier at Pak Bara, there are also occasional tour boats out to Tarutao but these are usually several hundred baht per person as they include a guided tour, meals, etc, though you may be able to hitch a ride on one for 100B or so. Your final alternative is to charter a boat with a group of people. The cheapest are the *hang yao* or long-tail boats, which can take eight to 10 people out for 500B from Pak Bara's commercial pier.

To get to Pak Bara from Satun, you must take a share taxi or bus to La-ngu, then a *songthaew* on to Pak Bara. Taxis to La-ngu leave from in front of the Thai Niyom hotel when there are enough people to fill a taxi for 20B per person. Frequent buses leave from the same place for 10B. From La-ngu, songthaew rides to Pak Bara are 7B and terminate right at the harbour.

Places to Stay – Satun

The *Rian Thong Hotel* (English sign says 'Rain Tong') is located at the end of Samantapradit Rd, next to the Rian Thong pier, embarkation point for boats to and from Malaysia. Large, clean rooms here are 90B. The *Satun Thani* near the centre of town is OK, with 100B rooms. Also in the centre of town is the not-so-clean *Thai Niyom* with rooms from 60B. Top end in Satun is the *Slinda Hotel*, which caters mostly to Malaysian tourists. Rooms start at 100B but are not very well-kept.

There are a couple of cheap hotels in the small town of La-ngu, too.

Getting There

A share taxi to Satun from Hat Yai is 35B. The taxi stand in Hat Yai is opposite the post office near the railway station. A bus is about half that. From Kuala Perlis in Malaysia boats are M$4.

YALA

จังหวัดยะลา

Yala is the most prosperous of the four predominantly Muslim provinces in south Thailand, mainly due to income from rubber production, but also because it is the number one business and education centre for the region. The fast-developing capital is known as 'the cleanest city in Thailand' and has won awards to that effect three times in the last 25 years (its main competitor is

Trang). Yala is a city of parks, wide boulevards and orderly traffic. During the dry season there are nightly musical performances in **Chang Phuak Park**, located in the south-east part of the city just before the big Lak Muang traffic circle, off Pipitpakdee Rd. The new **Phrupakoi Park**, just west of the *lak muang* or city pillar, has a big man-made lake where people can fish, go boating and eat in floating restaurants. Yala residents seem obsessed with water recreation, this may be a consequence of living in the only land-locked province in the entire south. There is a public swimming pool in town at the Grand Palace restaurant and disco.

One of the biggest regional festivals in Thailand is held in Yala each year during the last six days of June to pay respect to the city guardian spirit, Jao Paw Lak Muang. Chinese New Year is also celebrated here with some zest, as there are many Chinese living in the capital. The Muslim population is settled in the rural areas of the province, for the most part, though there is a sizeable Muslim quarter near the railway station in town – you'll know it by the sheep and goats wandering in the streets and by the modern mosque – Yala's tallest building and the largest mosque in Thailand.

Outside of town, about eight km north off the Yala-Hat Yai highway, is **Wat Khuhaphimuk** (also called Wat Naa Tham, 'the cave-front temple'), a Srivijaya-period cave temple established around 750 AD. Inside the cave is a long reclining Buddha image, Phra Phutthasaiyat. There is also a small museum in front of the cave with artefacts of local provenance. To get there, take a *songthaew* going towards Hat Yai and ask to get off at Wat Naa Tham – fare is 5B. Two km past Wat Naa Tham is **Tham Silpa**, a cave with murals from the Srivijaya era.

Further afield in the opposite direction is the well-known village of **Sakai** สะกาย in Tharato district about 60 km from Yala on the way to Betong at

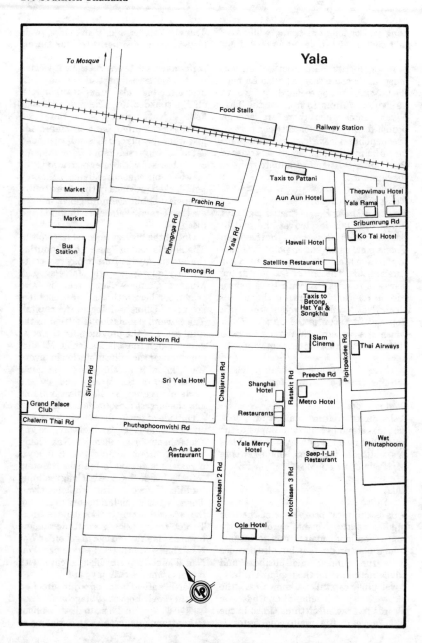

the Malaysian border. Sakai is the home of some of Thailand's last remaining Ngaw tribes, called so because their frizzy heads and dark complexions remind Thais of the outer skin of the rambutan fruit (*ngaw* in Thai). Anthropologists speculate that the Ngaw people are the direct descendants of a Proto-Malay race that once inhabited the entire Thai-Malay peninsula and beyond (also called Negritos, 'an aboriginal jungle race allied to negroid pygmies found in the Philippines, New Guinea and parts of Africa', according to George McFarland) but was subjugated by more advanced Austro-Thai cultures from the north. At any rate, the peaceful, short-statured people of Sakai still lead a traditional village life of hunting and gathering, practice very little agriculture and express themselves through their own language, music and dance. Also in Tharato district is **Tharato Falls**, which is now being developed into a national park.

Betong อำเภอเบตง is located 140 km south-west of Yala city on the Malaysian border and is Thailand's southern most point. The area surrounding Betong is mountainous with jungle and both Thai and Malaysian authorities believe that the Communist Party of Malaysia has its hidden headquarters somewhere in the vicinity. Occasionally, there are joint Thai-Malaysian military operations here in search of so-called 'Target 1', so this is a bit of a hot spot – a large contingent of Thai troops are in fact stationed at Camp Sirinthorn, an Army base near Yala. Malaysians are allowed to cross the border at Betong, so the little town is often crowded on weekends as they come across to shop for cheaper Thai merchandise, including, for the Malay men, Thai women. The town of Betong is famous for *kai betong*, a delicious local chicken dish and roast or fried mountain frogs, which are said to be even more delicious than the mountain frogs of Mae Hong Son. A share taxi to Betong from Yala is 50B; bus is 25B.

Raman รามัน , 25 km south-east of Yala by road or train, is well-known as a centre for the Malay-Indonesian martial art of *silat*. Two very famous teachers of silat reside here, Hajisa Haji Sama-ae and Je Wae. If you're interested in pure Thai Muslim culture, this is the place.

Places to Stay & Eat

Yala has quite a few hotels at all price levels. Starting from the bottom, the *Shang Hai*, *Metro* and *Saen Suk* are all nearly identical Chinese hotels with Chinese restaurants on the ground floor. All are on the same block on Ratakit Rd in the business district, not far from the train station. All three have rooms from 60B; the Saen Suk is a bit cleaner than the other two, and their restaurant is also better, specialising in generous plates of chicken rice.

At the next level, there is the *Sri Yala* (tel 212815) at 16-22 Chai Charat Rd (street sign says Chaijarus) with clean rooms for 100B, a restaurant and a popular coffee shop. The *Hawaii* and *Aun Aun* hotels on Pipitpakdee Rd might be the first hotels you see as you walk into town from the station, but are not worth the 100B rates. Better is the *Thepwiman*, a left turn from the station on Sribumrung Rd, across from the Yala Rama, which has rooms from 100B, AC for 200B.

Moving up a bit more, the *Yala Merry* is a good place at 120B for a very nice fan and bath room (150B for two beds), or 170B for AC. The Yala Merry is clean and quiet, but beware of the English menu in the coffee shop downstairs – the prices charged are higher than printed (eg, Kloster beer quoted at 50B is actually 65B) – they haven't got round to changing the prices on both menus yet.

Top end is the *Yala Rama* on Sribumrung Rd near the station. Here a room with fan and bath is 179B, while AC rooms are 250B to 292B. All rooms have two beds. The coffee shop and the night club here are quite popular.

There are plenty of inexpensive places to eat in downtown Yala near all the hotels, especially Chinese restaurants along Ratakit and Ranong Rds. The *Saen Suk* hotel restaurant has good *khao man kai* and the food stall next door, *Mae Prapai*, has good curry and rice plates for 8B, both Malaysian and Thai curries. The *Suay Suay* indoor/outdoor restaurant on Sri Bumrung near the Rama Hotel and the big *Satellite* restaurant on the corner of Pipitpakdee and Ranong Rds specialise in steamed cockles. On Phuthaphoomvithi Rd between the Yala Merry Hotel and Wat Phuthaphoom is *Laila*, a Muslim garden restaurant and, directly across the street, *Saep-I-Lii*, a small, cheap, north-eastern Thai restaurant.

On Kotchaseni 2 Rd, a couple of blocks down the street from Sri Yala Hotel, is *An An Lao*, a large garden restaurant specialising in *kai betong*, quite good and reasonably priced. The *Grand Palace*, at the end of Phuthaphoomvithi Rd in the opposite direction from Wat Phuthaphoom, serves fancy Thai and Chinese food at fancy prices.

Getting There

From Hat Yai, ordinary trains are 23B third class and take three hours. By share taxi the trip is 50B and takes about one hour. From Sungai Kolok at the Malaysian border, trains are 22B for a 2½ hour trip, or 60B by share taxi. There are AC buses between Bangkok and Yala for 364B.

PATTANI
จังหวัดปัตตานี

The provincial capital of Pattani provides a heavy contrast with Yala. In spite of its basic function as a trading post operated by the Chinese for the benefit (or exploitation, depending on your perspective) of the surrounding villages, the town has more Muslim character than Yala. In the streets, you are more likely to hear Yawi, the traditional language of Java, Sumatra and the Malay peninsula (which uses the classic Arabic script plus five more letters), than any Thai dialect. The markets are visually quite similar to markets in Kota Bahru in Malaysia. The town as a whole is as dirty as Yala is clean.

The centre of this concrete town is at the intersection of Thanon Naklua, the east-west road between Yala and Pattani harbour and Thanon Ramkomud, which runs north-south between Songkhla and Narathiwat. Inter-city buses and taxis stop at this intersection. Thanon Ramkomud becomes Thanon Rudee after crossing Naklua and it is along Thanon Rudee that you can see what is left of old Pattani architecture – the Sino-Portuguese style that was once so prevalent in south Thailand. Pattani, in fact, was until rather recent history, the centre of an independent principality that included Yala and Narathiwat.

Thailand's second largest mosque is in Pattani, a large traditional structure of green hue, probably still the south's most important mosque.

There are no fine beaches in the immediate vicinity of Pattani town and the harbour is not very impressive, but outside of town north toward Songkhla are km of deserted beach. There are even more beaches on the way to Narathiwat and the best is probably **Haat Patatiman**, near the town of Saiburi 43 km south.

Places to Stay

The *Chong Are Hotel* is a Chinese place on Thanon Preda with rooms for 60B without a bath, 90B with. A bit nicer is the *Santi Suk* at 1/16 Pipit Rd with rooms for 80B without a bath, 100B with. As in Yala, Narathiwat, Satun and Trang, all street signs are in English.

Getting There

Pattani is only 40 km from Yala. Share taxis are 18B and take about half an hour. From Narathiwat, taxi is 35B, bus 18B. There are also boats between Songkhla and Pattani, the fare depends on the size of the boat.

NARATHIWAT
จังหวัดนราธิวาส

Narathiwat is a pleasant, even-tempered little town, perhaps one of Thailand's smallest provincial capitals, with a character all of its own. Many of the buildings are old wooden structures a hundred or more years old. The local businesses seem to be owned by both the Muslims and the Chinese, and nights are particularly peaceful because of the relative absence of male drinking sessions typical of most upcountry towns in Thailand. The town is located right on the sea and the prettiest beaches on south Thailand's east coast are just outside of town. Just north of town is a small Thai Muslim fishing village at the mouth of the Bang Nara River, lined with the large painted fishing boats called *reua kaw-lae* which are peculiar to Narathiwat. Also peculiar to Narathiwat is the Bangsuriya palm tree, a rare fan-like palm named for the embroidered sunshades used by monks and royalty as a sign of rank.

Near the fishing is **Haat Narathat**, a sandy beach four to five km long, which serves as a kind of public park for locals, with outdoor seafood restaurants, tables and umbrellas, etc. The constant breeze here is excellent for windsurfing, a favourite sport of Narathiwat citizens as well as visiting Malaysians. Almost the entire coast between Narathiwat and Malaysia, 40 km south, is sandy beach.

The tallest seated Buddha image in Thailand is at Khao Kong, six km south-west on the way to the train station in Ton Yang. Called **Phra Phuttha Taksin Mingmongkon**, the image is 25 metres high and made of bronze.

Places to Stay

The cheapest places to stay are all on Puphapugdee Rd along Manao Bay. The best deal is the *Narathiwat*, a yellow-painted wooden building with brown trim and no English sign, which is quiet, breezy, clean and comfortable. Rooms on the water front cost 60B. Another nice place across the street next to the Si Ayuthaya Bank is the *Bang Nara* – friendly staff and large, clean rooms for 60B. A last resort is the *Cathay*, on the same side of the street as the Narathiwat, with rooms for 80B and 100B, but not so special.

The *Rex*, at 6/1-3 Chamroonnara Rd, is a fair place with 100B rooms. Similar rooms for the same rates, but not quite as quiet, are at the *Yaowaraj* on the corner of Chamroonnara and Pichitbumrung.

Top end is the *Tan Yong* on Sophapisai Rd, with fan-cooled rooms for 250B, AC rooms for 340B. Most of the guests are Malaysians and Thai government officials.

For eating, the night market at the intersection of Sophapisai and Puphapugdee Rd is good. There are also several inexpensive places along Chamroonnara Rd, especially the *Bua Din* for curries. On Puphapugdee Rd, there are some old wooden Chinese restaurants that are very cheap – one sells good *khao yam* in the mornings, a southern Thai breakfast specialty which consists of a mixture of dry rice, lime leaves, bean sprouts, shrimp, toasted coconut and lime juice tossed together.

Getting There

Share taxis between Yala and Narathiwat are 50B. Bus is 30B. Train is 13B third class to Tanyongmat, 20 km west of Narathiwat, then it's either a 15B taxi to Narathiwat or 8B by *songthaew*. From Sungai Kolok, buses are 20B, share taxis 30B.

SUNGAI KOLOK
สุไหงโกลก

This small town in the south-east is a jumping off point for the east coast of Malaysia. The river forms the border here and Rantau Panjang is the Malaysian border town on the south bank of the river. There is a fair batik (Thai: *pa-te*) cottage industry in town. The Thai government has a project currently underway to move the border crossing from here to Ban Taba in Tak Bai district on the coast 32 km east.

Places to Stay

There are plenty of cheap hotels in town for 40B and up. The *Savoy Hotel* has rooms from 70B to 160B and the *Thailieng Hotel* next door is about the same. Just a 10B rickshaw ride from the border or five minutes' walk straight ahead from the railway station. More expensive are the *Thara Regent*, the *Merlin* and the *Lilla* from 130B to 400B or more. There are lots of cheap restaurants – for an economical and delicious breakfast very early in the morning try coffee and doughnuts at the station buffet.

Getting There

A share taxi from Yala to Sungai Kolok is 60B. Taxi between Narathiwat and Sungai Kolok is 30B, bus is 20B.

FURTHER SOUTH

Bus or Taxi

Share taxis are a popular way of travelling between Hat Yai and Penang. They're big old Thai-registered Chevys or Mercedes which depart from Hat Yai around 9 am every morning. You'll find them at the railway station or along Niphat Uthit 2. In Penang you can find them around the cheap travellers' hotels in Georgetown. Cost is about 220B or M$22 and this is probably the fastest way of travelling between the two countries and you cross the border with a minimum of fuss. Cheaper and more comfortable, though less fast, are tour buses between Hat Yai and Penang. Hat Yai Tour (also called Yee Seng Tout), downstairs from the Cathay Guest House in Hat Yai, has buses for 200B which leave at 9 am daily and arrive in Penang five hours later.

There is also a daily bus running Alor Setar-Hat Yai-Kota Bahru and reverse. You can also cross the border by taking a bus to one side and another from the other but don't take the most obvious direct route between Hat Yai and Alor Setar.

This is the route used by taxis and buses but there's a long stretch of no-man's-land between the Thai border control at Sadao and the Malaysian one at Changlun. Finding transport across this empty stretch is difficult. It's much easier to go to Padang Besar, where the railway line crosses the border. Here you can get a bus right up to the border, walk across and take another bus on the other side.

There's also a road crossing at Keroh (Thai side – Betong), right in the middle between the east and west coasts. This may be used more now that the Penang-Kota Bahru road is open. See the Sungai Kolok section below for crossing the border on the east coast.

Train

Bangkok to Butterworth/Penang Monday, Wednesday and Saturday the International Express leaves Bangkok's Hualamphong station at 4.10 pm, arriving in Hat Yai at 10.15 am the next day, and in Butterworth, Malaysia, at 6.45 pm (Malaysian time, one hour ahead of Thai time). Fare to Butterworth is 846B for first class, 397B for second, plus a 25B Express charge. There is no third class on the International Express.

Bangkok to Kuala Lumpur Same train as above, changing to the Malayan Express in Butterworth, departing there for Kuala Lumpur at 10 pm, arriving in Kuala Lumpur at 6.35 am the next day. Fare is 1228B first class, 577B second class.

Bangkok to Singapore Same procedure as above, final leg leaves Kuala Lumpur at 9 am, arriving in Singapore at 5.15 pm. The entire two-day journey costs 1646B first class, 774B second class, plus 80B for a sleeper, plus 25B for the Express train. If you're going straight through, when you get to Penang get off quickly and rebook a sleeping berth to Kuala Lumpur (M$2 to M$3). In Kuala Lumpur you have to get a second class seat allocation – insist on second or you'll be fobbed off with third.

Bangkok to Sungai Kolok If you prefer the east coast passage to Malaysia, there are International Express trains to Sungai Kolok on Sunday, Tuesday, Thursday and Friday at 4.10 pm, arriving in Sungai Kolok at 2.55 pm. Second class fare is 378B plus 30B Express charge.

It's about a half km (maybe nearer a km) from Sungai Kolok town or railway station to the Malaysian border. You'll most likely have to walk. Coming from Malaysia just follow the old railway tracks to your right or for the town turn left at the first junction and head for the high-rises. Be prepared for culture shock coming from Malaysia, not only are any signs in Thai script but nobody speaks English around here. Third class rail fare to Hat Yai is about 40B.

Air

Phuket to Penang Tuesday and Friday Thai Airways flies to Penang at 12.50 pm. Arrival time in Penang is 2.40 pm. Fare is 1030B.

Sea

Coast Route There are several ways of travelling between Malaysia and the south of Thailand by sea. Simplest is to take a long tail boat between Satun, right down in the south-west corner of Thailand and Kuala Perlis. The cost is about M$4 or 40B and boats cross over fairly regularly. Kuala Perlis is the departure point for the ferries across to the Malaysian island of Langkawi. There are immigration posts at both ports so you can make the crossing quite officially but they're a bit slack at Satun (since they don't get many foreigners arriving this way) so make sure they stamp your passport.

From Satun you can take a bus to Hat Yai or even head directly for Phuket by taking a bus first to Trang or Krabi. Hat Yai is nothing special after all. It's possible there may be a boat route into Thailand from near Kota Bahru as well when the Ban Taba crossing opens in Narathiwat.

Ocean Route An alternative sea route is to travel by yacht between Phuket and Penang. The *Szygie* sails from Phuket to Penang periodically between 1 December and 30 April. Contact the operators at Restaurant Number Four, Patong Beach, Phuket or J Travel, Chulia St, Georgetown, Penang. They sail Phuket-Koh Phi Phi-Langkawi-Penang.

You can also find yachts going further afield, particularly to Sri Lanka. December and early January is the best month to look for them. The crossing takes about 10 to 15 days.

Glossary

achaan – respectful title for teacher, from Sanskrit *acharya*
ao – bay or gulf
amphoe – district; next subdivision down from province, sometimes spelled *amphur*
amphoe muang – provincial capital

ban – house or village
bhikku – Buddhist monk
bot – central sanctuary or chapel in a Thai temple

chaihat – beach
chedi – stupa; monument erected to house a Buddha relic; called *pagoda* in Burma, *dagoba* in Sri Lanka, *cetiya* in India

doi – peak, as in mountain

farang – foreigner of European descent

haat – beach; short for *chaihat*

isaan – general term for north-east Thailand, from the Sanskrit name for the mediaeval kingdom *Isana*, which encompassed parts of Cambodia and north-east Thailand

jangwat – province
Jataka – life-stories of the Buddha

keo – also spelled *kaew*; crystal, jewel, glass, or gem
khlong – canal
koh – island

laem – cape (in the geographical sense)

mae nam – river; literally 'mother water'
Maha That – literally 'great element', from the Sanskrit-Pali *mahadhatu*; common name for temples which contain Buddha relics
mondop – small square building in a *wat* complex generally used by lay people as opposed to monks; from the Sanskrit *mandapa*
muang – city

nakhorn – city; from Sanskrit-Pali *nagara*
nam – water
nam phrik – pepper sauce

nam plaa – fish sauce
noeng khao – hill

phaakamaa – piece of cotton cloth worn as a wraparound by men
phaasin – same as above for women
phra – monk or Buddha image; an honorific term from the Pali *vara*, excellent
phuu khao – mountain in central Thai
prang – Khmer style tower on temples
prasat – small ornate building with a cruciform ground plan and needle-like spire, used for religious/royal purposes, located on *wat* grounds. From the Sanskrit term *prasada*

rai – one *rai* is equal to 1600 square metres
rot thammada – ordinary bus (non air-conditioned) or ordinary train (not rapid or express)
rot thua – tour bus; any air-con bus. Also called **rot ae** (air vehicle)

sala – an open covered meeting or resting place
sala klang – provincial offices and/or city hall
samlor – literally 'three wheels'; three-wheeled pedicab used prominently in provincial Thailand
sema – boundary stones used to consecrate ground used for monastic ordinations; from the Sanskrit-Pali *sima*
soi – lane
soon – centre; from the Pali *sunya*
songthaew – literally 'two rows'; common name for small pick-up trucks with two benches in the back, used as buses/taxis

tambon – also spelled *tambol*; next subdivision below *amphoe*; 'subdistrict' or 'precinct'
thale sap – inland sea
thep – angel or divine being; from Sanskrit *deva*
tuk-tuk – motorised *samlor*

wat – temple-monastery; from Pali *avasa*, monk's dwelling
wiharn – counterpart to *bot* in Thai temple, containing Buddha images but not circumscribed by *sema* stones. Also spelt *wihan* or *viharn*; from Sanskrit *vihara*

Index

Temperature

To convert °C to °F multiply by 1.8 and add 32

To convert °F to °C subtract 32 and multiply by ·55

Length, Distance & Area

	multiply by
inches to centimetres	2.54
centimetres to inches	0.39
feet to metres	0.30
metres to feet	3.28
yards to metres	0.91
metres to yards	1.09
miles to kilometres	1.61
kilometres to miles	0.62
acres to hectares	0.40
hectares to acres	2.47

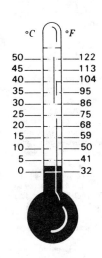

Weight

	multiply by
ounces to grams	28.35
grams to ounces	0.035
pounds to kilograms	0.45
kilograms to pounds	2.21
British tons to kilograms	1016
US tons to kilograms	907

A British ton is 2240 lbs, a US ton is 2000 lbs

Volume

	multiply by
Imperial gallons to litres	4.55
litres to imperial gallons	0.22
US gallons to litres	3.79
litres to US gallons	0.26

5 imperial gallons equals 6 US gallons
a litre is slightly more than a US quart, slightly less
than a British one

Lonely Planet

Lonely Planet published its first book in 1973. Tony and Maureen Wheeler had made a lengthy overland trip from England to Australia and, in response to numerous 'how do you do it?' questions, Tony wrote and they published *Across Asia on the Cheap*. It became an instant local best-seller and inspired thoughts of a second travel guide. A year and a half in South-East Asia resulted in their second book, *South-East Asia on a Shoestring*, which they put together in a backstreet Chinese hotel in Singapore in 1975. The 'yellow bible', as it quickly became known, soon became *the* guide to the region and has gone through five editions, always with its familiar yellow cover.

Soon other writers started to come to them with ideas for similar books – books that went off the beaten track and took an adventurous approach to travel, books that 'assumed you knew how to get your luggage off the carousel,' as one reviewer described them. Lonely Planet grew from a kitchen table operation to a spare room and then to its own office. It also started to develop an international reputation as the Lonely Planet logo began to appear in more and more countries. In 1982 *India – a travel survival kit* won the Thomas Cook award for the best guidebook of the year.

These days there are over 60 Lonely Planet titles. Nearly 30 people work at our office in Melbourne, Australia and another half dozen at our US office in Oakland, California.

At first Lonely Planet specialised exclusively in the Asia region but these days we are also developing major ranges of guidebooks to the Pacific region, to South America and to Africa. The list of walking guides is growing and Lonely Planet is producing a unique series of phrasebooks to 'unusual' languages. The emphasis continues to be on travel for travellers and Tony and Maureen still manage to fit in a number of trips each year and play a very active part in the writing and updating of Lonely Planet's guides.

Keeping guidebooks up to date is a constant battle which requires an ear to the ground and lots of walking, but technology also plays its part. All Lonely Planet guidebooks are now stored and updated on computer, and some authors even take lap-top computers into the field. Lonely Planet is also using computers to draw maps and eventually many of the maps will be stored on disk.

The people at Lonely Planet strongly feel that travellers can make a positive contribution to the countries they visit both by better appreciation of cultures and by the money they spend. In addition the company tries to make a direct contribution to the countries and regions it covers. Since 1986 a percentage of the income from each book has gone to aid groups and associations. This has included donations to famine relief in Africa, to aid projects in India, to agricultural projects in Nicaragua and other Central American countries and to Greenpeace's efforts to halt French nuclear testing in the Pacific. In 1988 over $40,000 was donated by Lonely Planet to these projects.

Lonely Planet Distributors

Australia & Papua New Guinea Lonely Planet Publications, PO Box 617, Hawthorn, Victoria 3122.
Canada Raincoast Books, 112 East 3rd Avenue, Vancouver, British Columbia V5T 1C8.
Denmark, Finland & Norway Scanvik Books aps, Store Kongensgade 59 A, DK-1264 Copenhagen K.
Hong Kong The Book Society, GPO Box 7804.
India & Nepal UBS Distributors, 5 Ansari Rd, New Delhi – 110002
Israel Geographical Tours Ltd, 8 Tverya St, Tel Aviv 63144.
Japan Intercontinental Marketing Corp, IPO Box 5056, Tokyo 100-31.
Netherlands Nilsson & Lamm bv, Postbus 195, Pampuslaan 212, 1380 AD Weesp.
New Zealand Transworld Publishers, PO Box 83-094, Edmonton PO, Auckland.
Singapore & Malaysia MPH Distributors, 601 Sims Drive, #03-21, Singapore 1438.
Spain Altair, Balmes 69, 08007 Barcelona.
Sweden Esselte Kartcentrum AB, Vasagatan 16, S-111 20 Stockholm.
Thailand Chalermnit, 108 Sukhumvit 53, Bangkok 10110.
UK Roger Lascelles, 47 York Rd, Brentford, Middlesex, TW8 0QP
USA Lonely Planet Publications, PO Box 2001A, Berkeley, CA 94702.
West Germany Buchvertrieb Gerda Schettler, Postfach 64, D3415 Hattorf a H.
All Other Countries refer to Australia address.

Guides to South-East Asia

Bali & Lombok - a travel survival kit
This book gives detailed information on the Indonesian islands of Bali and Lombok. Bali is a picturesque tropical island with a fascinating culture. Lombok is less touched by outside influences and has a special atmosphere of its own.

Burma - a travel survival kit
Burma is one of Asia's friendliest and most interesting countries, but for travellers there's one catch - you can only stay for seven days. This book shows you how to make the most of your visit.

Indonesia - a travel survival kit
This comprehensive guidebook covers the entire Indonesian archipelago. Some of the most remarkable sights and sounds in South-East Asia can be found amongst these countless islands and this book has all the facts.

Malaysia, Singapore and Brunei - a travel survival kit
These three nations offer amazing geographic and cultural variety - from hill stations to beaches, from Dyak longhouses to futuristic cities - this is Asia at its most accessible.

The Philippines - a travel survival kit
The 7000 islands of the Philippines are a paradise for the adventurous traveller. The friendly Filipinos, colourful festivals, superb natural scenery, and frequent travel connections make island hopping addictive.

Also Available:
Indonesia phrasebook, *Burmese phrasebook*, *Pilipino phrasebook* and *Thai phrasebook*

Other shoestring guides

South-East Asia on a shoestring
For over 10 years this has been known as the 'yellow bible' to travellers in South-East Asia. It offers detailed travel information on Brunei, Burma, Hong Kong, Indonesia, Macau, Malaysia, Papua New Guinea, the Philippines, Singapore, and Thailand.

North-East Asia on a shoestring
Concise and up-to-date information on six unique states, including one of the largest countries in the world and one of the smallest colonies: China, Hong Kong, Japan, Korea, Macau, Taiwan.

West Asia on a shoestring
A complete guide to the overland trip from Bangladesh to Turkey. Updated information on Bangladesh, Bhutan, India, Iran, Maldives, Nepal, Pakistan, Sri Lanka, Turkey and the Middle East. There's even a section on Afghanistan as it used to be.

South America on a shoestring
This extensively updated edition covers Central and South America from the USA-Mexico border all the way to Tierra del Fuego. There's background information and numerous maps; details on hotels, restaurants, buses, trains, things to do and hassles to avoid.

Africa on a shoestring
From Marrakesh to Kampala, Mozambique to Mauritania, Johannesburg to Cairo – this guidebook gives you all the facts on travelling in Africa. It provides comprehensive information on more than 50 African countries – how to get to them, how to get around, where to stay, where to eat, what to see and what to avoid.

Eastern Europe on a shoestring
With all the facts on beating red tape, and detailed information on the GDR, Poland, Czechoslavakia, Hungary, Romania, Bulgaria, Yugoslavia, Albania and the USSR, this book opens up a whole new world for travellers.

Lonely Planet Guidebooks

Lonely Planet guidebooks cover virtually every accessible part of Asia as well as Australia, the Pacific, Central and South America, Africa, the Middle East and parts of North America. There are four main series: 'travel survival kits', covering a single country for a range of budgets; 'shoestring' guides with compact information for low-budget travel in a major region; trekking guides; and 'phrasebooks'.

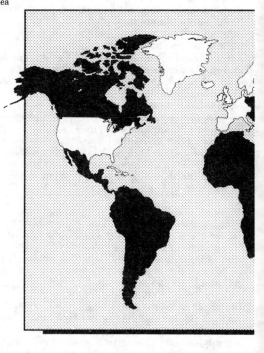

Mail Order

Lonely Planet guidebooks are distributed worldwide and are sold by good bookshops everywhere. They are also available by mail order from Lonely Planet, so if you have difficulty finding a title please write to us. US and Canadian residents should write to Embarcadero West, 112 Linden St, Oakland CA 94607, USA and residents of other countries to PO Box 617, Hawthorn, Victoria 3122, Australia.

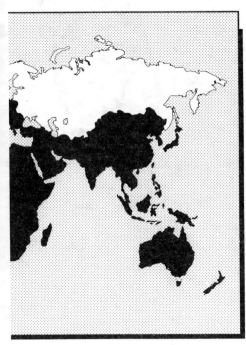

Lonely Planet Update

We collect an enormous amount of information here at Lonely Planet. Apart from our research there's a steady stream of travellers' letters full of the latest news. For over 5 years much of this information went into a quarterly newsletter (and helped to update the guidebooks). The paperback *Update* includes this up-to-date news and aims to supplement the information available in our guidebooks. There are four editions a year (Feb, May, Aug and Nov) available either by subscription or through bookshops. Subscribe now and you'll save nearly 25% off the retail price.

Each edition has extracts from the most interesting letters we have received, covering such diverse topics as:

- how to take a boat trip on the Yalu River
- living in a typical Thai village
- getting a Nepalese trekking permit

Subscription Details

All subscriptions cover four editions and include postage. Prices quoted are subject to change.

USA & Canada - One year's subscription is US$12; a single copy is US$3.95. Please send your order to Lonely Planet's California office.

Other Countries - One year's subscription is Australian $15; a single copy is A$4.95. Please pay in Australian $, or the US$ or £ Sterling equivalent. Please send your order form to Lonely Planet's Australian office.

Order Form

Please send me

☐ One year's sub. – starting current edition.　　　☐ One copy of the current edition.

Name (please print) ....

Address (please print) ....

....

....

Tick One

☐ Payment enclosed (payable to Lonely Planet Publications)

Charge my 　☐ Visa 　☐ Bankcard 　☐ MasterCard 　for the amount of $ ....

Card No .... Expiry Date ....

Cardholder's Name (print) ....

Signature .... Date..

US & Canadian residents
　Lonely Planet, Embarcadero West, 112 Linden St,
　Oakland, CA 94607, USA
Other countries
　Lonely Planet, PO Box 617, Hawthorn, Victoria 3122, Australia